CADEL
EVANS

CADEL EVANS

THE ART OF CYCLING

ABC
Books

The ABC 'Wave' device is a trademark of the Australian Broadcasting Corporation and is used under licence by HarperCollins*Publishers* Australia.

First published in Australia in 2016
by HarperCollins*Publishers* Australia Pty Limited
ABN 36 009 913 517
harpercollins.com.au

HarperCollins*Publishers*
Level 13, 201 Elizabeth Street, Sydney, NSW 2000, Australia
Unit D1, 63 Apollo Drive, Albany, Auckland 0632, New Zealand
A 53, Sector 57, Noida, UP, India
1 London Bridge Street, London, SE1 9GF, United Kingdom
2 Bloor Street East, 20th floor, Toronto, Ontario M4W 1A8, Canada
195 Broadway, New York NY 10007, USA

National Library of Australia Cataloguing-in-Publication data:

Evans, Cadel, author.
  Title: The art of cycling / Cadel Evans.
  978 0 7333 3462 7 (hardback)
  978 1 4607 0551 3 (ebook)
  Subjects: Evans, Cadel.
  Tour de France (Bicycle race)
  Cyclists – Australia – Biography.
  Bicycle racing.
  Mountain biking.
796.62092

Cover and internal design by HarperCollins Design Studio
Front cover photograph: © Jérémie Reuiller / BMC
Back cover image: Cadel Evans family collection, image supplied by Helen Cocks
Typeset in Sabon LT by HarperCollins
Printed and bound in Australia by Griffin Press
The papers used by HarperCollins in the manufacture of this book are a natural, recyclable product made from wood grown in sustainable plantation forests. The fibre source and manufacturing processes meet recognised international environmental standards, and carry certification.

For Robel.

Life is like riding a bicycle. To keep
your balance, you must keep moving.
– Albert Einstein

Contents

Prologue – So It's Over   1

PART 1: THE CLIMB

1   The Single Track   11
2   Racing on Dirt   23
3   Getting Serious   32
4   Europe   45
5   Transitioning to the Road   59
6   Mapei–Quick-Step   82
7   The Giro   95
8   T-Mobile   112
9   Lotto   133
10   The Tour   147
11   Dark Days at the Tour de France   162
12   Twenty-three Seconds   183
13   Stuck in Second Place   197
14   Losing Support   216

PART 2: TAKING THE LEAD

15   The World Championships   237
16   BMC   249
17   The Curse of the Rainbow Jersey?   271
18   'What's Going on with Cadel?'   292
19   Chasing the Yellow Jersey   304
20   Into Paris   321
21   You're Only as Good as Your Last Race   338
22   Beginning of the End?   353

PART 3: FINISHING THE RACE

23 The Decision   375
24 The Final Season   394
25 The Last Race   410
26 A New Life   418

Epilogue: For the Love of Cycling   432
Author's Note   437

SO IT'S OVER

2015

FOR 20 YEARS, MY bicycle has been an extension of me.

I don't want to count up the hours I've been on it, near it, fixing it, washing it, thinking about it, obsessing over it, straining to hear and feel any malfunction or glitch. From the earliest days of my career I could sense any tiny change in a bike's setup, any variation in its efficiency, any moving parts that needed cleaning or lubrication. An unfamiliar noise is often the first indicator of something about to go wrong – a part working itself loose, tyres that are getting old and dry, a hairline crack in a component or frame joint, a drivetrain that's worn or in need of a fine adjustment. I've become so attuned to the feel and movement of my bike that anything out of sync drives me a little crazy.

Sometimes my highly sensitised antennae have been detrimental to my psychology. When you're racing and you think, 'Hang on, what's wrong?', it can get in the way. I like to take the time before a bike ride to have everything just perfect.

You come to know your bike in minute detail. It's an exacting relationship. The bike is my tool, and I am intimately in contact with it. It is part of me, we are one.

I concern myself with tiny intricacies that someone from outside the sport would never notice. It could be the thickness of the tape on my handlebars, or the way they curve under the palms of my hands. My left brake lever has to sit a few millimetres higher than my right lever because of my battered and shortened left shoulder; both my brake hoods must be angled slightly inwards to align with my shoulders, which have become more and more rounded after thousands of hours of sitting on a bike.

If your bike is an extension of yourself on the road, then your clothing is too. Everything has to be balanced, even the objects in my pockets. I care that my socks are the same length, the shoes on both feet fastened at equal tension. I try to keep my helmet and sunglasses straight on my asymmetrical skull – a result of a childhood injury.

I care because, like millions around the world, I'm a cyclist. And being a cyclist comes with a mentality that is a cocktail of habit, routine, professional pride, a touch of obsession and a small element of superstition. I am well aware of the cyclist's many tics and quirks because, while I've ridden as a professional for 20 years, I always was and still am a passionate cycling fan, with a strong instinct for the cyclist's occasionally ludicrous obsessions.

If you want to be a cyclist, don't ever consider wearing underwear under your shorts. If your calf muscle touches a dirty chain that marks the skin, clean it off immediately!

Cyclists worry about their tan line. You don't want to change the length of your shorts or jersey sleeves and expose a white stripe next to tanned skin. That's a sign of a hubbard – an Australian cycling term for a novice or beginner.

Everyone learns what style of jersey they like, how high the pockets are, how long the sleeves are. Cyclists know exactly how long their shorts should be, what chamois they prefer – the point of contact between the 'undercarriage' and machine. These are the things you get used to over time and to change them becomes difficult.

All cyclists have their fixations, some with particular shoes, some with particular saddles, the particular fit of their bike. I'm particular about the soap I use to wash my training and racing gear. I'm careful not to mix the colours of my undershirts even though I have access to as many as I need for the year. I wash my whites separately; I wash delicate Gore-Tex and reflective materials by hand, trying to avoid the dryer whenever I can. All my clothes are carefully folded to preserve them and help them fit as well as possible.

Professional cycling is about order and reliability. You need to know that every piece of clothing, every component, every element on or around your person, is working. Working like it did yesterday. Working like it did the day before. And will work like that again tomorrow. Surprises aren't what cyclists enjoy – in a race there are plenty of those already. The margin between success and failure is too small to allow for any unknowns to enter your world, when you're coercing the bike down steep, narrow, slippery mountain passes where unpredictable brake performance, restricted visibility or a moment of poor judgment can be the difference between staying in front or lying injured on the side of the road. Climbing at the limits of your ability in the cold, under snow, where a poor choice in clothing saps your body of the energy to keep warm or restricts blood flow to your extremities that you need for shifting gears, braking, eating and drinking; as opposed to staying with the best riders in the world and maintaining the general classification (GC) ranking that your cycling year is going to be judged on.

Thing is, other cyclists understand. We spend a lot of time riding in close proximity to each other. Eventually someone will say 'Your socks aren't straight' or 'Why are you wearing those short socks? They're ridiculous' or 'Why is that cable outer so long?'

Three weeks of racing in a Tour de France with the same 180 riders is a lot of time to familiarise yourself with a teammate's pedalling style, a change in the muscle tone of a close competitor, a variation in a team's racing style. 'Is my teammate tired? Is the change in my competitor's position in the peloton (main group)

3

because of good form, bad form, or nerves? Is the change in his muscle definition due to dehydration, weight loss, lack of recovery, an illicit substance in the body?'

Cyclists evolve into this after hours and hours of unbroken riding, years and years of sitting on their bike. Outside the small bubble of professional cycling these obsessions seem bizarre. Inside the bubble they are unnoticeable norms. Constants become instinctive and invisible, the new and unfamiliar become obvious and unsettling.

SO, HERE I AM, getting ready for another race.

Getting dressed, or 'kitting up' in modern Lycra is now like applying adhesive material to your body. Professional competition clothing is now very well cut, tightly fitting, and so aerodynamic that it needs to put on and taken off in a certain order.

We put our clothing on carefully because our colleagues, competitors and cycling fans will look at what we do and pay attention to what we're wearing. There are people who take photos of professionals to make sure they are not wearing any brand of clothing that they are not contracted to wear. Observers of cycling are, well, very observant. They notice anything that is out of the 'ordinary'. I have been analysed for many years now, so I know, I have been conditioned.

But today is the last day I put a number on. Today is the last time people will be photographing me from every possible angle, the last time observers will be looking at my facial expressions, the last time commentators will be analysing my result. Did I win or lose? Could I have done better? Where did I make mistakes?

Today is the last race of my professional career, and like in every other race I've competed in over the past 20 years, I want to do everything as well as I can.

HOURS LATER, I CROSS the finish line for the last time. Geelong, on Victoria's Bellarine Peninsula, is wet from morning rain but the sun is out now. For me, as a Melburnian, this is not a surprise.

I can hear the race commentators on the PA system, calling the names of the riders as they come in. They call my name, but I can't hear what they're saying. I can hear people cheering, though, for me and for all the riders.

It's early February 2015 and I've just ridden the inaugural Cadel Evans Great Ocean Road Race. It's my last professional race on a bike and I'm not sure what I feel. Relief, excitement, confusion, sadness, pride? Or all of these?

As well as competing I am a race organiser so I want it to run smoothly, of course, but I also want to finish off my career fighting all the way for the win.

In the end I come fifth, a respectable result. Big crowds have braved the rain. I feel a gratitude and respect that I am profoundly touched by.

Among them are my mother and grandmother. I have ridden more than 750 professional races around the world, and my Australian-based family have only been able to attend a handful of them.

The race is over and a new chapter in my life has begun. It's fitting that the first person I spot waiting for me at the finish line is my four-year-old son Robel. I haven't seen him for three weeks while I've been in Australia, preparing for and helping organise this event. I lift him into my arms and we move through the crowd as the media and cycle fans gather round.

There'll be plenty of time later to reflect on this day. I can't fully absorb the poignancy of having raced my last race, because all my attention is on my 'little man' in my arms, whom I have missed so much. And too much else is happening right now. There's the presentation on stage in front of 20,000 people. The Mayor of Geelong asks me to sign a now empty bottle of champagne for his office. There's a media conference, my last ever as a rider, something I will probably not miss. Some quick hellos to friends and family who have travelled from various parts of the world to see me race. A few more media interviews. A run to the hotel for a shower, a change into something other than Lycra and some sustenance to see me through until the evening.

At my request, there's a small celebratory drink with the staff and other competitors to thank them for making the trip out and being part of the first Great Ocean Road Race.

Like every race, it's been a big day, but in the sweep of my life it's an enormous step.

A big week. A big 20 years.

I LOVE THIS SPORT.

I love the freedom you feel when you're out on a bike, the solitude when you're riding along a quiet trail in the forest listening to the birds sing, the feel of the warm sun or the cool breeze on your skin, the deep connection you develop with your bike.

These things are what attract me to cycling. These things are what I love about the sport.

Cycling has given me thrills, it's given me opportunities, and it's taught me important lessons in life. Cycling has given me everything.

That's why I am forever grateful.

That's why I don't hold any grudges.

What other people did, in an era when doping dominated the sport, I can't change that.

My mindset as an athlete was: 'Don't think about the drug cheats because otherwise you're going to psych yourself out before every race.'

There are many joys in a life of professional cycling. I have loved the camaraderie with teammates, the great friends you make, the endless enjoyment of being on a bike.

And then on the other side there are the cheats. The ones who let us all down.

As a young rider I would look up to older riders and be inspired by them. Then I'd find out that what they were doing wasn't ethical, or was illegal. That happened many times. My earlier admiration for these riders turned into a sense of disappointment, frustration and sometimes anger.

What other people do – they have to live with that. You can't go through life thinking about other people. You just have to live your own life in the best way possible.

This is me. This is my reason for being.

PART ONE

The CLIMB

CHAPTER 1

THE SINGLE TRACK

2015, 1977–1991

A FEW DAYS AFTER the inaugural Cadel Evans Great Ocean Road Race I fly to Stabio, the little Swiss town just near the border with Italy that has been my home for the past decade.

There's a strangeness in being home and knowing I don't need to prepare for a race. I don't need to train. It doesn't matter what I eat. I can sleep in. I am free of the strict regimen of an elite cyclist.

But with that freedom comes strange pressures. I am no longer Cadel Evans, professional cyclist. I am now Cadel Evans, father, son, friend. After 20 years, it's a change that will take some time to get used to.

But I'm still me. You don't change overnight. And that means I am programmed to get on the bike every day. It's February and it's snowing, but I still wake up and do some core and postural corrective exercises that are so important to the long-term health of an elite cyclist and ride the rollers, the indoor bike, just to maintain a bit of fitness.

As the weather warms, a '29er' mountain bike, a neglected Christmas present from my racing team BMC, is calling me from the back of a row of bikes that crowds my garage. I wonder what it would feel like to go for a ride, just a long ride through the countryside in the hills around my house. For years now, out training, I would often see a trail out of the corner of my eye and think, 'I'd like to ride that some time.' Then I would snap back to prescribed training: speed, watts, cadence and heart rate.

When I started mountain biking at 14, I couldn't quite pinpoint what I liked about it. I remember loving that first mountain bike. It was not expensive. It was not a very good bike at all – too big for me. Still, it did the job.

I started reading mountain-bike magazines and it was all about the 'single track', a trail only wide enough for one rider at a time. I got out my new mountain bike and came across some single tracks around my house and it was as though I'd found my calling.

Over my road career I've never just gone out mountain biking and explored the area where I lived. As a professional, if you have the energy to go riding after training or racing, it probably means you are not training or racing hard enough.

Fast-forward to 2015. I'm 38 and finally I have time to explore. Isn't that ironic? That my exploring years are happening at the *end* of my career?

Mountain bikes have continued to evolve since I last rode them professionally. The wheels are bigger. The suspension travels further and is greatly improved. Overall, the bikes are much easier to ride fast and are more fun.

I go out and discover new trails right near my home in Stabio. One day, in the forest above Morcote near Lake Lugano, I find a really fun but challenging single track about 17 or 18 kilometres from my house with a beautiful view over the lake. It snakes between huge and majestic trees and follows the contour of the hill. I'm able to ride up most of it, though for safety I dismount much more often than I used to.

I'm thrilled at this re-discovery. I'm tearing along, left, right, through a couple of rocky sections, and the bike's sliding and bouncing around, over tree roots, through switchbacks.

No one is watching. No one is judging me. No one cares how long I take. No one will analyse my power, cadence and heart rate. Riding down this single track, the thrill is there again; the adrenalin and the speed and the sensation of flying through the forest. I'm back in love with mountain biking and it feels fantastic.

And then I realise I want to share this. Since I've retired I've been enjoying the solitude of just being outside, riding alone for enjoyment or fitness. But these trails are too good not to share. So I decide this is where I'm going to take my friend Australian rider, Simon Clarke, who is a relative newcomer to mountain biking. We've been close since our first meeting as roommates at the 2009 Road World Championships, where he was key to my success. Simon's a rider who has dedicated the best part of his career and his ability to the success of his various team leaders.

After everything that's happened over my career, after all the ups and the downs, after all the care and attention I've put into my body and mind, after the hundreds of races and thousands of hours of training, after all the experiences that have made me the bike rider I am today, this is the freest I've felt in years.

I've competed in nine Tours de France and four Olympic Games, and won the Tour de France, a road world title and two Mountain Bike World Cups. To come back and reignite my passion for cycling by getting on a mountain bike again, to have that same thrill that I experienced as a 14-year-old, has made me feel quite young again.

IT'S 1991. IT'S 5.30 in the morning and the hills are shrouded in a midwinter fog, which sinks into the valleys and sits heavily upon our house and the paddock that surrounds it. The house is quiet. Mum's asleep and so, presumably, are the horses under their rugs in the paddock.

It's quite beautiful at this time of day, almost haunting. School doesn't start for another three hours, so there's plenty of time for a ride as the sun rises.

Our house is frustratingly close to the road and even at this hour I can hear cars passing by. If I catch the sound of swishing water under car tyres, I shudder in my bed, knowing it's going to be wet and cold and unpleasant out there.

It's on those days that my stretching ritual takes a little longer; I am subconsciously procrastinating. I don't particularly want to go out in the rain, but I have an internal drive that is stronger than anything else I have ever known. I am not going to be beaten by the elements, however wet and unpleasant they may be.

We don't have a lot of money so I can't afford up-to-date cycling clothes. But at 14, I don't know any better. Not that anyone is up at this hour to judge me – or, in Australia in 1991, even to care about judging a young teenager with a dream to enter a sport that most people don't know exists.

All the same, this dream is driving me and the only gear I have to make it happen is a Gary Fisher Lycra jersey and shorts, Shimano mountain-bike shoes and a Bell helmet. On colder days I improvise: I find that two pairs of heavy black women's stockings almost look like cycling tights when worn one over the other. They'll do; it's those or get *really* cold.

I pad quietly across the tired grey lino to the rear door, with the floorboards creaking under my feet, holding my one pair of prized cycling shoes and a water bottle. Under the house is my mountain bike, a used and very tired turquoise Specialized Rockhopper. I put on my shoes and rain jacket, take a deep breath and clip my feet into the pedals.

As I pedal away from the house the tyres crunch through the gravel, the only sound I can hear apart from the occasional car. I ride off, exhaling steam as I cross the road and start the clock.

The time trial starts. The faster I ride the warmer I will be, the more time I'll have to enjoy breakfast, the less likely I am to be late to school, the harder the ride will be, the better the training will be, the better the cyclist I might become ...

The loop through the back roads of rural Plenty, Diamond Creek, Nutfield and Hurstbridge will take one hour and eight minutes on a good day. And it's on this day, this bitter winter morning, I realise that I have found something within me, around me, that might change me, change my path, change my life.

They say knowing at a young age what you want to do in life is a great gift, so this is a big moment for a 14-year-old. It's a strong sense that I've discovered something, and am about to discover many more things, about the world and about myself. Graham Greene once wrote: 'There is always one moment in childhood when the door opens and lets the future in.' For me, as I push away on the pedals over the steepest and hardest climbs in the area, taking in the most challenging and enjoyable single-track descents, this is that moment.

While other sports have never worked for me – not Australian Rules, not cricket, not basketball – I've found a sport that does. It's one that suits people who don't mind – indeed, enjoy – being on their own, one that requires truly hard work, continuous commitment and dedication. It's one where you need the physical strength to get yourself through every kilometre, over every incline, and the mental strength and concentration to keep going through the pain of exertion, to extract every molecule out of yourself and put it down into the pedals and onto the road.

It's at this moment, on this little turquoise bike, amongst these quiet peaceful hills, in that crisp, clean air, feeling that surge of adrenalin, that I dream my life is about to change. And an adventure is about to start.

I WAS BORN ON Valentine's Day 1977, in the hospital of a remote Northern Territory town called Katherine. My first cycling-related memory dates from 1979. My dad Paul and I are in a bike shop and he asks me which one I want. There are two bikes in the smallest size, a red one and a yellow one. Inside me, I know I want the red one, but the yellow one is closer so I point at that. Now I have my own 16-inch BMX.

I spend hours hurtling around the isolated town where we live, red dirt flying everywhere, with the family dog, Woofie, following me in a protective motherly role. Not that traffic or people are the danger; snakes and spiders are much greater threats. We live in an Aboriginal community called Barunga, about 80 kilometres south-east of Katherine, on the south-eastern edge of Arnhem Land. It has a population of just 700, nearly all of them Aboriginal. My young parents moved here for the adventure and a different experience. I have vague memories of some of the Aboriginal people – the smiling mothers, the children who ran round with seemingly unlimited amounts of energy, the young guy who could lift his fingernail up and show what looked like bones underneath.

Mum and Dad take a photo of me on the little yellow bike, smiling. Soon I feel as comfortable on two wheels as I do on two feet.

When I'm four, we move to Upper Corindi, a collection of houses and farms 40 kilometres north of Coffs Harbour in New South Wales. My parents have decided they want to live near the ocean so they've bought 240 acres of virgin bush 10 kilometres from the coast. My father makes a horse float for the 3500-kilometre trip down from the Northern Territory, a steel-framed tin box that sits on the back of our blue Dodge Canter truck and houses our two horses and all of our belongings.

It's a very basic life in Upper Corindi. Initially we sleep in the float while my father clears the land for farming then builds a house from the very trees he's cut with his chainsaw. I wander around and ride my BMX along the dirt tracks that connect one landmark with another.

One day I walk outside and my mum, Helen, is talking to a stranger. This man is riding what must be a racing bike; I've never seen anything like it. I look at the pedals and see the toe clips and think, 'They must be to hold your feet in.' But I wonder, 'How do you get off when you stop?'

It's a happy, energetic childhood. My mother takes me to preschool balanced on the grey metal tank of an XT Yamaha motorbike. And as more people move to the area, we car-share on the dirt roads to the bus stop for the further 15-kilometre bus trip to Woolgoolga Primary School. The longer travel required in Australia shapes me from an early age.

At primary school, we wear a uniform of grey shorts and grey collared shirts. There's one grumpy teacher who's particularly strict about this, boasting that everyone in her class gets a stamp when they wear their uniform to school.

One day I'm not wearing my uniform and she rouses on me: 'Tell your mother to put your uniform in the washing machine!'

'We don't have a washing machine,' I reply, and I never get roused on again.

We eventually get solar-power electricity, and telephone and even a TV – a little portable black and white thing, with access to just one channel, the ABC. As a family we watch Richard Morecroft read the news, and on Sunday evening we watch Molly Meldrum on *Countdown* and that's it. On the weekends, I spend my time with the only boy who lives in the area, Simon Skerry – he's a year older than I am, and a much better bike rider. I can never do skids as long as the ones he does.

One day at school when I'm in Grade One, our teacher, Mrs Schute, takes the class up to the TV room in the library to watch something educational. It's a documentary about the Tour de France.

There are crackly old images of the riders sitting down to lunch, passing down a basket of bread to other riders … 'Hmm,' I think, 'that looks like nice bread, I'd like some of that.'

There are images of a lot of guys riding racing bikes around France. Mrs Schute talks us through the basics. 'See the rider in the yellow jersey? That means he's leading the race.'

She explains that all the riders are part of various teams and that one rider can win and his team can win too. Some riders help other riders by riding beside them and protecting them from the wind. As they tear down the hills alongside each other, it looks glamorous and fun, and a little bit dangerous.

I think, 'Hmm, I'd like to be the guy wearing the yellow jersey.'

While Dad grows vegetables for the market and does mechanical work from home, Mum is more academically minded, motivated to make a career for herself. So when I'm six years old, they decide to go their separate ways. I move with my mother and her new partner, Trevor, to Armidale in northern New South Wales, where my mother has been studying Australian politics and philosophy by correspondence at the University of New England.

The separation doesn't work out too badly for me; in fact, I like sharing my time between the different houses. It's nice to able to experience two different lifestyles simultaneously.

I spend the school term with Mum and Trevor, who becomes a second father figure in my life. Living in a rented house on a small sheep station, we don't have a TV or a telephone. Mum loves her horses. Trevor chops firewood and tends to the horses in the afternoons, then cooks dinner on an open fire; in the evenings we play cards and read books.

As an only child, I've learnt to make my own fun; I'm used to being alone, and I've always been fine with my own company. I consider it a lesson, practically and emotionally, to live in reasonably isolated places where I have to rely on myself for entertainment.

Trevor is a joiner who loves his work. After building furniture with machines all day, he'll often come home and continue working with wood by hand. On the weekends, we will be fixing or servicing one of his cars, or playing cricket or soccer together in the paddock.

We have a workshop and bellows in the backyard. Sometimes I help him hot-shoe the horses. I'll pump the bellows and he'll hammer the nails into the horses' hooves as the hot shoes sizzle a mould on each hoof.

Trevor does things the way they were done 100 years ago; I'll watch him French-polish a cabinet and meticulously dovetail joints, all by hand, and only in daylight hours, of course. Or he'll create hinges or gate latches with simple blacksmith's tools. He makes many of the objects around our home – windows, doors, fences, sheds, toolboxes, wooden cooking utensils. He works with the old-fashioned values of an artisan, with a real pride in his work, and a touch of teenage adventure still in his blood. He's a fantastic role model for a boy, and a living history lesson at the same time.

In the school holidays I go and visit my father, normally by bus. The ticket costs $12.50. It's a trip of around 200 kilometres that takes about three and a half hours each way. It's a beautiful drive down from the Northern Tablelands region of New South Wales, past Dorrigo Mountain, a mountain on the Great Dividing Range. It's probably one of the most beautiful roads in all of Australia.

My father's work ethic is in stark contrast to that of my mother and Trevor. Mum is driven, it's about seeing how far she can go in her chosen career, and she encourages me to work hard and succeed, to prove myself to those who doubt me. Mum always tells me, 'If you're going to do something, do it properly.'

Dad is the complete opposite. He prefers a modest life, with less work and a minimum of complication. 'Don't give me stress,' he'll joke about anything that requires a reasonable amount of effort.

Spending time with both teaches me a lot. With Dad, it's manual farm work and mechanical stuff. Living in the bush with leeches, goannas, spiders and snakes. We have to raise our voices in the evenings to hear each other over the screech of cicadas. The water pumped from the nearby river is murky and green; we drink rainwater from the roof that tastes better but still has tiny 'wrigglers' in it.

In school holidays, from the first day to the last, my hands will be stained with grease. It takes me at least a fortnight after I leave to wash off all the marks. We'll be pulling out tractor gearboxes, or switching engines or diffs between the very interchangeable Holdens of the time. Or we'll be seeding 200 kilograms of potatoes, or planting or weeding Dad's market garden. Weeding more than a hectare of corn, peas or potatoes takes hours.

Trevor shares some of Dad's interests, but on the whole, my other life in Armidale is quite academic and methodical. Life is all about school, books and learning. By the time Mum graduates from university, she's very well read. I haven't inherited her love of horses, but I am grateful to be influenced by her thoughtfulness, her interest in the world and her social conscience.

These two contrasting lives are undoubtedly shaping me. I'd like to think that they're helping me to be versatile and practical.

ON 25 FEBRUARY 1985, I nearly die.

The stitches on my scalp leave an obvious mark, but what happens on this day stays with me for much longer.

I'm eight years old. It's early, before school. We're packing to move to a new house in town and Mum is going through some stuff in a drawer. She asks me to bring the horses up from the paddock. There are four horses plus two foals. They usually come up by themselves, but for some reason this morning they've chosen to stay down in the paddock.

As I walk behind one of the foals to shoo it towards the house, it kicks out with both hind legs in excitement. One of its hooves strikes the right side of my skull.

I spend seven days in a coma in Newcastle Hospital. The doctors say I'm lucky. I could have been brain-damaged or paralysed down one side of my body.

I come out of hospital slimmer and weaker, with one half of my head shaved, unable to walk for lack of strength. Slowly I regain enough fitness to walk continuously. Still under heavy medication, I develop a series of headaches that strike me for years to come. Once or twice a week they hit, often when I'm sitting in class at school. They really nail me; sometimes the pain is excruciating. Different things will trigger the waves of debilitating pain – excessive exposure to sun, changes in temperature. If I don't wear a hat in the sun the headaches will usually start. I learn to avoid these situations but the headaches don't go away for years.

There's a big scar on my head where the neurosurgeon, Dr Bookallil, lifted the piece of skull touching my brain back into place. It required 28 stitches to close the incision. If I ever bump my head on that spot there is the most agonising pain.

The accident teaches me lessons about pain and discomfort that I don't forget.

I AM TWELVE YEARS old. After a short period living in the big city of Melbourne, we move to Plenty, a semi-rural suburb 28 kilometres away from the city centre.

It's hilly where we live, with trees everywhere, and big, wide-open skies. There are dirt tracks on the sides of the roads, magpies in the trees, horses in most of the paddocks, and a horse float parked alongside nearly every one of the widely spaced houses. In the early morning or late evening you'll often see kangaroos, or a sly fox slinking into hiding. It's nothing like the suburbs of Melbourne. We're in the country – no public transport, no socialising with the neighbours over the fence after school.

Plenty is to be my home for nine years. I detest it initially, being a teenager dragged away from my friends. Mum loves riding her horses but horse riding isn't my thing.

My school, Eltham High, is about 10 undulating kilometres away. Mum and Trevor work full-time and are preoccupied with their horses on the weekends so they can't drive me around a lot. One day I overhear them talking. Trevor says to Mum, 'If he wants to get fit, he could ride to school.'

Something strikes me about the idea of being independent. And wet days aside, as an alternative to two bus journeys and a train trip each way, it's convenient. So I try it on my basic white, green and blue road bike. It takes a long time, and I'm tired all day at school, but it doesn't put me off the idea of riding again.

The trek takes me across hills, along a series of dirt paths. It's pretty safe, but still, it would be much easier with a mountain bike.

Mountain bikes are a novelty, but something about them attracts my attention. In Greensborough, on my way home from school, there's a bike shop. I often go in there and look at the bikes and admire them.

One day I see a bike reduced from $519 to $375, more than my Mum can realistically afford at the time. It's the wrong size, and I don't like the colour, but thanks to the surprising generosity of my father, it's attainable. I don't see him as often these days – he doesn't have much involvement in my life after we moved 1500 kilometres south – but when I mention it to him in one of our weekly or fortnightly phone calls, he offers to buy it for me.

Soon I'm doing 100 kilometres a week, to and from school and rides through the countryside on the weekends, which is a big step up from doing nothing. It's tough with all my heavy schoolbooks sitting in my backpack. But it feels good, charging along on the bike.

A lot changes when I get that mountain bike. I'm old enough to ride satisfying distances and in great need of connecting with people my own age. But what I thought would be convenient transport to get to school and visit friends turns into a pastime in itself. Suddenly, I'm only interested in hanging out with friends who want to ride. Then to ride again the next day, and the next …

Soon I'm riding to school not to get there, but to get in as much riding as I can. Soon, I'm sitting in class waiting for the hours to pass so I can get back on my bike.

CHAPTER 2
RACING ON DIRT

1991–1993

FIVE OF US HAVE gathered at the BP service station in the pre-dawn chill on our bicycles, rubbing hands, stamping feet, adjusting gloves, our breath little clouds of steam. It's 6.30am in Diamond Creek, a little town that's just a short ride from my house in Plenty.

In the group is Kevin, a chiropractor, Luke Bond, a bike mechanic, Marcus Walker, who owns a bike shop in Montmorency, and a good friend of mine called Matt Farrell. There is also Kieran Ryan, an extremely fit cycling coach in his 40s. And me.

It's 1991 and I'm 14. Riding is starting to dominate my life. For me it's the biggest thing going on. I'm spending a lot of time at bike shops where I meet others with a similar passion. There aren't a lot of mountain-biker groups around, so I've been lucky to meet some like-minded people. Through this group I meet another group of riders who do solid rides two mornings a week, Tuesdays and Thursdays.

It's fun, but it's also about learning. I question anyone that has more experience than me on tips for training, racing and equipment. We'll often race each other on the climbs and maybe on the downhills. We start to push each other in the spirit of collaborative competition.

I start to hang out a bit more with Matt. He knows about cycling and I absorb his views and ideas. Matt encourages me to go on my first real mountain-bike ride, a nice loop around Kinglake, through some pretty awesome bushland. We start riding together often, using simple, very basic equipment, and no proper clothes. Just a bike, a helmet and shoes with toe clips.

Matt suggests we have a go at a mountain-bike race at Janefield, 10 kilometres from Plenty. Sounds cool.

There are about 10 people in the race. It isn't very well organised, and the course markings aren't very clear.

I fly over the bumps, ride the landings, take the turns easily. At one turn, seven of the others go the wrong way, which means I come second.

I get home a few hours later. Mum is making coffee.

'Did you enjoy it?' she asks.

'Yeah, it was great. I came second.'

'How did you find it?'

'Like the hardest thing I've ever done, Mum.'

'Would you like to do it again?'

'Oh yeah, I think I would.'

In fact, I do it again that afternoon. This time the race is in Blue Lake. I come 10th. I get home exhausted but exhilarated.

I start riding in some novice races and win a couple. 'Wow!' I think afterwards, 'that wasn't actually very difficult. I know how I can get better. I can go harder if I'm fitter.'

KIERAN RYAN IS THE first serious cyclist I've ridden with. He has such well-defined calves and when he rides it seems effortless. I want to be as fit as he is. He's quite an inspiration to me in building tone and aerobic capacity.

I start asking him questions about training. He sees the passion in me, the desire to improve. He offers me advice on tapering and training loads, how best to prepare for competition, what to eat and when, how to rest and for how long. He opens up a new world for me, a world where being organised and prepared means you'll have the best chance of winning a race.

It's the beginning of 20 years of commitment to the routine of training.

At this stage it isn't structured training by any means. I do hilly loops on dirt roads around Plenty, first with the group and then by myself, long treks through the countryside, every day the rides get longer. Soon I'm doing three- or four-hour training runs.

Riding is teaching me a really important lesson about sport, and life. It's teaching me that the more you put in, the more you get out. I find it so satisfying that the hard work and the training are making me stronger and fitter. I see that cycling is about putting the time and energy in – and it's just a matter of prioritising things to make it happen.

I go from a couple of rides during the week, and then on the weekend, to riding every day on my own. I really like it. I start getting in a good volume of training at the start of the day. It's not easy getting up that early, but it's so nice to be out riding on the country roads around Diamond Creek, Arthurs Creek, Kangaroo Ground, Hurstbridge, Strathewen, St Andrews. I ride past Peter Brock's house in Nutfield and the first intervals I ever do are on the very hill in Plenty where Craig Lowndes, the V8 supercar driver, lives.

A beautiful part of the world, and I feel very much a part of it on my bike.

THE TOUR DE FRANCE: the biggest event in the sport of cycling. If you know no other cycling race, you know this one. It's a reference point, used as a metaphor for something that's extremely demanding or difficult.

I'm intrigued. How do riders get fit enough to ride through France for three weeks with virtually no respite? How do they build that type of endurance? How do they manage to keep going mentally?

Matt's a huge Greg LeMond fan. The charismatic American is in the last years of his Tour career after winning it three times. Matt's family don't have a TV, so when the highlights of the Tour de France are shown at 6.30 each evening Matt rides over to my house to watch them on SBS. Apart from that documentary at Woolgoolga Primary, it's the first time I've ever seen the Tour de France. Each night there's a distilled 25-minute version of the day's racing, so it's pretty intense.

Matt knows a lot about the sport and he'll explain some of the strategies and nuances to me – when a rider will attack, which ones are the climbers, which ones are the experts at riding on the flat, who are the *domestiques*, the support riders for the team leader. I learn about time trials and the gruelling mountain stages and spectacular sprints, and about the sheer craziness of racing 3700 kilometres through France.

I love it, I soak it all up. I look at the faces of the riders as they toil away, and watch the spectators with their signs and deckchairs, and I love the châteaux and vineyards they ride past.

The program is hosted by the renowned cycling commentator Phil Liggett and his colleague former British cyclist, Paul Sherwen. Together the pair have educated nearly every English-speaking cycling fan in the past 30-plus years. I am one of these millions of fans, so it is all fascinating talk to me. But in Australia it isn't easy to find stuff out. All Matt and I can do is buy the cycling magazines and read the very brief reports about the races weeks after they have occurred.

This year – 1991 – the Spanish rider, Miguel Indurain, wins the Tour for the first time. The Big Mig – as he is universally known – has a certain mystique that makes him all the more fascinating. He's so dominant and composed. When he races he looks like he isn't suffering at all. My impression is of a machine of a man who's dominating the Tour de France. He becomes my first road-racing idol.

I find out whatever I can about him. One time I see a little documentary piece on him, narrated by Phil Liggett. Phil says, 'He still lives on the farm with his parents. The only difference now is there's a Mercedes Benz parked out the front, by the tractor.' I think, 'Isn't that nice.' Watching this documentary is a key moment for me.

There are even Australians in the Tour. Phil Anderson is a great pioneer in Australian cycling and for me, he's a legend. He's certainly getting towards the end of his career and past his best years performance-wise, but he seems to be our best rider. There are other Australians like Stephen Hodge, Allan Peiper and Neil Stephens racing, but Phil is the guy who'll go out and fight for stage wins.

The challenge for riders like Phil is that there isn't much racing they can do when they come back to Australia. It's all in Europe. I read that Phil likes to go back to the Australian countryside in the off season and just quietly train and stay out of trouble, stay away from all the fuss and the attention.

Because there's not so much interest in cycling here, Phil isn't really seen by many in Australia as the champion he is. But I'm sure he inspires a lot of riders of my age. When I see him on TV I get really excited: 'Phil was on TV, Phil was there!'

Phil Anderson and Miguel Indurain have really inspired me to think about Grand Touring. They've placed a seed in my mind that I'd like to ride the Tour de France one day.

For now, though, mountain bikes are my main obsession. I already have mountain biking idols I've read about in magazines and so on – Ned Overend, John Tomac and Swiss rider Thomas Frischknecht, whose results make him the best cross-country rider of his generation.

All of them are professionals. But in Australia, even within the small cycling community, the notion of making it as a professional is scoffed at. Phil Anderson, Neil Stephens, Allan Peiper and Stephen Hodge are the only four riders competing on big professional teams in Europe, and they're all road racers. When I tell people my dream of turning professional as a mountain biker, they think I'm a little bit crazy. I refuse to let it discourage me.

A friendship forms with one of the employees at the local bike shop, Russell Collet. I tell him my plans and ask him for his thoughts. 'What would I need to do to become a professional mountain biker?'

He looks at me, and I see a lot of doubt in his eyes. 'You're going to have to train a lot. A LOT.'

'Oh, OK.'

And so I start training hard. Very hard.

TODAY DURING TRAINING I give myself a two out of five.

It's not a great score, but I have to be honest with myself. It went OK on the bike today, but it could have been so much better. I could have gone harder, could have managed my time better to allow me to ride longer. I should have returned from the ride with nothing in the tank except the knowledge that I had extracted everything out of myself.

So today it's two out of a possible five.

The next day I get up a bit earlier and get on the bike. I've got a plan to ride hard along the tracks around home. And a plan to eat really well. And to go to bed a bit earlier.

The plan works well. It's a very good day. So for training I give myself a five out of five. For diet and self-discipline? A four. For rest and sleep? Recovery was maximised, I got my self-evaluated minimum of eight and half hours of necessary uninterrupted sleep. A healthy five. All in all, a good day. A day that I used to its maximum potential to improve myself.

I write the scores into the little notebook next to my bed. It's a simple book, with lined pages and a blue cover. It's my training notebook. I write in it every day, because at 15, I have become my own psychologist and motivator.

I put down my hours of sleep, quality of sleep, training volumes, training values, and average heart rate. I write: 'Train harder. Don't eat dessert. Go to bed earlier.' Sometimes I go to bed and realise I haven't written in my diary, but I remember every detail by heart, so I update it the next day.

And the thing is, I never cook the books. As one of my teachers and role models, David Lawrence, once said, 'If you don't touch the telegraph pole at the far end of the cross-country course, you're only cheating yourself.'

The training diary formalises my regimen and helps me prioritise everything in my daily life. And it creates my mindset. Over time, I develop discipline and motivation and the ability to make sacrifices, because I have practised how to do it. By writing it down, I formalise what I'm thinking, put a structure on it. The more I get used to writing down the score, the less I'm inclined to veer from my targets.

Every day I ask myself: 'What did I learn today? What could I do better tomorrow?' It helps me become a disciplined, determined, efficient and effective athlete.

I gain knowledge in any manner possible – by talking to people, by reading any information I can find. I learn from nearly everyone I meet, from the first guys I ride with, to the elite and semi-professional riders I sometimes have the opportunity to drill with questions.

As a cyclist, the first thing you have to learn is to deal with fatigue – waking up tired, then going out and making yourself even more tired. As you progress, you learn more about your body. You learn what training works for you, you learn what recovery methods work for you, and also the timing – quantity and duration of training versus quantity of recovery required.

Diet fuels you. You need to learn what, when and how to eat properly to allow it to get you through long stints on the bike and to maximise your recovery periods. What you choose to eat has an effect on you physically but also psychologically. Knowing you're eating healthily and well can aid your concentration.

I'm not a skinny kid, so I have to change my body type by changing my metabolism. That takes a lot of work and concentration. Maintaining a very low body weight and watching nearly everything I eat every day has a big effect but mentally it is very draining.

To train well you need to be mentally focused, because that allows you to train hard and, in competition, race hard. You learn what's generally good for you, but then also you have to learn what's specifically good for you because every individual's different. And it takes a long time to learn what really works for *you*.

Once you've learnt what's good for you, the challenge is to fit that in with your daily lifestyle, your family situation, your life at home.

Up at 5.30, do some stretching. Take off on the bike for a one-hour loop, timing myself. Have a shower and some breakfast, get my schoolbooks, get back on my bike and ride to school, another 10 ks. Get to school at the very last minute, do all my classes. At lunchtime (or during a spare period in my senior years), go to the library and do my homework so it frees up time for the afternoon. Or go to a gym down the road from school, do a gym session and come back to school for more classes.

My new life of blending schoolwork and cycling requires one main ingredient: good time management. I need to be super-organised. But it also means that this is all I'm doing. School, riding, eating, sleeping. A real structure has developed in my life.

A lot of my friends are starting to go out to parties, smoking cigarettes, drinking alcohol. I don't miss drinking or smoking, I do miss the socialising, but that isn't a priority right now. In the bigger scheme of things, when I'm talking about following dreams, it's not a huge gap in my life.

I'm getting more and more serious about pursuing mountain biking as a career.

Damian Grundy is a national-level mountain biker who has opened a bike shop just down the road from my high school, Eltham High. I start spending a lot of time at the shop, asking questions, learning, improving.

In early 1992, my mother takes a few days off work to drive me up to Thredbo in the Snowy Mountains, so that I can compete in the Under 17 (sub-junior) category at the Australian Mountain Bike Championships, my first national-level race. It's by far the biggest test I've faced up till this point in time. I'm hoping to finish in the first 10 and do well in the hill-climb event.

I end up winning the hill climb and coming second in the cross-country event, behind Hugh Morgan. As anyone feels when they come second, I'm disappointed not to have won, but really happy to get a good result at my first nationals.

Damian Grundy is watching with his fiancée Rachel from their hotel apartment. Rachel spots me, 'Oh there's the kid who comes into the shop all the time.'

'Cadel Evans? How's he going?' asks Damian.

'Well I've only seen one other rider come through so he must be doing pretty well.'

Damian greets me at the end of the race, 'If you are interested in any help with your training, come in and have a chat with me.'

That's how I get my first coach.

WITHIN A COUPLE OF years we've set some major goals:

Try to compete at the World Cup.

Try to compete at the World Championships.

Try to compete at the Olympics. (Mountain biking has just become an Olympic sport; 1996 in Atlanta is going to be its first outing at the world's biggest sporting event.)

It's now 1993 and I'm 16. It's probably good that it's just the two of us having this conversation. Anyone else might think we're being absurdly ambitious, especially as we're aiming to do well in these events, maybe even win.

The thing is, we don't know how difficult these goals will be to attain, so we're not intimidated by them.

I've developed a reasonable understanding of my aerobic capacity and my ability to keep going when it gets hard. I've done enough riding to know what might be required. I'm already asking: 'What needs to be done next?'

CHAPTER 3

GETTING SERIOUS

1993–1997

DAMIAN BRINGS DIRECTION TO my cycling – goals to work towards, a base of knowledge to start from, some contacts in the cycling industry so we can arrange some sponsorship. It's my first lesson on the professional side of the sport – keeping sponsors happy, becoming a valuable marketing tool. I race at the Under 17 Australian Championships again in 1993, and this time I come first.

Driven by my own desire, and helped by Damian's advice and encouragement, I also start racing some local criteriums on the road – small circuit races that are run in disused industrial zones or sports facilities where traffic is not an issue. Damian explains that learning how to ride on the road is the best form of training for mountain biking. 'But who knows?' he says. 'Maybe one day you'll want to race exclusively on the road.'

In 1994, thanks to the good work of a soon-to-be-close friend, Martin Whiteley (the founder of the Australian Mountain Bike Association), Australia is chosen to host a round of the Mountain Bike World Cup. It's Australia's first international mountain-bike race, to be held in Cairns, in Queensland's far north, in July. It gives me a chance to compete in my first international race.

This is a chance to medal or maybe even win at junior (Under 19) World Championship level. At Martin and Damian's suggestion, I decide to specialise in cross-country events from this point.

I increase my training, increase my focus and have a bit of a review of all the equipment I'm using. Being a teenager of course I've always wanted the good equipment, but I haven't had the funds to buy the higher-performance products.

I've started out with the slowest and most basic friction-shift gears, old cables, worn tyres; it's taught me to ride smoothly and delicately, forcing me to be physically stronger and technically more proficient. And to appreciate every piece of equipment I own.

With the prospect of racing in the World Cup, all that is changing. I have great support from a local bicycle manufacturer, Apollo Bicycles. They don't make the highest-level bikes but they're a really good professional sponsor for me and they help me out with all my equipment. Together, we assemble a competitive bike for the race. It's more than good enough to ensure I'm not going to be disadvantaged.

I'm finding my niche quickly, by training harder and preparing more carefully than my fellow competitors, and I'm unbeaten in the juniors for the entire season. So to push me harder at national events, Martin and Damian put me into the elite (senior) class, against the men, a year early. I'm doing Year 12 this year, but I train hard before school most mornings. I'm pretty motivated for it, and concentrate on getting a good result.

In July I fly up to Cairns with textbooks in my bag, very excited and ready to test myself against international elite competition. I can say with certainty that the level isn't quite what it would have been had the race been in Europe, but at the same time, as a junior I am fortunate just to get a start.

The race goes well, and I come fifth. It's a big achievement: I'm the first Australian to place in the top 10 of a cross country World Cup. At Martin Whiteley's request, the organisers decide to expand the podium from three to five. They feel it's great that an Aussie has placed so highly. So there I am, up on the podium, a kid in a men's event. The international mountain-bike community starts to learn how to pronounce my name.

After this, Mountain Bike World Cups always have five riders on the podium: a smart move for the sport because it gives more sponsors exposure.

IN SEPTEMBER I HAVE another chance to be part of an international race, this time the Under 19 cross-country Mountain Bike World Championships in Vail, Colorado.

In the mountain-bike magazines I read, Colorado seems the centre of the mountain-biking world. I've read that a lot of the top bikers live in a town called Durango, in the southwestern part of Colorado.

We have a training camp with the national team near Durango, and stay in a ski resort town named Purgatory. One day we're out riding and we see John Tomac coming back from a training ride. I think, 'Isn't this amazing!' I can see why so many mountain bikers live here. The natural terrain and the weather – at altitude – are really well suited to mountain biking. And the trails are well maintained too.

I love the experience. I'm missing some weeks of Year 12. I take my schoolbooks to study, but I don't open them once in six weeks.

I spend time talking with the most experienced rider on the team, John Gregory, from Tasmania. He's one of the first riders I've met who has raced in Europe. His amazing dedication to training, diet and racing, impresses me. He teaches me to concentrate on just doing my best, otherwise riders with more talent or other assistance will always best you and demoralise you. This plants an important seed in my mind, one that develops into a mentality that will get me through many, many difficult situations.

One day he says to me, 'Road cycling is chess on wheels.' It stays with me. I'm learning that cycling, on the road and within the team, has a lot to do with strategy, tactics, and about knowing your place on the board. I don't know how to play chess, but it is evident that I have a lot to learn about road cycling.

I think a lot of people have been expecting me to win, but I come second to French rider Miguel Martinez, the diminutive son of Tour de France rider Martino Martinez. He's on a different level from me on the day, but it's the start of the longest rivalry in my career.

I'm happy with second. Again, I have a good race and I get everything on the results sheet.

IN LATE 1994, CYCLING Australia is setting up a mountain-bike squad at the Australian Institute of Sport (AIS) in Canberra to train riders in the hope of winning medals at the 1996 Olympics. As well as selecting the riders with the most potential, the squad needs a coach. Damian is probably the most successful coach in the country and is chosen to lead the squad.

I'm 17, the number two junior in the world, and if I can get the results at national senior level I could be selected for the AIS, which would be a stepping stone to being able to race internationally. In November, in between my final VCE exams, I'm invited to an AIS training camp that will help them determine who gets into the squad.

Then it happens. I'm offered an AIS scholarship. It's a big moment for me. Being able to train full-time is a huge step. It means great opportunities to go overseas and race, and it's the best path towards becoming a professional mountain biker.

Everything is falling into place.

IN MARCH 1995 I fly to Canberra to start my training. I've just turned 18 and it's my first time living away from home, but that doesn't faze me; I'm focused on fulfilling my potential. Finally I can dedicate my entire day to training on and off the bike. I learn how it feels to do five- or six-hour training rides, and I learn that if you recover well you can make big improvements. The AIS training system is based on principles developed by our East German coach Heiko Salzwedel: very high volumes of training without a great deal of specificity. Or, as AIS physiologist Dave Martin describes it, 'like baking a cake: the fewer ingredients you put in, the less chance there is for something to go wrong'. The big training loads serve as a great base, both physically and mentally, for the years to come.

It's an environment where I can satisfy my desire to learn more from the most qualified people in Australia. I have my first chance to talk to a nutritionist and a sports psychologist, and I start reading my way through the AIS library. They do a series of physiological tests that show I have a rare combination: a high lung volume combined with a capacity to absorb more oxygen in a breath than 99.9 per cent of the population. It's the best result they've ever seen.

I'm very enthusiastic but in need of experience. The first serious rider I get to spend time with on the national team is John Gregory. Tasmanian-born but very Swiss-influenced, he's not the most famous or the most successful rider, but what I learn from him – about diet, dedication, off-the-bike training – shapes me as a cyclist. He teaches me some of the fundamental philosophies of being a rider. Always focus on getting the best out of yourself, not on the result. Judge other riders by their professional decisions and results, but judge them as human beings separately. This becomes very helpful later in my career when I have to compete against and deal with individuals who use questionable methods to achieve results.

In April 1995, I go to the US with Damian and the rest of the new Australian national team – Paul Rowney, John Gregory, Rob Woods, Janine Feyaerts, Jane McDonald and Rachael Bruce – to compete in cross-country rounds of the Mountain Bike World Cup. I'm the youngest in the group by about seven years, but I'm not homesick or nervous. I'm just so motivated to ride and realise my dream.

I meet up with them again in Europe for the remaining World Cup races and World Championships of the season. In the middle of all that, in July, I take a break from mountain biking and travel on my own to join the junior road track squad in Italy. I fly to Venice where AIS junior road coach James Victor and team manager Nino Solari pick me up from the airport. We drive 100 kilometres to Bassano del Grappa for a training camp in preparation for the Juniors Track World Championships in San Marino, my first serious competition on the road. I end up coming third in the time trial – won by fellow Aussie, Josh Collingwood – but crash out of the road race, injuring my hip.

At the camp I meet junior track endurance coach Shayne Bannan, a man of few words, with an air that's partly serious and partly about showing his authority over those he's coaching. There's a bit of fear towards him on the rider's side because of how careful he is with his communications. He isn't cold, but he's firm. He's one of the most serious adults I've met in my life, a professional coach doing his job, and doing a good job.

One day Shayne and I are riding near camp and look over at a magnificent ruined castle. Shayne says, 'That's probably Marostica. The castle's over 500 years old.' I'm amazed that something so sophisticated by modern standards could be so old, compared with what we Australians are taught to believe is 'historic'. I'm awestruck by being in Europe, by the ancient villages and the castles and the sense of history all around me. Up till now, the possibility of going to Europe has existed only in my dreams, and here I am, riding in Italy, the heart of international cycling culture.

In Australia I'll see one cyclist out a week and I'll wave; here two or three will pass by every five minutes and I'll wave at each one. I'm surprised when none of them waves back at an 18-year-old Australian with a huge grin on his face.

Racing with the Italians certainly is something. Here's a country that is, by most people's standards, very religious, but let's just say that after one junior road race, my vocabulary of Italian expletives is well developed.

And the food ... how good is even the simplest dish of pasta? And the coffee? Disappointingly, with Australia's strict stance against drug use, as juniors we're only allowed one espresso for the entire three week trip, the morning of the time trial.

I grow to love the food, wine, fashion, cars, bikes, and the fast-paced lifestyle, even though it's frenetic. The life of a rider in cycling-obsessed Italy is exciting. So is the way Italians speak with such passion, the way they don't take life *all* that seriously. It's the beginning of a lifelong love of all things Italian.

THE FOLLOWING YEAR, 1996, I'm approached to join a US mountain-bike team called Diamondback International (sponsored by Diamondback Bikes). The team manager, Keith Ketterer, has been on the lookout for talented young riders coming through, and scouts from Diamondback have been observing me ever since the Cairns World Cup in 1994. One of the attractions for them is that I'm an English-speaking cross-country rider from a good athletic background, which is attractive to the American market. They think I have the potential to be a good competitor in World Cups. For me, a major reason for joining Diamondback is to increase my chances of getting to the Olympics later in the year.

As a first-year pro rider, the expectations on me are fortunately not that high. I'm still finding my way as a serious professional athlete, and an adult for that matter. It's my first experience on an international team, and at 19 I'm learning a lot. I'm noticing that Australians will 'say it like it is', while Americans soften things a bit. Coming from that Australian culture of bluntness is probably helping and hindering me in equal measure.

There are two Italian riders on the team who are particularly good, World Cup podium level: Hubert Pallhuber and Alessandro Fontana. They've both been coached by a man named Aldo Sassi. They're much more experienced than I am and I learn a lot from them. They give me considerable help with my dedication to training, preparation and ultimately competition. Hanging out with them, I also start to learn to speak Italian, learn to cook Italian, learn about the Italian lifestyle.

Hubert Pallhuber is in his early 30s – quite old by riders' standards – but we get on well. Because he speaks some English, I ask him a lot of questions. We cook together in the apartments we stay in, travelling round America. The thoroughness Hubert puts into his training extends to selecting the best and freshest ingredients in the kitchen, and preparing them really well.

Hubert changes the way I think about diet. At the AIS it was all about reducing fat to get skinny. As an athlete, you think, 'Reduce it? If I cut it down to zero then I'll definitely get skinny', because you have the mentality that if something's good, then more is better. Extreme measures.

But for me, especially for my body type, it doesn't work, because keeping fat levels low makes my skin very dry and hard. I think what happens is it changes the way your body deals with fat: because you're not having much of it, your body seems to hanker for it, and you're always hungry.

With Hubert, all of a sudden I'm getting filled full of olive oil every day. And as well as being really good for my skin, it helps satisfy my appetite, so I'm eating less and I start to lose what many people would refer to as 'puppy fat', which of course helps me perform a lot better. The European way of life seems to suit me.

But I'm still learning about my body, how it reacts to different types of training and how to reach and maintain my optimum weight. I'm discovering it takes a long time to learn about your own physiology. You start to understand it, but then it changes and you have to relearn. It's a constant process of re-evaluating what your body needs, how far you can push it, when it needs rest and when it can be pushed harder.

IN JULY I RETURN to the Australian national team to compete at the Atlanta Olympic Games. This means switching back from a professional organisation to an amateur team, and I let this undermine my confidence.

Since it's the first time mountain biking has been a medal sport, none of us knows what to expect. I go to Atlanta focused on getting the best result I can; later, I wonder what my result would have been if I'd just gone there to enjoy it.

Before the opening ceremony, the athletes around me are so keen to be on TV and they're getting into all the glamour and excitement. I think, 'Well, they're making such a big fuss, I'd better go along and see what it's all about.' But I've grown up in a household where we never watched much TV, so I've never seen an Olympic opening ceremony, and I struggle to connect with it all.

I find the actual race a bit strange; because it is a small field it doesn't quite have the depth of a World Cup event. I race reasonably well, and get close to the front at one point. But I'm 19 years old, the second youngest person in the race, and I was never going to win. The main idea is to gain experience. In the end, I come ninth.

Afterwards I get straight back into it, travelling to the next round of World Cup races in France and continuing my season.

IN SEPTEMBER, THE MOUNTAIN Bike World Championships are held in Cairns. It's the first year of the new Under 23 category. Miguel Martinez and Canadian, Roland Green are fighting it out for the lead during the first half, then Dario Acquaroli comes out of nowhere to seize victory. I'm third behind Miguel. At the press conference afterwards, I accidentally sit in the winner's chair: a sign of how much I still have to learn.

I come out of the 1996 season with renewed focus and determination. By the end of the year, back in Australia after a season of following an Italian diet, I've lost a lot of weight but my body hasn't had time to adjust to the thermo-regulation effects of losing so much fat. In early 1997 I compete in a race at the Thredbo ski fields. Even in summer, it's freezing cold; it actually snows on us during the race and I'm struggling. I get a 'hunger flat' – I completely run out of energy because I cannot keep my body warm.

A few people from the AIS are shaking their heads in disbelief. How can I perform properly at that weight? They think I've ruined my career. I don't feel I can speak to them because they're so dismissive of the approach I've been taking in Europe. The nutrition experts at the AIS are saying, 'Cut fats out of your diet', and here I am with the Italians, drizzling my salad with olive oil. But it's been working well for me and my recent performances reflect that.

I talk about this with Mum and she suggests I write a letter to Damian. So I sit down and write out my training goals. I'm keen to take another step in the sport, to go to a higher level. I tell Damian: 'If you want to be a part of it, I'd love to work with you. If not, thanks anyway.' I'm 19, and I'm standing up to the national coach, who's also one of the main selectors for the Olympic team, so it's a fairly bold move.

I hand the letter to Damian after a small club criterium in Melbourne. We speak on the phone a few days later, and Damian says he'd be delighted to help me get where I need to go. He writes me a training program that I stick to for the next three years.

I adhere to it to the absolute letter. Rain, hail, shine, appointments, social engagements – nothing stands in the way. It's quite stressful and requires a lot of concentration, but I learn a lot from it. Among other things, it teaches me to be effective with my time and energy. I'm told that when you work like this for eight or nine years you keep the benefits for the following ten.

IN 1997, DIAMONDBACK HAS suddenly moved to a whole new level and we're racing to win the World Cup. It's a pretty ambitious goal.

And here's where the tricky politics of being in a team begin to reveal themselves. On the strength of my 1996 season, this year I'm a real contender for the World Cup.

But the marketing department of Diamondback decide that rather than race for the World Cup lead, I should go and compete in California, largely for promotional reasons, because that's where the Diamondback factory is. So, because I'm trying to act like a professional I think, 'I don't want to, but OK, I'll do as I'm told.'

Things get better a few months later. In April, the team sends me to compete in a round of the World Cup in Wellington, New Zealand. It's a good place for me to race. The people and culture are similar enough to Australia that I feel at ease, almost like I'm back home. Meanwhile my North American and European competitors aren't used to the crippling jetlag that comes from flying across so many time zones, but for me that's been a fact of life for a couple of years and I am able to recover quickly.

It's a fairly typical World Cup course: 8.4 kilometres over gravel, grass and sandy clay; dodging rocks and roots with a 350-metre ascent over each of the six laps. I've learnt that preparation is the key to a good race. I research the course obsessively, especially the downhills and other technically difficult sections. I get to know individual tree roots, rocks and other obstacles. I decide on the best lines, alternative lines and the most promising places to pass.

Because the bike I start with must be the bike I finish with, I check that every part of the machine is ready for some 50 kilometres of punishing riding. If something breaks, I've got to be able to fix it myself – fast – with the tools I'm carrying. Mountain bike racing demands self-reliance.

The starting gun fires and I make a good start. This is key. Unlike road racing, where it's typically the last 300 metres where you need to get in a good position to launch your sprint; here, the sprint that can make the race is at the start. You want to be among the leading riders when you reach the first section of narrow, non-passing track, otherwise you'll really struggle to pass enough riders to win.

Italian rider, Dario Cioni, is leading for most of the race but I'm hard on his heels along with two experienced French riders. One is the current World Champion the other is last year's World Cup Champion. At the end of lap four Cioni starts to flag. I'm a bit nervous about being done over by the other two, but I'm feeling good so I decide to attack and I overtake Cioni.

Being in front can be a stressful place for a young competitor – suddenly you've got everything to lose. But I manage to stay calm, keep my lead, and cross the finishing line over a minute clear of the second placegetter.

I'm 20 and it's a big step for me: my first international win. I am the youngest rider ever to win a Mountain Bike World Cup race. It's a huge milestone, and a welcome reward for my hard work with Damian.

It's proving to be a breakthrough year for me. I back up the win in New Zealand with a second World Cup victory in the US in July. I've gone from a top 20 competitor to number one in the world. I'm starting to feel as though I could go anywhere in this sport.

After these wins I notice something: the attitude of people in the cycling world has changed. Even the behaviour of people close to me is different, including Damian. Before the wins, if I made a comment about anything, people were dismissive of me. Now, all of a sudden, whatever I say is gospel. It feels very strange to me.

I'M ALSO GETTING MORE and more racing experience on the road. In the breaks between mountain-bike races, I travel to Italy to join the Under 23 Australian road-racing team, based in a town called Quarrata, near Pistoia in Tuscany, and twinned with an Italian Under 23 team. Organised by Shayne Bannan, the move to Italy is the first big step in bringing Australia in line with the best cycling nations in the world. It means I'm getting big blocks of training, and it's the highest quality of racing anywhere in the world outside of professional ranks. To have the exposure and experience to race against the highest calibre of Under 23 riders in the world is a huge boost to a whole generation of Australian riders.

I'm racing against guys like Danilo Di Luca, Ivan Basso, Rinaldo Nocentini. Some are incredibly good. Ivan and Rinaldo are talented, but still have to prove themselves. Danilo Di Luca seems to win every race he competes in; he's just amazing. I keep thinking, 'How can I beat this guy?'

The Australian team live in Italy for four or five months a year. It's a small professional operation, with a team house, vehicle and uniform. The main sponsor is a local furniture manufacturer. It's another step in adapting to European culture: seeing how the other Aussies fit into life in Italy, going to the local café to be told by the old men that you are hopeless for coming second. The *signora* who looks after the house who will not give you dinner if you are more than five minutes late.

This involvement on the road means putting in a lot of time and energy. It's a big commitment, given that I'm travelling the world with my mountain biking as well, competing in about a dozen races a year, accumulating points for the overall ranking of the Mountain Bike World Cup. It's my performances at the mountain-bike events that are paying my salary at this point. Meanwhile, the road racing is to help prepare me for the mountain-bike races, and gain experience for a possible road career at some point in the future.

Racing in two different disciplines of the sport has its difficulties, though. Aside from the commuting required between the US and Europe, a fair amount of training and preparation is needed every time I switch between the sports, despite the sometimes impossible time constraints.

I still want to base my mountain-bike career in Australia, but competing in so many international events means it's no longer practical to live there all year round. I need a base in the northern hemisphere. The easy way would be to go and live in California or Colorado, and ride the nice trails there and hang out in the great weather. That would be the fun option, but I want to be able to perform at the highest level. The best riders in the world are all Europeans. Europe is a bigger culture shift to make, but to be exposed to the best level of competition, in both mountain biking and road racing, it's the place to be based.

After my performances this year, I'm in a good position to choose a team, and a place to live, and further enhance all aspects of beginning a profession on the road. It's time to decide on my future.

CHAPTER 4
EUROPE

1985–1989, 2004, 1997–2000

THERE ARE TWO FIGURES in my life I've always looked up to. The Dalai Lama is one, Tintin is the other. It's meant as no disrespect to His Holiness that he shares my admiration with a cartoon character.

I'm eight when I see a Tintin book in the school library for the first time. It's called *The Black Island*. On the cover is a young man driving an old wooden boat towards an island, and inside there are animated scenes involving planes and forgers and a ferocious gorilla. I borrow the book and take it home, reading the 62 illustrated pages just in time to get it back to the library before the due date. Interested, I borrow another, and another, until within a few weeks later I'm reading one of Tintin's adventures a night, often for the fourth or fifth time over.

And it isn't long before I want to be him. The intrepid kid reporter with the red cowlick and plus fours, accompanied by his little fox terrier Snowy, roaming the world having the most amazing adventures. He becomes my first idol, because he is everything we all hope to be in life: intelligent, brave, strong, fair, and smart enough to triumph over the bad guys.

He stirs a curiosity inside me; I want to go where Tintin goes. I want to explore the world, meet different people, learn from incredible experiences. Tintin is Belgian – as was his creator Hergé. My fascination with these characters quickly leads to a fascination first with Belgium and then with Europe. How they dress, how they live, how they speak. Something about Europe has me in its grip. The history, the culture, the languages, the exotic food, and the pictures I've seen of ancient bridges across rivers flowing slowly through medieval cities.

So, at 12, I make up my mind: one day I'll live there. And I vow that I'll visit all the amazing places where the adventures happened in the books.

One image in particular sticks in my mind. Tintin is walking down the street with a baguette on his shoulder, Snowy by his side.

Some twenty years later, it's 2004, and I'm walking back from the bakery in a Swiss village with my little dog Molly, carrying a baguette. My 'cowlick' of hair is not so pronounced, and plus fours have long since gone out of fashion, but here I am, living out that scene from the book.

But it's been a long journey to reach this point.

IN SEPTEMBER 1997, I compete in a round of the World Mountain Bike Championships at Château-d'Oex in Switzerland, second again to Miguel Martinez. I am exhausted after a long season, completely emptied of adrenalin from the huge step up I've made over the past year, since beginning Damian's training program. I renounce my commitment to compete in the Men's Under 23 Road Race at the World Road Championships, which would have been a valuable experience, but I'm totally depleted.

During the week at Château-d'Oex, I'm approached by cycling legend Stephen Hodge, one of the first Australians ever to join a European road-racing team. He's just retired from professional cycling and is working with sports agency International Management Group (IMG). I know Stephen only through seeing him on TV in the Tour de France, and spending a small amount of time with him at the Atlanta Olympics last year.

Stephen is a very sincere person and I like and trust him from the outset. He's new to the world of mountain biking but sees potential in me, and he knows I want to be a road rider as well as a mountain biker. As an Australian, he understands the difficulties of living on the other side of the world, away from family, friends and other support networks. He asks whether I would like him to manage me. My earnings are increasing, so I'm becoming more attractive to managers. He offers to look after things for me, and it's exactly what I want. I'm so focused on the riding side of my life that I can't cope with the other aspects.

Finding somewhere to live is the first thing. As a foreigner, I could start anywhere, but if you're a rider, you base yourself where you have contacts. In this case, Stephen is my point of contact in Europe. His idea is that I should base myself in Switzerland.

I find an apartment in a little village called Lugnorre, on the side of Mont Vully in French-speaking Suisse Romande, on the border with the German-speaking western part of Switzerland.

Suisse Romande could hardly be called the most glamorous or sought-after part of the country, but that isn't what I'm after. Lugnorre has all the charms of a small village. It's a couple of hours' drive from the IMG offices in Zurich, but fits in with my need to live the quiet and committed life of an athlete. It has beautiful views and fantastic mountain roads to train on. On the downside, the drive to Geneva Airport takes its toll, and because it's north of the Alps the weather can be a bit unkind – but in good conditions it is one of the most beautiful places in the world to ride.

I've come to Europe for very good reasons, and rationality has guided where I've chosen to live. It's all about performance and being a good professional. Where's the best exposure to the best quality racing? Where's the best place to train? Where is practical? And for a young professional this village is the best base.

This year I also need to lift things a little higher than Diamondback is capable of. Volvo–Cannondale, another US team, is the biggest and best team in the sport of mountain biking. On the back of my recent results, they're happy to welcome me on board for 1998.

In November, I get a call from Stephen Hodge. He's decided he doesn't want to continue in sports management. While the role of supporting riders can be very gratifying, he's realised that the marketing–salesman side of it is not for him.

It's been a short association, just two months, but Stephen has done a lot in that time to set the future direction of my life and career. Stephen's colleague at IMG, Luxembourger Marc Biver, takes over his managerial responsibilities.

I go back to Australia for the off season, to finalise the details of my relocation and change in teams, see my family, and have a much-needed rest. When I leave for the 1998 season in February, I say to Mum, 'I'll see you in October.' It becomes an annual occurrence from then on.

Mum and I are both saddened by the prospect of being apart. I'm an only child, and we're such good friends. The empty-nest syndrome kicked in pretty early for her when I lived at the AIS in Canberra, but my move overseas is much harder. At the same time, she's always wanted me to follow my dreams, if that means going away then she'll learn to cope. We speak a lot on the phone.

I move into the apartment in April 1998 in between various rounds of the Mountain Bike World Cup in northern California, Portugal, Hungary and Germany. I've just turned 21, and I soon realise that living overseas is going to be more difficult than I expected.

The language is one of the first things to deal with. The local people are very polite and respect my privacy, but this is a small farming village and not many people speak English. I don't speak any French. I studied French at high school for a while but I didn't like it so I stopped doing it as soon as I could.

But language is only the beginning. I arrive with just my suitcase and my bike bag. No knives and forks or towels or sheets or anything like that. I definitely need some help.

I find that in Madame Petter.

Someone is smiling on me the day I become Madame Petter's tenant. She's a charming, warm and motherly presence. My own mother is a long way away, and while resilient, I'm a long way from being fully 'domesticated'. Madame Petter makes sure I feel secure and looked after.

As soon as I arrive I go away to race. I get a call from one of the IMG staff. 'You've found yourself a real European mum here in Switzerland, your apartment's ready to go.'

Madame Petter has spare furniture and saucepans and kitchen stuff, and when I come back she's set up the whole apartment for me. She's put in a chair and a table, and the bed has pillows and sheets, and the covers are folded back. She's put bread in the cupboard and milk in the fridge. She's my saviour.

While Madame Petter speaks French and German, her husband Michael was originally from Ticino, an Italian-speaking region in southern Switzerland. Because I've been racing with Italian teammates, I've been able to polish my Italian from school days. So I speak to Michael in Italian and he translates into German for her.

'Can I hang a picture up on the wall?' I'll ask in Italian, then he'll translate it into German and she'll reply to him and he'll translate back into Italian for me.

This is how we start.

I'm in apartment number 10 of 10 apartments, so every 10 days it's my turn to wash in the communal laundry.

With Michael's help, I tell Madame Petter, 'I'm a cyclist. I train every day so I need to wash nearly every day otherwise my clothes get stained.' It looks as though I'm going to be washing a lot by hand. I'm living in an apartment with just a sink, no laundry.

Madame Petter says, 'Oh, it's OK, you leave the clothes in a basket on the corridor, I'll wash them for you.'

The next day, I go to the shop and when I return there's a basket of folded clothes outside my door.

I go and find Madame Petter. I tell her, 'Thanks for doing my washing, I really appreciate it.'

'If you have any more just put it out,' she says.

Mum comes over to visit. She has brought me up to be independent, and I'm not sure what she'll think of my landlady doing my washing.

I say, 'Mum, you know, to do the washing I just put it out and Madame Petter washes my clothes for me, because it's a communal laundry and I'm only allowed to wash every 10 days. You're only going to be here for a week, you won't have time to wash your clothes, so Madame Petter said she would do them.'

The clothes come back the next day, washed, and folded – including Mum's. Mum doesn't say anything, except to thank Madame Petter.

IT'S NOT JUST THE Petters who help me adjust. Here I am, in a village where everyone around me speaks the purest French in northern Switzerland. I've improved my Italian through socialising, but Italians are very open and talkative – the Swiss are not! Bit by bit, though, talking to the baker, the hairdresser, the lady in the patisserie, I start to learn some French and get going.

I rely on Marc Biver and his staff for a lot of things too, such as paying my bills. And being on my own in Switzerland I appreciate his support. It's good to have the company of another Australian.

I've always tried to take the best things from every country I visit and learn from them, and to me Switzerland is an amazing country. But I'm finding out that in Switzerland there are systems for every aspect of life, in contrast to the more freewheeling ways I've got to know in Australia, Italy and America.

Seemingly small things can become big hurdles. When I first arrived in Switzerland I would get back to the hotel at 2pm, hungry after training, just as *all* of the restaurants were closing. Coming home to an empty house after a week or so away racing is a similar affair. There are no shops or restaurants open after 8.30pm – very difficult if you have raced 200 kilometres that day. Recycling can only be deposited on Friday afternoons and Saturday mornings.

Hairdressers are closed on Monday, and need at least a week's booking in advance. The post office closes twice a day, and only takes cash.

I quickly learn that you have to plan every small errand well in advance, and to be sure to check all of the office opening hours, to take cash, and not to dare think of arriving at a place of business within 10 minutes of closing time. Switzerland is really designed for couples, you need two people to manage everyday affairs.

People in Switzerland are wedded to routine. They might get up at 7 o'clock every morning of their life. They don't even need to set an alarm. You know that saying you can set your watch by someone? The Swiss are perfect for it. They don't even look at their watches because they're so regular with everything they do. It's funny that in the land of the Swiss watch, no one actually needs one.

THEN THERE ARE THE hard parts of living on my own that no one can help with. I have accidents that drag me down in performance and which I have to deal with alone. My mountain-biking competitors will train for races, and in between they'll go home. But I go and join the national Under 23 road-racing team in Italy and race with them on the road. In some ways it works well because I'm getting a great training load, but mentally and logistically it's tough. Instead of having a rest and spending time with family, as the others do, I'm in Switzerland by myself with no family to support me.

And sometimes I get homesick. Normally I don't miss Australia, mainly because I don't think about it; I'm focused on other things. But every now and then a little reminder pops up – an Aussie accent, the smell of eucalyptus, the taste of Australian wine if you're lucky enough to find it on a European menu. These small cues help me remember how good Australia is.

But I am here in Europe for a reason, and I am going to follow that through to the end. I'm determined to do everything I can to become the best bike rider I can be, and to try to answer the question: am I good enough to be the best in the world?

TINTIN HAS GIVEN ME the curiosity to travel and an open mind towards other cultures that have brought me to live on the other side of the world. He's also given me a belief in the fact that good guys do win. All these ingredients have come together to make me the rider I've become.

I don't want to overstretch the symbolism here. I'm not Tintin in the world of bike racing. But after I move to Europe, there are moments when the challenge of resisting the bad guys isn't totally lost on me.

I've come into cycling at the end of a very bad period. Of course I've heard rumours about doping by professional road racers, but I'm so far away from that world that it all seems pretty removed from what I'm doing. Racing on the road as an Under 23 rider in Italy, I've heard a lot of stories but I don't know how many of them to believe. I have to say, though, the level of racing in Italy is incredibly high – a little bit *too* high.

A few months after I move to Lugnorre, a scandal breaks that becomes a big turning point for the sport. In early July, three days before the start of the Tour de France, a Belgian *soigneur* (assistant) from the Festina team is stopped by police. Inside his car is a load of anabolic steroids, growth hormones and masking agents. It says a lot about cycling culture that he's more worried about the injection he's had to help him stay awake than the load of performance-enhancing drugs he's transporting.

The team is later expelled from the Tour. The incident becomes known as the Festina Affair. When the scandal breaks, no one can stop talking about it.

I'm so green as a road racer that I'm struggling to understand the implications. It's hard for me to imagine what pressures some of these riders might be facing from their teams. I know one day I might make the switch to the road and I think, 'Well, that's a bridge that maybe I'll have to cross one day.' It's certainly intimidating, but what can I do about it? Until I have to confront it, I'm not going to let it worry me. I'm in Europe trying to fulfil a long-held dream.

My response is – as it has always been – to forget the rumours and get on with the job.

I'm comforted by the fact that Volvo–Cannondale have chosen me not just because I speak English, but also because they have faith that I'm a clean rider.

BY SEPTEMBER, I'VE ACCUMULATED enough points to become the overall winner of the cross-country Mountain Bike World Cup, the first Australian to achieve this. I've reached a huge goal in my career, but it's actually been quite a long process: six months of racing before you know if you've won or not. So the 'winning feeling' is also spread out over a long period. But it's great to realise I'm officially the best in the world at what I do. I've reached my peak as a mountain biker.

MY FIRST PROFESSIONAL ROAD race is in January 1999, at the first ever Tour Down Under in Adelaide. I now have my feet in two different camps. The first is the sport I've spent nine years working so hard at and the other is my new life, road racing.

The Tour Down Under is Australia's first 'big race', a sign that we've arrived on the world stage as a major cycling nation. South Australia has created a unique event, one of the most enjoyable stage races to ride because of the layout of the race. I don't say that because I'm Australian, I say it because it's in a beautiful part of the world, the Adelaide Hills, and at a time of year that is perfect for racing. Because the stages are relatively short and within close proximity, riders get plenty of time and energy to enjoy the race. And because it's during the summer holidays, people are in a great mood, and the ambience is fantastic. It's immediately well received by both international and national riders, and the Australian public.

I'm really happy with my performance at this event: I come 12th overall and win the jersey for best young rider.

On 27 January, three days after the Tour Down Under, a team has been formed for the Tour of Tasmania, one of Australia's few road races with a decisive climb. Phil Anderson is one of the team directors. Here's someone I used to really look up to, now he's in the car behind us. Fantastic!

For the time trial, Phil says, 'Oh, man, you spin your gears too much. You need to ride a big gear, you've got to look at those guys like Indurain. When you go against those guys, they'll eat you for breakfast.'

'OK, Phil.' I take in everything he says.

I win the uphill finish to Mount Wellington, and take the overall lead. As I'm riding away from the rest of the field on the upper slope, Phil Liggett tells the TV audience that one day I'll win the Tour de France.

I smile when I hear this. I'm flattered that a veteran cycling commentator sees something in me. But for an athlete, it's the hard work that matters. If I get that right, the results will come.

IT'S A YEAR OF near-constant motion. From Tasmania I travel to California for the Sea Otter Classic in Monterey and the first Mountain Bike World Cup race of the year in Napa Valley. Then it's straight back to Australia for the second round in Sydney. From there, I head north again for a gruelling spring season in Europe, racing both mountain and road bikes in Spain, Germany and England.

In June, shortly after training in the mountains of Switzerland with Matt Wallace, I fly to Big Bear Mountain, California for round six of the World Cup. It's hot, dry and very dusty. California and Colorado tend to make for dusty conditions which are tough on bikes and riders alike – at times it's a struggle just to breathe.

On the final lap I am battling it out – a minute ahead of the rest – with a younger Swiss teammate, Christoph Sauser. We pass the team manager and I am expecting him to give an order to Sauser. Nothing. Sauser sits on my wheel and then attacks and beats me to the finish. While I would like the win, I am happy for Sauser, and second place keeps me well ahead on points for consecutive World Cup victories. This starts some friction within the team.

From Big Bear Mountain, the circus moves on to Canmore, Alberta for round seven. It's mid-summer, but freakish weather has brought colder conditions than any Melbourne winter's day. Snow two days before race day has turned to intermittent rain and the course is a mire of freezing, fluid mud.

I usually perform well in mud, but there's no denying that the conditions are horrible. I wear latex surgical gloves under my racing gloves for extra warmth and spikes on my shoes for extra traction. Nothing on the bike works well in the mud. Picking up the bike and running is the fastest way through several sections of the climb.

I spend most of the race in a three-way battle with Christoph Sauser and Frenchman, Miguel Martinez, but none of us can catch frontrunner Thomas Frischknecht, a former Cyclo-cross junior World Champion who literally runs away from the competition on lap one. I manage to hold off Sauser and Martinez for another second place. One of my better performances in the coldest and wettest conditions I have experienced.

IN SEPTEMBER 1999, I join the Saeco–Cannondale road team – linked to my mountain-bike team, Volvo–Cannondale – in the lead-up to the Under 23 Road World Championships in Treviso and Verona, Italy. At this point I'm riding for Saeco as a *stagiaire* (in Italian a *stagista*). This is an internship, in which you work for free to gain experience and in return, the team sees how you are as a rider and may offer you a contract. At the races as a *stagiaire*, you're the work-experience kid. You have to go and get everyone's lunch or clean the toilets, and you're the butt of many jokes. But I don't mind so much – it's so exciting to be mixing with the professionals that I have only seen on TV and read about in magazines.

It was around this time that Marc Biver at IMG recommends that I get a manager who can be more focused on my career. He suggests former Swiss-German rider Tony Rominger who has his own company, Tony Rominger Management. It's the start of a 16-year partnership.

I am aware of Tony's cycling career, I've seen him on TV and read about him in magazines, but I never knew him when he was a rider. Racing from the late 1980s to late 1990s, he won the Vuelta a España (Tour of Spain) three times and the Giro d'Italia (Tour of Italy) twice, and twice broke the hour record.

He was there in the mountains, but it was at the time trials that he really excelled, in fact, he was perhaps the best time trialist of his generation. I ask him, 'How did you win so many Tours of the Basque Country?'

He says, 'It always had an uphill time trial and I always won it there.'

We're similar kinds of riders but we aren't the same. He could race well in the bad weather; I race well in the warm weather.

Cycling has changed so much since he was riding, but he always understands what a cyclist goes through. He understands the life of an elite cyclist, how it feels, how much work is required.

Tony is very fair, well respected by the teams, honest and upfront, and looks after me well. It isn't just looking after the professional side of things, Tony helps me with general living as well, things like ensuring the rent and bills are paid while I'm away. I'm living alone, a young man in a foreign place. Tony makes sure I'm never overwhelmed.

Some of it is just day-to-day living. Stuff that rattles me. The car registration office, for instance, loses my number plate. Tony goes out of his way to get me some other number plates so that the day I arrive back from a race outside Europe I can drive my car around and get on with my life. He bends over backwards to help me out when he really doesn't have to.

We start out as colleagues but over time we become good friends. In my experience, Swiss-Germans can be quite closed people, but when you gain their trust then you really have their trust for a long time to come. He gives me the most professional service a rider could ever hope to have within the sphere of cycling.

Tony guides my career, and his help is invaluable. Tony can see I can be a good road rider, but how good we don't yet know.

With Tony by my side, I manage the juggle between mountain biking and the road. The question is, how long can it last?

Combining both sports is gruelling, an endless round of driving, flying, competing, recovering then doing it all over again. Sometimes my head spins with all the commitments. I seem to be constantly on the move, and constantly exhausted. I seem to have no time to myself, and not even enough to flick the switch between the sports.

On top of this, I am falling out of love with mountain biking. I'm able to accumulate enough points to win the World Cup for the second year running, but emotionally, the sport that has dominated my life for at least a decade is losing its grip on me. The mountain-bike races I'm competing in just aren't as enjoyable any more. As the 1990s draw to a close, mountain biking is going through a decline in popularity and interest. And maybe I'm feeling the same way about the sport I've loved for so many years.

Unity in the Volvo–Cannondale mountain-bike team is poor. There's a lot of friction between the riders and a bit of internal politics going on. I have the feeling that some of my teammates are more interested in being the best rider of the team rather than the best rider they can be. It's a strange type of competitiveness, and I don't find it a healthy one. All this negativity is hindering my performance.

The team managers are also expressing disappointment with me because they think I'm focusing more on the road. And some of their equipment choices seem to be more about marketing than about helping our performance. When a guy from marketing comes in and tells me, 'No you've got to ride this bike that weighs more or doesn't have as much energy-efficient transfer as that one', that's no way to run a sport. It undermines my whole philosophy of being a professional: the first priority should be doing everything to get results.

In my life of constant sport switchbacks, I'll go off to the road-cycling team and really enjoy it. There isn't the same pressure to win any races. Every time I go to a road race I'm motivated and ride well, and this of course means that the team is happy.

And instead of travelling back and forth from Australia, I want to move to Europe permanently. As well as the opportunities Europe offers, cycling is so much a part of the culture, and road cyclists are treated with real respect. To me this is alluring.

The contrast has become quite stark.

At this point, one environment is clearly more conducive than the other.

CHAPTER 5

TRANSITIONING
TO THE ROAD

2000–2001

'WE SAW YOU ON TV, in the opening ceremony!'

An excited phone call from Martin Whiteley, who's now living in Spain. It's September 2000, and I'm at the Summer Olympics in Sydney, the biggest sporting event on the planet.

'They were showing all the pretty girls on the Australian team, then they showed you. You looked good!'

I'm not sure I looked all that excited, though, probably because I wasn't. At 23, I'm already hard-wired to judge success by results not by how much you enjoy an event. That night, I didn't live in the moment. I couldn't – or wouldn't let myself – take it all in: the stadium lit up with all the photo flashes, the cheers, the banners, the sense of the world sporting community coming together to compete. None of that really moved me. I was thinking, 'Yeah, but my result, that's all that matters – my result, my result.'

Leading up to the Olympics I've had to deal with setbacks through injury. I don't have much experience in this and I've found it very unsettling. I've gone in with really high expectations, and

I'm getting a lot of media attention. But I don't have the experience to deal with these expectations. I let external factors affect me.

This mindset is a shame, because it means I'm not allowing myself to soak in this amazing experience. I'm not sure I fully appreciate what the opportunity means – after all, I'm only going to do one home Olympics in my whole life, aren't I? And I've come into it acting as if my life depends on it, which is not the best mental approach to have.

Anyway, in the end I get walloped, coming in sixth in the cross-country mountain-bike event, with Miguel Martinez winning once again. And I don't enjoy the race because everyone's expecting me to win a gold medal, and it sours the whole experience for me. My benchmark is pretty straightforward: did I perform well or not? No. Therefore, did I enjoy it or not? Well, not really.

But there's one massive takeaway from the experience. All the athletes are offered mentors, people you can talk to, and one of them is motor-racing legend Peter Brock.

As a lifelong petrol head, I regard 'Peter Perfect' as a hero, probably my favourite Australian sportsperson. One day in the athletes' village, he gives a talk about the first time he drove a Holden Torana GTR XU-1 in third gear around the circuit in Sydney, which isn't there any more. I grew up hearing stories about Trevor's 1972 XU-1. And the fact that Trevor – who was a father figure to me – loved this Torana, makes Peter's words even more special.

Thinking about my childhood idol, who grew up not far from me, I realise there are many similarities between us. Peter was also a young hopeful forced to race on inferior equipment that helped him become an even better driver.

To spend time with him is a privilege. For me it's the best thing about the Sydney Olympics.

I'M LEARNING A LOT, quickly. This new sport is different. It's not bull-at-a-gate. It's such a change from the nonstop world of mountain biking.

In mountain biking you start fast and you keep going fast. You set a pace and stick with it. As a self-driven athlete, you have to have your foot on the gas all the time to stay at the top of the sport. As a road rider, though, you've sometimes got to go into neutral and put your foot on the brake. Often you've got to do a complete U-turn. For someone who's so used to going flat out, it's a big challenge. I'm going from a sport with one speed to one with many, and it's a lot to get my head around.

I come into professional road racing with some experience from racing with the Under 23s, with a high level of fitness, a low level of endurance but a lot of drive and enthusiasm. As I start my road career, this often leads to being close to big results but being frustratingly let down by lack of experience. I've built my physical base off road, and my limited road experience in the juniors and Under 23s is not as thorough a school as most of my competitors have passed through.

Most others spend years gaining the knowledge and experience of racing against the pros on the road as they build their fitness, allowing them a longer learning curve. By the time they get to the elite level, they've already done some years of racing full-time, as professionals and before that as Under 23s and maybe even juniors. So they are practised in this art. Also, most have raced many of the big races already and know a lot of the climbs, a lot of the descents, whereas I'm having to learn all this quite late.

Road racing is all about history and tradition, very different from the young sport of mountain biking, which is still evolving and is changing constantly.

Mountain biking is a sport that is mainly individual, in the sense that everything you do, you do with your own two legs and your own mind and matter. You have help from your team during your preparation, and your coach has input at the beginning and end of the race, but *during* the race it's all up to you. There's no race car or radio to fine-tune tactics along the way. As a mountain biker you have to be very self-disciplined and internally very driven.

So coming to the road there is a mentality switch, stepping into a majority team sport. But it's interesting, because there are times when it drifts between a team sport and a very individual sport. And this can change from one second to the next. It's about knowing how the race is going and what the team is planning to do, but being prepared to switch back suddenly into a self-reliant, individual mode.

It's also about learning how to be a teammate. You get used to each member of your team, how they ride, when they attack, how they position themselves, who gets protected and why. Who is strong enough to be there in front when the going gets really hard and fast. You also learn about the strengths and weaknesses of riders on other teams, how to understand the politics and clashes of egos that influence the outcome of many races. And all that takes a little time.

Then you learn your own role – you're the team leader, or maybe you're the first guy to ride – as in, the first guy to sacrifice himself for the leader – or maybe you're the last or the second-last guy to ride. Again, this changes with each race and with each moment of the race itself. Tactics have to be continually adjusted. Messages are sent and you need to respond to the race director's orders. Getting used to a team dynamic is quite physically and mentally draining.

It's generally believed that as a mountain biker you're automatically going to be good at descents. When you're on your own on a 'slow' technical road descent, the skills are similar. But it's so different descending on the road tightly packed among dozens of other riders. It requires trust and faith in others' abilities and judgment. I find my mountain biking hinders my road-descending ability because I have a mountain biker's habits. It's like a touring car on a race circuit compared with a rally car – they're both cars, they're both going quickly, but they're very different.

You need to learn about positioning in the peloton – judging when to be in front or when to ease to the back, knowing how to move into position without wasting energy. Especially at the elite level, positioning in the peloton is much more difficult than people would think. Often by the time you realise you need to move it's already too late.

The concentration required for mountain biking is huge. The racing is much more intense. One mountain-bike race is like racing three or four days on the road in terms of what it requires mentally. So I've never been able to do more than 21 good mountain-bike races a year – whereas to race 60 days on the road is actually not that hard. It's much more tactical, though: you need to conserve mental energy for later in the race when it's really necessary to be alert.

There's also the endurance aspect of road racing. Regular, intermittent bursts of high speed and power over a long period of time require the body to efficiently metabolise fat as fuel whenever possible, reserving valuable stores of glycogen for the big moves required at the business end of a race.

I haven't changed my physique, my metabolism hasn't changed, but road racing is different in so many ways. As a mountain biker I have an engine that's used to doing a one-and-a-half- or two-hour event once a week. You're training to perform at maximum capacity for a short period of time, operating at constant high intensity. You're training your body to use sugar as fuel, and to have it available to use and empty yourself in that one-and-a-half- or two-hour event. And I've been working this way for years, and tuning my body very specifically for this routine.

Now, on the road, I'm preparing for a chance to ride a Grand Tour, an event in which you ride for five or six hours a day for three weeks. These are dramatically different demands.

The shift to intermittent bursts of intensity, sometimes higher and sometimes lower, over a much longer period of time each day, almost every day for three weeks, takes a lot of getting used to. You're having to train your body to use added fuel in order to continue to perform over this duration. So I have to change my physiology.

Part of this is changing my diet. On the road you're riding much further and burning more calories and more fat, so you have to eat a lot more carbohydrates and a little bit more fat. If you're racing for five or six hours, you need a substantial amount of food so you can recover then race again, always remembering that a bike rider has to stay very lean; your body weight counts for more because you've got to go uphill. And this is where it gets really tricky, because obviously you're burning off the calories, you put fuel in, you recover, you train hard and you have to be very careful not to eat too much, because to get really, really lean – and I'm talking below four per cent body fat – to get down there and stay down there can be very difficult.

I love good food, good wine too. I also love dessert. That's OK, though, because obsession with a perfect diet isn't going to get you to where you need to be. What is going to do that is a sense of perspective. Food gives you a great deal of pleasure and satisfaction. Having to refuse things is sometimes difficult to deal with, particularly in Europe, where eating is a central part of social interaction. And following a really strict diet is really draining. I've seen people concentrating so much on their diet that when it comes to racing hard or going out training in the rain or the snow, that toughness that they need, that hard edge, isn't there. The mental energy required to do that has already been consumed in refusing dessert for several years. To achieve a diet that's balanced and synthesises with all your social interactions, that's hard to manage.

To make matters worse, I'm still juggling the two disciplines of mountain biking and road racing. And it's not just about the sheer demands of both sports. It's about the effort in making the switch between them. For the road racing I'll have to get the endurance thing switched on, and then going back to the mountain bike I'll have to get the intensity thing going. I always have a smaller race before the important ones in my race program, because every time I make the switch I need at least one race to really get going.

By early 2001 I am no longer under 23 so I'm entitled to race under a professional licence with my mountain-bike team, Saeco–Cannondale, and with the Saeco road team. It's a hectic time.

In June, riding for the Saeco team, I compete in the Tour of Austria, a very hilly seven-stage race. The mountain stage involves the Kitzbüheler Horn, known as one of the steepest mountain roads in Austria, so we all know it's going to be tough.

On the first day there's a big break really early, a group of about 15 riders. I bridge across to it, but we slow down and lose 10 minutes.

The mountains are intimidating everyone. My German teammates, Fabian Wegmann and Torsten Hiekmann tell me, 'We hope you're climbing well, Cadel, because no one else has a chance to do anything here.'

Then on stage four, the mountain stage, I'm just about to start my climb when I twist my chain. I only have one bike, so I'm thinking, 'Oh, this isn't good', because you can't ride a bike with a twisted chain.

The support guys in the car are saying, 'Quick, get on this bike.' They hand me a bike I've never ridden before.

I jump on it and a couple of the other Saeco guys wait and bring me to the back of the lead group. I pass everyone in the group, get to the front as it's starting to split, and ride away and win the stage, taking the leader's jersey beside the Kitzbüheler Horn. The guys in the team seem very happy about it. I think, 'It'll be good if I can keep it.'

And I do. I keep the jersey till the end, and win the race.

No one has been expecting much of me. I haven't been expecting much either, but I'm just really happy that my training is paying off.

At Saeco I've found myself in a great environment, where everyone in the team wants to help me and is happy when I do well. It feels nice – very different from my mountain-bike team.

It's my first major road win, and I'm still perceived as a mountain biker. When I win the fourth stage, reporters refer to me as 'Volvo–Cannondale mountain-bike racer Cadel Evans'.

Winning the Tour of Austria is more than just an announcement to the world of cycling that I have talent. It highlights how much I enjoy being on the road. Something big is happening: my future is being paved for me. It seems I've made the right decision in taking up road racing.

This is confirmed for me the following month, when I ride an invitation-only Swiss event called the A Travers Lausanne (Across Lausanne). It features two uphill time trials, each one 6.85 kilometres.

I've been called in to do this event because it's organised by my former management company IMG. David Millar – one of the few English road racers at this point in time – has pulled out and they need a rider to fill in. I live nearby and they ring and ask if I'll ride it. 'Why not?' I tell them. So I'm here wearing the number of David Millar.

Someone in the crowd calls out, 'Hey, David!'

'David!'

I say, 'Excuse me, I'm not David Millar.'

They keep yelling at me. 'Yes you are! Look, it says so here in the newspaper!'

It's the first time I'll be racing against Lance Armstrong, who won his third Tour de France just two days ago. As a lifelong fan of cycling, I've followed his incredible journey to the top with admiration.

I'm pretty sure he's exhausted after a three-week tour, but being the competitive animal that he is, he'll probably want to win this event too.

The two time trials start at the centre of Lausanne, ascending the hill above the city, past the Olympic Museum. I've ridden it once before so I know the climb.

In the first time trial I feel good. I'm climbing well. And as I climb everyone seems quite excited. When I get to the finish there's some enthusiastic commentary. I still don't understand French very well; I hear my name mentioned but not much else. It makes me think I must have done a good time.

After lunch, I put my time-trial skinsuit back on for the second time trial, thinking, 'OK, this time I'm going to put everything into it.'

So I go flat out. I ride to the finish and it turns out I've won it. Lance comes in fifth. I've beaten the best Tour rider in the world.

It feels like one more brick in the road of my cycling career. When you race against a big star in cycling and you beat him, it stays there forever in history.

THERE ARE A LOT of young road riders trying to be noticed by professional teams, hoping for a break. Getting spotted is a sell-job. Tony Rominger and I often discuss ways to do this.

I need to know: is it worth giving up a good career off the road to try racing on the road? Switching to the road has its obvious attractions, but it means going from being at the top of one discipline of the sport, to starting almost at the bottom of another. If I take several steps back in results, earnings and reputation, how many steps forward can I eventually go? Will it be worthwhile?

After my testing at the AIS, I know about my body's capabilities and have a reasonable idea of how my own talent stacks up against those racing at the top level of the sport. In the summer of 2000, though, my results at the AIS stand for nothing in the conservative and Eurocentric world of pro road racing.

Having the ability to concentrate, make sacrifices and dedicate years to training and preparing for events means little. The thing that counts is what the decision-makers of the sport think you can do – the team managers, whose perceptions are influenced by the top coaches. And at the international level, in the biggest races, the most influential opinion of all is that of Italian coach and doctor Michele Ferrari. If Ferrari says you're a good rider, worthy of investing x number of dollars in and capable of earning x amount, you'll probably get all the opportunities that Ferrari thinks you're worthy of.

Ferrari has worked with several high-profile clients – including, most famously, Lance Armstrong, winner of last year's Tour de

France. No one knows exactly what Ferrari's methods are, and even though Armstrong is starting to dominate in a way that is causing some concern, he's never tested positive.

I discuss this with Tony, who suggests I approach him. The motivation is simple: I'm interested in Ferrari's analysis of me because while I am quite sure that I can be a good road racer, the world of cycling will need some convincing. The AIS testing doesn't count inside the small bubble of pro cycling. Within the world of road cycling, I feel Ferrari is the key person who can tell me whether it's worthwhile giving up my mountain-bike career and switching to the road.

And to do that he has to perform a physiological test. I'm confident I'll get good results, and that if he sees I have good physiology he's going to tell the teams, and that when it comes from him, the teams will listen.

I have access to Ferrari through Marc Biver – General Manager of IMG Switzerland – and also through Tony, who worked with Ferrari before breaking the Hour Record. Tony requests a meeting and Ferrari agrees to test me. In July 2001, Tony and I meet Ferrari in St Moritz, Switzerland, at the Albula Pass, a mountain I've always enjoyed riding.

We arrive at the base of the mountain and Ferrari explains how the test will work. I will ride up a hill five times, do a loop, and then do the same test in a fatigued state. He will take lactate, time, heart rate, watts; all the usual measures.

I find conversation with him a bit awkward. When I ask him who else he has been working with, he looks embarrassed that anyone would ask him such a question and says nothing.

I think, 'Okay, he's a doctor, I guess that could be confidential.'

I tell him I will be seriously considering moving from mountain bikes to the road and can he recommend any teams for me? He says something dismissive of Mapai and mentions that he cannot work with any Italian teams, which seems odd.

.But the test goes well, and Tony and I receive the answer we want. Ferrari tells me: 'I think you should invest your time and effort in becoming a road rider.'

Ferrari's endorsement of me has probably put up my potential contract value to a team by three to five times. As a 24-year-old, this is, of course, very appealing to me: annual earnings of three to five times more ... for doing the same job.

If cycling is chess on wheels, I've just been promoted from a pawn to a knight in an instant.

IN JULY I FLY back from the Mountain Bike World Cup in America and come home on a Sunday to an empty house. I'm hungry, tired and a little frustrated. I've been away for two or three weeks, so of course there's no food in the fridge. If you get home on a Sunday in Switzerland, there are no shops open. All I have in the cupboard is some chocolate and some potatoes that have grown long tendrils.

The next day I do four hours' training in the early-morning rain, then get in the car at 7am and drive four hours down to Bergamo in Italy to arrive by 11 o'clock. The team has given me only one bike, so I've got it in the car, but of course I've been training on it for four hours and it's filthy.

When I arrive in Bergamo the team managers are waiting. 'Come on, come on, you're late, let's go.'

I've just driven 400 kilometres, I was on the plane before that for 10 or 12 hours, plus 100 or so kilometres of training. And then I get there and we jump in the car and drive another 400 kilometres to the race.

They tell me I should go for a little ride to roll the legs out. Sure! I've already done 800 kilometres in the car and 100 on the bike. Another ride would be nice. Again, in the pouring rain. Still, I get changed and walk out to go for a ride.

But the mechanic isn't happy. I've arrived with a dirty bike and he doesn't want to clean it. I'm thinking, 'Oh man. Exactly when did he think I would have found a minute to clean my bike?'

Next day I wake up sick. I've ridden in the rain while jetlagged and am a bit run down. I can't follow the best guys in the race and I have to pull out. It's one of the first times in my career when I've done that. It leaves me feeling guilty.

This isn't working. It's literally making me ill. It's not just the packed schedule or the empty house that's wearing me down. I'm serving two masters and it's exhausting me. Too many flights, too much driving, too many demands, and a lack of support from team members like the mechanic who didn't want to give my bike a wipe.

Cycling can be a tough sport at the professional level. Expectations are something that you only ever satisfy briefly. The moment that you achieve a goal or objective, another one is added to your list. For as long as I competed in two disciplines, this treadmill has been running twice as fast.

Life is so fast for me that I rarely have a moment to just stop and think. But occasionally, as I deal with the frustrations of my life as a part-time mountain biker and part-time road racer, I have moments of great clarity about my future.

I can visualise continuing to ride well on the road, using the training base I've developed, and harnessing my innate competitive spirit. I can see in front of me a successful future, and I find that inspiring.

The win in Austria and my disillusionment with mountain biking are drawing me away from one sport and towards another. Tony Rominger understands my feelings well, and is also looking towards the future.

A few weeks later I say to Tony, 'I want to change to the road.' It's time. As soon as I get through this season, I want to focus on one sport.

JUST A FEW DAYS after the 9/11 tragedy in September 2001 I ride the World Mountain Bike Championships in Vail, Colorado. After watching the terrible images on TV of the planes flying into the World Trade Center we are struggling to concentrate.

But I want to give it my best because I know it may be my last major mountain-bike race ever.

Maybe there is something symbolic about how it ends. I think Chistoph Sauser, my Swiss teammate, wants to be the first Volvo–Cannondale rider, or the first Swiss rider, or both, to cross the line, so he wants to beat me. His countryman, Thomas Frischknecht, is also gunning for first-Swiss status so he's focusing on Christoph. I just want to get the best result I can. Meanwhile Roland Green is riding away from us, to cap off a dominant year.

In the final stages I'm racing for second. I'm doing a descent and I come into a really technical section.

All of a sudden my bike just stops. What the hell?

Somehow the bunting – the thick plastic tape that marks the borders of the course – has done a loop around my bike's seat pole. I try to pull it off but I can't break it.

I'm forced to dismount and reverse to get some slack into the tape so I can untangle it. As I'm doing this, Christoph and Thomas Frischknecht go past me. I get going again and race towards them but they're in a sprint for second and third. I finish just behind them in fourth.

It's Roland Green first, Thomas Frischknecht second, Christoph Sauser third. And me. No podium, no prize. Fourth. The wooden spoon.

That's the way I finish the last major event of my mountain-biking career. Of the many great memories from my nine years in the sport, this is far from the best.

I've come close, but I've never won a World Title. I don't think I had it in my legs today to come first, but were it not for all the infighting, I could have done better than fourth.

I'M LYING FACING SKYWARD in a ditch, my bike next to me, wheels still spinning. Around me are the seven other members of a breakaway. It's early October 2001 and I'm racing the professional four-day Giro della Provincia di Lucca in Tuscany, a lead-up race to the Road World Championships.

The Tuscan sun is not shining today. The road is wet and slippery, and judging by the random nature of this crash, it's not just from the rain.

We're on the last descent, only six kilometres from the finish. I'd started to back off on the descent, thinking, 'These guys look like they're going a bit too quickly.' I came around the corner and everyone in the breakaway was lying on the side of the road. It didn't look good.

Everyone has been risking it on the descents to keep away from the main group just behind us. But it seems like there is some oil on the road, hidden under the water. As soon as the breakaway touches it, they all go down, sliding along on their backsides, shoulders, knees, heads. I can't think about braking. Next thing, *Boof!* I'm down as well, sliding along the chunky bitumen into the ditch and towards everyone else. Everyone's hit the deck, sprawled on the side of the road.

The first guy to get back up is star German rider, Jan Ullrich. He rides away and wins the stage. I get back on my bike and finish in sixth place, less an uncomfortable amount of skin.

I don't mind the occasional scrapes and crashes. We are racing in some beautiful quiet back roads in Tuscany. I have had a long mountain-bike season, and I am extending it by participating in the last few road races of the year.

Also riding for my team at the Worlds is another superstar, Mario Cipollini. With his long hair, they call him 'The Lion King'. But all the Italian riders refer to him as 'Cipo'. Riding alongside Cipollini is more of a culture shock than a sporting experience.

I'm in the Saeco camper, maybe I'm the last to arrive. There is one vacant seat at the front so I take it. A couple of the riders are talking to each other in Italian. There's an Austrian rider who'll translate for me.

The Italians are speaking quietly to each other and looking over at me.

I think, 'What's going on here?'

The Austrian rider leans over. 'That's Cipollini's seat.'

'Oh. I should move, then.'

'Yeah, you'd better.'

Suddenly the other riders in the bus are excited. One claps his hands and announces Cipo's arrival.

'*Eccolo qui, Cipollini! Cipo! Cipo!*'

I move seats pretty quickly and sit in the back somewhere.

Learning to become a road rider is not all about what you do on the road. A lot of it is about knowing who's who. And getting out of their way if you need to.

Later I have another intimate moment with Cipollini. A bit *too* intimate, actually.

At the end of one stage I walk into the bus and there's a *soigneur* wiping Cipo down, head to toe. Yes, head to toe. When you're really exhausted the *soigneurs* have been known to give you a bit of a scrub, because the diesel on the road can stain the skin. If you've done a really hard race you usually don't have the energy to scrub yourself. So they use wipers soaked in alcohol that wash you down really well. Then you go and clean the rest of you yourself.

Not Cipo. Cipo is being scrubbed, head to toe, fully naked.

I think, 'This isn't an example of what I want to follow, not just in bike riding, but also in human engagement.'

THE LONGEST TIME I'VE ever spent continuously on my bike is at Paris–Tours, a one-day race between Paris and Tours in the Loire Valley that is always among the last rounds of the World Cup. The course is very flat, it's quite long and there's one little hill right at the end.

In 2001, the race is held just two days after the Giro della Provincia di Lucca. There's a headwind all day, and after about 20 kilometres, French breakaway specialist Jacky Durand attacks –

along with countryman Richard Virenque, which you wouldn't expect. They've collaborated really well.

They take a large gap early in the race and they manage to stay away from the bunch for most of the day. Because there's a headwind and there are only two riders in the breakaway, the main group – especially the Rabobank team, who are there to defend their Word Cup lead – let the gap go.

We race for over 250 kilometres and finish at dusk. In the final kilometres, Durand tires and falls back while the main group gains on Virenque. But the Frenchman holds on to win in a time of just under seven hours, two seconds ahead of the bunch.

It's now Sunday and I'm due to compete at the Road World Championships in a week's time. Early on Monday, I get in the car and drive 650 kilometres from France, home to Switzerland to take a plane from Geneva Airport at nine o'clock on Tuesday. Because of the crash in Lucca, I've got ripped skin on one side of my hip, so I'm not sitting very comfortably in the car. I eat at an uninspiring roadside stop, walking gingerly.

I make it home by 1am, put a bit of disinfectant on my wounds and go to bed. I've got to get up at 6am to drive to the airport, which is 130 kilometres away. I get up, arrive at the airport to fly to Lisbon, Portugal, with a bit of time to spare for a last training ride ahead of the World Championships.

I'm grumpy because I'm exhausted. At the airport I'm in the queue to check in and just in front of me is a young Swiss rider named Steve Morabito who's there with his family. He has a big smile on his face, happy to be going to the World Championships. He looks as proud as punch. I can see that his bike and all his bags are packed neatly and his dad's there and his girlfriend and sister too, all helping carry his luggage. And I'm looking at them with just a little bit of envy.

I get to Lisbon, and because it's the Worlds I'm racing with the Australian team, and my roommate is Dutch-born Australian Patrick Jonker. He's an experienced rider and it's interesting talking to him. We go for a last long ride on the Wednesday, on the outskirts of Lisbon, to be ready for the men's road race on Sunday.

I'm not in the best mood. The leadup to the race has not been ideal. It's disappointing because it's such an important event. I've prepared badly, so I'm probably going to perform badly. I'm nursing injuries and exhausted after two big races and countless hours of travel in the past two weeks. It's my first World Road Championships, but I'm not looking forward to it at all.

Later that day, one phone call changes my mood completely. Tony Rominger wants me to meet with the biggest cycling team in the world.

IT TURNS OUT THE Italian Mapei–Quick-Step team have been observing me since I was an Under 23 racing on the road. Mapei's well-known coach, Aldo Sassi, has been following my results for three or four years.

We get together the night before the race in the lobby of the team hotel. So often in the world of professional cycling, the important meetings are held in very inconspicuous places, away from the eyes and ears of journalists and fans who are keen to gossip. So it's just a very small meeting. Team manager Alvaro Crespi, Aldo Sassi, Tony Rominger and me.

Alvaro gets straight to the point. 'How would you like to join us and develop into a Grand Tour rider?' Mapei will take me on as a 'neo-pro', a first-year professional – the top team in the world with the best coaches, facilities and most importantly, the best mentality.

I think, 'My God, this is exactly what I've been waiting for my whole cycling career.' It couldn't have come at a better time. And it couldn't have come from a better team.

Here's a group of people who want to work with me, and who have the same outlook I have: work hard, do everything required, train as best you can for the biggest races in the world. The races I really want to ride in.

'Yes, of course I'd like to.'

'Do you have a contract for next year?'

'Yes, I do.'

'Can you get out of it?'

'Um, I think so.' And that's where the conversation ends.

As we go our separate ways I'm thinking, 'Wow, this is fantastic.' I'm 24 years old, I'm still young enough to have a full career on the road, I've already had seven years in international mountain biking, in World Cups, World Championships, Olympics.

This is an opportunity to have a second career in sport, and not just to compete, but to work with the best professional cycling has to offer, in an ethical environment that's possibly unique in cycling.

Recent setbacks aside, I'm in a good place physically. I've had the opportunity to race and fight for victory in the best races the discipline of mountain biking has to offer, and now I have the chance to race with the best team in the world and to work towards a new set of goals in a stimulating and refreshing environment.

Some in the peloton don't like the team: the training programs are too hard, the testing and monitoring too controlling. But more forward-thinking riders would kill to ride with Mapei, including me. They're known to do things properly and professionally. And my introduction to road racing is going to be guided by the strong-willed, sometimes intimidating, slightly obsessive Aldo Sassi, a man known as a visionary in his outlook on how to prepare, a man who is going to show me how to be an elite bike rider.

The Mapei offer gives me all the things I've been looking for: new motivation, a new environment, and a new challenge. The whole idea is really invigorating.

NEXT DAY I RACE in the Worlds. It's a really hilly course. And because it's so hilly we all race very conservatively.

It becomes very strange when the Italians start attacking each other. Italian rider, Gilberto Sironi, is in a breakaway and one of his teammates attacks him from behind, which helps bring the breakaway back. It gets very messy in the Italian team and it sets the dynamics for the rest of the race.

In the downhill finish, I'm distracted, trying to work out what's going on with the Italians. And I can't put enough on the road today after racing so many events in quick succession.

The race is won by Spanish Mapei rider, Oscar Freire, his second title. I finish in 26th place. I come away a little disappointed.

That's OK, I'm excited about the Mapei offer. After the meeting last night, my mind is focused on my future.

Of course, I have to keep it all to myself for now; for months I'm making life-changing decisions and I can't speak to anyone about it except Tony Rominger.

And first I have to get through the rest of my season with Volvo–Cannondale and Saeco.

THE REMAINDER OF THE year doing both sports is all-consuming. In the background I'm sorting out contracts and my future. While I'm riding races I'm imagining what I might be doing next year ... the Giro d'Italia? the Tour de France?

After the Worlds, I have a sleepless night thinking about the future and going over the race a hundred times in my head: analysing, reliving, taking note of the decisions made, and what to improve on next time.

I am out of bed early and make my way to the airport for another flight. I have an argument with the Swiss passenger behind me, who has trouble understanding why I'd want to go to sleep at nine o'clock in the morning while we're stuck on the tarmac. 'This is not the time to be sleeping!' he says. In the past 48 hours I've spent more time racing my bike than sleeping. I need to get home to start preparing for the Giro di Lombardia (Tour of Lombardy) on 20 October, just a few days away.

This 242-kilometre event, founded in 1905, is the race of Italian legends, Fausto Coppi and Alfredo Binda. Coppi won it five times (1946–1949 and 1954) and Binda four times (1925–1927 and

1931). Italians have won it 67 times. It's also called 'La Classica delle Foglie Morte' ('The Classic of the Falling Leaves') because it's in autumn. With its variable conditions it's often known by other names: we bike riders sometimes refer to it as 'The Classic of the Falling Rain' because if it's raining it's horrible and wet and cold. Or even 'The Classic of the Falling Snow'. Its course winds around Lake Como, past some of Italy's most gorgeous scenery. Lombardia is where you see the real passion of Italian cycling because they understand the sport so well they have a genuine appreciation for the cyclists' efforts.

It's considered the world championship for climbers because it's very hilly, the closest 'classic' to my home for climbers. It's one race that I would really love to win. But it's at the wrong end of the year for me – it's one of the season-closers and I nearly always get there exhausted.

True to the race's reputation, I finish in the pouring rain, minutes behind Danilo Di Luca.

I STILL HAVE ONE final mountain-bike commitment. After riding Lombardia on Saturday, I hop in the car and drive to the south of France to do a mountain-bike race next day, the main race of the Roc d'Azur, a mixed pro–amateur race. I didn't want to ride it but the team have asked me to. I can't understand why, because they have another rider who lives close by in Switzerland with fewer commitments than me. I want to leave Europe, race the Japan Cup Cycle Road Race on my way home then do the Noosa Criterium as an end to my season. But I have to stay on and head to France and I'm not very happy about it.

I arrive about 1am at the hotel where the team is staying. The race starts at 9am. Again, not ideal preparation.

I start in the front and ride about 10 of the 42 kilometres before getting a puncture; I haven't had time to check my equipment. My spare tyre fails too, and I have to flag down a willing competitor to lend me tools to repair the puncture so I can ride back to the start.

That's where my mountain-bike career finishes, pretty much.

I return to the hotel in Fréjus, wondering why I've bothered driving all the way to the Côte d'Azur for a few ks of racing. In town I run into a friend of mine, a girlfriend and manager of one of my teammates. I haven't seen her in a while. It's nice just to sit down and talk to someone. It's not like I've actually spent time with any friend for quite a while. We sit and have a cup of tea and chat for a bit. I'm grateful for the company and the chance to talk about something other than cycling.

THERE'S A DINNER THAT night for the Volvo–Cannondale team to celebrate the end of the mountain-bike season. All the riders and team members are there and everyone's quite jovial. It's a little awkward for me, though, because I have so many possibilities awaiting me in the future, all of them away from this group of people and this environment. No one knows I am leaving mountain biking and joining a road team, the contracts certainly haven't been signed and I don't want to tell anyone until it is official.

At dinner I sit next to Beppo Hilfiger, Cannondale's head of marketing in Europe. Beppo asks what races I'm planning to do next year. I mumble something noncommittal then make my excuses. I tell Beppo I've got something going on tomorrow morning so I have to leave early. I head out of the restaurant around 10.30pm and drive 200 kilometres to a roadside hotel.

What I have on is a meeting with Mapei, at nine tomorrow morning.

NEXT DAY I WAKE early, jump in my little blue Audi and drive the last few hundred kilometres to Sports Service Mapei, the team research centre northwest of Milan, to get things in place for the following year. I am measured for my clothes and bikes, have my photo taken for promotional material, and a host of other things. At the Mapei centre I meet up once again with Aldo Sassi.

Among young Italian riders Aldo's known as a very tough customer who expects his crew to give him everything they have. A few can meet the brutal training loads he hands out to his cyclists. Most can't.

I'm about to find out whether I'm one of the ones who can.

Mapei is the only team with a lab, and Aldo is keen to use the facility. I arrive on time with two one-day races in two different sports and many hours of driving in my legs all within the last two days. I'm sitting there in Saeco shorts. A few of the other riders that Aldo coaches have come in. One of them is fellow Aussie, Michael Rogers ('Dodger', as we call him), who's only a few years younger than me, and whose career has paralleled mine. Dodger brought his skills over from the track to the road, just as I brought mine over from mountain biking. We first spent time together on the Australian Under 23 team based in Quarrata, Tuscany. Now he's part of the Mapei GS3 team, Mapei's development squad.

He sees me. 'Are you lost?' he asks with a smile.

We laugh. He's onto me.

I see Aldo approaching. *'Hai gli scarpe in macchina?'* he asks. Have you got your shoes in your car? *'Faremo un test.'* We'll do a test.

Aldo can determine a lot about a rider's capabilities from just one lab test. I wasn't expecting to go straight to a test, but this is how Aldo likes it. He wants to test me when I don't know I'm going to be tested.

He checks body weight and skin folds while one of the lab assistants sets up the ergometer to my riding position complete with the same pedals and seat as my own bike.

He puts me on the ergometer for an endurance test. Within a few minutes I'm sitting at 5.2 watts per kilo.

Aldo tells me, 'If you stay below four millimoles of lactate in this test you can ride in the first ten at the Grand Tours.'

My body is so exhausted it can barely produce lactate. I've produced something like 1.8 millimoles, so I have haven't even got halfway to Aldo's cutoff point.

I'm in the top 0.1 per cent of the world's aerobic endurance athletes but Aldo is giving nothing away.

Joking, I say to Aldo, 'Do I still get a contract?'

He smiles and grunts, 'You still get a contract. But you've got some work to do.'

He's not kidding.

CHAPTER 6

MAPEI–QUICK-STEP

2001–2002

AT THE END OF 2001 I formally retire from mountain biking. I'm 24 years old and at the start of a new career. And I've just signed with Mapei, which sits proudly at number one team in the world, not just in rankings and size, but also in organisation, motivation, and most importantly, mentality. This is a team ten years ahead of its time, although this is not appreciated or understood by most of the world of cycling.

Given most of my racing is now in Italy, an important switch I make is thinking in Italian. In the Mapei lab all the staff speak Italian. The race meetings are in Italian. The race radio is in Italian. Learning the language is an important element in transforming into a full-time road racer.

It's a deeply significant time for me. I'm focusing on a new sport and I'm also adjusting to a new team environment.

Mapei want me on board because they'd rather have a rider who's doing the right thing than a rider who wins Grand Tours doing the wrong things. I've always felt I was in the minority for wanting to do my best while staying clean. It's hard to deal with when you're attacked in the newspapers for being beaten but can't speak out against other riders, even when they may be doing things they shouldn't.

Mapei have faith in the future; they're working towards a better situation than the one the cycling world is in. They want success without cheating. But not every team is like that and that's why people are being pushed and pressured into doing things they shouldn't. I have neither the need or desire to speak out against any of them because I can't know the pressures they've been under to make the decisions they've made at the time they needed to be made.

My commitment from the moment I became a professional cyclist has been to try to get everything out of myself, and do everything possible to get the best results for the team. Enjoying it has always been secondary for me.

This mindset is welcomed at Mapei. I find myself in the ultimate environment to work in.

We work seriously, though many of the riders can't help but have fun racing: Paolo Bettini's constant joking and smiling every minute of the day; Andrea Noë (nicknamed *il Brontolo* – Grumpy Dwarf) whose derogatory non-stop commentary on life can only be laughed at; the two loudest riders in the peloton, Paulo Fornaciari and Davide Bramati, amongst my best teammates ever with their boisterous voices that need to be heard to be believed. They are a very diverse mix of personalities but all with one common goal.

At Mapei it's thought that one glass of wine is medicinal. More? No. So everyone has one glass of wine for dinner; that's the rule. A glass of wine after a monster day on the bike is a tonic, not just physically but mentally too. I'm finding it tough enough to wind down from the day without having to deny myself in the evening.

MY PASTA WITH PESTO arrives at the table, together with Aldo Sassi's fried mixed seafood and chips. Aldo looks at my plate. 'Pasta with pesto, Cadel? That's not really a plate for riders.' He calls to the waiter. 'Can you take this back? He'll have some *pasta bianca*.'

At Mapei, you don't have sauce on your pasta, you have it *bianca* – white – with just olive oil and cheese. If you eat rich food all the time you're only satisfied with rich food, but if you eat plain food all the time you're satisfied with plain food.

My pasta with pesto is taken away and the new, less interesting plate arrives. As Aldo starts eating his fried seafood, a look of envy creeps across my face. Aldo says, 'Do as I say, not as I do.'

I start cooking *pasta bianca* at home because I become so used to having it plain. It makes you very fastidious about eating pasta that's perfectly cooked. You also switch on very quickly to what the best olive oils are and develop a real palate for them. And you only want the best cheese, like *Pecorino* or quality *Parmigiano-Reggiano*, maybe *Grana Padano*.

If a climber's body fat gets up to four per cent Aldo will scold, 'You're eating well, you're enjoying life!'

Enjoying life? I had some pasta! OK, and some cheese. And I had a glass of wine. Wow, this guy is tough.

I feel I am already living a fairly strict, ascetic life, not monk-like but very careful. I almost never have dessert.

But Aldo is raising the bar.

AT THIS POINT IN time, the whole area of cyclists' preparation and training is badly due for an overhaul. Training schedules haven't been maximising riders' potential. Riders come along to races not as fit as they could be. Many are not as professional as they should be.

Aldo wants to change this. He feels things can be done differently, that preparation can be more scientific, that with more effort in the lab, road racers can make improvements in their physiology that will make them better riders. He's well ahead of his time.

Aldo's vision of how cyclists should prepare has found physical expression in the Mapei research centre, founded in 1996 to support the athletes of the Mapei professional cycling team. The centre has since expanded to offer training help to cyclists from all teams as well as athletes from other sports.

Aldo is the leading figure at the centre, leading research initiatives to help athletes and coaches achieve their potential through developing their physiology, biomechanics and nutrition. Aldo is a big reason why Mapei is number one, and the riders are happy to be part of it.

Aldo is a man who wastes nothing, not words and certainly not time. His view of professional cycling is clear: you do the work, you prepare properly, you succeed. Lots of riders are talented, but it's the ones who work hard and work *smarter* who get to the top. And if you happen to be one of his protégés you do it his way or no way. He often tells riders that if they're not prepared to follow this philosophy, they'd better look for a new coach.

Like most, I find Aldo a little bit intimidating, although those who can't do the set training loads have better reason to be nervous. And I'm insulated to some extent by my underdeveloped Italian skills. I miss the nuances of addressing people, and speak to him using the familiar *tu*, like he's one of my mates. I think Aldo, and even team owner Dr Giorgio Squinzi, enjoy this because everyone else is so formal with them, except for the Aussie protégé.

It might even be breaking down any barriers between Aldo and me as master and student – because that's what we're becoming. I am in Aldo's inner group, and privileged to be so.

I'm already competitive by nature. I already have an inner drive to do anything to improve my performance – not just because I think I should, but because I want to. Aldo sees in me someone who has the physical capacity to work hard and race hard, but also the mental capacity to back that up. He'll often say the mind is as important to a rider as the body. He is combining my natural ability, racing nous and desire to win with his knowledge and experience of the scientific side of cycling. I've found the ideal partner for my journey on the bike.

I've always thrived on work. He pushes me hard, but because of the commitment to training I developed as a young rider, I cope all right. I train a lot, maybe sometimes too much. But unless you are breaking world records, Aldo is always asking for more. Usually I turn myself inside out for Aldo, but sometimes we all – me included – come up short. I'm trying, but sometimes, according to Aldo, not hard enough.

One day he sets me a ridiculously arduous threshold training load (training at my lactate threshold). When I point this out to him, he says, 'But this is the training load of a junior! What do you mean "less intensity"? It's nothing!'

I know it's not nothing but that's Aldo's way of getting more out of an athlete. That's OK, I don't mind being pushed. The thing is, he's an unnerving figure, so when he says 'It's nothing', even though you know it's not nothing, you listen.

Aldo has methods that every rider on the team is required to adhere to. Riders will send him data about their training, and after looking at the numbers he'll email them with feedback and suggestions. Aldo is a scientist, so he analyses numbers. But numbers do not measure other factors like stress, personal life events and their effects on emotions, motivations and consequential effects on performance.

We share an important philosophy: 'Train when it's miserable outside, train in the rain, train when it's the last thing you feel like doing. That way you'll be prepared for terrible conditions'.

The training loads are in a three-day block that he's developed. It's strength and effort on the first day, intensity on the second and endurance on the third.

I don't think Aldo is respected enough for how much he's doing for the sport. At the beginning people thought he was a little bit nuts. Pioneers are often thought of this way. Not many people realise how intensely he's involved in the science of our sport. He's ahead of his time in terms of training and his approach to the sport and how to run a team. He writes programs for riders that take account of VO2 max (maximum rate of oxygen use) and power output and anaerobic thresholds. Most riders have never even heard of these.

Aldo is about to exert the biggest influence of anyone on my cycling career. He's about to transfer my desire, motivation and capabilities from the mountain bike track to the road. He's going to show me how to train properly, how to prepare for races, how to shape my body, and how to pay attention to the smallest detail that will give me even the tiniest advantage on the bike.

Aldo is about to change my world.

IN ADELAIDE IN JANUARY 2002 I win a stage of the Tour Down Under. It confirms the big pre-season training and adaptation work I have done under Damian Grundy's guidance and my place in the team. I always prefer to get a result or at least a good performance immediately upon joining a new team. It works wonders in convincing those you work with more than anything else. I feel fit and confident; maybe it's the new environment at the Mapei team. The better I perform, the happier the team is; the happier the team is, the better I perform. The transition from mountain biking to the road is going to plan.

ON BECOMING A PROFESSIONAL cyclist, you quickly learn if you can ever be good enough to be a team leader riding for general classification (GC), or if you'll play the role as a secondary leader, opportunistic rider for breakaways, or what has come to be known as a *domestique*.

The best *domestiques* win races for their team leader. My new teammate, Dario Cioni, is one of these; he's committed to looking out for the GC guy. *Domestiques* are motivated just to be there and take the leader to the right place. Some say, 'Yeah, I'm here to help so-and-so', but when they're needed they're sitting at the back of the peloton talking to their friends instead of paying attention to the race. It's the *domestiques* you see jumping in early breaks, taking their leaders to the front in the crucial moments of a final that are the guys that make a difference.

To be a great *domestique* you need to be psychologically driven to work for someone else. That's never been my strong suit. I always ride for the result of the team but sometimes I admit I need to work pretty hard to be motivated enough to work for someone else. But if that other rider is there to win and that win could be compromised by me, well, then I'll easily find the motivation.

When you're the leader you have to help the *domestiques* be motivated, show that you deserve the sacrifices they're making for you. As a leader, you get told off for not getting the result, but when the riders on your team who were meant to be there to help you weren't, you often have to take the blame for them as well.

You need the team structured so the riders are acknowledged for the work they're doing and the contribution they're making, whether that's in the respect they receive from the team or in proper financial rewards. The best results happen when the whole team is awarded respect. In the best teams, in the best victories, everyone knows their roles, and exactly what's expected of them, and that is key to binding the riders and building team unity.

Being a *domestique* sounds unenviable, but the leader has to deal with most of the consequences. The leaders are often thinking, 'Wouldn't it be nice to go to a race and just ride in the services of someone else and not have all those expectations placed on you? To be able to enjoy the race more, because at the end of the day, the press don't come to you and say, "You didn't win, what did you do wrong?"'

As a GC rider you have to be able to adapt to the different types of races. A time-trial rider needs a mentality like that of an engineer or an accountant. It's all about numbers and data. A sprinter is much more like an artist, more impulsive, going on feel, less calculating.

I'm finding a time trial is a lot like a mountain-bike race, where you have to be perfectly primed so that when you start you can instantly put everything down on the pedals. There is no hiding in the wheels or risking everything on the downhills to make up for lack of legs. That's why the time trial is called 'The Race of Truth' – because you can't succeed by being clever. There are tactics within it, but basically it's going fastest from point A to point B. It is quite draining mentally because it requires a lot of concentration to extract absolutely everything out of yourself – whereas in a road race you're following others and the weight of the difficulties and challenges ahead are shared.

Often you come across time trialists who are really talented riders but not always the strongest individuals mentally. They are so rigid in their thinking that they can't adapt to a bad moment or a bad day. They often over-analyse, whereas most sprinters are more instinctive. They may not feel they're riding well but they'll perform fine when it counts. However, they won't be able to consistently repeat the performance because of a lack of structure in their preparation.

I like to think of myself as a versatile bike rider, switching between the different mentalities as required. I'm probably too muscular to be a pure climber, but I'm a decent descender and I'm developing my time trial abilities so that I can be an all-round rider and have the makings of a GC rider and team leader.

But first I've got my apprenticeship to finish.

IT'S A WHOLE NEW world I've found myself in. New places, new races, new faces; a whole new set of challenges to work for and a whole new environment to work in.

Similar to the world of mountain bikes, it's 'See you next week', 'See you in France', 'See you in Italy', 'See you in Switzerland', 'See you in Poland, Portugal, Spain, Germany, England, Ireland' as we leave to go home before the next race.

THE MAPEI TEAM IS highly organised and each day you know exactly what your role is. This structure suits my personality; I like order and knowing where I stand in terms of the season, the team, in fact any situation that relates to my performance.

My race program includes the climbers' Spring Classics in April – the Flèche Wallonne and Liège–Bastogne–Liège – and then I'll concentrate on the Giro d'Italia in May and June.

Until the 1990s the biggest names in cycling would enter all of the big races: Classics, Tours, Grand Tours. Then guys like Greg LeMond and more so, Miguel Indurain, started focusing on the Tour de France and the Monuments – the oldest and most revered one-day races. After that, riders and teams were more selective: they would match riders with races, realising that some riders were better suited to the three-week races and some to the one-dayers.

The Spring Classics (which include the five Monuments) are the major one-day races in the calendar from Milano–San Remo in early March to Liège–Bastogne–Liège in late April. For three-week specialists, the Spring Classics are increasingly seen as opportunities to sharpen up for the Grand Tours.

Cycling is becoming more and more specialised; it's rare now for a rider to be competitive in both the Grand Tours and the one-day races. They're such different disciplines.

In the three-week tours, it's about being consistent over 21 days of racing, one after the other. For one-day races, its about getting everything right, and usually everything out of yourself on just one day, with maybe three or six days to recover and train for the next Classic. A Classics rider may focus an entire season on just the Tour of Flanders and the Paris–Roubaix.

The team's challenge each year is to match their riders to the right races – juggling riders' wellbeing and training programs with the needs of the team and its leaders.

For me, the Giro is the really big goal of 2002, to perform at my first Grand Tour. But before that in early May, and after the Classics, is the Tour de Romandie, racing through the French part of Switzerland, my home away from home for four years now.

IT'S THE COLDEST I'VE ever been in my life.

I ride through the snow and it's zero degrees and I can feel my clothes hanging heavily on me. I'm finding it hard to see ahead. Every time I wipe my glasses they fog up again, I try removing them but the sleet against my bare eyes is too painful to bear.

The roads are soaked with ice-cold rain and snow. We're sliding all over the place. My hands in my wet gloves seem to be paralysed. The cold wind ensures they are not going to get warm any time soon.

At a certain point your body starts to shut down the circulation to your extremities to keep your organs warm. Riders begin to lose dexterity, forcing them to shift gears with the opposite hand because their thumbs don't work. It's tricky having to brake from your shoulders because your fingers can't bend enough to squeeze the levers, especially on the long downhill stretches.

Normally, there would be a battle in my head: the will to keep going versus the reasons to quit. Not this week, as I happen to be reading *Mawson: A Life* each night after the stage. The stories of Antarctic hardship make my conditions feel insignificant and get me through.

My face is numb. Riding well in this race is my first big goal for the year, the precursor to the Giro d'Italia. And here I am, constantly soaking wet, almost paralysed with cold and concerned for my health. And playing tricks on my mind to avoid quitting.

The problem is that I am not used to this excessive cold. It's my first full-time year on the road and my physiology is still changing. I still have a mountain bike rider's body with slight quantities of muscle mass and fat, so the cold is biting into me without the protective insulating layer that would help me in these conditions.

Being over- or under-dressed can have a big impact on your performance. If your feet and hands and head are warm, then your body's warm. If your neck is covered, your resistance to illness is greatly reduced. In your cycling wardrobe, you need clothing for every variation in temperature and humidity. Getting out on the bike missing one piece of clothing means you might be cold for the whole ride and it's not very nice. And to go out overdressed and sweat excessively is not very nice either. So you need to be quite fastidious about which undershirt to wear. It's about breathability, because when you climb you have slow wind speed and higher energy expenditure, but when you descend you have higher wind speed and lower energy expenditure so you're getting colder. These are things that a young rider has to learn.

You need three or four different sock choices, for example: very hot, in-between, cold, really cold. You need socks made of wool and thick cotton socks and thin cotton socks. You need black socks when it's muddy or when it's raining. White socks are traditional in cycling but they never stay clean, especially in Europe where there are a lot of diesel cars and the exhaust fumes stay in your socks and they become grey. Fortunately cycling fashion is starting to adapt.

In extreme wet and cold conditions basics like cling wrap are great. Put your shoes on and wrap cling wrap around your shoes – excellent protection from the rain. Then maybe a pair of shoe covers made from wetsuit material to keep the water out. Your feet are going to be wet but at least the sweat is going to be warm because you've got cling wrap around your feet.

Freezing cold? Wear two or three pairs of gloves, first maybe normal road gloves, then latex gloves like surgeon's gloves, then warm waterproof Gore-Tex gloves over the top of that. You put those on last because once you've got those on you can't do much.

If it's really cold, you might also put heat patches in your vest, your gloves or shoe covers. Oil rubbed into your legs, arms, even your torso will encourage the water to run off your body. Anything to keep warm.

As important as the equipment is the setup: the angle of the bars, the height of the brake levers, the saddle position and the cleat position. Because of the repetitive nature of cycling – 3500 to 4000 pedal strokes per hour – even a slight change in cleat positioning is a huge adjustment for the body to make. When you ride a lot and you make one small change, your body struggles to adapt, especially mid-season when your body has acclimatised to what you've been using.

The components of the bike, especially those you have contact with, whether they be made of carbon fibre, aluminium, rubber, steel or titanium, become part of you.

I'm learning pretty quickly by watching and listening.

In a mountain-bike race I wouldn't even adjust my gloves or shoes during a race. I'd have everything perfectly prepared at the start and I wouldn't touch anything for the entire race.

With road racing there's a subtlety to the timing. In the snow and sleet the peloton will stop by the side of the road and change all our clothes – pants, undershirt, jersey, everything. (Preferably where there are not any members of the public, and away from the TV cameras.) We'll all stop in a tunnel and get changed, and then we'll all start again at the same time.

You have to take your sunglasses off, then your helmet, then your jersey, then your braces (in bad conditions you may have five layers to peel off). Then you can put your new undershirt on, put your braces back on, put your new jersey on and put your helmet and your sunglasses back on. That's a lot of time lost. But no matter how well you've prepared, you're so ridiculously cold that this is the only way you can go on.

Right now, at the Tour de Romandie, I've lost all feeling in my hands and feet. My eyes and head have started to hurt.

My childhood friend Simon Skerry was out riding with me once and got so cold he couldn't manage to say, 'My eyeballs are frozen.' Instead, 'My ice balls are frozen' came out. That's how mine feel at the moment.

It's the final stage and we're riding up a hill, and of course the higher we go the more it snows and the colder it gets.

Now I'm losing the feeling in my ankles and the cold creeps up and up. It's a bit of a strange sensation, because my legs are going flat out towards the hilltop finish, but I only have feeling down to my knees. Everything below is numb. It's like I don't have feet and ankles. At this point I hope I don't start shivering, because that costs too much energy, which I desperately need just to stay warm.

I feel like I'm riding with all the flexibility of a store dummy. My hands on the grip remind me of *The Thunderbirds* on TV, where wooden puppets walk around with a complete lack of flexibility.

Immobilised by the cold, somehow I manage to hang in with Alex Zülle for the finish. I get out of the saddle to sprint to the line but my rear wheel slips in the ice and snow. Alex stays seated, perhaps too cold and exhausted to stand, and edges past me for the stage win. The team is really happy with such a good result in such tough conditions.

As soon as I cross the line a *soigneur* grabs me, wraps a jacket around me and guides me to the bus, helps me up the stairs, takes me to my seat, sits me down and starts peeling my cold, soaked clothes off. I can't do it for myself. I'm sitting there on the bus with my blue hands extended in a frozen paralysis. I'm disappointed to lose the stage, but bewildered more than frustrated by the extreme conditions.

Some time that evening in my hotel room, after a cool shower, warm fluids and a hot bath, some feeling returns. Stories are traded among teammates. Everyone is convinced that this is the coldest race they have ever experienced, which I find reassuring. At least when it was cold in mountain biking the race was over quickly.

I'VE ALWAYS SEARCHED FOR ways of improving myself. Since I was a schoolboy I've always wanted to be as well informed as possible. In my lunch hour at high school I would either go to the gym or I would go to the library and read books on physiology and training and nutrition.

So much of Aldo's work is based on utilising the best scientific testing and knowledge to train smarter, to perform better for a rider who wants to compete over three weeks. The challenge of the three-week tour is what drives him.

I think Aldo's ultimate dream is to find a rider he can develop to win the Tour de France. He sees in me a rider who can do this; he thinks we can do it together. Not that we speak about it much. We quietly work together, step by step, towards the ultimate goal without actually discussing it. It quietly becomes a shared dream.

But there's another Grand Tour to conquer first.

CHAPTER 7
THE GIRO

2002

MAPEI'S MOST IMPORTANT RACE – with Mapei being the Italian sponsor and the main Italian team – is the Giro d'Italia. Being part of it is an honour I can't yet comprehend. The Giro has a rich history and a deep significance for Italians. And it's the race in which I'm about to make my Grand Tour debut.

After the Tour de France was set up in 1903 to promote *L'Auto* newspaper, young Italian cyclist Armando Cougnet wondered in 1908 whether Italy should have its own national race.

The idea was well received. An administrative director on the newspaper *La Gazzetta dello Sport* – where his father also worked – Cougnet successfully organised the first Giro d'Italia in 1909. He remained in overall charge of the race for 50 years, until after World War II.

On 13 May 1909 the first Giro d'Italia set off from Milan. The bikes had fixed gears, forcing the riders to pedal constantly, unable to rest on descents.

Almost a century later, the owners of the newspaper continue to run the Giro. It's the main bike race in a country with a profound love of cycling. It is a much-loved annual sporting event, an important piece of Italy's culture, and second only to the Tour de France in significance.

The conditions in the Giro are much harder than at the Tour de France; it has the steepest climbs, the narrowest roads, the worst weather. Everything's harder in the Giro. If you want to see what the very best equipment is, look at what's winning at the Giro d'Italia – tyres, brakes, components, raincoats, gloves – because it's not going to have a harder test than that.

The Giro is also known in Italian as La Corsa Rosa, The Pink Race. While Tour de France leaders wear the yellow jersey, it's a pale pink one (in Italian the *maglia rosa*) at the Giro. The pink matches the colour of the pages of *La Gazzetta dello Sport*.

The Italians love the Giro. They grow up hearing about it, knowing about it, seeing it on TV and going out to see a stage. Over time, everyone in Italy sees the Giro pass near where they live or work. They're passionate about it, and when they have a brush with it they remember it forever.

It's followed intensely by millions of Italians. In cafés in Italy when the Giro's on you often see the classic double: people sitting with an espresso and the pink newspaper, perusing the previous day's results. The race is ingrained in everyone in some form or another, even if they have no direct interest in it. It might become ingrained in you because your road is blocked, or you get stuck in a traffic jam because of it.

But for many Italians it's the race itself that matters, a race in which a handful of cycling heroes have become legends. Their names are permanently linked with the Giro. Alfredo Binda, who won five times, Fausto Coppi (also five wins), Gino Bartali (three).

And here I am, a kid from Australia, about to ride it for the first time. Not only am I from a country without much of a cycling heritage, but I'm not even from this sport. I grew up on a mountain bike. My knowledge of Italy and its culture is still developing. Unlike the young Italians I'm riding with and against, for me at 25, Binda, Coppi and Bartali are just names from history.

It isn't the culture and the history that are driving me. I'm more interested in answering some questions: How will I cope in the all-important third week? How good a Grand Tour rider am I? The only way to find this out, though, is to ride one. The only way to gain the physical and psychological fitness for three-week races is to race some.

I don't know how I'll be accepted. Coming from the world of mountain biking, undoubtedly I will be looked down upon by some of my colleagues.

But what is undeniable is that I can climb. Many in road racing may dismiss mountain biking, but in terms of my fitness and aerobic capacity it's given me a great base, especially for climbing, and an abundance of steep climbs is why many riders consider the Giro the hardest of all the Grand Tours.

To prepare for this challenge I've done an enormous block of training. I've crammed a lot of work in the two months before the season start in an effort to change my physiology and increase my efficiency so I can perform well in a longer event.

I'm charged by the attitude at Mapei. I'm beginning to realise that this team enter each race to win. Everyone – the staff, mechanics, *soigneurs*, and all the riders – put absolutely everything they've got into every race.

Even though I haven't raced a single tour, some of the other riders are thinking it's possible I could be a team leader. I'm discovering I have the legs to be in front. I've won some respect from some of the top riders in the team because I'm consistently climbing with the best.

At this stage of my progression as a rider I don't feel any need to get a result, but Aldo has taken me aside and told me to 'Be there just in case'. I try not to place too many expectations on myself. If the time comes to race for the win, OK, I'll race. But I'm here to race for the team.

As the Giro approaches, my main reassurance comes from within. It isn't my tactical skills or experience that's going to set me apart. It's what the cycling world hasn't seen yet: my undiscovered capabilities. I might be an inexperienced Australian, but I'm feeling strangely comfortable heading into my first Grand Tour. I keep my feeling to myself though, I don't want any expectations beyond my own.

IT'S 11 MAY 2002. I'm in the team bus at the start of stage one of my first Grand Tour. I look out the window. There are people everywhere – fans, media, locals in dress-ups, officials with clipboards, the motorcycles getting ready with the cameramen on the back.

I am trying not to be nervous, to do the job I've trained to do. The main challenge is to stay calm. My exhausting pre-season, and heavy early season are helping me with this.

While I'm trying to calm down, everyone around me – the team and the staff and the managers and the directors – is nervous. The people who've come to watch the race – who may have travelled from Australia or America to be here – are really excited but I prefer to keep to myself, to save some energy and excitement for when I need it most.

The most effective way for me to distract my mind is to sit down and prepare every little detail, very thoroughly. These last moments before a race are a time to ensure that you have everything you need and that not even the tiniest thing has been overlooked. That way, you can ride off and do what you've trained to do with a clear mind. Focus on the detail and the rest will take care of itself.

I check the map, check the times, check the distances, check where the feed zones are, check the weather, check the humidity. And prepare accordingly. Because at kilometre zero, if the race just goes absolutely crazy, there might not be time to correct an error.

I sit calmly in the bus until the last minute, have a coffee, put sunscreen on, use the bathroom and check everything again. Then I do something monotonous: I fold up my shirts neatly and put them in my suitcase ready for when I come back. It's about 'separating', finding a way of stepping back from the stress. My suitcase is already immaculately neat, and folding everything again won't actually make a difference in the race, but that moment of calmness might.

In the team bus on the wall is a notice indicating time trial start times. This is key to everyone's day. For the time trial warm-ups I prefer to have the notice and the clock right there in front of me. I am often so focussed on the warm-up, reviewing the course and breathing calmly that it's easy to let details like my start time slip my mind.

The first stage is a Prologue, a short individual time trial to work out which rider will wear the leader's jersey for the first stage. Only seconds will differentiate the places, and seconds conceded are seconds lost on the stage and the GC.

MY ROLE IN THE Giro is to be there for our GC rider Stefano Garzelli, a hero to the Italians. He won the Giro in 2000 and joined Mapei–Quick-Step last year.

On the bike he's very small and slight. He has a surprisingly fast finish for such a slight build and moves very delicately on the pedals. He rarely wears a helmet; instead, he wears a bandana on his head, one on his sleeve and a third in his pocket. He regularly switches between them to keep his hairless head dry and warm.

Coming from mountain biking, I'm used to racing with a helmet on – but also because of having had a close call with death after a head injury 17 years previously, and Australia's particularly prudent approach to bike safety. My home state of Victoria was the first place in the world to make it mandatory to wear a helmet while cycling. Helmet laws have reduced some people's enthusiasm for cycling, but the statistics clearly show they've had a huge effect in reducing severe injuries, particularly brain injuries, in cycling-related accidents. And around the world, people's mentality toward them is changing.

Coming into my first Giro, my aim is to do my best, enjoy the experience and hopefully get a clearer idea of how good a rider I can be. It's not going to be me doing the winning. Not this time.

As the start time looms I feel a mix of excitement, trepidation and a degree of fatigue from the work already done this year. This is huge for me.

My instructions for the race are clear. Aldo has told me, 'You ride in support of Garzelli but stay on GC in case something happens.'

Well, everything *does* happen.

EVERYTHING GOES WELL DURING the first few stages. Then at the end of the first week there's a stage finish coming into the town of Liège, in Belgium. I've come into the last corner and done my job, leading Garzelli out, and he wins the stage.

I don't quite sit up but I don't keep sprinting. I leave a gap and lose a few seconds.

In the hotel that evening a couple of us are congratulating Garzelli. He's tired but pleased with the result.

The pink jersey is sitting there. I think, 'I might try this on', so I do.

'What do you reckon, guys? This look good?'

Garzelli looks at me blankly while Cioni beams a big smile agreeingly.

Putting on the pink jersey is just a bit of fun. But Garzelli is riding so well I'm thinking, 'We're a chance to win this Giro.'

And then the bombshell.

After stage six, the Union Cycliste Internationale (UCI), the sport's governing body, conducts a retest of urine samples taken earlier in the tour. An earlier positive dope test after Garzelli's victory in stage two is confirmed by the analysis of a second sample, and Garzelli is put out of the Giro.

The tests show slight traces of the diuretic probenecid. It's been known to be used as a masking agent, but at 29 nanograms it's not enough to mask any drugs that might be performance-enhancing. The whole thing is quite bizarre. Stefano has no idea how it got into his system. It's particularly hard for an ethical team like Mapei to deal with.

I sit in a meeting where the team discuss this. My Italian still isn't so good, so South African Robert Hunter is translating for me. Naïvety is helping me again.

When everyone hears the news of Garzelli, it's as if a close relative has died. Everyone is devastated.

The role of team leader will fall to my Italian teammate Andrea Noè or me. Here I am as a neo-pro and Noè's done a dozen Giros; he won stage 11 in 1998 and finished fourth in 2000 and sixth in 2001. He has the experience, I'm the newbie, so of course he's the natural option.

After the 10th stage, the team's plan is to ride for both Noè and me through the mountains. The result after the stage 14 individual time trail will determine who leads Mapei to Milan.

So Noè and I ride to the mountains knowing we both have a chance at leading – an idea Noè finds quite amusing. He shakes his head, says, 'Evans, *capitano*.' As in 'How ridiculous.' The dismissiveness oozes from that basso profundo voice.

And to the world of professional cycling it does sound ridiculous. Here I am, potentially about to be asked to lead my team to the finish in my first Grand Tour – the Giro, the biggest, most important race for the number one team in the world. A skinny kid still in the throes of changing my body to meet the requirements of the road, and especially a tour. Usually it takes four to five years full-time to get to this stage; I've had four to five months. It's been a steep learning curve.

But even if Noè is dismissive, probably only for his own self-confidence, I do have support in other quarters. I'm rooming with the English-born Italian rider, Dario Cioni, another former mountain biker. When we were both mountain biking I didn't know Dario beyond a friendly 'hello'. He was among the first to successfully switch from cross-country mountain biking to the road. I was soon to follow, and before we knew it we were becoming close friends on the Mapei team. We've often traded stories in confidence about the ludicrous amounts of training Aldo sets us, and the lukewarm compliments he gives us when we can actually complete them.

Dario has a swimmer's build: long limbs, broad shoulders, large feet, but a huge aerobic capacity. He's one of the gentlest people in the peloton, a serious and sincere individual whom I feel I will stay in contact with even when my cycling career is over.

Dario is a great help to me in trying to understand everything that's going on in the team and within the race. He translates for me, tells me what I'm doing right and occasionally what I need to improve on. We talk for hours in the hotel room, lying on our beds after the long, tiring days shared together.

I am in such unfamiliar surrounds, among people who are in very familiar surrounds. So I have to be a bit careful. If I have a question or a doubt, I go to Dario or Aldo. Apart from that I try to keep my mouth shut and head down.

NEXT DAY IN THE time trial, I get third place behind American rider Tyler Hamilton, a teammate of Lance Armstrong in the 1999, 2000 and 2001 Tours de France, who's riding GC for Saxo Bank. He has a distinctive style on the bike, holding his head quite high. He is a rider capable of good results, though he does seem to have more than his fair share of crashes. Sergie Honchar, riding for our arch-rival team Fassa Bortolo, takes second.

Momentum is swinging my way. My time-trial result puts me second on GC which automatically promotes me to team leader. And the peloton is noticing. I also get the impression Noè may be feeling a bit of jealousy. At least my performance in the time trial reduces the sneering and criticism.

I'm suddenly in a position to possibly win the race. Of course, this wasn't the original plan. I'm green, a neo-professional, and what happens is that neo-professionals don't normally take the lead.

It's on stage 16, the second-last mountain stage up the Passo Pordoi, that my big chance arrives. I'm right behind Julio Alberto

Pérez; I'm riding for GC, while he's riding for the stage, which is frustrating. He leaves me exposed trying to reel in Italians, Francesco Casagrande and Dario Frigo. Then Casagrande is disqualified for causing a crash and putting Colombian, John Freddy García out of the race. I can't be sure that the decision is the right one, but clearly things are going my way.

The moment that reinforces I'm going well comes when I'm riding with all the GC riders and I hear our group referred to not as the breakaway group but as 'Il Gruppo Evans', 'The Evans Group'.

Frigo finishes third behind Pérez and Italian, Paolo Savoldelli. I come in ninth but it's enough to put me in first place overall.

I'm 25 years old and I'm about to wear the leader's *maglia rosa* in my first Grand Tour, with only four more stages to go.

I'M PROUD BUT ALSO calm about wearing the pink. I've only found myself in a position to win it because of Garzelli's departure. No one was expecting it, least of all me. But I'm certainly happy to be having this experience.

I don't realise at first how big a deal it is for Aldo to have his Australian neo-professional straight out of mountain biking take the *maglia rosa*; a lot of people have probably questioned what he has been doing. In a way, I'm vindicating Aldo's decision to invest and believe in me. It was meant to be a learning experience, but it's turning into a chance to win my first Grand Tour. Aldo has seen the future.

At a press conference the reporters ask me for my thoughts on the Giro as a cultural institution. I was born on an Aboriginal settlement on the other side of the world – I don't know what to say. I've come from mountain biking and have found myself in the bubble that is road racing. I've come with an Italian team to an Italian race where everyone speaks Italian and has been watching, analysing, living this race for years. I'm quite taken aback by how insulated they are from the rest of the world of sport, and the world in general.

I also have no idea how mean-spirited this world can be. As I progress and succeed and perform beyond the capabilities of others, the belittling, criticism and questioning accumulates. It isn't just my teammates like Noè who are giving it to me. American, Tyler Hamilton seems to have a real problem with me in the Giro. He's been belittling me, saying how could a first-year professional and an ex-mountain biker possibly lead a team at the Giro?

Tyler doesn't come across to me as a particularly sincere person. I don't find him to be someone I can trust. He's nice to me only when it suits him and it isn't suiting him right now. These comments are pretty heavy-handed, very mouthy and consistent with a snide attitude towards mountain bikers. It's also maybe a tactic to put me off.

Well, it doesn't work. I take it as an indirect compliment on my abilities and it makes me even more determined to succeed.

But what happens next – in the final mountain stage – underscores how a relatively modest base of road training and racing, combined with big ambitions can have unintended consequences.

You could say that ignorance is bliss. Because I'm ignorant about all the expectations around me, and about everything I am doing. So the fact I've been riding so hard doesn't faze me.

At this point I'm only thinking about taking the pink jersey to the finish in Milan. I've been racing without considering my physical limits. While that has allowed me to get into the lead, it's also my undoing.

THE BIGGEST THING I'M learning about being in a Grand Tour is how tired it's possible to be. The first two weeks are one thing. The physical and mental expenditure is gruelling, exhausting. But in the third week you experience a fatigue that no training block or training camp can prepare you for. And until you've done a three-week tour, you have no idea what's coming.

The fatigue you feel in that third week is unlike any fatigue you feel in any other form of cycling. The level of fatigue you get is actually quite bizarre.

It's week three at the Giro and I'm lost in a hotel.

Well, not lost as in 'Where the hell am I?' Lost as in 'Where is my hotel room? What floor is it on? What number is it? Is it 302 or 402? Hang on, it was 302 yesterday …'

Time is passing and all I want is to be horizontal in the room where I left my stuff. I'm finding out that things that sound so simple – like remembering today's hotel room number – are beyond me in the third week of a Grand Tour.

The routine is that after a stage you go back to your hotel room and have a rest waiting for the *soigneur* to come and get you when it's your turn to have a massage.

Normally each *soigneur* in a Grand Tour will have two riders, and you'll either be first or second, depending on what time you get in. So you just sit in your room and wait, which is fine, because all you want to do is rest. Or you use your phone or check the weather or watch TV, or read a book if you've got the energy.

So the *soigneur* comes and gets me from my room and I follow him down to his room, get onto the massage table, have a massage.

I walk back to my room. But I can't find it.

I try again and I'm back at the *soigneur*'s room.

Which way did I come?

I'm so tired I can't even find my own way back to my own room. Is this normal?

I'm hangry – hungry and angry. Walk down the wrong corridor and I'm furious. 'That's five minutes more I could have been lying down. How could I be so stupid? How could I be so tired!?' I just want to go to dinner then go to bed. Hopefully I can soon vent my frustration, or have a laugh, or even just sleep.

This condition is what I call Zombie Mode. I'm told it kicks in at about stage 12 or 13 of any Grand Tour and it lasts for days afterwards. It's when you see the riders in the hotel and they just have a blankness in their eyes. Zombie Mode usually means my patience and tolerance levels are hugely diminished. There is no energy for anything other than racing, eating and sleeping. Other details are dealt with by instinct and possibly a grunt.

After a day of hard racing your body and mind are still functioning, but not at a very high level. Internally they're screaming at you to lie down, not to move. They're saying, 'After what you've done to us today, you owe us this much.'

Three-week races take a lot of getting used to. They're an adventure in every way. The first thing you learn is about your physique, because you've never done a block of riding like this before in your life and nothing can replicate it.

There's the excitement and nerves of the first week; by day four or five, people start to feel mentally fatigued; by the second week the lack of concentration's really starting to kick in; and then after day 13 or 14 everyone's just so exhausted they switch into survival mode. By this stage, everyone's getting tired – the drivers, the motorbike riders, the photographers, the journalists, the directors, the race organisers. There's a cumulative fatigue. We are all on the same downward plane.

You see the riders losing their edge because of mental exhaustion. Occasionally they'll allow themselves a lapse in concentration to recharge mentally. What happens in that minute is *Bang!* Traffic island, touch of wheels, big pile-up.

In the second week, riders and directors require their teams to 'Ride in front, because people are starting to get tired and there are going to be stupid crashes.' This actually increases the stress and nervousness of the group and almost certainly the risk of crashes.

Riding for GC, you have to concentrate from kilometre zero right to the finish line, and many in the team don't realise just how draining that is. You're exhausted physically and mentally, and sometimes you're travelling at 70 or 80 kilometres an hour and it's pouring rain. I have a reasonable ability to concentrate but it could be improved.

In the third week, in Zombie Mode, you learn to ration your energy. You only have so much and you need it use it very carefully. So you don't care about anything but rest. If you're lying on your bed and you unwrap a packet of food, you don't put it in the rubbish bin because that would mean getting up and walking to the bin and back, which sounds very lazy, but that's where you are.

You may need to go to the bathroom but you're too tired. Or you have a massage appointment with the *soigneur*. So you say to yourself, 'I'll go to the bathroom then so I've only got to get up once.' Or, 'I've got to get something out of my bag – oh, no, I'll wait until I need to go to the bathroom.' Just to move your body off the bed can sometimes be too much.

The team gets used to riders when they reach this point. They know they need to approach them carefully, sit down next to them, speak slowly, move quietly, be aware of their frazzled state. Maybe open the bottle of water for them at dinner, anything to help.

The team will put Parmigiano-Reggiano on the table. They'll buy a big block in a vacuum-sealed bag. You know you're tired when to grate cheese onto your pasta is a real struggle. When a rider arrives at the breakfast table with their shirt inside out or an ear plug still in their ear, which happened to an American teammate of mine, you know they are in for a tough day.

It's a circle: you don't realise how tired you are because you're so tired, so you have to look for your own signs to work out your state: 'Am I nervous? Am I exhausted? What am I showing to whom? Who can see how tired I am? Do I need to mask this feeling, or is everyone else exhausted enough not to notice?'

When someone comes to the Tour for the first time and they're all energetic and excited. I'm saying, 'Calm down, calm down', because the excitement is just too draining.

But the biggest surprise at my first Grand Tour isn't so much the fatigue. It's the fact that I'm able to deal with it and keep pushing myself.

Even though my body is completely exhausted, my youthful enthusiasm and the success thus far stimulates and motivates me day after day to keep pushing, to keep fighting. It's a revelation. It means that instead of emptying myself and struggling, I manage to empty myself beyond empty. My body keeps going and going, pushing through pain and fatigue barriers I didn't know existed.

It's the mystery of a Grand Tour: how a human being can keep going when every fibre of their body is telling them to stop.

IT'S THE 17TH STAGE, and I'm in the *maglia rosa* with one mountain stage to go. Frigo and Hamilton are still in contention. My plan is to try to finish in the lead group and retain the pink jersey, if not increase my lead on GC before the final time trial.

I ride on Frigo's wheel. I feel I am covering him. And then he blows up. We've gone 211 kilometres in the mountains and it's having an impact.

I'm exhausted, and so is everyone else, it seems.

On the second-last climb on Passo Bordala, Dario Cioni is alongside me, setting a good tempo for the team as I have asked him to do so in an effort to tire out the others before the final climb. Unknowingly I've blown up on the second-last climb, but faced with the next climb I power on even though I am completely devoid of energy. I'm in a catabolic state. My body has switched to emergency mode – burning muscle for the energy to ride on, saving all the sugar left in my system for the brain to operate on. The only thing keeping me going is my tenacious motivation and unfamiliarity with these new-found depths of fatigue. I think to take the last bar out of my pouch but the downhill is too fast and winding.

On the Passo Coe, the last climb, involving nine kilometres of steep uphill, I'm riding beyond my limit. Savoldelli attacks me and I try to respond. But I've got nothing left. Frigo is the first of the contenders to blow, then Hamilton, then me. I'm now delirious. I can hardly function.

Dario is encouraging me. I can see his mouth moving but I cannot hear what he's saying. Then I realise how bad a state I am in. I'm delirious and just clinging to an awareness of my state. I'm so exhausted from turning myself inside out that I'm losing connection with reality.

I get to the finish line and I am so insensible that I just keep riding up the hill for about 400 metres. People are wondering what I'm doing. I'm not riding consciously, I just can't stop pedalling.

It's not an experience I would wish on anyone. I've lost 15 minutes on one climb, with nine kilometres to go. I've gone from first place on GC to 15th.

I'm devastated.

After the race people are confused. Some ask me if I've eaten properly (I have). They wonder why, when I've looked so strong, I haven't finished it off.

I know what's happened. I've pushed things way too far. I've done an enormous amount of training in November and December and now I'm paying for it. I've been racing absolutely flat out since the first races of the season. As Aldo described it, I'm a mountain biker coming into a three-week road race with a Formula One engine and I'm driving like it's a mountain-bike race, riding like there's no tomorrow.

My body is well trained at burning sugar for fuel and my fat system isn't as efficient as someone with years of long road racing in their legs. But my biggest problem is that I've had no idea how exhausted I am in this third week, so I've kept riding and pushing myself.

I've been road-racing full-time for just six months and I've found myself the leader of the biggest team in the world, in first place at one of the most important and difficult races in the world. I'm learning lessons that most people get to learn only after several years in their profession. And I've had to learn them very quickly.

MY EFFORT IN THAT last stage quickly becomes a byword in cycling for an effort that might have killed a nice boy from Australia who went too hard. Afterwards, it's amazing how many people come up and say, 'You know what? I never usually watch sport, but I watched you in that Giro and I cried on my couch for you.'

The whole thing appeals to the Italians. Here's this young cyclist from a foreign country leading their biggest race of the year and look what's happened to the poor guy. It appeals to people outside sport because of the human element to it.

I was concentrating on winning the Giro d'Italia rather than looking after myself or considering my fatigue.

It was an extraordinary feeling to have worn the jersey, and to have been within striking range of victory. As the first Australian ever to wear the jersey I'm extremely proud. But in hindsight, it would have been so much better for me to stay out of the results, to watch and learn, then maybe the next year have gone for the Giro d'Italia on my own, with enough experience to win it.

Was I swept up in the moment? Maybe.

Was I tempted by the chance of winning the first Grand Tour I'd raced in? Of course.

Was it a foolhardy approach? Probably not. I'm a bike racer. My instinct is to win, to keep going, to defy the odds, to push myself past the point where pain is an issue.

This was the Giro. I had a chance to win it. Why wouldn't I take it?

It was all captured on TV for everyone's viewing pleasure. It was a very good example of learning in public.

There are mixed emotions afterwards. It was a steep learning curve. I think for young riders in their first year who are getting a little bit frustrated because of their big ambitions, sometimes it's better to take a year or two, to sit back, to watch and learn so they can get even bigger and better results later.

I win a lot of respect from the road-riding world after that result. From the outside it may have looked as though I was trying to make a big statement. But I was just concentrating on doing my sport. I was proving myself to the cycling world of course, but more than anything, I was there to prove myself to *me*, what I could do. I wanted to prove what Aldo Sassi saw in me – that I could be a Grand Tour rider.

Although I haven't won the Giro, I've definitely shown the cycling world what I can do. Now they're looking at me, and the sport of mountain biking, in a different light.

CHAPTER 8
T-MOBILE

2002–2004

IN OCTOBER 2002, A few days before flying back to Australia for the off season, I meet Chiara Passerini, a 23-year-old who lives with her family in a town northwest of Milan called Gallarate. We're introduced by a trusted mutual friend in the good old Italian way.

Chiara is studying American Literature and Italian, Swedish and English at university in Milan, and also doing a diploma in classical piano at the Giacomo Puccini Music Institute in Gallarate. It's always refreshing to meet new people from outside the sport – but something particularly strikes me about the Italian student, pianist and singer.

We stay in contact over the next few months while I'm away in Australia, but it's only much later that our relationship becomes something stronger than a friendship.

Being Italian, Chiara has grown up knowing about cycling. When she was younger, she used to go and watch Tre Valli Varesine (Three Valleys of Varese), a Summer Classic held around her home in Varese province. As a teenager Chiara would wait on the side of the road for her favourite rider, Stefano Zanini, and cheer him on, even though as a sprinter he was nowhere near the front. I've got to know Stefano as a teammate at Mapei; Chiara was almost intimidated by the fact that I was good friends with one of her childhood heroes.

She tells me about the day the Giro went through her town, and came close to her house. 'Oh, the Giro, the Giro once passed through Gallarate!'

Of course being in a serious relationship changes my life, and it changes how I go about my training too. It has to. As an athlete you have to organise your life around your performance, which of course, means it's all about you.

I'm sure this seems – and is – very egotistical. To be in a relationship with an athlete would probably drive me crazy. You're doing a job that demands so much, very different from most jobs where you can walk out of the office at the end of the day and hopefully forget about work till the next morning.

As an athlete, everything you do every hour of the day contributes to your performance. This can lead you to worry excessively about seemingly trivial things, like what you eat when you go out for dinner, being on your legs for a particularly long time, being out in the cold.

I became very self-reliant and independent at a young age, which is good for a cyclist travelling around the world competing, but it's not conducive to a balanced life. I've spent quite a few years almost completely dedicated to my sport. This is great for my performance, but is not ideal for growing into a balanced, well-rounded individual who needs to perform at a high level for years to come. Chiara gives me stability and brings in a bit of perspective from the world outside cycling at exactly the right time in my life. Becoming part of her family helps me to feel more at home in Europe.

AS 2002 DRAWS TO a close, I look back at it as one of the best years of my life so far. I've met Chiara, I've started a new career in a new sport, I'm riding for a great team, and I've made my mark in my first Grand Tour. It's such an exciting time for me.

After the experiences I've had on the bike, I feel I'm set for a really strong 2003. But what's about to happen reinforces a cyclist's mantra: Be very careful about looking too far ahead.

In late 2002, the owner of Mapei, Dr Giorgio Squinzi, decides to shut the team down. I never find out exactly why.

It's the end of a very happy chapter in my life. Tony Rominger has been in negotiations to renew my contract for the next four or five years. I thought Mapei was the team I'd ride with for my entire career. Then, out of nowhere, we get this very sad news.

The Mapei company is happy to honour all of the riders' contracts, and keeps the sports research centre going. All the riders are given one more year's access to the centre even though they will ride for another team.

Aldo decides to appoint two ambassadors to promote the Mapei centre: a Classics rider and a GC rider. I don't initially appreciate what a great opportunity he has given me when he appoints me as the GC ambassador. It means my working relationship with him continues as strongly as ever, and if anything, my visits to the Mapei centre increase. This becomes the backbone of my success for the next 13 years.

Considering my results this year, especially at the Giro, finding a new team is not a problem. The question is whether I'll be able to find another team like Mapei.

The market for GC riders is lucrative but small, there aren't actually that many teams actively looking for a potential Grand Tour winner. All the teams want one, but whether they're willing to invest in and commit to one is another issue. Tony presents me with three options, and recommends Team Telekom.

This German team have lost their star rider, countryman Jan Ullrich, who left after receiving a six-month ban in June for testing positive for amphetamines. They've decided that instead of placing all their hopes on one rider, they'll take on three, including an up-and-coming GC rider to fulfil their Tour de France hopes.

That rider is me. They offer me a healthy three-year contract. On Tony's advice, I sign for two years.

All I know about Ullrich and the banning is what I read in the media. Since his Tour de France win in 1997 and his gold at the 2000 Olympics, Ullrich has been going through issues in his personal life. So I'm convinced the positive drugs result had nothing to do with the team, and I feel completely comfortable riding for them.

As 2002 ends with me in new team colours, I know I'm going to miss that one great, happy year with Mapei. What I don't know yet is how much.

FOR, ME ULLRICH'S DEPARTURE from Team Telekom is a real opportunity. But I've only been in the sport full-time for a year, so I'm still on a steep learning curve.

My first race with the team, the Tour Down Under in January, is OK. There's a good group of guys, friendly and welcoming. I'm sharing a room with an American teammate, Bobby Julich, and it's nice talking to someone whose first language is also English. Bobby and I have a fun race.

But there's one incident early in the 2003 season that for me encapsulates the reputation of Team Telekom. We go to Spain in February to race the Vuelta a Valencia and I see an Italian rider I always say hello to. So I happily go up to him and he looks at me with a blank face.

Then he sees who it is. 'Oh, Cadel. Sorry, I didn't realise it was you. How're you going?'

He hasn't recognised me because I'm now wearing a Telekom jersey. The other riders are so used to being ignored by the Telekom riders they don't even bother to say hello. And all of a sudden, just because of a change of jersey, no one socialises with me. I find it very disconcerting and it's a little more isolating than is comfortable.

There's such a different mentality on this team: 'Don't speak out of line, don't make any jokes.' This is epitomised by German rider

Erik Zabel, a very serious, dour individual. When he's at a race, no one smiles or laughs, which makes being at a race a disappointingly tiresome chore. It isn't long before I'm not enjoying going to any of the races and my performance shows it.

BANG!

This cannot be happening.

I have bounced and then skidded along the road on my front and side, and there's a sharp pain in my shoulder area.

Surely not the collarbone! Not the collarbone that's just healed! I'm too nervous to touch it and check.

But I don't really need to. Denial lasts a few seconds. Reality will last some time longer.

This cannot be happening. Again!

The first time was in April at the Amstel Gold in the Netherlands, the first of the Ardennes Classics. I saw it as a good opportunity to fine-tune my fitness with a Grand Tour just a few weeks away and familiarise myself with the particulars of the Amstel Gold.

In cycling, don't rely too heavily on your plans.

At the precise moment I shouldn't have, I reached for my water bottle. As I did this, the peloton in front of me all braked suddenly. As I headed into the wheels and the inevitability of a crash, I didn't even have time to put my hands on the handlebars. And the next moment I was sprawled on the ground in pain, knowing I'd broken something.

It was such a stupid little crash. And I was amazed I'd injured myself so easily.

Four weeks after the accident, the doctors said the injury had healed to the point where I could race again, so I rode the Tour of Bavaria in Germany in late May, part of the team's preparation for the Tour de France. Then, a week later, I am entered into the Rund um die Hainleite, a small one day race in Germany.

I'm in the breakaway in the final circuit with German rider Fabian Wegmann. I'm following him and we're going pretty flat out in an effort to win the race. I'm riding behind him thinking, 'Isn't there a traffic island somewhere here?'

At that moment he darts to one side and I slam straight into the road sign on the traffic island. My bike comes to a complete halt and I go sailing through the air – which is fine, until I hit the road on my left side at about 50 kilometres an hour.

BOOF! Once again I land on the shoulder that had not fully healed.

I lie there not quite believing what has just happened. Have I really crashed again? As I struggled to stand up I feel a sharp pain coursing through me. Can I really have broken the same collarbone?

The doctors confirm this quickly. And this time I've *really* damaged it. I can feel part of my clavicle stretching, almost piercing, the skin on my shoulder. The bone was still healing from the first crash and it broke in the same place.

I'm shocked, disappointed, angry, frustrated. What makes it worse is that the first crash was a stupid one that should never have happened.

It's the start of the most unhappy period of my career.

I'M TAKEN TO A hospital in Germany near the Swiss border with only a day bag containing a pair of pyjamas and a magazine. Chiara is deep into her exams in Milan. Fortunately, she's been able to take time out and come to Germany to visit me in hospital. Now she has a new role, as my consoler. She keeps telling me the injury will heal and I'll be back on the bike soon. I'm really grateful for her support but I find the situation extremely depressing.

Chiara then she goes back to Italy to do her next exam.

I'm strapped up in bandages with nothing to do but stare at the white wall day after day, and unable to talk to anyone because of my limited German. At one point I wonder, 'Is this actually worth it?' The only person who seems to care is Chiara, and she can't be here.

The reason I'm in this hospital is that one of the team doctors works here as an orthopaedic surgeon and he's helping me with my recovery. But that's the extent of the team support. I don't get any calls from the team to see if I'm OK – not from riders, not from staff, not from anyone – and it's demoralising.

Lying in hospital I feel my chances of starting my Tour de France career slipping away.

I try to be upbeat, but it's hard. It's amazing the impact an injury has on an athlete. So much of your self-perception is tied up in your physical prowess. At times you think that you are how you ride, that your capacity to jump on a bike and do well helps you know who you are. I am not saying this is healthy, but it's how an athlete learns to rate himself.

Lying in bed unable to move is a real low point.

But 2003 is about to get worse.

TWO MONTHS LATER THE collarbone has mended enough for me to race, so the team make plans for me to compete in the Vuelta a España, the Tour of Spain.

Inspired by the strong following of the French and Italian national tours, the Vuelta was launched in Spain in 1935. Just as the other two big races were launched by newspapers, the Vuelta was established by the Spanish newspaper *Informaciones* to attract advertising and boost circulation.

Of the 50 riders who started in the first Vuelta, just 29 finished. The legends of the race are the three who have each won it three times – Spain's Alberto Contador and Roberto Heras, and Swiss rider, and my manager, Tony Rominger, whose three victories were consecutive, in 1992, 1993 and 1994.

I've heard that to ride the Vuelta is nice, because the crowds aren't generally very large so you can concentrate on the racing. The Vuelta has quite open, sparse stretches, so sometimes you're riding along for 100 kilometres without passing a town or village.

Since 1995, the Vuelta is raced in September, finishing before the World Championships. Because it's late in the year, the pro peloton is usually very fatigued, so, unfortunately for the Vuelta, the standard of racing probably isn't as high as at the Tour de France or the Giro d'Italia. Still, I'm keen to prove myself, to come back in at a high level and get some results at the tail end of the season.

A lot of riders like to ride the Vuelta in training for the Worlds. It has a looser vibe, a lower level of nervousness. In terms of the importance for the team or the sponsors, it's not like the Tour where they're watching every minute of what everyone's doing. At the Vuelta the attitude is 'If you can win, great, and if you can get some points, great' … making it a more relaxed race to ride.

I'M RIDING IN STAGE four, back among the cars getting water bottles before re-entering the group. There's one rider just in front of me. I look over my shoulder to see where my teammate is. As I do that, the rider in front, not knowing anyone is behind him, veers right, taking my front wheel down. I fall and land on my left side again.

Of course everyone's an expert afterwards on why the crash occurred. But for me, this time it was pure bad luck.

What is happening? It's my third significant crash in a five-month period and each one has been for a completely different reason, but all three have brought me down heavily on my left side.

It's the beginning of the breakdown of my relationship with the team.

The first two accidents have already changed the way I ride, and not for the better. They've made me too cautious, which has had a spiralling effect on my risk-taking and decision-making. When you become nervous your body becomes more rigid and you cannot control the bike as proficiently, which makes you even more nervous, so it's a vicious circle. After a string of accidents you don't want to risk anything. And the constant risk assessments you're making mean it's difficult to ride with purpose.

Then the rehab from this third injury is tough. When you have one shoulder strapped it's really hard to put your shoes on or open a jar of honey or have a shower or go to the toilet. Some mornings it's tough just putting one foot in front of the other. You're not racing, you can't train, you can't even get on a bike. You go from being an elite-level rider to what feels like an invalid, which for an athlete is very difficult to deal with.

I've already had two lay-offs and two operations before this one, and each time it happens I need more hours in surgery, and the longer the surgery, the longer it takes to come back.

I know this accident means the end of my season. It's time to cut my losses and start thinking about 2004. But because of these three accidents, the team have lost faith in me and my ability. Because I'm being more cautious, there comes a point when I'm not taking enough risks to get the job done.

I also feel for Chiara. She's met some guy who's having the most depressing year of his life. She's only known me as an unhappy rider, riding for a team where there isn't a great deal of passion involved. She must be wondering what she's got herself into. But she's certainly there for me, encouraging me to stay positive, trying to cheer me up and see me through this low period.

It's at moments like these that you really feel the lack of family and a support network. The riders from Europe can never get their heads around this, the challenges we non-Europeans face. We're here on our own pursuing our dream to become professional riders, and when things aren't going well we feel pretty alone. Chiara and Aldo are all I have.

My selection for Team Telekom is now looked at as a bad decision. Not that I know this for sure. I just know there's a big silence from those who might be offering some support right now. I don't receive a single phone call. Not to check up on my recovery, not even a call just to see how I'm holding up. It seems like they've well and truly given up on me.

So I accept my situation and commit myself to recovering from my injuries, and planning for 2004 and my debut in the Tour de France. That will be my main focus for next season.

Meanwhile, it's about recovering and not being miserable.

BY JANUARY 2004 I'M ready for the new season. Team Telekom – now known as T-Mobile – decide not to compete at the Tour Down Under, so I'm sent to an altitude training camp in Tenerife with teammates Alexander Vinokourov, Paolo Savoldelli, Mario Aerts and Matthias Kessler. Then it's off to Spain for the Vuelta a Valencia in February, and the Vuelta a Murcia in March.

After a year racing for Team Bianchi, Jan Ullrich is back at T-Mobile. I haven't got to know him well; he has so much fuss going on around him all the time wherever he goes.

It's at this race that I first witness the extent of Jan's celebrity.

The team say, 'OK, we'll go here, we'll go there, we'll get everything ready and then we'll go to the start at the last minute.'

I'm saying, 'Why don't we just go there and chill out? It's just a small race.'

'Oh no, no, with Jan, you'll see.'

And sure enough. Mobbed. The whole team is mobbed because Jan is there and we've all got jerseys on the same as Jan's. I'm thinking, 'Hang on, I just want to go to the start and sign on.'

Jan has an amazing amount of talent. Lance Armstrong has often said, 'Jan Ullrich's the most talented bike rider in the world.' Jan has a pretty fast finish and quite a good eye for tactics. He has an incredible cycling acumen and despite the fame that comes with that, he's remained a simple, easy-going guy. He comes from a relatively humble background and I don't think he's ever felt comfortable with the stardom that's been thrust upon him.

I'm at Murcia racing for GC. I finish third overall: a satisfying comeback after such a bad 2003. There are some tensions among the rest of the team, which I find disappointing. It's as though my doing well is showing up their lack of motivation.

'AREN'T YOU GOING TO send me my flight details? Don't I have to go to Holland and Belgium?'

It's early April 2004. I'm in training for the Ardennes Classics later in the month – the Amstel Gold in the Netherlands and the Flèche Wallonne and Liège–Bastogne–Liège in Belgium. I'm on the phone to Mario Kummer, head director of T-Mobile. I want to know the details of my travel so I can organise my training and my life. Initially, I get one or two phone calls a year; apart from that it is just an email with an air ticket attached. But I haven't heard from them in quite a while. I'm in limbo with these guys. It would be nice to know where I need to be.

The team manager tells me, 'We've decided we're going to send you to the Tour of the Basque Country.'

The Tour of the Basque Country? Oh. That's not what I want to hear.

This is the moment I know for sure that T-Mobile have lost faith in me. The constant injuries in 2003 have cruelled me in their eyes. I am now just a number in this team.

Aldo, with all his experience at Mapei, will probably be a better judge of this than I am.

I ring him up. 'Aldo, I've just been told I'm not going to the Ardennes Classics, I'm going to this other race.'

'Oh.' He sounds very disappointed for me. We chat for a while and he encourages me to stay focused on the Tour de France.

A month before the Tour I am preparing to race in Austria. In a rare moment, face to face, I ask Mario, 'Is there some doubt about me going to the Tour?'

'If you perform well in the mountains in the Tour of Austria, then you go to the Tour,' he says bluntly.

'OK,' I think. 'So apparently there *is* some doubt.' At least now this is clarified.

So I go to the Tour of Austria. I have good memories of this race, because it's where I had my first professional road win back in 2001.

I've been training well since the injuries last year and I'm in good shape. Just like in 2001, I'm able to win the mountain stage on the Kitzbüheler Horn and take the overall lead. The team are very happy, and they ride on the front to defend my lead. We win the race and I ride home thinking, 'This is good. Just what Mario wanted.'

In fact, it's more than Mario wanted. I didn't think I had to prove myself again but now I've definitely earned my Tour de France selection.

A few days later I go to a stage race in France, the Route du Sud (Route of the South), my last race before the Tour de France.

Mario and I meet after the race. 'What's happening with the Tour?' I ask expectantly.

Mario pauses awkwardly. 'You're not going to the Tour.'

What?!

I'm shocked. Speechless. Ever since my year with Mapei in 2002, I've been working towards the Tour de France. The whole of my 2004 season has been about debuting at the Tour. I cannot believe what I have just heard.

I find out later through indirect means that the team decided back in November that I wouldn't be part of the Tour de France. But they didn't tell me until three weeks before the event. Not ideal behaviour, but not uncommon in the world of professional cycling.

A cyclist's life is entirely geared around certain cycling events. You plan your training load – and your whole life – around competing in those events, to make sure you're ready both physically and psychologically. To have your schedule changed can really compromise your ability to peak and perform. A team can easily destroy your season if they want to.

Once more, Aldo is supportive. He may be tough on the surface, but the thing that really makes the difference for me is that in the bad times he's there. When I was coming back from injury last year and no one believed in me, he never for a moment lost faith in me, even when I was starting to lose faith in myself. It's those moments that are the most crucial in the making of a top rider – those moments when you need the help and support and you get it.

And then something happens that I've never experienced. All of a sudden I lose all my motivation. For anything.

I don't have any reason to get out of bed in the morning. I sleep until really late, sometimes 11 or 12. It's very strange. Normally I'm the guy who snaps up out of bed, uses every minute to train and perform, recover, do whatever needs to be done.

But that has changed nearly overnight.

For the first time in my cycling career my adrenalin has deserted me. I feel numb, listless. From being almost obsessively active and routine-based, all of a sudden I become the most sedentary person ever. I don't even know this person.

The sense of exclusion has utterly rocked me.

I go out on the bike, but don't ride hard. It is just to cheer myself up. On the day the Tour starts I watch the prologue on TV. It's strange, given I thought I'd be there. I feel strangely disconnected. I need a distraction, something to ground me.

That distraction is Molly.

Of all the sacrifices I have made to get this far in my career, the one thing I have missed the most is having a dog in my life. As our relationship has strengthened, Chiara and I have been going to dog pounds, looking around for a suitable puppy.

One day, while I'm still staying with the Passerinis and out on a ride, Chiara calls me. 'Come to the market, there's something I want to show you.'

At the market, Chiara points out a puppy, that has a remarkable resemblance to Hobie, a Kelpie cross I had as a kid 15 years before in Armidale. In the heart of Europe, Chiara's found a funny, skinny little Aussie. 'A bit like me,' I think.

We take the puppy home. We call her Molly and she does her job of distracting me. I spend the next few days settling Molly in, and watching bits of the Tour de France on TV. Not obsessively as I usually do, though. Missing the Tour start this year no longer seems as significant.

Molly sits on the floor, biting me, like the faithful companion that only a dog can be, beside me every step of the way, through good and bad, blissfully unaware of my results. I know that if everything else in my life changes, she'll still be there, supporting me like a faithful therapist.

BEING OUT OF CYCLING for a while has its good side. It means I can attend events I otherwise couldn't have. Chiara does her final exam for classical piano and I'm able to be there to support her during that. And taking a break from this team environment is always helpful.

But soon I'm back into my training. In July I go to do a camp at altitude at Livigno in the Italian Alps, near the Swiss border. In classic T-Mobile style the team sends me an email while I'm there, saying team rankings are below expectations so come to Germany and join *our* training camp. I've just arrived in Livigno with the puppy and Chiara to keep me company, and they say I've got to go to Germany – tomorrow.

So I go. It's not at altitude. They're not training hard. They're not even training well. So I've left an altitude camp for this.

It's typical of T-Mobile. They've completely misjudged me as a rider and a human being.

This is best illustrated by the fact that the mechanics in the team appear not to care whether my bike seat is the right height. They're insulted when I check my seat height with a tape measure. They say, 'That's close enough', and it's five millimetres too low. They regard me as demanding and particular.

One day a T-Mobile mechanic complains because I want to change a wheel. He tells me, 'There's nothing wrong with this wheel.'

But there's glue on the brake service so the brakes are grabbing. I need some maintenance done so I can ride my bike properly.

I've brought attention to some sloppy work and he's not happy.

So I'm the problem? I want a bike that works for me! Is that so bad? To get back at me the following year he goes to my new team manager and says 'Good luck with that Cadel – he's difficult'.

In a nutshell: I want to do everything as professionally as I can, so at T-Mobile that makes me a fish out of water. Now I cannot wait for the season to end.

Fortunately, quite a few teams are interested in having me; my good results in the past haven't been forgotten by team managers and the rest of the cycling world.

In August, Tony and I have an initial meeting with Marc Sergeant, manager of Belgian team Lotto–Domo, and Marc Coucke, owner of Omega Pharma and its brand Davitamon. They want to form a new team in 2005, Davitamon–Lotto.

There are already two Australians on the Lotto team – Robbie McEwen and Nick Gates – so unlike at T-Mobile, the team managers have an idea about what Australians are like. Lotto is built around the Classics, and supporting Australian, Robbie McEwen in the flatter races and the sprint stages at the Tour de France, vying for the sprinter's green jersey. To my mind Australia's best sprinter, the short, stocky, dark-skinned Queenslander with a very strong character is probably the best in the world at positioning himself in a final to go for the surge to the line. Always suntanned, and with a particularly muscular build for a cyclist, he always looks fit and ready, year in, year out.

I immediately ask Marc Sergeant: 'Why do you want me on the team?'

They have clear goals: they want a presence in the hillier races and need a good GC rider to achieve that. This is coming from the new sponsors, who want the added TV exposure. Until this point in time, the team has been almost invisible in the hillier races.

Teams earn their money through sponsorship. And a team sponsor goes into cycling with a view to gaining publicity. Just as you can buy advertising time in newspapers or on TV, you can buy a space on a cycling jersey. Basically, riders' jerseys are billboards for corporations, products, organisations or even cities (like Astana). But just as with other forms of advertising, you can't be sure how many people are going to see it or how effective it's going to be.

If you're sponsoring a team that goes to the Tour de France and they get in a breakaway on one day, the company logo and colours are broadcast to millions of spectators around the world, so all of a sudden it becomes a very valuable, quality investment.

Having Robbie win the green jersey is great, but sprint stages only make up five to seven of the 21 stages at the Tour de France, and over time, this number seems to be decreasing. Lotto want a presence during time trials and mountain stages. If you're in a breakaway in the mountains for a couple of hours, the TV coverage is equivalent to a couple of sprint stage wins.

I will be leaving a team that is full of riders for the races that suit me and going to a team that has no riders for the races that suit me. At T-Mobile I haven't even been selected to go to the Classics or the Tour because they have so many good climbers and GC riders; at Lotto, I'll be free to do every hilly race I want to. I'll have a great opportunity to get back to racing at the front in big races. Lotto are not experienced with GC racing, so I can help shape their plans. It will be a mutually beneficial arrangement.

I've had two bad years and I don't have a lot of results to show. Subsequently my value is half what it was two years ago. So I'm hoping I'm good value for money.

But money isn't what's motivating me. At 28, I'm in a hurry. For two seasons I've been held back by injuries, bad luck and team constraints. I'm highly aware that it's late to be starting a tour career and now I just want to get on with it.

IN SEPTEMBER I RIDE the Vuelta again.

Just three days in, six of T-Mobile's nine riders are mysteriously sick.

I'm sharing a room with Colombian rider, Santiago Botero, a gentle, soft-spoken guy. He gets up in the middle of the night, then accidentally wakes me up as he comes back to bed, and he's full of apologies. 'Sorry to wake you up, sorry to wake you up.'

'What's the matter, you OK?'

'No.' He's been in the bathroom for hours, very ill. He pulls out of the race, along with another rider. Another two drop out within a couple of days.

Now I'm sharing the room with Alexander Vinokourov. He's been ill too but has managed to stay in the race. His incredibly tough mindset and desire to be ready for the World Championships keeps him going.

I'm riding GC and pretty much on my own. We are down to four riders in the race: Germans, Stephan Schreck and Erik Zabel, Vinokourov and me.

The morale among the remaining riders is low, even by T-Mobile's depressing standards.

I'm begging Vinokourov not to leave because the two Germans aren't talking to me. He shows a trace of sensitivity and tells me with a smile, 'It's not that bad.'

I'm hanging inside the top 10 on GC until the time trial at stage 15 when I lose about a minute and half to a Spanish rider, Manuel Beltrán, who's a very light climber, not of a time-trial build. I'm demoralised. I think, 'I rode a good time trial, how come these guys are so fast?'

I give up riding GC; instead, the next day I help Vinokourov get to the front, then I just sit up and ride in the group, my first ever experience of the *grupetto*. I feel way out of my depth in this level of competition, but I know I still have a week of a Grand Tour to ride. The misery of being in this environment is torturing me.

Then after stage 18, Vinokourov leaves the tour. Stephan and Erik and I sit on the bus and in the evening, at the dinner table, in complete silence. I talk to assistant manager, Giovanni Fidanza for company and a bit of a morale boost, I speak to the *soigneur*, the bus driver, maybe briefly to some riders from other teams and that's it for the day. It's pretty lonely, not a nice ambience to be a part of.

At meals I go and sit with my old team, Saeco. At least *they're* friendly. I can see the other two guys, resentful as they watch me getting along well with the Saeco guys, talking, laughing, enjoying life for a moment.

The Saeco guys can see from a distance how cold it is in our team. Everyone can see I'm just moping along in the race, and they can see exactly why.

Meanwhile, Lotto is still sounding me out.

One day at the race I see Lotto manager, Marc Sergeant.

'Marc this is killing me being here,' I tell him. 'I can't stay.'

Marc says, 'You've got to do it, for next year. Just a few more days. I know it's hard but hang in there.' Marc also knows that I need a Grand Tour in my legs for the next year.

TWO WEEKS LATER I go to the Worlds in Verona, where I raced as an Under 23 back in 1999. I'm riding on the national team for Stuart O'Grady.

The Australian team have their bikes stored in the garage of a hotel; sometimes you're not allowed to take bikes into the rooms. Mine has special race wheels I've bought for it. Two nights before the race, I look at the bikes sitting there and think, 'This doesn't look very secure to me.' I take the wheels back to my room but leave my bike there with all the others.

When we come out the next morning all the bikes have been stolen. For us professionals it is, of course, frustrating, but we know the team will replace them all. For the poor juniors, though, whose parents have bought their bikes and have to pay all their own expenses to get here, it's a real loss, and they still have to race the next day.

Chiara is coming to watch the race so she brings over my training bike from home. I ride it in the race and it's fine.

So often in Italy bikes get stolen, but not just one or two; they'll steal 20 or 30 bikes from a hotel, probably selling the components on some kind of black market.

I'm still tired from the Vuelta, but it's nice to be back in a team environment where people are happy to be there and show it openly. The next day in the race I ride alongside Stuey for as long as my legs can last.

The red-haired, fair-skinned Aussie is sometimes referred to as 'The Freckle'. He started racing in 1995. I still don't know Stuey very well at this point; I've ridden with him only once before, at the 2002 Commonwealth Games where he reconfigured the team's tactics to suit his own desires. But I've seen he has a great eye on the road, he's great to have on the team, and he's an incredible team worker. He's got one of the best riding styles of anyone – a true 'natural talent'. Along with his smooth, clean pedal stroke, he's a graceful rider. One of my strength and conditioning coaches considers him the example of perfect posture on the bike. He's also one of the most hilarious guys I've met in cycling. It's so refreshing to have someone who's funny around the scene, especially after the company I've been in.

I can see he's really motivated for this race and the course suits him. I know I'm probably not going to perform as well as he is, so I just stay by his side and do whatever he requires in the race. He comes in fourth; I don't even finish the race.

A week later, I spend more time with Aussie riders when I go to Lotto to do the team meeting for next year. I'm now officially part of the team.

I drink beer with Robbie McEwen and Nick Gates, and spend the evening laughing, joking and breathing many sighs of relief.

I BEG AND PLEAD with T-Mobile to do the last race of the year, the Tour of Lombardy in October. By now, everyone knows I'm going to another team. When you're leaving you're usually not allowed to race in the big events because they think you won't perform.

But I end up finishing fourth. For my own experience and satisfaction, I wanted to have one result at an international race for the year, and the more results the better as far as I'm concerned. It is a big race, and in sport a good performance is rarely a bad thing.

Ironically, the points I get mean that T-Mobile win the team rankings for the year. This is important for them and the sponsor.

After the race, my last day at T-Mobile, I turn up with my bike, the one I've looked after and respected for so long as if it were my own. Strictly speaking, of course, it's their bike, but I clean it regularly and make every effort not to scratch or damage it if I have to travel with it somewhere.

I always race with my Polar heart-rate monitor and an altitude cadence (pedalling rate) sensor so Aldo Sassi can collect data and make calculations. These are attached to the bike.

The T-Mobile mechanic comes up to me and points at the monitor and sensor. 'Are these yours?' he asks.

'Yes.'

He cuts the cable ties, gives me the sensor and monitor and takes the bike away.

'My bike!' I watch him wheel it rapidly away – it feels like it's being stolen. Despite its flexible front end and high speed instability, I have an attachment to the bike.

It's a metaphor for my time at T-Mobile. It started with a jersey delivered to my house for a magazine photo shoot with my name spelt incorrectly on the back. Now I go home and realise I don't even have a bike to ride on.

I'm leaving the team knowing I have critics, no doubt. But the way I see it at this point is that to be criticised by T-Mobile is a compliment. If I was ever to have fitted in with that team, I would have had to compromise many of my life principles, and if that is the price to pay, I'd rather not fit in.

But the result is I now have a reputation in the cycling world. Everyone who rides has one. Mine is pretty clearly defined. It derives from my wanting to be professional and wanting those I work with to be professional too. But at T-Mobile, this was not appreciated.

AFTER A QUIET DEPARTURE from T-Mobile, I'm looking ahead to a new start at Lotto and the simple goal of regaining the habit of racing at the front in big races. And a new house is nearing completion in Australia – in a town called Barwon Heads, near Geelong on Victoria's Bellarine Peninsula. It's a small town made famous as the setting for a TV show called *Sea Change*, in which a female magistrate (played by Sigrid Thornton) moves from Melbourne to a coastal town for a lifestyle change or 'sea change' as it becomes known.

I get to soak up the great beachside culture while being close enough to Melbourne to be in touch with family, friends and racing contacts, but still far enough away to train without interruptions in the pre-season.

I can train in the morning, sit in a nice café or restaurant over lunch, then head to the beach. Or I can ride into Geelong to see specialist doctors and sports physiotherapists, then do a training session at the Geelong Cats Football Club to work on injuries. Or I can get in the car for the hour-long commute to Melbourne to take care of whatever media or sponsorship requests need attending to.

It's a chance for me to enjoy being Australian a little more – coming back in the off season, and having a place I can truly call home.

I'm looking forward to enjoying a new lifestyle. And at Lotto, I'm looking forward to a new set of teammates, a new race program, and reinvigorated motivation.

CHAPTER 9
LOTTO

2005

IT'S LATE AFTERNOON, A luminous day, and the green of the new spring leaves is stark against Lombardy's blue sky. I'm descending slowly, squeezing the brakes, winding my way down from Val d'Intelvi with its small hotels and restaurants hugging the mountainside, to Morcote on the shores of Lago Lugano.

This is becoming one of my favourite training rides in the world, just a half an hour from home. Sometimes the roads here can be slippery from the crushed chestnuts or the sap that drips from the trees. It sounds autumnal and evocative but it can make the roads extremely dangerous. But if you can avoid the dangers, then these curvy mountain roads, winding through lush forests, combine an excellent training environment for the legs with some of the most beautiful scenery in southern Switzerland to feed the soul.

But the slippery roads are not the only danger. After spending time here you grow wary of the grumpy old men in their Fiat Pandas, and not just because of their bad driving. It's likely they are on their way to their secret fungi spot. Around here, fungi are gold.

Don't let them know you know where they're going, and definitely don't follow them. It could end badly for you. I've heard that the tyres of those who venture too close to these secret spots are slashed, as a not-very-subtle warning to stay away. Who would have thought a mushroom could inspire such violence?

It's on these roads that I escape into the hills and mountains around Como, Varese, Lugano and the lower-lying lakes that divide the beautiful peaks. It's an escape from everything. From the noise and demands of life as a professional cyclist. From the judgements of the press desperate to fill empty news space. From the expectations on me. I feel happy out here riding my bike – unburdened. I can put into perspective the expectations, conditions and circumstances that high-level competition can bring.

The expectations are a consequence of the precious opportunity that I have to make a career out my passion. My job is to get results. Results are achieved, time passes, results are soon out of people's minds, and new results are required to justify your place in the team, the team's existence, and the future of your career.

Put all that aside for a moment and look around. Descending, you catch flashes of blue from the lake as you ride over ancient stone bridges and through medieval villages clinging to the mountain – past kids on their bikes, past a balcony where a man is reading his paper with a grappa on the table next to him.

My thoughts jump around. I sing a few bars of Bruce Springsteen's 'Glory Days'. I love Springsteen, a great American poet. Then I sing the chorus of Crowded House's 'Private Universe'. I love Crowded House too. I'm no singer, but there's no one around so it doesn't matter, and these are great songs that suit the moment.

I pedal along the shores of Lago Lugano, the grumpy fungi hunters are forgotten. Now I must avoid the well-to-do housewives 'sciura' in their big SUVs. Today's been good, all the efforts completed without completely emptying me. I get home, wipe the chain clean, make a chamomile tea overflowing with local honey to enjoy in a hot bath – warming inside and out.

SINCE COMING TO LIVE in Switzerland in 1998, I've always passed through the Mendrisio region, in the canton of Ticino, on my way to and from Italy. Often I'll stop at Meride, a small town on the shore of Lake Lugano looking across to picturesque Morcote, not far from the border with Italy. It's usually around dinnertime when I reach Meride, and there's a great pizzeria a minute away from the freeway exit with a view over the lake and mountains. I'll sit there and think, 'This would be a great place to live. Swiss efficiency, Italian style: a perfect European blend.'

It's only because of residency complications that I haven't done it earlier, but in 2005, to be closer to Chiara and her family, and to Aldo and the Mapei centre, I finally move south of the Alps to enjoy a friendlier climate. I take the advice of Daniele Nardello, my teammate at Mapei and T-Mobile, and a native of the Varese region like Chiara. For geographical practicality, he suggests Stabio: 3500 inhabitants, and the last Swiss town towards Italy.

I find myself a small apartment, register with the local cycling club, Velo Club Mendrisio, and start life as a honorary Ticinese – or more specifically a Momò, as the people of Mendrisio call themselves.

AT DAVITAMON–LOTTO, THE 'TRAITS' of my character that caused me grief at T-Mobile are a good fit with a group of guys who ride bikes for a living, but above all want to have maybe a little too much fun. It's not just the balance of riders and the new opportunities that are attractive. Like at Mapei, I've found a team that actually encourages feedback and ideas and leadership. There's a spirit of camaraderie and optimism. The culture of the team is very likeable.

T-Mobile was elaborate on detail. Everything seemed to be overly controlled. At press conferences I just wanted to answer questions naturally and spontaneously, but they wanted to give me all the questions beforehand with suggested answers. It was as if I was being discouraged from being myself.

At T-Mobile you had timetables and instructions to follow. For team photos you'd have make-up and a professional photographer. It took three or four days to get them done.

At Lotto, things are done quickly and efficiently, without any fuss: 'Here are the clothes you'll need, here is your bike, off you go.' No mucking around. Everything's done in a day and then in the evening we'll go out and have some beers together.

By contrast to the palaver at T-Mobile, Lotto meetings are small, simple, quick and easy. I find the team managers a little bit more open-minded, willing to listen to suggestions for improvements.

T-Mobile had the best equipment and clothing, high-quality natural supplements, a T-Mobile phone, an Audi. Lotto doesn't have the budget of T-Mobile but what the management lack in budget, they make up for in careful decisions about rider selection and spending. They get on with the job without fuss. They're my kind of people.

Lotto are behind the times in training and nutrition but their approach towards doping is ahead of the times. That is to say, they want nothing to do with it. This is never spoken about directly, but it's obvious from their approach to preparation and races. They want you to do well in the Tour de France but they don't expect you to win it. The general mindset in this period is that if you expect to win the Tour de France, you cannot do so drug free. Lotto understand this, and they don't want to go there. For me this is a great relief.

It's an environment I've needed for a long time. I haven't been this happy in more than three years.

This is what cycling *should* be about.

MY FIRST RACE WITH the team is the Australian National Championships in Adelaide in January 2005, 182 kilometres around the town of Echunga in the Adelaide Hills.

I'm in a breakaway with Robbie McEwen, but he's made his own arrangements for the race. He's a rider who doesn't need a team to position for a sprint; he can do it better on his own. He's the opposite of most sprinters, who like to have the best possible lead-out team around them. Robbie always has a small team around him but he uses the other teams more effectively than anyone.

Already Robbie and I are working pretty well together. We're completely different kinds of riders, so we can't always do much to help each other. But on this occasion I drive the four man break to the finish so we can win, which I think puts me in good stead with the team. It's Robbie's second national title, after his victory in 2002.

I come in fourth. I could have acted selfishly and surely been capable of a better result, but at this point in my career getting the confidence of a team around me is more important for the grand plan. I have bigger fish to fry.

I've come to *his* team and of course I want to create good relationships for the years to come. My thought is 'I'm just going to keep my mouth shut and do what I'm told here.'

I'M RIDING FROM WHITTLESEA, an outer east Melbourne suburb, towards the city. I've finished a training ride and I'm on a commuter road, which I usually try to avoid, but it's the only road that will get me from the hills of Kinglake and Humevale to my mother's house where I am staying for a visit.

I feel the rush of a car passing me, really close. I look out of the corner of my eye and see the car is towing a trailer. The trailer's mudguard has brushed my calf. It hasn't grazed my skin, but it has passed right next to me.

I have nightmares about it for months. If I'd been riding five, six, seven centimetres further to the right, I might have lost my leg, or at least had my calf muscle ripped apart.

This person is driving along, maybe they're speaking to the person next to them, talking on the phone, listening to the radio, maybe they just haven't noticed the bike rider ahead – no idea. Whichever the case, this incident – stemming from that person's moment of inattentiveness or lack of thoughtfulness – nearly cost me my leg.

I don't know a bike rider who hasn't had an experience of this kind. The stories are endless. It's the really scary element of our sport. The thing that frightens me the most is the idea of a driver who's not paying attention and cleans you up from behind. You need eyes in the back of your head. You're probably not even going to see the car that does it.

The dangers exist for all cyclists every minute they're on a bike. And one of the problems is that drivers don't respond well when their poor and dangerous driving is brought to their attention. If someone makes a mistake driving and you go up and tell them, 'Hey, how about watching where you're going?', their spite and anger are only amplified.

Of course, there is anger and frustration toward drivers. There's a proportion of drivers who don't like cyclists, or anyone for that matter. They either don't think they should be on the road at all or think that they are easy picking for some seemingly playful but cowardly and often dangerous harassment.

Many drivers don't seem to notice bike riders, or have enough appreciation of how vulnerable they are. We're meant to be sharing the roads, but often it seems to be an unequal relationship; one risking commuting time and paintwork, the other risking life and limb.

IN FEBRUARY, I RACE the Vuelta a Andalucia in Spain, more commonly known as the Ruta del Sol (Route of the Sun), or 'Route Without Any Sun', as too many very wet days lead us to call the race.

We're riding down a wet descent through olive groves that's not particularly difficult. And then, all of a sudden, the front half of the peloton have all fallen down on the road. 'What's everyone crashing for?' I think.

Just as I contemplate braking *Poff!* Down I go. Fallen olives crushed by passing traffic have put oil all over the road!

Here we all are, lying on the ground or trying to get back on our bikes. We can't walk on our cleats, they're too slippery, so we're struggling just to stand up on the road.

I'm pushing my bike sideways along the road, feeling how slippery it is. A mechanic from the team car comes along with spare wheels and he's in running shoes and *he's* slid over on the road; it's so slippery you can't even walk in normal shoes.

Then there are the hazards that occur more often. I'm riding along in the peloton talking to Robbie McEwen one day. Jan Ullrich is in front of us. Jan moves off to 'answer the call of nature', and Robbie says, 'Look out. Jan's a sprayer.'

Sure enough, we narrowly avoid being gifted a moist moment by German superstar Jan 'The Sprayer'. I'm thinking, 'Robbie's such an experienced rider he even knows our competitor's natural habits!' The things you learn in this profession.

In a race you have to choose your moments carefully if you feel you need to make a stop. Sometimes you're on your bike for five hours or more and you're drinking a lot of liquids, so at some point it's going to have to come out the other end, maybe more than once. You can stop on the side of the road and make sure you do your business before the end of the convoy comes. Or you can, as you're rolling along, look for a place where there are no spectators on the side of the road, ideally going slightly downhill, not too fast, with no need to brake, then urinate while you're riding along. That way you don't lose much position.

For the most part it goes well. I suppose I'm always extra-careful because I just can't imagine a more embarrassing thing than crashing while doing that. How would you feel at the medical car getting those grazes tended to?

IT'S A FEW DAYS away from my second Liège–Bastogne–Liège, in April. The Liège is a much-loved race in Belgium. Belgian legend Eddy Merckx won it five times and countryman Philippe Gilbert, later, three times. It's a popular classic for Tour contenders because it's got more hills than other Monuments like the Tour of Flanders or Paris–Roubaix.

I'm focusing on being ready for the Tour, so I've had to be really careful about the volume of training I've done coming into Bastogne–Liège which is a demanding 260 kilometres.

My teammate Christophe Brandt, a Belgian rider who's joined Lotto from Saeco, is also in the race. I've always liked Christophe. He's my age, a friendly guy and always up for a chat even before we were teammates. But I don't know him all that well. That's the case between most of us: mostly we're friendly with each other, but often don't get a chance to find out whether we have anything in common. Life as a cyclist is often too busy for that.

The team put me alone in a hotel on the banks of the Meuse in Liege; I am spending the week there for the Ardennes Classics. Christophe lives five kilometres away so he comes down to give me some company and take me for a ride. I get a guided tour of his hometown; the school he went to, the house he grew up in, the house he is building for his young family. We say hello to Philippe Gilbert's father who is working outside in his garden as we ride past his house. Christophe explains some of the roads that the various editions of 'L-B-L' has taken over the years, they seem like insignificant variations in the race to me.

I say, 'You know everything around here. Please tell me about the Bastogne–Liège, this is only the second time I've been to the race.'

'Sure. I've been to every Bastogne–Liège since I was three.'

Christophe is 33. He's been to 30 Bastogne–Lièges. He was going to Bastogne–Liège before I knew what it was.

'Who won the first year you saw this race?'

Christophe says the name straightaway.

It certainly shows the difference in our upbringings.

Australians come into cycling not knowing much about the history of the sport. Most Europeans have a much better understanding of the history of cycling because of their upbringing. It's an entrenched part of their culture. When I was five at primary school no one knew what the Tour de France was.

Australians moving into cycling have got to find our own way right from the beginning, without the framework of that tradition.

We might develop an interest in cycling at age 12 – reading the magazines, watching highlights packages on TV, becoming fans of particular riders as I did. Increasingly, though, with the internet, young riders and fans can grow up with cycling and be well-informed at least.

But there are also advantages in not having this history. Not being immersed in this culture can help you to move beyond the tradition, to be better at adapting to the evolving nature of cycling. In Europe there is something of a blind adherence to what has always been. There are always exceptions, Aldo Sassi being the first and foremost amongst the coaching and team management side of the sport, although he was ostracized for it.

Here's where being an outsider helps me. I don't have all that cultural weight in my saddlebags. I'm not hidebound by rules that have always been there. I'd be the first to say how much I admire and respect European cycling culture. It is and has been for over a century the abiding culture of our sport. European tradition is fantastic. It's what led me to come and live in Europe and try to succeed at 'their' sport.

In the small bubble that is cycling, though, over 100-plus years, there haven't been that many changes. For a long time it has seemed that cycling hasn't evolved a great deal. But then, all of a sudden, since around 2000, there've been a lot of changes. And it's been the Americans, the British and the Australians who have led the way, while the Europeans have been playing catch-up, because the riders from the US, the UK and Australia haven't been held back by preconceived ideas about preparation, training, diet, nutrition, mindset, rider selection, team culture, equipment preparation and testing. Every aspect of the sport.

This might have parallels in the cultures and mentalities of the countries from which professional cycling has grown. Switzerland, the country where I live, functions very well because everything runs on a system. But trying to get something done outside that system is really difficult.

Many Swiss riders share a similar approach to their training. My experience in a German team reflected this. Don't even think about questioning the system!

I see older riders who've done things the same way for so long they have difficulty adapting, whereas change is easier for younger riders because they don't have to reform old habits.

In 1994, I read an interview with Lance Armstrong. In the article he was portrayed as arrogant and disrespectful towards the Europeans and certain riders in the peloton who should have commanded respect. When I was a young *stagiaire* I was once yelled at by the Belgian rider Johan Museeuw because I passed on the right in the feed zone. I had no idea that I shouldn't have done this. I was young and naïve and rightly got told off by a veteran. I learned my lesson and never forgot it.

While it was uncomfortable reading Armstrong's quotes, I also realised that it was this brazenness that was helping him win. Armstrong arrived at the 1993 World Championships aged 21, racing against Miguel Indurain. If he'd had respect for what riders like Indurain had contributed to the sport he might have felt intimidated. But I'm guessing he didn't have that respect and he thought, 'I'm American, I'm better, I'm going to show you.'

And he did. With all his brazen cockiness, he went on to win the World Championships, dropping Miguel Indurain on the last climb in the rain in Oslo, Norway.

Armstrong was disrespectful, sure. But he also wasn't hidebound by history and tradition. He was the new face of cycling, and that face wasn't there to respect his elders.

Armstrong helped change cycling in the 1990s with his brashness and desire to win at all costs. He regarded himself as an innovative trainer, and marketed this well for many years.

In interviews, he says, 'I go and do course reconnaissances and train specifically for specific events.' Accordingly, European journalists ask me, 'Are you going to go to course reconnaissance, like Lance Armstrong?' But actually most of the top riders are doing this. It's frustrating that it's presented as something Lance has virtually invented. In the world of mountain biking, virtually no one competes at any level without having seen the course.

IT'S SUITING LOTTO WELL having me in the team, I am keen to race a lot and be at the front again. Of course, I'm on the hunt for results, and two years of not even being selected for suitable races have left me even hungrier.

At every stage race I go to I finish in the top 10 and Lotto gets ProTour points, which delights the team so they send me to every stage race possible to get more points. I'm quickly becoming their go-to points accumulator.

But it's started to become a problem. Before I know it I'm racing *too* much. I'm not being left with enough time to train specifically. And it's very taxing riding GC at every race.

I'm trying to start focusing on the Tour de France, and to do that the team and I need to be strategic about how much I race and which races I ride.

At least I have some good company on the team. Back in November there was a criterium in Brisbane, which is where Robbie McEwen is from, so he invited Chiara and me to stay at his place so he and I could train together. We hung out for a week, training hard and having barbecues and drinking beer together.

Australians, Henk Vogels and Nick Gates – very typical Aussies whose company I've always liked – were there too. Henk was about to be a teammate, Nick had already been with Lotto for some time. I knew Henk when I was with the national AIS team as a mountain biker. I think I first met him in 1996, after he'd just become a professional with Rabobank.

Henk, along with Stuart O'Grady, was the first of my AIS generation to go to Europe and be a professional. At Lotto we room together. And that is where you get to know someone a bit better because you talk to them, you hear them on the phone to their family, and you learn all their habits – not all of them good. Henk is the sort of guy who curses his shoes for being wet and smelly in the morning. I would have to tell him 'Henk, of course, your shoes are going to be wet and stinky if you leave them wet in your bag overnight.'

Henk is just hilarious. He always says, 'If it wasn't for descents, I never would have made it as a Pro.' It's true he isn't the greatest climber; he's a very talented rider but he doesn't work to maximise his potential, nor look after himself very well. Some are happy to make a career accepting what they get out of the sport for minimal effort.

One night over an amusing dinner Henk and I are talking about my time at Telekom. Henk says, 'You came fourth at the Lombardia? That result alone could make you a team leader.'

'Fourth? Well, I am sure I can actually do better than that.'

I'M 28 BUT ONLY in my fourth full-time year on the road. And this is the season in which I'm finally about to start my Tour de France career.

I've always felt my destiny, my raison d'être as a road rider was to be a Tour de France rider. For me, it's always been first and foremost about the Tour de France. Every other event is secondary to that.

After terrible years in 2003 and 2004, I feel the significance of this great opportunity to race at the highest level. But there is not a great deal of interest in me coming into my first Tour. My years at T-Mobile have been seen by the somewhat short-sighted cycling world as proof that I can't compete at that level. I am not concerned about the minimal interest from the press and public. I am only interested in my performance.

Going into the Tour, Robbie is always the first priority in the team, and rightly so. He's fighting for the green jersey and stage wins. One of the great things about riding alongside Robbie is that he is very good at dealing with pressure and expectations. It's one of his great qualities, alongside his incredible ability to position in a sprint. It's been interesting to see his work up close.

But as well as supporting Robbie, I am there to work as a GC rider, because, reasonably untried as I am, that is my only reason for being in the team.

I am keen to get this Tour started so I can finally see how I measure up as a GC rider. And to do this, I'll have to be a little bit selfish, to save all of the energy I can. I'll be going up against Lance Armstrong, Jan Ullrich and Alexander Vinokourov, the best of the current Tour riders, who all have dedicated and specialised teams committed to one goal: them.

My approach is 'I'll see how I go in 2005, and from that, I'll have a measure of how good a Tour rider I can be'. If I finish in the top 10 it could be a launching pad for the future. It might be my last opportunity to show the cycling world that I can be a true Tour contender. I need to find out how good I am, to test myself in one of the toughest sporting challenges there is.

So I go to the Tour starting almost from scratch.

Physically I'm a little underprepared: On Friday the 13th of May, some weeks before the Tour, while motorpacing after the descent of the Col d'Aubisque on the road in Pau, I hit a patch of gravel and came down hard. I hit the tarmac at about 50 kilometres an hour falling on my left side and breaking my frail left collarbone for an unbelievable sixth time. It's the only bone I have fractured in 14 years of racing. After my bad luck with injuries in the previous year I can hardly believe it has happened to me again.

So coming into the Tour I've had to deal with rehab on an injured collarbone that has mended slowly. I've also had to change my race program and my lead-up to the Tour, and reduce my amount of racing to have more time to do specific training camps and course reconnaissance.

Squeezing in all of Aldo's training requirements has proved to be a bit too much. But I'm getting great assistance from David Bombeke, an osteopath and physiotherapist with an incredible knowledge of his job, a calm demeanour and inexhaustible motivation that make him a pleasure to work with. I met him for the first time at Paris–Nice back in March and we got along well. Since then, David has been at all my big races and important training camps as an osteo, as a *soigneur*, but most importantly as a friend. A special bond is built between rider and *soigneur* as often the post-race massage is the only relaxing time a rider has during some very stressful and tiring days. They become part physical therapist, part mental therapist and often a friend after good and bad days are experienced together.

I do what I can after the setback, knowing of course it's the Tour de France so it will be hard, but for me, the most intimidating aspect is that I may not turn out to be the Tour rider that I've always hoped I would become.

CHAPTER 10
THE TOUR

2005

THE TOUR DE FRANCE was born out of a meeting in a Paris café between two journalists and an accountant from the newspaper *L'Auto*. The idea of a bicycle tour was suggested by a young journalist, Géo Léfèvre, who thought a bicycle race around France would boost circulation and help *L'Auto* compete with its rival *Le Vélo*.

Léfèvre's boss, Henri Desgrange, liked the idea. On the day of the first stage of the first race in 1903, Desgrange wrote a rather bombastic mission statement:

> *With the broad and powerful swing of the hand which Zola*
> *in The Earth gave to his ploughman,* L'Auto, *journal of*
> *ideas and action, is going to fling across France today those*
> *reckless and uncouth sowers of energy who are the great*
> *professional riders of the world ... From Paris to the blue*
> *waves of the Mediterranean, from Marseille to Bordeaux,*
> *passing along the roseate and dreaming roads sleeping*
> *under the sun, across the calm of the fields of the Vendée,*
> *following the Loire, which flows on still and silent, our men*
> *are going to race madly, unflaggingly.*

Over the 102 years since then, an awful lot of riders have raced madly and unflaggingly. They might be what Desgrange called 'uncouth sowers of energy', but there have always been many in the crowd who also match that description.

Just like the Giro in Italy, the Tour de France is a race deeply embedded in French culture, celebrating as it does perseverance, endurance, courage and extreme physical resilience, often in atrocious conditions; an extraordinary physical and psychological test; in the end a test of character.

On paper, the course of the Tour is easier than the Giro or the Vuelta but the depth of the competition is what sets it apart. The best GC riders, *rouleurs* and time trialists are all at the Tour, in peak condition. At the Giro, maybe five people can win it. At the Tour, there are probably more who can win it, but crucially there are probably 20 riders who want to do the best GC effort they can.

In almost any other race – other than the World Championships or Olympics – many riders are there for training, or they're there to make up the numbers or take the place of an injured rider. The Tour de France is the one race of the year where everyone there is at the very best of their form. And they're there to give everything they've got, whether it's for themselves or their team on every breakaway, in every sprint, on every mountain. It's the race every rider wants to win, every day for three weeks.

THE MAJOR NEWS EVENT around the 2005 Tour is certainly not that it's my first – but that it's Lance Armstrong's last. At 34, Armstrong is riding what he and everyone else think will be his final Tour. That's what he's said. As the winner of the past six Tours, Armstrong is a dominant – and many say domineering – figure in world cycling.

At this point in time, Lance's domination is incredible. While some are sceptical, few speak out about him. Those that do seem to have very short careers. There are journalists writing stories strongly suggesting that there are irregularities in Lance's methods.

Some – such as the journalist David Walsh – have got very close to the bone, always irritating Lance beyond measure. Lance often seems to be denying stories about him, always with a snarl and sometimes with an attempt to demean the accuser.

It's well known that Lance receives the ultimate protection from his team. He will only ride in the safe slipstream of his teammates for the whole race. He always has one teammate in the wings from the first kilometre of the race to the last. All GC contenders are protected by their teams, of course, but Lance has teammates so strong that they can ride in the wind from kilometre zero to the end and Lance won't ever have to touch the wind, until he makes one of his devastating attacks. This protection also greatly reduces his chances of crashing. From memory, in the past seven years, I think he's only been in one crash, and it wasn't a pile-up. No other riders have teams that are strong enough to do that. Riding the Tour with Lance will allow me to see how he and his team operate up close.

Armstrong has taken the oxygen out of other teams' hopes. They're thinking, 'Oh we can't beat this guy at the Tour, whatever he's doing to win he's just going to keep winning, we don't have a chance.' All the riders have this defeatist mindset because Armstrong has always won so convincingly.

Expectations are not a problem for me at Lotto, fortunately. They want to have a GC presence at the Tour but they're not expecting me to beat Lance. That suits me just fine. I am happy just to have a *start* at the Tour and test myself.

While standing on the start line of one of the first stages, trying to step outside of the 'cycling bubble', I do look over at Lance and think, 'There he is, a legend of world sport, lining up next to me at the Tour. Maybe I'll have children and grandchildren in the future, and they'll ask, "Did you race against Lance Armstrong! Did you beat him?"'

And at that moment, I have my first realisation of the grandeur of the Tour de France.

MY TEAMMATE NICK GATES has ridden the Tour de France with Lotto in 2003 and 2004. He pulled out of the '03 edition after the 15th stage and the '04 edition after the first, but he's been there and experienced how it feels.

Nick tells me beforehand, 'You won't believe the Tour. People are hanging on the sides of the barriers, they're going crazy.' And soon I'm seeing it for myself.

More than any other bike race, the Tour is beyond cycling, beyond even sport. It's a crazy three-week festival. The riders are there to ride the world's most famous bike race, and they are all very serious about it. Fans, though, are there to have fun, get close to the cyclists, grab a photo or souvenir, have a quick chat. And they'll often do anything to achieve this without worrying overly about whether it might have an impact on the riders.

Sometimes you'll be riding along and an over-excited spectator will just jump out in front of you holding a sign or dressed in some sort of costume. (The crowds are becoming a bit more international these days; I even see a few Australian flags being waved.)

I love the passion of spectators. If I had time to read their signs I might even enjoy them. And the costumes can be funny. But when you're as focused as a rider needs to be, swerving to avoid crashing into someone is not something you want to have to do. You can actually hit a lot of people when you're racing.

The Tour does attract a different crowd from other races, much more mainstream – politicians, film stars, journalists from non-sporting media, all mixing with keen cycling fans. As they say, if going to the Giro is like going to the museum, then going to the Tour is like going to the zoo.

This is because the Tour de France transcends cycling. To many it's more of a cultural event. It attracts a different type of fan: someone perhaps there for the spectacle more than the sport.

This brings a whole different ambience to the race. Rather than being treated as a bike rider, you're treated as *the show*. Of course we *are* the show at a bike race, but I think it's different being in a show on the stage in a theatre or on a playing field, where maybe there is a fence, a barrier or at least some space that prevents the audience from reaching out and touching you.

Our 'show' is performed amid dogs running around, people wandering onto the road, riders getting hit by the crowd. Most bike races attract bike fans who understand the sport and are respectful of your space, but non-aficionados take a different approach. 'Oh, you're a Tour de France rider!' they'll say, and they pull your shirt and grab you. Many seem to leave their respect for privacy and personal space at home.

I have never been overly keen on being randomly grabbed by strangers. Some will try to steal your water bottle because they've got one from every other team but yours. Some will try to get a photo for their Facebook page so they can show that they met a Tour de France rider. Others will try to stop you when you're riding to the start line of a time trial or will abuse you because you *don't* stop.

On my first day of my first Tour an older woman is after a photo with Axel Merckx, the son of cycle legend Eddy Merckx and my teammate at Lotto. She's grabbing me. 'Where's Axel? Where's Axel?'

I don't know where Axel is, I'm not Axel Merckx, leave me alone. Before I know it, she has her arm around my neck, clinging on to my jersey yelling 'Where is Axel?'. I don't know how to get away without hurting her.

People at the Tour will get what I come to call Mad Tour Disease. They get to the Tour and are so excited about it that they forget they're human and it all becomes a bit of a farmyard.

I suspect many in the crowd have never been to a bike race before. And they want to see Lance Armstrong in the flesh in his last Tour. Eventually, that is all they are focused on, at the expense of everyone's personal safety.

One day we're riding towards the start of the Petit Ballon and the Grand Ballon in Alsace. The crowd is lining the sides of the road and as the peloton comes towards them, they have to step out of the way because they don't realise how much of the road we take up – as in, all of it.

Lance is leading with, as always, a teammate in front of him. I'm in the middle of the group. As we approach all the spectators step back. Except one man. A very large American, holding a camera. He's looking for Lance. Lance rides past and the man turns and stares, but remains standing in the middle of the road. We're doing 50 ks an hour bearing down on him and he's looking the other way. What amazes me is that he doesn't realise that there are 170 other riders in this race apart from Lance Armstrong, and about 50 of them are about to plough into him.

We ride towards him and shout to get out of the way, just before the peloton slams into him. He does not move and the peloton streams either side of him. Amazingly, nobody crashes.

I hope he got his photo.

MY FIRST TOUR DE France is proving to have a very steep learning curve. It's still a bike race but every aspect of the Tour is faster, harder, at another level.

On stage nine from Gérardmer to Mulhouse, I am following Robbie McEwen through the group. In the time it takes me to see a gap in the group open and close, Robbie has accelerated and moved though.

Your handlebars are 44 centimetres wide so a gap can be 44.5 centimetres wide; that's all Robbie needs. Personally I like 46 or 48 centimetres, but I'm not a sprinter – maybe that's why.

The sprinters have to make their risk assessments very quickly, even instinctively. They have everything to lose by not taking these risks. But that's what they're concentrating their whole career on. I'm just trying to stay safe in the finishes.

As I am riding without teammates in the finals, I find my own way in the finishes; searching for a place that is out of the wind, close enough to the front to be safe, while staying out of the sprinters' way.

If a gap opens and I have a chance to be in the front, I move there, and sometimes I can move up and finish near the front. But I would never get in a real sprinter's way. The only time I *will* get in their way is if we're going slightly uphill and they're starting to get tired and it's playing to my strengths. That's when I'll move in front of them and go, because there's every chance they won't be there in the final.

THE NEXT STAGE – AFTER a rest day – is my first Tour hilltop finish. My first real test to find out how good a Tour de France rider I can be.

I find my way to the back of the GC teams to position myself for the last climb of the day, my first Tour de France hilltop finish.

The whole Discovery team takes over. It's like riding behind eight motorbikes. They have their order that they ride in: the reverse order of the best climbers. So their *rouleurs* – all-rounders – will ride first. They'll ride fast to the bottom of the climb and then the next guy will do the first kilometre of the climb, then he'll pull off and ride easily to the finish while the third guy takes over. The rest of them are riding tempo so they can come up from behind.

At this point, I'm riding way beyond my limit. I'm recruiting every molecule of energy in my body just to get up the hill in as little time as possible.

Lance gets down to his last teammate, Yaroslav Popovych. Popovych is doing his turn, Lance is riding in his slipstream and the five or six who have not been dropped are following behind. There are now only eight riders left in the front of the race, and I'm eighth.

I'm seeing black and blue just trying to hold the wheel. I'm scared to take a breath of wind more than necessary for fear that it will mean the difference between staying in the select front group, and being dropped and throwing away all the work I've done to get this far. I can't hear for the effort of concentration and the pain

I'm in, and as I unravel, I cannot follow any more. I turn myself absolutely inside out, from there to the finish line, and finish eighth in the stage. Alejandro Valverde wins the stage, Armstrong is second. Then it's Rasmussen, Francisco Mancebo, Ivan Basso, Levi Leipheimer and Eddy Mazzoleni. Then me.

Armstrong is dominating this Tour, as he dominated the last six. Today I've seen that dominance up close. At first it bemused me, now I'm beginning to wonder...

Was Lance even hurting there in front?

AFTER THE STAGE I ride back to the hotel and get on the rollers for a little while. In 2005 people are surprised to see me doing this after a stage, but my entire body is aching, and it gives me a chance to reflect on things.

Relaxing during a Grand Tour is tough. To have that downtime so you can revitalise yourself mentally is critical, but hard to organise. It's a struggle to shut your brain down after an intensive day of racing. You're always moving around the country, so your environment changes daily, which makes it even harder. A lot of time is taken up travelling to and from the hotel and the start and finish of a stage. Most riders will share rooms, so it's important to have a roommate whose company you enjoy.

My best modes of relaxation after a stage are reading a book and listening to music (if you can find the time). The problem is I don't like wearing headphones much, and my roommate is nearly always around, so you can't just play music with another rider lying next to you on his bed. Unfortunately I never share a room with another Bruce Springsteen or Paul Kelly fan.

If I read a book, it will often be a factual book that will take my mind away from everything that's going on in the race. The more different the topic is from cycling the better. Reading is my biggest saviour. I find it critical in helping me get to sleep.

Getting good sleep is not as easy as it sounds, and it's extremely important. Sleep is actually one of the most under-considered aspects of cycling. People talk about good diet, good equipment, products and devices to help recovery. But you don't often hear about the importance of sleeping well. It's such a basic thing but it's one of the most important aspects of health and therefore successful performance. You have to learn for yourself how much sleep your body needs. Everyone's different.

Some riders perform well with eight hours sleep a night, others need ten or more. During a long race you want to sleep as many hours as possible, but just trying to do that in itself becomes a bit of a challenge.

My roommate will always turn his light off before me. Then I'll just lie there and read for 20 or 30 minutes. Distracting my mind away from the race. That's my form of escape.

TO FINISH EIGHTH ON a hilltop finish is unheard of for Lotto. After my performance in stage 10 there's a bit of a change towards me.

For me, eighth is good. It's not so far away from winning. I wanted to see how I measured up to the best riders in the Tour de France, the Tour specialists, and considering the long term view, it's a promising start.

Later that same evening I watch the day's race highlights. Lance is looking across at Valverde, who won the stage. As I watch Lance I'm thinking, 'This guy's not even struggling.'

During the stage, Aldo had me wearing a Polar heart-rate monitor, which registers speed, cadence, elevation and, of course, heart rate. Aldo will collate this information and calculate power output and VO2 max, a measure of the maximum volume of oxygen that an athlete can use. Then he'll use this data to analyse my performance.

The monitor reveals that I've spent two hours and eight minutes at or above my theoretical threshold of 175 beats per minute on that climb ... no wonder I was hurting. It wasn't as good as it could have been, but it wasn't bad at all. Normally, you'd finish a mountain climb like this on threshold. I was above threshold from start to finish. I read in the English press that I 'looked like a suffering dog going uphill'.

The next day I see Lance in the bunch during a moment of calm.

I go over to him. 'Lance, were you even *in medio* yesterday?' *In medio* means below threshold, expending relatively little energy.

Lance just looks at me and gives me a sly smile.

He's always professional and friendly to me but I try to leave him alone out of respect for his private space. I feel he respects me as a competitor. But I certainly wouldn't want to be on the wrong side of him, because he has a lot of power and influence in the sport, and I've seen what has happened with other riders.

Lance has a psychological grip on the peloton. He's a dominant presence, with an extraordinary record, and many riders are intimidated by him.

French rider, Christophe Bassons, once spoke out about Lance, and his career came to an abrupt end.

It's hard enough to make a career out of cycling without adding any more obstacles and challenges. For this reason, few riders have ever done what Bassons did. In the media, it's often referred to as an *omertà* – the name for the Mafia code of silence. But it's just going about your job without causing yourself unnecessary problems. We're riders, not governing bodies or anti-doping authorities.

The way the Discovery team is racing in this Tour is incredible. They're able to deliver their main rider to a certain point and then they'll just blow everyone else off the wheel. On the important stages, they will get to the front first thing and stay there all day in the wind. I spend most of the Tour looking at their backs, hiding in their slipstream. They'll glide up a climb, their smooth cadence unchanged, seemingly unaffected by the brutality of climbing a horrendous mountain stage. They seem to be able to ride the final stages as fresh as the first.

ALL OF US ARE devastated when we hear on the second rest day of the Tour – 18 July – that Australian national team cyclist Amy Gillett,

29, has died after six of the team were involved in a head-on crash with a teenage driver in Germany.

I don't know Amy, but her death has a huge impact on all the Australian riders at the Tour, and her name, through the Amy Gillett Foundation, will be forever associated with the need for drivers and cyclists to share the road safely and respectfully. Amy's legacy is a powerful one.

AS THE TOUR PROGRESSES, Robbie's long-time lead-out guy, American, Fred Rodriguez (known as 'Fast Freddie' for his sprinting prowess) is helping me out a lot.

Freddie sees I'm on my own and is able to give a little bit of help, which goes a long way. He takes me to the bottom of the climbs and positions me. I'm learning so much about positioning at this Tour because I've had to do most of it on my own. The other teams are very well organised, having five or six riders to help position their GC rider, and I have to go up against these guys with just Freddie. If it wasn't for him I would have ridden the entire Tour relatively isolated.

And then, in stage 16, my key moment. I'm following moves before the intermediate sprint, in Robbie's interest. There is a gap between those contesting the sprint and the group. Before I know it I get off the front with a small breakaway group and have a chance to go to the finish. The others in the group aren't riding very hard and are going to get caught. I ride alone on the front for the last six kilometres to go before the finish in Pau.

T-Mobile start chasing behind because I'm knocking on the door of Vinokourov's general classification and they need to protect that. It is quite a turnaround from the previous year.

I cross the line in fourth position which is enough to propel me from 11th to 8th on GC and I'm less than three minutes away from a top five finish in Paris. It's an enormous relief after two years of disappointment, finally, I am back on track again.

I CROSS THE FINISH line of the final time trial dehydrated, and completely depleted – physically and emotionally. I've turned myself inside out. The difficulty of completely emptying yourself in the last time trial of a Grand Tour is something only true GC contenders are familiar with.

I pass a row of team support staff and *soigneurs* waiting for their riders to finish. Many teams have left the finish area already. When all of the teams' riders are done, we typically race like idiots to the next hotel and get started on preparations for the next day. For the sprinters' teams, who may have all of the riders low in GC, this time trial is almost a recovery ride the day before the sprinters' big show on the Champs Elysées tomorrow.

I look around for the Lotto *soigneur* for some water and directions to the team bus. I can't see him so I ask a group of journalists, 'Have you seen anyone from the Lotto team?' They haven't. I ride around impatient and delirious.

Normally when you're a GC rider you cross the line and they take you and hold you up on your bike to prevent you from collapsing with exhaustion, and they give you a drink and make sure you're OK. Because Lotto don't normally do GC, the importance of the time trial is zero so the *soigneurs* don't bother sticking around.

People are starting to pack up because there are only seven riders to come in. Armstrong is 12 or 13 minutes away from coming in to win his seventh Tour de France and people have gathered to see that. But most of the teams and buses are starting to leave.

I'm insulted, offended, what? The team has forgotten about me? I'm that insignificant to the team?

Someone from another team sees that I'm exhausted and can't find my bus. He points it out to me. I get there and I bluntly let the team management team know how I feel about it. I lose it a little bit. I'm actually yelling.

'What the f—? Do I mean nothing to this team? You can't even wait for me at the finish to tell me where the bus is!'

I turn around. Eddy Merckx is right there, sitting on the bus. Because his son Axel is on our team, he hangs out on the bus occasionally.

On this occasion, I look at him and a little part of me dies. It's 'The Cannibal', staring straight at me.

Um, OK.

I've heard about Eddy a lot, especially working with Belgian *soigneurs* on various teams over the years. During his career, Eddy was a hugely popular figure in his native Belgium and across the cycling world. He is spoken of as the greatest ever stage race and Classics rider. He will always be remembered for winning his debut Tour de France in 1969 by almost 18 minutes, along with the points and mountain classifications. As well as his five Tour de France victories he won five Giro d'Italia titles, one Vuelta, 28 Classics and 19 Monuments, including seven Milan–San Remos, two Tours of Flanders, three Paris–Roubaix, five Liège–Bastogne–Lièges, three Flèches Wallonnes and two Tours of Lombardy. It's an extraordinary legacy.

I calm down a bit. If I'd seen him before I'm sure I wouldn't have spoken so firmly, although I don't know how much English he understands.

Eddy gets up and shakes my hand, and says in French, 'You did a really good ride.'

I reply, 'Coming from you, Eddy, that means a real lot. Thank you very much.'

I think anyone else could have said the same thing, but coming from him it carries far more significance. Not only is Eddy one of the greatest ever riders, he is a rare example of a champion on the bike and off it.

I'M VERY SATISFIED WITH how I've ridden during this Tour: I got maybe 99 per cent of what I had to give onto the road, and in terms of what's realistically possible that's a lot. Eighth place is a good starting point looking towards the years ahead.

I've learned a lot – about concentration and conserving energy and staying in a safe position, and balancing all three. I've learnt about positioning at the Tour which is different to other races. When you need to be in front, you need to be in front. When you need to save energy, you need to save energy. Riding the Tour is a constant balancing act and finding the right balance requires a lot of experience.

At the end of the Tour I'm pretty exhausted, but I've become the first Australian since Phil Anderson to place inside the top 10. After two years with almost no results, it's nice to be back where I want to be, enjoying getting great results at the big races. From eighth to the podium isn't that far.

MY CAREER FEELS LIKE it's back on track, and that settles me a lot … Now I can start thinking about the future, and the engagement ring I've been carrying around for several months.

The first quiet moment I have with Chiara, in the hotel room in Paris, I ask her to marry me.

'*Mi sembra di si*,' 'I think so,' she says though teary eyes.

We're married in her home town, Gallarate. It's a small affair, just family and friends. We enjoy beautiful Italian food and wine, and we both say a few words. It's a lovely way to start our new life together.

I know what I want in the world. I want to get the best out of myself, I want happiness on and off the bike, and I want balance. Some people can separate their career and their private life, but for me most of the time those two facets are intertwined, one affecting the other. If I'm riding badly I'm not happy off the bike, but if I'm happy off the bike I usually ride well. There's a pretty strong correlation there.

I'm dedicated as an athlete, and when you're living by yourself in another country I suppose you can be. But as with anything in life, you can be *too* dedicated. Cycling can consume you. It can rob you of time and energy and even opportunities to think and have perspective.

Having someone in your life who's not in the sport brings an important balance. Now, when I get on my bike I'm a rider, but when I put it away in the garage I try to step away from the sport. We don't have any cycling memorabilia in our house; we don't have any of my trophies on display. When I get away from training and riding I deliberately try to cultivate the other aspects of my life.

Chiara allows me to take my career a bit less seriously and not be so obsessive. Life isn't all about training and preparation. It's not all about tactics and team meetings and finding tiny new ways to create an advantage over other riders. Being one half of a couple shows me there's much more to life – sharing your thoughts, your experiences, your hopes, dreams and fears; and talking about anything but cycling.

Chiara not only makes me happier and more relaxed, she helps sustain me during my career.

CHAPTER 11

DARK DAYS AT THE TOUR DE FRANCE

2005–2006

AFTER THE 2005 TOUR, the world of cycling is paying a little bit more attention to me. It's encouraging that people might care, but on a human level, your sport and particularly your Tour result often overshadow you, the human being who actually does the work.

I am looking at improving for the 2006 Tour, working with the team to acquire teammates who can support me in the mountains. Looking at changes to make in the build-up to the season, adjustments in the racing program to permit me to arrive to the Tour fresher and more rested. Further optimising training, more specialised training camps, course reconnaissance and improving the efficiency in the day-to-day activities of an athlete, all with the idea of enhancing the quality of recovery, to ultimately improve the quality of the work required.

I'M GETTING SOME GOOD results in the months following the Tour despite being mentally fatigued from the season thus far. In August I come 15th in the one-day Clásica de San Sebastián in Spain, then second in the Tour of Germany. In mid-September I turn my thoughts to the Tour de Pologne (Tour of Poland).

Since 1993, Czesław Lang, the 1980 Summer Olympics cycling silver medallist, has run this event, which this year, largely thanks to him, has become part of the UCI ProTour. He was a good rider, well before my time, and he has achieved good things with this event in Poland.

The thing about racing there that makes it difficult, though – a little bit like racing in Australia in some ways – is that the towns are so far apart. To make a stage from one city to the other means there are very long stages.

We get to a stage finish late one day and it's nearly dark, which means they have to shorten the stage, so instead of six laps of the finishing circuit we do two. There's heavy wind and we're doing tight circuits on *pavé* streets – paved with stones – which are a bit dangerous. Normally with eight laps you'd start slowly and get faster and faster, and get to know how to handle the *pavé*. But when you only do two, there's inevitably a crash in the final. When it rains there, absolute disaster; the *pavé* roads get very slippery.

Some of the roads in Poland are new and very good but some of the roads are terrible. In one stage we're riding along on a dead-straight, beautiful new asphalt road, then suddenly we take a right turn and we're in the mud on a farm road that only tractors would use, full of rocks and holes.

We pass a particularly bad section of road and I'm watching my Belgian teammate Peter Van Petegem on the *pavé*. He specialises in the Classics; in 2003 he won both the Tour of Flanders and Paris–Roubaix (two of the 'Cobbled Classics', raced on cobbles even rougher than *pavé*). He's very good at positioning, so good that he can afford to be lazy, often riding in the last three of the group, but the second he needs to be at the front he'll move with lightning speed.

There are a lot of young Belgian riders who idolise him. They'll hang out at the back and talk to him and laugh at his many jokes.

Then he'll zip to the front and the young Belgians will all be stuck there because they can't move quickly enough.

Watching Peter pedal almost effortlessly over the cobbles, I'm thinking, 'I can see why he's such a good Cobbled Classics rider.' I ask him, 'How do these roads compare with Paris–Roubaix?'

He says, 'At least at Roubaix, you know where the cobbles are!'

Hearing this from a *pavé* specialist is comforting. The roads really *are* as bad as I thought.

Another time we're riding along through a town and the people on the side of the road are cheering: 'Oh wow, there's a bike race in our town.'

I'm riding along next to another rider and suddenly someone in a second-floor apartment has thrown an egg and it's hit the rider next to me on the side of the head and gone down his face. He's a bit shocked and very insulted. I find it very disrespectful. It's a reminder that Poland isn't a cycling nation in the same way as Belgium or France or Italy.

I end up pulling out before the end with stomach problems, and the rest of my season – at the Worlds and the Giro di Lombardia – doesn't go too well either. That's OK – I've been on the go since January and I'm thinking ahead to doing well in 2006, when the Tour will be a bigger focus.

IN MARCH 2006 I give a talk to a group of children at a high school in Lugano with former Swiss cyclist, Gottfried Weilenmann. Gottfried, a sprightly 86, won the Tour de Suisse (Tour of Switzerland) in 1949 and competed in the Tour de France five times and the Giro twice. The idea is for the students to hear about sport but also to hear how things have changed. Gottfried and I are the old guard and the new.

It's not just the students learning things today. After listening to Gottfried speak about cycling in the 40s, I learn that the basics don't change. The equipment changes. The average speed changes. Ideas about nutrition and race distances change. But in the end it comes down to whoever eats well, stays fit and lean and races with a hard edged desire and hunger to win. This hasn't changed in 50 years.

I used to look at photos of the Tour de France in the 1930s and think: 'How the hell did they ride those pieces of junk?' But I've still got my old mountain bike to look at. I was showing a photo of it one day to a young rider and he was laughing at me. It looks so dated, but at the time it was the bee's knees of equipment. As good as, if not better than that of my competitors' equipment.

It makes you realise that the guys from 10 or 30 or 100 years ago were all riding with the best support and equipment that were available at the time, and they were all riding flat out, at the limits of the best riders in the world.

IN APRIL, WITH QUITE a few races already under my belt, I compete in the Tour de Romandie, a reasonably big race in the ProTour rankings.

It was super-cold when I first raced it back in 2002, but it's a favourite race for many riders. Beautiful roads, beautiful climbs, an interesting time trial – a really enjoyable race. It's held after the Ardennes Classics, which are always a really big deal now I'm on a Belgian team. You go to Liège–Bastogne–Liège, the last of the Ardennes Classics, then you go to the Tour de Romandie and it's so nice to calm down and just race nice roads and a nice course, without too many expectations.

The race takes me to within a couple kilometres of Lugnorre, the village that I lived in for eight years. I look around and see the baker and the hairdresser and places I know. I really hope this race is able to survive in the cycling calendar because it really deserves to stay in the WorldTour for the fantastic race that it is.

In the final stage, I ride a time trial that's one of the best that I have ridden up until this point. We don't have very specific time-trial equipment at Lotto – something that becomes quite a disadvantage at the top level – but because I have good legs and the experience of two A Travers Lausanne races on the same course, I'm able get everything down on the road effectively. I win not just the time trial, but also the general classification, jumping from third place to first.

It's my first ProTour stage-race win: a quiet confirmation to myself, and a loud indication to the team of my capabilities. In the cycling world, unless you win a Monument, a Grand Tour or a World Championships, you're forgotten about very quickly.

It certainly wasn't expected that I'd win it. Lotto has been a sponsor of the sport for twenty years and I don't know if they've ever won a mountainous stage race in all that time. Slowly, the goal of having a greater presence on GC is being realised.

I DO A COUPLE more races during May and June, and before I know it July is approaching, and the prospect of my second Tour de France.

There's also a different attitude towards me from my team this year. Normally in cycling, you are only as good as your last race, but as a Tour rider you are as good as your last Tour. I feel they have more faith in me. And for the first time in years, the field for the 2006 Tour is wide open, because of Lance Armstrong's retirement. After seven Tours de France in a row won by the same rider, no one can nominate a favourite for 2006. Lots more riders have a chance but I don't consider myself a contender. I'm just hoping to improve on last year's result. We're aiming – if things go our way – for me to get into the first five.

Externally, there are increasing expectations of me after my eighth-place finish last year. From a purely athletic perspective, that does not change much. But it does have an impact on how I'm able to go about my work. A lot of people are wanting my time: journalists want interviews, photographers want to do a shoot ... there are more requests than I have time to fulfil. The team should manage these requests to preserve my time and energy. Unfortunately, Lotto have an attitude that more media coverage is better, regardless of the athletic cost. Personally, I prefer to get everything onto the results sheet and deal with the media requirements afterwards.

Put it all on the road. That's what I'm good at. One of my best qualities as a rider is that I have a finite amount of ability but I'm able to get nearly all of that ability out onto the road. I don't mind that at the end of the race I'm so exhausted I can barely walk. I don't ever want to finish a race with something left in the tank.

But for me to squeeze everything out of myself, I need to be very focused. If you forget one little thing, a course detail, a GC position, a feed, you'll compromise that focus. And at the Tour de France, the Giro or the Vuelta, that can happen easily, because everybody wants a little piece of you and your attention.

The media are a huge part of the world of cycling. They play a crucial role in bringing our sport to cycling fans, and usually they do a great job. I admire a lot of the cycling journalists who each year will travel to the Tour de France or the Giro or the Vuelta or the Classics and file their reports each day. Some have been doing it for more than 20 years; their knowledge of cycling history is superb, and some, even if they have never raced a bike, have a profound understanding of the sport.

Teams and riders need journalists; journalists need access to teams and riders to provide accurate and insightful reports: a seemingly harmonious relationship. But factor in deadlines, pressure from editors to cover particular subject matter, the reality of live television, and this relationship can be fraught.

The needs of journalists often conflict with the priorities of a rider. Every journalist requests a one-on-one interview with a Tour de France favourite. But a Tour de France favourite probably has more right to uninterrupted training for a Tour than anyone else. A rider who has just crossed a finish line after giving their all in a Tour de France mountain stage is unlikely to be able to give thoughtful insight on a race they have only witnessed from their bicycle. An exhausted rider is more likely to say something inaccurate. This often suits the media because an inaccurate statement or an offhand remark can only help stir up controversy.

Many in the mainstream media employ a tabloid style of journalism that appeals to the negative and cynical side in all of us. They exploit the bizarre human attribute of needing to think and speak badly of anyone or anything that appears to have achieved more than yourself. As a result, riders and those close to them become very reticent. Why even give an opinion when it's almost surely going to be twisted, exaggerated and used against you and your profession?

It's something that I have often struggled to distance myself from. I've never enjoyed living in a world of headlines; it doesn't suit my personality. Of course, as a professional athlete your job is to help with publicity for the team. It's not as though I don't want to do my duty with the media, but at a certain point it can grow to be too much for one person to manage alone.

Interviews with cycling insiders follow a very narrow scope, after so many years of these questions, it is not very thought provoking. However, interviews with 'outsiders' are refreshing. Those new to cycling will ask a question that we in the cycling world would never even consider, which encourages a different perspective.

One day at the Tour I find, to my cost, that satisfying the media can affect your performance very directly. I'm doing an interview with a journalist before the start. It suddenly strikes me that I may need to be at the stage start.

'Hang on,' I say. 'Isn't it starting time? Don't I have to go?'

She says, 'No, no, no, you've got plenty of time.'

'But why is everybody gone?'

'No, no, you've got plenty of time.'

But I don't. I have no time. I miss the fast stage start and I have to chase by myself for four kilometres. The problem is that it's a long, 220-kilometre stage with an uphill finish. So I'm going to the finish in the front group for the win and I blow up with 500 metres to go.

Considering how close I was to the line, it is very possible that if I hadn't had to do that four-kilometre chase at the start, I would have had enough in reserve to get me there and fight for the win. Instead, I finish fourth.

My reluctance to fulfil every journalist request grows …

MY BUILD UP TO the Tour has been trouble free and things are flowing nicely. After a lighter early season, I'm fresh and fit. Things are coming together. This year's Tour route favours non-climbers, all-rounders and good time trialists, which are all good things for me.

And then, just days before the Tour begins, the sport is in the headlines for all of the wrong reasons.

'Operación Puerto' is the codename of a Spanish police operation against the activities of Dr Eufemiano Fuentes, the doctor at Spanish cycling team Kelme. It began in 2004 after former Kelme rider Jesús Manzano exposed systematic doping within the team. In an interview, he spoke of blood doping and the use of performance-enhancing drugs.

The Amaury Sport Organisation (ASO) – organiser of the Tour de France and several other races – asks teams involved in the 2006 Tour to withdraw riders who have been implicated. On the eve of the prologue in Strasbourg, 13 riders are expelled. Among them are Jan Ullrich and Ivan Basso, two favourites to win the race, and rising star, Alberto Contador.

Out of the race is every rider who finished in the top five behind Alejandro Valverde and Lance Armstrong in the 2005 Tour: Basso, Mancebo and Vinokourov. Though not all were personally implicated, I am asked about how many of the seven riders who finished ahead of me in 2005 (Lance included) were actually clean. It's not something I want to consider deeply.

The 2006 Tour is suddenly an even more open race than before. Waiting for the start of the Tour, new teammate, Chris Horner and I are coming back from training and we pass the T-Mobile team hotel. I've never seen anything like it. Vans with satellite dishes on the roof, TV cameras on small cranes trying to get a view in through the windows. It's like a movie set – actually, it *is* a movie set.

Among the contenders, American Floyd Landis riding for Phonak becomes a hot favourite. He finished one place behind me last year. Leading into the Tour, Landis has been winning everything in sight. Every time he's come out to race he's won convincingly. This string of wins means that Landis is being spoken about as a successor to Armstrong.

I first met Floyd in 1997 when he was a mountain biker. I'd see his name in the mountain-bike results. Then he switched to the road and spent a few years on Lance's team, US Postal Service. I always knew he was quite a talented rider, but at Postal Service he never got many chances.

He first came to prominence on the road when he joined Phonak then won Paris–Nice. And everyone thought, 'Well he can't win Paris–Nice *and* the Tour.' And then he goes to the Tour of California and wins that. I'm thinking, 'If this guy can come back from that effort and ride a good Tour de France, I'm going to be really surprised'.

Because of the specialised training loads required to reach these levels then recover, I considered it impossible to come straight back to a high level and get through the whole of the Tour.

Off the bike he's known as a very talented joker, one of the funniest bike riders that ever was. I'm told he does a great Iggy Pop impersonation.

YOU CAN ONLY BEAT who's up against you. So I don't think too much about the riders who've been disqualified, and try to focus on those who are left. I never like to analyse or even consider that any of my competitors might be using illicit means to enhance their performance and therefore increase their chances of beating me. The base of an athlete's psychological strength is their confidence. Anything that can erode that confidence can weaken them. So it's best just to concentrate on the factors you can control, and hope that the regulators take care of the rest.

AS I FOUND OUT in 2005, the Tour is dangerous. Spectators lining the road, dogs, infants in prams, grandparents in wheelchairs. Cycling is a free public event, very accessible, but that can only work until the sport is a certain size. After a particular point, safety can become compromised. A moving peloton of 180 riders going at 50-plus kilometres an hour, using absolutely every centimetre of the road has its limitations.

Near the end of one stage I side-swipe a woman in the crowd. Everyone else has stepped back as we ride past, but she's taking a photo and looking through the lens of her camera, which completely distorts her sense of distance. I'm squeezed into a gap with nowhere to go. I try to curl over and not get her with my shoulder, but instead she connects with my back. It's all too quick. Apparently she just goes flying through the air. I'm told I was doing nearly 60 kilometres an hour.

It's the worst spectator incident I've ever been involved in. I check later and find out she's OK. Meanwhile, it has shaken me up and I have a very sore shoulder in the next day's time trial.

STAGE 11 TO PLA-DE-BERET in Spain is the biggest day of climbing I've ever done: 5500 metres of climbing on a very long stage. I'm pretty tired. I blow up about a kilometre from the finish and I'm furious with myself.

But it's in stage 17 that everything happens.

On the first climb of the stage, my teammate, Wim Vansevenant comes up to me. 'Watch out, Phonak's doing something, come on, get ready.'

'What? What are you talking about? It's the first climb of the day.' I try to calm him down, thinking he is panicking.

But Wim is right. Phonak have gone on the front, riding incredibly fast at the start of the first climb. I'm thinking, 'What the hell are these guys doing?'

Phonak have pulled something like a sprint lead-out at the start of the first climb and put everyone into the red, on the limit. Floyd

Landis is blasting away on the front. He's playing with everyone, provoking them to chase. He knows he doesn't have a very strong team. T-Mobile fall into the trap and start chasing. I'm thinking, 'What is Landis doing? He's just throwing the Tour away.' He's already eight minutes down after yesterday's stage.

One by one guys are dropping, until there's a group left comprising compatriot Michael Rogers, Russian, Denis Menchov and me, all about the same on GC. I'm staying on Menchov's wheel. Michael Rogers is in front of him. Landis is still riding ridiculously fast.

I look up at Michael. And think to myself, 'Let him go, what are you doing?'

I'm experiencing a massive calorie deficit just to be in the front group today, not because I've done anything wrong, just because it's been so ludicrously hard. We can never be sure who is listening in on our radio channel, so I use a little bit of code when I talk into it – nothing complicated, just vague phrases that have very specific meanings. Only Chris Horner and race director Hendrik Redant know the code. I have a code for flagging that you're in trouble: I ask for a 'calorie bomb', a high-calorie sugary mixture in a bottle.

I say on the radio, 'I'm going to need as many calorie bombs as possible today.'

Hendrik and Chris know I'm really in trouble because I'm only 50 kilometres into a 150-kilometre stage. Usually I'll ask for a calorie bomb with 20 or 30 kilometres to go. To ask for it after 50 ks and ask for as many as possible is a sure sign telling the director, 'Hang on, we'll have to be really conservative here.'

To follow Landis's effort on the first mountain of the stage has completely depleted me, emptied my energy stores. And I still have three mountains to go.

After riding the stage on the edge of going hunger flat, or 'blowing up', I've positioned myself well for the last climb up the Col de Joux Plane over into the little town of Morzine, in the Rhône–Alpes region. This town is significant to me because it was where my first European Mountain Bike World Cup event was held in 1996. I've done this stage in reconnaissance so I know the descent. I was dropped on the climb but I've managed to claw back some good time on the descent.

We've all over-expended ourselves on the first climb instead of the last, so virtually everyone is spent. T-Mobile and Movistar, are the only teams with numbers. Landis has been away solo for the entire stage.

Landis's performance is nothing short of eye-popping; riding by himself for 150 kilometres and taking 10 minutes, more than reversing the eight-minute time deficit from yesterday. Neither Movistar or T-Mobile behind can take any time back on him.

I'm at the back with Chris Horner, and Chris as usual comes through for me, nursing me through the stage, protecting me up the mountain. Chris knows when I need help; he knows what it's like to be having a bad day. I've tried to stay in the hunt on GC, but today I'm really on my limit.

The glowing assessment of Landis as Armstrong's successor is done no damage by Landis's achievement in stage 17 of the Tour. He rode everyone off the wheel on the first climb. Then he catches and passes a breakaway group and reverses all his deficit from the day before. Floyd charges back into the lead pack.

I manage to finish in the main group of GC contenders – but we're all still well behind Landis, who has powered ahead and ridden alone to the finish line in a performance no one thought was possible.

The reports are glowing. *Cycling News* says that 'without a shadow of a doubt, today will go down as one of the finest stages in modern Tour de France history', and that Floyd has 'staged a comeback that defied logic'. The site later says that Floyd's solo move on the first of the day's climbs 'quite simply looked irrational'.

A very accurate description from where I saw it. Many people describe Floyd's performance in stage 17 as 'superhuman', but Floyd claims it wasn't and that there were two stages in the 2005 Tour in which his watt average was higher.

I barely have the energy to ride the two kilometres back to the team hotel in Morzine, a modest uphill climb to a modest hotel. One aspect that makes the Tour de France less enjoyable than the Giro is the hotels you stay in. They are often owned by franchises rather than families and a lot of the staff are just there to get their salary, not to make people want to come back to the hotel. The level of friendliness and enthusiasm often isn't very high, if it's there at all.

As happened in week three of the Giro in 2002, I can barely muster the energy to locate my hotel room. Even that is a struggle.

It's one of the few days in my cycling career so far when I've walked into the hotel room and just lain on the bed in my cycling kit. I have no energy even to take my shoes or clothes off and have a shower.

Next day during a quiet moment I go up to Floyd.

'Floyd, that was the most incredible athletic performance I've ever seen in my life. Congratulations.'

He's is proud and looks chuffed.

Coming from someone who knows how hard the Tour is, I think he appreciates it.

The next day, in the final time trial of the Tour, I get a puncture. As a cost-saving measure, the team does not have a spare time-trial bike for me so we have to make a wheel change, which is a slow process on a time-trial bike. It's frustrating – a little ridiculous, even unprofessional.

I'm able to prove to the team that we have to do better than this, but I do it by actions, not words. They see what I have to go through because of this lapse, and the point is made. Actions are always a better way of asking for things to change.

FLOYD GOES ON TO win the Tour.

I come fifth, just inside our achievable, but not so easy goals.

As improbable as his comeback in the race is, none of us think any more about what Floyd has done. We don't think there's anything to think about, except having witnessed an extraordinary sporting moment.

Floyd's victory has become the feel-good story the Tour needed, particularly after the way the race began. All the cheats have been booted out, and Floyd, the big, brash American, has won the Tour with a remarkable finish.

But it doesn't take long for the truth to be revealed.

IN THE 2006 TOUR I again raced with a state-of-the-art Polar heart-rate monitor that measures cadence, altitude, speed and heart rate. After the Tour has finished I have all the files neatly downloaded onto my computer.

This is as accurate a physiological record as I can have. I go home, and there are no calls from journalists, no fanfare, so things are quiet for me. I notice a graph of Landis's effort has been published on the internet, but I don't pay it much attention.

Two days after the Tour has finished, I drive down to Aldo's office in Castellanza, outside Milan near the Mapei centre. We're due for a debriefing on my performance in the Tour.

I go into Aldo's office. 'Aldo, I've got the heart-rate files, and I see Floyd's figures for the stage are on the internet.'

Aldo's eyes light up a little bit. It's amazing for a physiologist to see these kind of revelations published.

He has a remarkable mind for mathematics and an amazing ability to interpret figures. He sits there with his calculator for a minute or two.

He looks up at me. 'Cadel, you reached a V02 max of 89 millilitres per kilogram, so that's a compliment to you and your training, your preparation. You prepared as well as you possibly could have and you reached your peak performance in that race.'

He pauses. '*E Floyd era dopato.*' And Floyd was cheating.

He says it so calmly. I just look at him, trying to contain my emotions. I'm speechless.

I also don't know what to do with this information. You can't accuse someone of cheating if it hasn't been proven in a court of law.

While I'm in Castellanza I decide to treat myself as a reward for my efforts in my career thus far. I've just parked outside specialist watch shop Veneruz when my phone rings.

It's a journalist I know. 'Cadel, there's been a positive test from the Tour,' he tells me.

I say, 'Oh, right. That's a pity.'

'He was in front of you on GC. It's a positive test from someone who was in front of you.'

'One of the four in front?' I say a name.

'No, not him.'

Then another. And another. There's only one name left: Floyd.

'No. You're kidding me,' I say.

It's true. Floyd Landis, the flamboyant American ex-mountain biker, has failed to pass a drug test. His Tour de France victory will be revoked.

Of course, the media go crazy for the story. It's the first time a Tour de France winner has been disqualified for taking drugs, though winners have been disqualified since the very earliest days of the Tour for other infringements such as taking trains and cars. Somehow being caught catching a train is kind of funny. But there's nothing funny about being caught doping 100 years later.

The 2006 Tour de France has been bookended by drug scandals. It is a kick in the teeth for all the good people abiding by the rules in our sport.

I came in fifth on that final day but now I'm moved up to fourth. It's not the first time it's happened to me and I'm guessing it won't be the last. It doesn't mean much. Adjustments in results after riders have been judged to have doped are classic hollow victories.

I KNOW THAT TO do better than fourth place I'll have to race less and train more specifically for the Grand Tours. I haven't actually been winning a lot of races: the more you're focused on quantity rather than quality, the more difficult it becomes to win. Lotto are generally happy with my results, but somehow I need to convince them that I'm not just there to earn GC points in every race.

Changing their attitude to me is going to take a while.

In August, they send me to the Tour of Denmark, which isn't a ProTour race. It's my first time at this event. One of my ex-teammates comes up to me and asks: 'What is a rider like you doing in a race like this?'

I find out later how much Lotto were benefiting for me to go there. They've said to me, 'You're the only rider that can get us some points, we just need one rider in the first 10.' So even though I'm exhausted, I have to stay there on GC right to the end, and I'm also going for the mountains jersey. I could have used the energy much more effectively elsewhere, but what can a professional do? Not much.

There are some challenges in the race too. In Denmark they put sand on the road to mitigate the winter ice. But in the sand are sharp seashells. Sharp objects puncture tyres. I speak with one of the team mechanics to get an idea of the number of punctures in the race. I'm told that on average each team is getting 8 to 12 punctures a day. Fifteen teams in the race, five days of racing. That's a lot of tyres.

I ask the team, 'How many tyres did you bring, are you going to have enough?'

I'm told, 'We've had to get some more sent here because we might run out.'

If every team is puncturing eight tyres, that's 200 tyres a day. That is an amazing number of punctures and a lot of tyres to throw away.

It's also my first encounter with an up-and-coming Italian rider called Vincenzo Nibali. Although lacking definition in his legs, he looks very delicate on the pedals, but as I find out, he can really race.

I'm riding to the start of my time trial, going backwards on the course but on the footpath. I've just come round the corner of a building and I'm thinking, 'No rider's going to cut this close to the corner, because that would be pretty extreme.'

Suddenly there's a flash in front of me – it's Nibali. We have nearly hooked handlebars. He's cut the corner so finely; I think, 'Shit, that is a real racer, he's using every centimetre of the road'.

At the end, at least Lotto are happy because I come 10th on GC.

A WEEK LATER I compete in the Clásica de San Sebastián in the Basque country of Spain. It's a ProTour one-day race, the first major event after the Tour de France.

It's my third time at this race and I usually have bad luck.

One day we're riding up the climb on the Jaizkibel and I'm away and we come across some Basque protesters. The Basques are a minority group within Spain and some of them are pushing for complete independence. They're protesting by holding a an enormous heavy chain across the road with links as big as your fist, at a height that means you can't ride under or over it.

The TV coverage of races in Spain is often of such poor quality that none of the race directors know anything about the protest. So after the race, the Lotto director says, 'What happened, why didn't you go away on the Jaizkibel?' It feels like I am being blamed for the team's lack of a big result.

'Well, I was away with a group and there was a protest on the road.'

'Oh, we didn't know that.'

As a rider you get judged on these things: 'Oh you didn't perform.' But what are you supposed to do? You go there, fit and prepared, you ride well, you do everything correctly and something like this happens.

On one of the previous times I raced San Sebastián, I remember being away with American Levi Leipheimer on the Jaizkibel, two of us away in front, and the TV motorbike's come up alongside me.

The guy is sitting on the motorbike with the camera lying on his lap, and he's leaning his elbow on the camera like he's leaning on a bar at midnight, waiting to order another beer.

I talk to the Lotto managers after the race and they say, 'The TV coverage was terrible', and I say, 'I can see that the coverage is terrible while I'm riding the race!'

THE 2006 ROAD WORLD Championships are held in September on the outskirts of Salzburg in Austria. It's a lumpy course, but not hilly by climbers' standards. When we ride the first lap of the course in training, I find it strange that we go through a tunnel-like underpass inside the last kilometre. I have one of those pre-race feelings and tell myself to be attentive there.

I'm surprised by how well I end up riding, following the last attack from Italian, Davide Rebellin in the final kilometres. In the sprint, passing through the underpass I felt was unusual, someone leaves a gap, which catches everyone off guard. Paolo Bettini is the first to see it and jumps across the gap, surprising fellow sprinter Erik Zabel and Paolo wins his first world title.

'STOP, COME AND LOOK inside the church. You'll be amazed, it's incredible.'

It's a chilly day in Lombardia in early October. I'm riding with my friend and colleague, Italian cyclist, Guido Trentin up one of the Giro di Lombardia's iconic climbs, the one they call Ghisallo.

Guido and I are doing reconnaissance for the Giro di Lombardia in a couple of days' time and we want to familiarise ourselves with its twists and turns.

I often get together with Guido – who won a stage in the Vuelta of 2002 – to train in the area around Lake Como, in between where we both live. The rides are useful to check out the descents, the climbs and some of the surprises along the narrow roads with their sharp, blind-sided switchbacks.

Sometimes Guido and I stop for a quick coffee at a little bar, always at my request, but mostly it's just business.

I think today is business. So when Guido asks me to look at the church I say, 'No, no, we're training, let's keep going.'

Fortunately, Guido resists this.

We ride up to the famously tiny chapel known as the Madonna del Ghisallo. What a setting for a church. Up here at 750 metres above sea level you can see the aquamarine blue of the Y-shaped Lake Como at the juncture where it splits in two.

The final stone of the Madonna del Ghisallo was laid by Pope John XI in 1672. In 1948, in his summer residence, Castel Gandolfo outside Rome, Pope Pius XII lit a lamp that was called 'the permanent flame of the Ghisallo'. It was taken to Milan and then by cyclists – including Italian legends, Fausto Coppi and Gino Bartali – in relay to the church.

The following year, the Pope officially declared that the Madonna del Ghisallo would become the site of the patroness of Italian cyclists.

As an Italian who grew up loving cycling and its history, Guido has visited the church before. All Italian cyclists – and many cyclists around the world – know it and make a point of visiting. Though I've never taken the time out to see it, I am aware of its importance.

Sitting on top of a large monument outside the chapel are two unknown cyclists in bronze, one with an arm raised exultantly, the other fallen on the ground and needing help. Beneath them is an inscription about the sweetness of sacrifice.

At the church entrance are plinths bearing the cast bronze heads of Italian cycling legends Gino Bartali, Fausto Coppi and Alfredo Binda, names that are deeply embedded in Italian sporting culture.

Inside it's a cycling mecca and, judging by the quiet respect of the small crowd here today, a place of reverence. There are no seats, only room for maybe 15 people standing.

There's a wall featuring many small framed photographs of Italian cyclists down the years. Mounted on the other walls are the bicycles and racing jerseys of some of cycling's most loved names. There's Felice Gimondi's bike from the Giro d'Italia of 1976, that of Maurizio Fondriest, World Champion in 1988, the bike Fausto Coppi rode in the Tour de France of 1949, a bike owned by Eddy Merckx, the bike used by Gino Bartali in his 1938 and 1948 Tour victories, and Francesco Moser's 1984 Hour Record bike.

It's intriguing to look at the bikes here. Bartali and Coppi's are almost agricultural by today's standards – simple but very robust. I imagine they'd weigh a lot but they could probably do 100,000 kilometres. Built to last. With today's bikes, you have to change the chain every 500 or 1000 kilometres: nearly as often as you change your clothes.

On these walls are triumph and tragedy. As well as the bikes of race winners, there are those of riders who lost their lives while racing, including Olympic gold medallist Fabio Casartelli, tragically killed after coming off his bike on the Col de Portet d'Aspet in France in 1995. This piece of sad cycling history is significant for me. When I first arrived in Europe in 1995 as a junior rider I watched the Tour de France live for the first time and I remember being shocked and saddened.

Standing in this small chapel, I'm moved by how much this country reveres its cyclists. As popular as cycling is now becoming in Australia, it's still nowhere near the popularity of the country's biggest sport of all, Aussie Rules football.

In Italy, people truly love cycling, idolise its champions, and have a deep respect for its history.

IN NOVEMBER, AUSTRALIAN RIDER Paul Crake is competing in a Tour of Southland in New Zealand when a fierce wind gust blows him off the road into a fencepost. He's unconscious for five minutes and scans later reveal major spinal injury. Paul, who was previously a cross-country runner who won the 86-storey Empire State Building Run-Up five times, is now in a wheelchair.

I met Paul earlier in the year in Salzburg, where he's based. Having come from a different sport he has an interesting mentality.

He's just met Daniella, a really nice Italian banker. She supports him through his recovery. They later move to Australia.

Everyone in the cycling world is shaken by Paul's accident. We all know that what happened to Paul could happen to any bike rider.

Paul's accident influences me heavily over the ensuing months, more than I first realised. There are several times when I think of Paul as I'm competing.

It might be raining or snowy, the most horrible day. And I'm riding along thinking, 'This is ridiculous.'

Then I think, 'Paul Crake would give anything to be here.' And I keep going.

CHAPTER 12

TWENTY-THREE SECONDS

2006–2007

CAN IT REALLY COME down to wheels? Maybe it can.

At Lotto we ride on Campagnolo wheels, very good road wheels for races like the Classics and the Tour. For the time trials, though, their wheels are not the most competitive. Late in 2006, at the team meeting for the 2007 season, I suggest to team manager Marc Sergeant that we buy some of the fastest time-trial wheels available, just in case. A more aerodynamic wheel can result in a two- or even four-second gain per kilometre in a time trial. We already know there'll be 110 kilometres of time trialling in the 2007 Tour. Why not be as competitive as possible?

'Hmm ... we'll see ...' is Marc's response.

We don't have a very good trial bike either, a fact I try not to dwell on. I'm trying not to dwell on it because I know other teams have better equipment. I've always believed it's important to find out about what our competitors are using, but it can also be demoralising.

Bike racing sometimes comes down to seconds, as I'll soon find out.

AS IS NOW USUAL, the Tour de France will be the main focus of my 2007 season. Having finished fourth last year, my aim for the Tour in 2007 is to get on the podium.

The first six months of 2007 don't bring too many big results. My best performances are seventh at Paris–Nice in March, fourth at the Tour de Romandie in May and second at the seven-stage Critérium du Dauphiné Libéré in mid-June. This is the first time I've ridden the Dauphiné and I find it a perfect lead-up to the Tour. It gives me a chance to ride in the French Alps, so it's a good warm-up for the Tour de France just three weeks later.

Leading into the Tour, equipment that's not up to standard isn't the only frustration for the team now known as Predictor–Lotto. In three seasons, Lotto have gone from wanting a presence on the GC side of things to having a genuine chance of reaching the podium of the Tour de France. We're stepping into another league, but the question is: are we ready for it?

IT'S THE YEAR THE Tour doesn't have a clear favourite, though Dane, Michael Rasmussen is incredible, snatching the yellow jersey in the second week.

One look at his legs and you'd never guess he was a bike rider. Even though he has a slight build, he doesn't have the muscle definition that some riders of his climbing ability get.

I raced against Michael for a long time as a mountain biker. We first clashed head-to-head in 1997, racing for the win in a World Cup event in Colorado. I won, he was second. Go forward a couple of years to 1999, and I was second to Marco Bui at the Under 23 World Championships. And then on the final day of the Men's Elite World Championships he was just untouchable; it was extraordinary. He became World Champion in the filthy Swedish mud.

And then he switched over to the road. I never spoke to him much because he doesn't talk a lot. When he came to the Tour in 2004 and was riding for the King of the Mountains polka-dot jersey, he was just incredible. He ended up winning the jersey in both 2005 and 2006.

But this year he surprises most of us and leads the race for nine stages. We knew he was good, but no one expected him to be so consistent and so strong on GC. Most of us realise we're racing for second because he is untouchable in the mountains.

I keep thinking, 'How can this guy go so fast? He doesn't even seem to have the muscle mass to push the gear he's riding.'

I'M SECOND ON GC when we head into stage 13, the second time trial of the Tour. I do have the advantage of being able to time-trial a bit better than my main competitors. But I'm racing on inferior equipment, and in the end, I can't hold off Alexander Vinokourov, who beats me by more than a minute.

The following day, I realise it's not just Rasmussen and Vinokourov I have to deal with; I'm also fighting a ragingly in-form Alberto Contador. He's very clever tactically, someone you have to pay attention to when you're going head to head with him.

With 10 kilometres to go he goes away with Rasmussen and I can't close the gap to them. For both of them, collaborating means they increase the time gap to me, and put themselves in a much better position.

It's in stage 15, to Loudenvielle, when I realise what I'm up against, racing against riders with better team support. At the insistence of race director Hendrik Redant, I ride a little more within myself on the climb to have something left for the final, rather than turning myself inside out staying glued to Contador's wheel.

In the last stage of the race I'm on a climb on my own. Chris Horner has been dropped. All of my competitors look to me to close the gap to Contador and Rasmussen.

I lose 56 seconds on that stage. It's my only significant time loss in the whole Tour. Afterwards I'm very frustrated. I go back to the bus furious at the error we have made.

Robbie McEwen tries to placate me. 'Cadel, the difference in Paris is going to be minutes, what are you worried about? Stay calm. It's not going to mean anything at the end of the race.'

I neither agree or argue.

IT'S BECOMING DEPRESSINGLY REGULAR.

The Tour de France is again rocked by doping scandals. On the rest day after stage 15, Vinokourov (Astana), one of the pre-race favourites and winner of two of the past three stages, has failed a drug test after the time trial in which I came second. This triggers the withdrawal of the entire Astana team, and for Vinokourov, a one-year suspension from the Kazakhstan Cycling Federation.

Vinokourov has done so much for cycling in Kazakhstan and for professionals from that country – sadly undermined by his behaviour as a rider outside of Kazakhstan, where he seems to have done more disfavours than favours for the world of cycling.

On the bike, he's the strongest competitor, mentally, that I've ever ridden with. If there's one guy in the race you can never give one centimetre of space to, it's Alexander, because he'll take that centimetre and turn it into a big win. His performances are incredible. It's how he's achieved them that I can't always endorse.

His team's withdrawal is another blow to the credibility of the Tour; there is even a suggestion that this year's race should be cancelled.

What can I do? Just get on with it. Play my own game. My only choices are to focus on other riders and be demoralised by it all, or focus on being the best Tour rider I am capable of being.

NEXT DAY, ON THE Col d'Aubisque in stage 16, Rasmussen is untouchable on the climb.

I'm hanging on, really at my limit. Rasmussen has attacked again, accelerated, and Contador is able to follow him, but I can't, so I'm riding for third and I'm trying to hold off Levi Leipheimer behind me.

Then Contador gets dropped by Rasmussen.

Watching the TV highlights later it's difficult to defend Rasmussen against the accusations that he is cheating. As Rasmussen accelerates on the climb the TV motorbike is struggling to accelerate with him. He is riding so effortlessly, seemingly not even breathing. The crowd on the side of the road is convinced that he's a cheat and they're booing. Watching this footage, after having raced against Rasmussen since the 90s, I'm just shaking my head in disappointment.

Rasmussen crosses the line with his arms in the air exultantly. He seems thrilled with his win. I wonder if he heard the booing – and if he did, what did he think of it? In a sport replete with deniers, can Rasmussen be that removed from reality?

I'm always trying to put out of my mind the thought that someone might be cheating, but today it's been tough. I was behind him when he sped up on the Col d'Aubisque. I was focused on my own race, but when I crossed the line, the crowd had made its decision, it seemed beyond question that the leader of the Tour was not racing within the rules.

It's the last stage of the Tour that he will ever ride and I saw it up close. After this stage his own team, Rabobank, throws him out of the race. One more step to a cleaner sport. One more example to the next generation.

It's a swifter-than-usual reaction to doping, and it means that suddenly the rest of us are racing for the win again.

It comes down to the final time trial in stage 19. I'm one minute 50 seconds behind and it's calculated that I'm going to be able to take this time back from Contador in the last time trial and win the Tour, which I think I can.

Contador is in yellow but there's nothing between him, me and Levi Leipheimer. Leipheimer and I are considered better time trialists than Contador – but they say the yellow jersey gives you wings.

I give everything to the time trial but Contador is better. I ride a good time trial. Contador rides an exceptional time trial. He beats me in the Tour by 23 seconds.

It helps him earn the title I believe he deserves: the best Grand Tour rider of our generation.

NATURALLY, TO LOSE THE Tour de France by 23 seconds is deeply disappointing. You want to win with all the want you have.

And I've put everything into it. I got 99.9 per cent of what I had in my legs onto the results board and that was enough for second place. It wasn't a win but it was a good performance.

As I've done in the past, I try not to learn too many details about my competitors' equipment. When you line up at the Tour de France time trial to win and you've got to make back a minute and nine seconds on Alberto Contador, and you know that the wheels he has are three seconds faster per kilometre, psychologically that doesn't help you.

When you're in there you need to be as convinced as possible that you can win. You don't want your belief in yourself eroded by the knowledge that it's not a level playing field.

This was just one of few things that Lotto could have done behind the scenes that would have made a difference. And a quantifiable difference too.

AFTERWARDS, IN AN INTERVIEW with ABC Radio, I touch on my frustration about the dopers.

> CADEL EVANS: *My only one regret was I had to rely on the team to chase in Loudenvielle [in stage 15], I lost 55 seconds to Contador and Rasmussen on the stage to Loudenvielle, and now I think everyone understands why I was particularly frustrated, and swearing and cursing after that stage, because ...*
> ABC: *So the riders who are riding dishonestly, it must make you furious?*
> CADEL EVANS: *I think they're all getting caught to be honest, and the UCI really is – the International Cycling*

*Union – really is doing a good job against the fight in sport
and …*
*ABC: So you don't think people are being stopped from
getting on the podium because of cheats anymore?*
*CADEL EVANS: I really don't know, to be honest.
But they're doing a much better job than any [other]
organisation in the world is.*

IT'S MY FIRST TIME on a Tour de France podium and I'm proud of that. However, I can't help but feel deflated by how our sport is being portrayed. Doping is entrenched in sport, a cultural reality. No one can plausibly deny that cycling has a massive image problem.

Big names in the sport are being eliminated. For many people, they were heroes. Kids looked up to them, admired them, wore the jerseys of their teams. You wonder how those kids will manage to keep the faith. I hope and trust they'll realise that it's not every rider who's doping.

The great irony is that the more drug cheats the authorities find in cycling, the less trusting the public becomes. Cycling should actually be *building* its credibility, because the drug tests are getting better so more cheats are being discovered. In its quest to rectify past problems, the UCI is transparent in its actions, which means every positive test is reported openly, which gives more fuel to the publicity fire. By making our sport cleaner, cycling is penalised. My hope is that other sports will soon come under the microscope.

One thing I've really noticed is that it's the most unfriendly and unreasonably nervous people who are, one by one, being taken out. In my first Tour de France in 2005 I was racing against a German rider from Liberty Seguros–Würth who was not all likeable. I didn't know anyone in the group who actually liked him. A year or two later he was caught up in Operación Puerto, his career was over and cycling never heard about him again. I don't think he was missed at all.

It might seem like fate or karma that the most unlikeable riders are being busted and removed from the sport, but maybe there is more to it. The business of organising these now illegal activities: purchasing, trafficking and consuming drugs, combined with the high chance of being caught, must surely be stressful. Perhaps this stress has a negative impact on the personalities of some riders.

These riders have most likely been convinced, almost brainwashed, by people who have a lot to gain from them. They've been told that they cannot win without the help of medical assistance and that they will not get caught. After all, if 'everyone' is doing it, obviously not everyone is getting caught. By winning, they will be wealthier and celebrated more than they are now. And surely that's a good thing.

When I first came to Europe the first question I was often asked was how many races I'd won. The focus was too much on coming first. And because it's all about winning, if the only way to win is by cheating, they do. By that I don't necessarily mean taking drugs but also doing things incorrectly. I'm not talking just about riders here. I'm talking about everyone around them who was also cheating.

Sometimes I wonder whether dopers ever stop to think about how they'll be regarded after their racing careers have ended, what their legacy will be, how they'll explain their behaviour to people they meet, or think about what it's doing to their sport.

Every athlete has to ask themselves each time they are beaten, 'Why?' Are those ahead of me training harder? Are they smarter tacticians? More talented? Or is it something that cannot be seen? Cutting a course? Hanging onto a car in a difficult moment of a race? Competitors that are paid off to lose? Or the pharmaceutical assistance flowing their bloodstreams?

Cycling has created its own culture, a small world, a closed environment, revolving around riders, sports doctors, *soigneurs*, team managers, sponsors, press, the public and the desire to win. Applauding the winner, not the second, third or fourth placegetter. Everyone's perspective has been distorted by the desire to win.

That's the case in Europe, anyway. In Australia it's a slightly different story. I think in Australia we have a really healthy mentality where we often cheer for the underdog, the one who's done the hard yards. We're applauding the guy who's had the hardest road to travel, not necessarily the one who wins.

The most talented rider on the biggest team is not always the one who works the hardest or has to make the most sacrifices, and it's great that Australian sports fans understand that.

I am often asked about drugs in sport and particularly cycling. It's my least favourite subject, not for the subject itself, but because it's a subject where anything you say is likely to be reported out of context by those who want to create an issue rather than report on one. What the sport needs now is an example to follow. I am well positioned to do that, supported and honoured to do so. Actions speak louder and much longer than words.

In the face of cheating all I can do is go about my business, train and perform as well as I can. My philosophy is: Don't look at other riders because you can't control their actions. Or as Aldo Sassi would say, 'Have faith in what you do because you're doing all the right things.'

I GET ON THE plane at Charles de Gaulle heading to Milan and home. I have my trophy for coming second in the Tour. I had to take it out of my bag to go through security. It's small, so I put it in the seat pocket in front of me.

The woman sitting next to me speaks English. 'What do you do?' she asks.

'I'm a bike rider.'

'Oh, we were here to watch the Tour de France.'

'Oh, I watched it too.'

'Yes, I saw your trophy. Did you win that trophy in the Tour?'

'Yeah, I did, actually.'

I think, 'That might be the best Tour result I ever get, and there's the trophy in the seat pocket.'

JUST OCCASIONALLY, DRUG TESTS are weird. *Very* weird. And this one in Beijing is far and away the strangest drug test I've ever had.

It's August and I'm at the Beijing Olympic Test Race. Since the Tour, it's been the normal ridiculous travel schedule. I raced criteriums in Austria, France and the Netherlands then jumped on a plane to China, jetlagged and exhausted as usual.

There's not a huge culture of cycling in China. I was obliged by the Australian national team to go to this race. I've fulfilled my obligations in the podium ceremony and given time to the small media contingent present at the event. I walk into the room for the drug test and I'm filling out the forms and carefully checking everything, as you always do. And then before I've gone in to pee into the sample container, the male official says:

'Go into the room and put your hands on your head, and turn around three times, slowly.'

Um, OK, if that's what you're asking.

I go into the room and there are mirrors on two walls and windows in the other two.

I'm thinking, 'This is a bit strange.' It makes me feel a little uneasy.

A voice.

'Pull your pants down, put your hands on your head and turn around three times – slowly.'

It reminds me of a scene in the movie *Starsky and Hutch* in which Hutch is being asked to do weird things by a prisoner he's trying to get information from. It's a hilarious scene. But this one's not so funny.

I follow the path of least resistance. I pull my pants down a bit and put my hands on my head and starting turning around.

The voice again.

'Turn around slower. Pull your pants down lower.'

'Hang on,' I think, 'am I allowed to take my hands off my head?' I don't know.

I pull my pants down even further, put my hands back on my head and turn around again.

'No, slower!'

So I'm turning around slowly.

This is ridiculous.

When I recount this story to colleagues later on, they say, 'Yeah, yeah, they were putting one Euro coins in the slot on the other side – didn't you know?'

IN SPITE OF THE weirdness, we are the overall winners of the weekend's long stage race.

Then in September I ride the Vuelta. The team arrive in Galicia in the north of Spain, my first time in this area. Chris Horner is rooming with me, which is always welcome. I raced against Chris in the US domestic series in the 1990s. He would rather have a McDonald's burger than a massage after a stage. We got along on the team because we both liked to race well and train hard. We would go back to the room and have a sort of debrief on our day, a very friendly and passionate discussion. And then Chris would reach over to his suitcase and pull out a pile of Mustang magazines. We'd each pick up a magazine and start talking about cars. It was a mutual passion; we both have classic Mustangs. We wouldn't speak about bike racing again until the meeting the next morning.

One thing about Chris that always impresses me is how much he loves riding his bike. The team are all out training two days before the start of the race, and after we've done about 95 kilometres, most of us want to head back. Chris looks at me and says, 'I'm going to keep going.'

The rest of us get back to the hotel, shower, change and eat, then finally Chris comes back. 'Were you missing some ks?' I ask.

'No, I just wanted to ride. It was such a beautiful day out there.'

How fantastic! Here is a 36-year-old pro, lining up for his second Grand Tour of the year, with probably around 30,000 kilometres in his legs for the season, and all he wants to do is ride his bike!

The race gets underway and we adjust to the cruise pace of Spain and the Vuelta. There's great scenery as we ride along the quiet coastal roads. At one moment I have a déjà vu experience: we're riding up a small hill and it looks identical to the road leading north out of Coffs Harbour, the nearest town to Upper Corindi, where I lived between the ages of four and six. It puts me at ease with the race.

As we reach the second week of the race, Denis Menchov is incredibly strong, holding not just the overall leader's jersey but the climber's and all rounder's jerseys as well. As I follow him I notice how lean he is: I can see the veins on his glutes through the Lycra. Veins even on his bum – now that is lean!

In the mountains in stage 15, we're passing over the Alto de Monachil in the Sierra Nevada, before turning left down towards Granada. As I crest the climb, having just been dropped by the main contenders, I have to squeeze everything out of myself to stay within striking distance. Hendrik Redant counts down the seconds as I come up to the King of the Mountains line. I know I have a short downhill, one more steep climb and then the long descent to Granada.

I completely empty myself on the last steep incline, cramping as I sprint to start the downhill with as much speed as possible. I've thrown my spare water bottle away at the start of climb to save weight. There are still 20 or so kilometres to go, and I haven't got a drop of liquid to help ease the cramps. The only guy in the group with a bottle is Menchov. I ask if I can have a sip, but he just smiles at me coldly and keeps riding.

Stage 19 finishes close to the beautiful monastery town of San Lorenzo de El Escorial; it's the location of what was possibly one of my best Mountain Bike World Cup victories in 1999. It's very wet, and I see Menchov look around at me. Concerned that he's about to attack, I try to move through the small group close behind him. Manuel Beltrán seems to intentionally block me in against the embankment at the side of the road.

'Get out of the way!' he yells at me.

'Beltrán, you can't get out of your own way,' I think angrily.

Meanwhile, Menchov rides away, gets third place and holds on to his Tour lead.

In the last time trial the next day, I lose my spot on the podium to Spaniard, Samuel Sánchez. Coming fourth isn't a very satisfying position in any competition where there's a podium of three.

Still, at least I'm getting points for the ProTour. With just one race left for the year, the Giro di Lombardia, I am sitting second in the world rankings behind Danilo Di Luca. A few days before the race I am riding up to Cuasso al Monte, just over the border in Italy, not far from home. An SMS message arrives on the small phone I carry with me when training. I glance at the message: the Italian Olympic Committee has given Di Luca a three-month ban for doping offences. I am now training to be number one in the world.

I take sixth at the Giro di Lombardia which gives me enough points to win the UCI ProTour overall, the first Australian to do so. It's the road equivalent of the World Cup, which I won twice as a mountain biker. It indicates the consistency of my performances throughout the season. It's the highlight of my year, and one of the highlights of my career so far.

But at this stage I'm often accused of not winning much. As the UCI media officer is presenting me with my trophy after the Giro di Lombardia, he says 'But you didn't actually win anything.'

'Oh, who won two time trials at the Tour de France?' I respond, which prompts cheers from those in the crowd who understand. Another (ironic) sign of the lack of perspective in the world of pro cycling.

Anyway, big changes in the sport are happening. Once you were judged by how many races you won but that's not necessarily a sign of how good a rider you are these days.

Twenty-three seconds is the second-smallest winning margin in the history of the Tour. As my good friend, Martin Whiteley said to me afterwards, 'A lot can happen in 23 seconds.' Or, as the title of Lance Armstrong's autobiography so appropriately states, *Every Second Counts.*

I have fulfilled my aim of standing on the podium of the Tour de France and indeed come so close to winning it. Twenty-three seconds is cruel, really. As resilient as I always strive to be, it plays on me for a long time to come. Actually it plays on me in various ways for a lot longer than that. It's the birth of an ongoing narrative about me and my career: the gritty rider relying on courage and perseverance.

I can't control what they write, and I try not to take too much notice. For me it's all about improving things for next year, focusing on the basics.

Lotto's lax attitude to equipment has been proven wrong. My Tour result has reaffirmed that there are always things you can do to improve your performance. In every aspect of equipment, training, planning, racing, there are always things that can be done better.

And I am going to spend the off season doing just that. I am going to use every bit of the frustration of this loss. It is not going to eat away at me, it is going to sit there as motivation. Motivation to work smarter, to perform better.

It reinforces the philosophies Aldo has always taught me. Reinforces our shared belief in what is possible, what it's possible to do at the Tour though talent, persistence and hard work.

CHAPTER 13

STUCK IN SECOND PLACE

2008

EVERY YEAR MY GRANDMOTHER calls me on my birthday, 14 February. I'm 31 today. I'm at home in Stabio, expecting the call.

The phone rings. It's not Grandma. It's a journalist. He says, 'Astana's been disqualified from the Tour, which means you're now the race favourite. How do you feel?'

Great. Another doping scandal, but worse, I am now the default favourite for the Tour.

How do I feel? I feel frustrated that the news about our sport is being dominated by cheats. I feel frustrated that the biggest news in the world of cycling seems always to be bad news, news that means those who ride clean have to waste precious emotional energy having this stuff in their heads, and having to deal with it as the topic of conversation over breakfast, lunch and dinner, at the coffee shop, in the aeroplane – anywhere you are in contact with people.

But I don't say that. Instead I say a few bland words, something about how I'll just concentrate on my own race because that's all I can do. Saying anything more is going to drag me into a discussion

I don't want to waste time having and away from exactly that – being focused on my own race.

The ASO has banned Astana from all of its events, stemming from Astana's previous doping infringements.

What it means is that Alberto Contador, race favourite until now, won't ride. And now that Contador is out, the media focus on the rider who came second to him last year: me. This means I'm the one journalists want to talk to, the one everyone is looking at …

I say a few more things about being well prepared and that it doesn't matter who I'm riding against, I'll just ride the best I can, thank you, then sign off.

The phone rings. Another journalist.

Can I get off the phone? It's my birthday, leave me alone. Thank you.

The phone rings again, and again. I don't get to speak with my Grandmother, I even have to cancel my afternoon physio appointment so I can fit my training ride in.

Eventually, Chiara and I get out for a nice dinner, away from the journalists and the questions and the speculation.

A few days later I receive a letter from the UCI informing me that because of Alexander Vinokourov's doping bust, I have been officially awarded first place in the 2007 Tour de France individual time trial in Albi. Talk about a hollow victory. It's my first Tour stage win and it comes to me while I am alone, standing by my letterbox.

THE FIRST MONTHS OF my year go well. I win stage two in the Ruta del Sol in Spain and stage four of Paris–Nice in France. Often known as 'The Race to the Sun', Paris–Nice began in 1933, and runs in eight stages from the often freezing roads of Paris down to the warmth and sunshine of the Côte d'Azur. In recent times it has come to be known as Sean Kelly's race after the Irishman won it seven times in a row between 1982 and 1988. I win a stage on Mont Ventoux, while riding in the services of Yaroslav Popovych.

He's just joined the team this year and finishes in third place overall at Paris–Nice.

The Tour of the Basque Country is held in Spain in early April and has UCI ProTour ranking. It's six stages over 800-plus kilometres. Some good multi-day race riders have won this race, including Sean Kelly (three times), my manager, Tony Rominger (three times in a row, 1992–1994), and other GC riders like Alex Zülle, Andreas Klöden and Denis Menchov.

There are some races you like to ride and there are some races you never like to ride. This is a race I've never liked to ride but it's really good timing in the lead-up to the Ardennes Classics.

The Basque people are very enthusiastic, and love cycling, but the rain can be so heavy. You either have to take your glasses off and get water and grit in your eyes, or leave them on so you can't see anything.

One reason I don't like it – other than the horrible weather and the narrow tiny roads – is that even though I tend to do everything right, I almost always have really bad luck there, a bit like at the Clásica de San Sebastián, held in the same area.

In stage five, the day before the final time trial, I'm coming to the end of the stage and there's a small climb then a short downhill, right turn, flat to the finish.

I'm second to Contador on GC. I've managed to get rid of him on the last climb but I've gone away with another rider on the downhill. It's pouring with rain and I come into the last right-hand turn. We've had to do this section already in the stage, so I know that there are some big stone blocks on the road ahead that can be quite slippery. And they're at the apex of a 90-degree turn, so I've come in very cautiously. I've dropped the rider I was with on the downhill but he's come back to me as we reach the flat. He's gone to pass me on the inside of this last corner, thinking that he can beat me in the sprint to the line. Suddenly, *Crash!* he's taken me down.

Italian, Damiano Cunego is just behind us, and rides past from behind to win the stage relatively easily.

Afterwards, team director Roberto Damiani comes over. 'Hey, what'd you do? What happened in the finish?' There's an overtone of 'Why didn't you win the sprint?'

'Well, didn't you see it on TV?' I reply.

'There was no TV coverage.'

Because it's so soggy and wet they couldn't film from the helicopter to show what happened. Here I am getting blamed for losing the stage after someone has taken me out from behind. The 'fault' for not winning is pinned on me.

But being taken out from behind isn't the only danger. A doctor tells me the riders who come to the Tour of the Basque Country often get sick. Local farmers put cow manure onto the fields to fertilise their crops and it rains so much the cow manure can get washed onto the road. As you ride it comes off the wheel of the rider in front and into your face. And mouth.

Consuming manure is not really ideal athletic preparation.

After crashing in stage five, I'm hoping I'll be able to come back to Contador in the time trial. But I get to the first time check after four kilometres and Contador has taken a minute on me.

I'm thinking, 'This is impossible – how can you take so much time in such a short distance?' I ride exactly the same speed for the rest of the trial as he does, even marginally quicker.

Once again, Contador has surprised me in the final time trial. I never find out how he did it. Still, second on GC is my best result at this race. Aldo Sassi has ideas as to how and why, none of which are at all complementary to Contador.

It's not my last second placing, either. I come second at La Flèche Wallonne in April, and the Critérium du Dauphiné Libéré in June. In between, I place seventh in the Liège–Bastogne–Liège.

La Flèche Wallonne ('Walloon Arrow') is an Ardennes Classic one-day race of 200 kilometres in the French part of Belgium. It attracts really passionate cycling fans who've been going to the Flèche for years and know the race so well.

It's a semi-classic that finishes on a climb. It's very short, it's very steep, and positioning into the climb's very important. You almost win it all on the positioning to the start of the climb rather than on the climb itself.

On the day of the Flèche it's raining once again. Some riders really suffer in the cold and wet; I can handle it reasonably well, but others, like Luxembourger, Kim Kirchen, grow wings. Seeing him ride in the Tour of the Basque Country a week ago has convinced me of this.

Coming into the last climb up the short but very steep Mur de Huy, I've gone away early, but am looking good for the win. As I exit the last narrow right bend into the final few hundred metres to the line, Kim bursts past me to take the win.

Liège–Bastogne–Liège is the last chance of the season for a Classics team to win a Classic. More often than not, Lotto (now called Silence–Lotto) will get there having not won a Classic thus far, so there's a level of pressure that swings my way.

I always work for the Classics, but not so much that it will compromise my performance at the Tour in July. So while I can go and be competitive at the short La Flèche Wallonne, at Liege-Bastogne–Liège I'll usually get over the big climb of Côte de la Redoute then find myself running on empty for the last 40 to 50 kilometres.

This year, though, there aren't many expectations on me outside of the Tour. I'm already gaining a lot of press in the Belgian papers (important for the Belgians), and Lotto are thrilled with the attention on me being Tour favourite. There seems to be an air of complacency, putting about the idea that, 'We're going to win this Tour.' It's a terrible way to think. My attitude is 'It's not over until it's over, and a lot can go wrong, so let's be really careful.' Being in front is one thing. Racing for the win and bringing it home is something else.

A DIFFICULTY WITH BEING race favourite, aside from the pressure it may put on you, is the sharply increased media interest, which takes time out of your training and personal life. And if you don't cooperate with the media they seem to create more problems for you. They'll write about you disrespectfully because you didn't answer to their every demand. You try to be the good guy, but you're in a demanding profession that takes up time and energy and you can't be available 24 hours a day.

Lotto's attitude towards the media seems to be: 'The more the better.' I'm thinking, 'Yeah, OK, but if we win the Tour we're going to get plenty more, so why compromise our chances by expending all this time and energy for the media now?' I don't mind fulfilling that aspect of my job, nor being on TV or in the newspapers. What I do mind is having the quality of my professional and personal life compromised by one aspect of my job.

An example of Lotto's misplaced media management is their decision to make a documentary about our Tour without telling me. I was due at a track in Belgium to test some time trial equipment. The day before I clearly said that the next day was to be testing only – no TV, no media, no journalists. I told them we were there to work and that was it.

I arrive to find a TV crew there. I confront the assistant manager.

'No, no, they're not journalists,' I'm told, 'this is just an in-house video we're making.'

'Well, we're here to do testing for the equipment and that's it, OK?'

'That's it, sure.'

So I do the testing.

The media manager arrives looking slightly sheepish. 'Cadel, just five minutes. The film crew's been waiting all day, can you give them five or 10 minutes?'

They want the footage to be part of a documentary, *Yell for Cadel*, to be made without my approval, and which they want to sell. At that moment, I feel more like a commodity than an athlete.

Another frustration quickly emerges. At the Tour de France the crowds are always intense. And as race favourite, there is a lot of attention on me. It's harder than ever to get to the start line with the crowds pushing and pulling at you.

Lotto suggests a bodyguard be assigned to me. I have a feeling it's not so much that they think I needed protection, it's more that they want to create media interest, so when I turn up at the start of the race with a bodyguard the TV crews film it.

To me it seems completely unnecessary. Serge Borlee, a Belgian ex-policeman, is a very nice guy, but I don't feel any more secure with him around. It's quite draining for me always having him around. He'll wait for me outside my room and take me down to breakfast. And if there are people around he'll hold them back. As a private person, who values my personal space, I find this unnecessarily taxing. Fortunately I have my twin therapists: osteopath, David Bombeke at the races and four-legged, Molly at home.

I tell the team, 'I don't want this. I just want to be a normal person and ride my bike in the race.' But I lose that battle.

DESPITE ALL OF THE external distractions – and there have been many – as preparations go, I haven't done too badly. Each time I have got on the bike, it has more and more become my sanctuary and I am riding very effectively.

The team have some good riders – Yaroslav Popovych, Robbie McEwen, Mario Aerts, super-trusty and reliable, Wim Vansevenant, tall and lanky, Johan Vansummeren. We've lost Chris Horner to Astana, the team led by Alberto Contador, but Lotto feel that it's their best Tour team ever.

At the Tour, one indication of people's expectations of you is the number of journalists at your pre-race press conference. On my first Tour rest day in 2005, three or four journalists wanted to speak to me; now the team are delighted to have a press conference for 100 people or more.

I'm up against three main GC riders in the Tour, all riding for CSC–Saxo Bank: the Schleck brothers, Andy and Fränk, from Luxembourg, and Carlos Sastre from Spain.

I've raced against the brothers from Luxembourg for a number of years. Fränk, the older of the two, is not as gifted but gets more out of himself as a rider. Andy, younger but more talented, doesn't often get everything onto the results sheet. The brothers are very close, both as riders and as friends. Fränk tells me that they call each other at least once a day. It's not something I can relate to, being an only child.

The early stages of the Tour are flat, and the yellow jersey is worn by a few different riders, but by stage six, Kim Kirchen is in the lead and I'm second on GC.

On the 224-kilometre stage nine from Toulouse to Bagnères-de-Bigorre – the first stage in the Pyrenees – I'm riding down one of the many tactically unimportant descents. The rider in front of me, from Euskaltel–Euskadi, crashes for no reason at all, it seems. I'm right behind him and career into him at 60 kilometres an hour. *Boof!* I slide along the road, watching as the gutter heads towards me.

I'm stunned and lying on the road. I feel the pain of dirt and sweat entering grazes in my legs, elbow, shoulder and back. My helmet's smashed up and my bike could be damaged, but I'm not certain of that yet. I'm thinking, 'Please don't let this be the end of my Tour.'

After a moment I've sorted myself out. I'm missing skin and bruised but I don't think I'm badly injured. I manage to get back on the bike and chase to rejoin the pack led by Euskaltel–Euskadi, and with some good team support I catch them.

I make my way to the doctor's car. Robbie McEwen is there, firmly but concisely barking instructions, do this, do that. He's been here before, and knows what's at stake.

I ask Robbie, 'Who's riding on the front?'

'Euskaltel.'

I can't believe it. The very same people who have taken me out are now riding on the front while I'm at the doctor's car getting anti-inflammatories and being patched up. I have torn skin, a lot of bruising, holes in my jersey, holes in my shorts, a broken helmet – and they're riding on the front. It's not sporting. What little respect I had for the team is diminishing even further.

Soon I'm back in the main group and Italian, Riccardo Riccò of Saunier Duval–Prodir attacks, I don't follow him because he isn't riding for GC. Riccò, he's a good rider on a good day but there's really not anything else nice to say about him.

I turn myself inside out and I make it to the finish. I'm last in the GC group and exhausted. This stupid crash has really cost me. After the stage, David Bombeke does what he can to patch me up.

I'll have to make up for the drop in performance with the only thing I have left: sheer determination. I'll have to push even harder, race even more efficiently – but as a rider who's dedicated his entire career to learning how to squeeze everything out of himself, it's not like I have much in reserve. To exacerbate the difficulties, continuing to race will have a cumulative effect on my recovery. The more fatigued I get, the more recovery will be required.

I think the only person who understands how hard it is for me is David Bombeke – someone who has a much better idea about stress- or fatigue-related tension in my body than I do, but also someone who knows me as the rider I am away from the races.

The next day I don't know whether I'll be able to start, but David gets me in OK condition to race. Stage 10 to Hautacam, in the Haute-Pyrénées, is a short but intense 156-kilometre day in the mountains, a category-three (lesser difficulty) climb. I am pretty well placed on GC. I go for a ride before breakfast to loosen up. David is in the car, following me to see if I can sit squarely on the bike.

After the ride, I go back for some more treatment from David. It's enough to get me to the start line, but my body is feeling pretty tired by this point and the bruising from the crash has really knocked me around.

In the stage I'm by myself at the back, with New Zealand rider Julian Dean. The peloton is spread out in a line and I'm second last.

Julian and I are getting dropped off the back. Here I am, riding for GC, and I can't even get through on the category-three climb. I suspect Julian might be sick, because he's getting dropped off the smallest rises, and I'm getting dropped with him. I don't have any teammates with me.

By the bottom of the last climb, Hautacam, I start to feel OK. There's a sprint against Andy Schleck and at the last minute, I slip in and take the yellow jersey by two seconds. I was just trying to ride for GC but I end up with the yellow jersey, becoming just the fifth Australian to win it. From being one of the worst climbers at the race at the start of the day to climbing into the race lead at the end of the day, I am more than relieved to receive my first Crédit Lyonnais lion and yellow jersey.

With my injured shoulder and all the bruises, I can hardly put it on. I'm in some pain when I get off the bike and make my way to the team bus. I'm missing skin underneath the jersey. People are patting me on the back to congratulate me. It bloody hurts.

Then someone grabs me, right on my left shoulder, where pus is leaking through a bandage and my jersey.

What the hell? It hurts badly and I react. I can't do anything to keep away from people, it's painful and infuriating.

ONE RIDER I SEE for the first time at the Tour this year is Kenyan cyclist, Chris Froome, racing at his first Tour de France. On one stage, I notice he's really struggling to position well in the peloton. I'm amazed at how well he performs given how badly he positions. He's started so far back in the climb but he still manages to get to the front and climb.

He's very lean and skinny, and holds his elbows out very widely. I don't know why. His riding style is quite particular. He looks a little like a praying mantis on the bike, not quite straight.

But I'm impressed by what I've seen of him. I say to team manager, Mark Sergeant, 'I think this is a rider we should consider getting on the team.' He seems to be a guy with a lot of talent but just needs some time to develop. Who knows how good he could become.

STAGE 15 IS UP the Col Agnel, a 2774 metre high mountain pass in the Cottian Alps. On one side, coming from France, it's hot and humid. Then we go over the top into Italy and there's a storm and it's quite cold on the descent.

I'm soaking wet from climbing up and getting sweaty and not having enough rain protection on the way down. I am wearing the yellow jersey which is not nearly enough. A race organiser gives me a yellow rain jacket but I'm still wet and cold. Evidently the most sought after jersey in the race, the yellow one, is not very warm.

On the descent Oscar Pereiro crashes. We slow down to wait for him while he gets back on his bike. I go hunger flat from the cold and I can't follow the attacks from the Schleck brothers and lose the yellow jersey to Fränk who gets eight seconds on me. I've held the lead for five stages and I'm deeply disappointed.

There's more tension when we have drug control at the end of the stage and I discover I'm to be tested by someone who doesn't understand the protocols for drug testing. When you're being tested you have to follow every rule to the letter, because if anything goes wrong your career is on the line.

So I'm in there being drug-tested by someone who's never even done a drug test before and doesn't know the rules. It's a little bit frustrating. I get into an argument because they have a lot of extra forms that I have never seen before and they don't have enough chaperones for all the riders they're testing.

This guy's asking me all these questions, being really rude and trying to speak to me in English. I say, 'But you're Italian.' So I start discussing firmly with him in Italian what's going on. 'OK. Do we do this by the rules or do we get someone else to do this?'

He's really offended. I think he's an Italian policeman, helping with the Spanish Operación Puerto investigation. I don't think he likes being told what to do and how to do his job. The problem is that this isn't his job; he's not a drug tester, and he doesn't know how to do it. Any mistake in this now very simple administrative procedure could have devastating consequences for me.

It's quite a heated conversation, but in the end I do the test and fill out the forms as they should be done and off I go.

STAGE 17 FINISHES ON the infamous Alpe d'Huez. This mountaintop is above the treeline, and there are no barriers on the sides of the road, just rocks and barren ground, so on TV from the helicopter it looks quite spectacular. The reality of racing, though, is that all this beauty tends to pass me by when I'm focused on riding. And I'll need to concentrate even harder today because of my injuries.

At the foot of Alpe d'Huez, Carlos Sastre attacks. I'm watching Fränk Schleck, who's in the yellow jersey and in a great place to win the Tour. There's only a small group following, including Fränk and Andy Schleck, who are Sastre's teammates, plus a couple of Spanish riders. I realise that neither of these Spanish guys is going to chase down a Spanish rider, because if they make him lose the Tour they're going to be crucified by the Spanish press. No one in the group has an interest in closing the gap.

Race director, Hendrik Redant is on the radio. 'Come on, you've got to ride, you've got to ride!'

And I'm thinking, 'I've got a long way to go and I'm not actually feeling that good, so it's not like I'm going to be able to do much.'

I start accelerating at three kilometres to go, where it gets a bit steeper, and where I think I can ride fast to the finish, but with this injury it's tough. And these Spanish riders sitting on the wheel do not help. But I have to get on the front so I just ride and ride.

This stage to Alpe d'Huez is the single most difficult day of my career thus far, the hardest I've ever pushed myself on the bike, because I'm here for the win. If it was for third or fourth I'd never find the strength to fight so hard, and go so deep.

But it's not enough. Sastre wins the stage and I limp to the finish in seventh place.

After the stage I go to do a drug test straightaway. They say, 'You can take a test now or you can wait. But if you wait, you might be here for an hour.'

I'm on top of Alpe d'Huez, I've just done the single hardest ride I've ever done on my bike in my life, and I just want to go back to the hotel and recover.

But I take the blood test and my urine is bright red – not a healthy sign. It's the first time this has happened to me and it worries me.

After the test I'm so depleted I'm struggling to walk down the steps of the drug-testing caravan.

That evening the team, and especially the other sports director, Herman Frison, are furious with me. 'Why didn't you close that gap? Why didn't you organise the other guys to chase?' Again, the blame is on my shoulders.

I'm thinking, 'If I'd stayed back with the others and tried to motivate them to chase, apart from the fact that they weren't going to because Sastre was too fast, I would have lost another 30 seconds.' And of course it's me who's got to take back all this time over the remaining stages.

In the final 53-kilometre time trial everyone is expecting me to take back time from Sastre to win the Tour.

They say wearing the yellow jersey lifts you. Having never time trialled with the yellow jersey I can't say for sure.

But the injury has got me. I'm missing that five per cent that Aldo identified.

I start one minute 34 seconds behind but I can't do it. I ride quite a good time trial but Carlos Sastre rides what, for him, is an extraordinary time trial.

Sastre wins the Tour de France. I'm second again, this time by 51 seconds.

CSC–Saxo Bank have had a very strong team this year, and although they initially worked to set up victory for Fränk Schleck, Carlos's attack at the foot of Alpe d'Huez turned out to be the best ride of his life. He went on to time-trial well above his norm. Despite what the world of cycling was expecting, I couldn't get the time back to pass him on GC. He hasn't won a lot of races in his career but has become a Tour de France winner nonetheless.

Of course I'm shattered. How could I not be? I've lost two consecutive Tours de France by a total of 1.26 minutes. This time I've raced injured and, again, without ideal team support. Silence–Lotto recruited stronger mountain climbers to support me, but when it came to crunch time in stage 17 my teammates were not even there.

Afterwards, when there's a quiet moment, I start to analyse my performance. Had I not crashed early would I have won? Aldo calculates that the crash cost me five per cent in outright performance, and I'd say a lot more in stress and frustration. Had the team been better able to support me, would things have been different?

I've been pushed to the limit nearly every day since mid February, and since the crash in the first week, I've been pushing myself beyond my limits, so I'm happy that I got everything out on the road that I could. I feel I had the legs for fourth or fifth, and I got second. It's a good performance, despite what's being said in the bubble of cycling.

What is frustrating is that the team is disappointed in me. On the final day, Lotto seem to lose faith in me and after that, things start to unravel. They think that if I couldn't win the Tour this year then I'll never win it. I find that hurtful, because I don't believe the team provided an environment that helped me. It seemed to be all about making a movie and making me ride so many races in the lead-up to the Tour.

We didn't have the strongest team by any means, because if you can't control the breakaways on the flat in the Tour de France your chances of winning the race are not great. And they expected me not only to win but to perform exceptionally off the bike as well. The team scheduled a program that drained energy away from me. I was riding the Tour de France for the win, I needed as much energy as I could get. Instead, I was overloaded with other commitments.

And now in their eyes I'm the guy who's just lost the Tour de France two years in a row. Placing second by a matter of 51 seconds isn't enough to make the team happy. At the end of the day, they're furious at me because I didn't win.

I prefer to look at it another way. Without much team support, I missed winning the Tour by just a few seconds. Actually it was an incredible performance, against the odds.

I'm not going to deny that losing hurts, and, of course, the poignancy of such a narrow loss makes it tougher. It's a bitter letdown that I'll have to absorb and learn from so I can reload and go again. I'm convinced within myself that I can do better than second but that's not how the world of cycling sees me.

An article on the Fox Sports website is headlined: 'Is Australian Cyclist Cadel Evans Unlucky or Is He His Own Worst Enemy?'

While I have to cope with it on both a personal and a professional level, for the public and the media there's an epic quality to it all. Journalists have always written about me as a hardworking, well prepared, intensely focused athlete. Now they're starting to characterise me as cursed, the guy who constantly just misses out.

I can see why the journalists are doing it. Undoubtedly, it's dramatic. It's true that my story is starting to be all about near misses. And on top of this narrative there is undeniably an overlay of dopers placing ahead of me.

There's nothing I can do about the dopers. That's for others to deal with. But I *can* do something about the stereotypes people are starting to force on me. I've gone from 'Hardworking Cadel' to 'Unlucky Cadel'.

Riders can't afford to deal in stereotypes. It's dangerous to allow yourself to indulge in them, because they have the potential to become self-fulfilling prophecies.

Sure, it could be said that luck hasn't gone my way, two years running, at the most famous road race in the world. Accidents and injuries are bad luck. Lack of team support and poor decisions by team directors are, I suppose, bad luck. But the concept of 'luck' doesn't fit with the way I've approached my career. If you let the concept of luck– or lack of it – attach to you, it may rob you of the qualities that made you what you are in the first place: a rider relying on preparation and hard work to succeed.

Coming second at the Tour de France, it feels like you are the most criticised rider in the race. That side of it bothers me more than not winning, because I'm basically happy with my performance. Still, all people can say is that I've 'lost' the Tour de France.

Now everyone's asking: 'Can you win it? Can you win it?' It's not just the journalists, but the people I meet in the street, in a café, in a bar, in the supermarket, out riding on the road; they're all asking me this same question.

It just gets so repetitive that your own mindset can actually get dragged down. And that's when you start asking yourself: '*Can* I actually win it?' There is only one way to find out.

The question always puts me back where I don't want to be. I want a break from talking about the Tour de France. I've done everything I can, I'd rather not think about the Tour de France again until it's time to come back in 2009.

Chiara had the foresight to bring our beloved dog, Molly to the race this year. Molly is the only one in my life who *doesn't* ask me about the Tour de France.

THE REST OF THE world may be talking about my 'loss', but for me, there isn't much time to dwell on it. The Olympic Games are due to begin in Beijing in two weeks' time and I've been selected for Australia's men's cycling team. It's a chance to ride well for my country and have a bit of fun with a big group of athletes from around the world, an experience I don't want to miss.

Lotto were convinced I was going to win the Tour so they've organised an end-of-Tour party for the team and sponsors at the Hard Rock Café in Paris which I am expected to attend. This seems to me like a crazy piece of hubris: organising a victory celebration in anticipation of the victory. Talk about tempting fate.

But I think, 'Well, they've put on a nice party, best I take an hour out of my professional life to enjoy this.'

Chatting to some guests of the team, I turn abruptly, feel my heel slide on the wet floor, and suddenly feel a severe pain in my knee.

After so many years of avoiding dodgy riders in the peloton (they know who they are), tearing down dangerous descents along slippery roads and surviving pack crashes, I can't believe I've injured myself by falling over in a bar.

And it's not just a small injury. It turns out I've ruptured my anterior cruciate ligament (ACL). If a footballer did his ACL he would almost certainly immediately have a knee reconstruction and would be out for 6 to 12 months. For a cyclist, a damaged ACL means the knee loses stability, but surgery isn't necessary because there are no sharp lateral movements in the action of pedalling.

I can't walk very well. I'm on crutches for four days and unsure whether I'll be OK to fly to Beijing and compete. I'm due to ride in a criterium in Holland before I go, but obviously I can't. Despite my sending a letter from my surgeon stating that I'm unfit to ride, I read in the Dutch newspaper that I'm 'unprofessional' for not turning up. I try to contact the team to help me, but all of the management are on holidays.

Normally, going to Beijing would be out of the question, but I have a fantastic physio and orthopaedic surgeon helping me out – Luca Ruiz and Danilo Togninalli. Danilo assures me that he once saw a skier who sustained exactly the same injury and two weeks later won the downhill world championship. He gives me a lot of hope.

Chiara drives me back and forth on visits to Danilo, the hospital and Luca four days in a row as I try to get the knee right for Beijing. By day four, I'm pain-free and I think I might be mobile enough to race. I do a little test with Australian Head coach, Shayne Bannan and the cycling team doctor and I get the thumbs-up. I'm soon on a plane to Beijing.

I GO INTO THE Games with no expectations. Apart from the knee injury, I always feel constrained going to the Olympics. As a professional athlete, you like to have the best team of people around you, the best teammates, the best staff, and the best equipment to perform at the best of your abilities at the biggest and most important races. Yet at the Olympics, although we have a team of great riders, we may never have raced on the same team together, we work with staff we may never have met, and receive tactical orders from a team director who may not even know our strengths and weaknesses. And we only have a few days and the race itself to get into the swing of things.

Beijing turns out to be a bizarre Olympics, the 'rent-a-crowds' strangest of all. We're riding along in the road race and we finish a circuit and there's one screen for us and one screen for the spectators. I look at the screen for the riders; it's got the times of the breakaway and how many laps to go and so on. Then I look across at the other screen; it says 'Cheer', and all the Chinese people stand up and cheer. I've heard rumours that they've had to have lessons. They certainly don't have a cycling culture, but they don't even seem to have a passion for sport.

I ride the 245 kilometre men's road race and finish 15th, 22 seconds behind the winner, Samuel Sánchez. I've underestimated my post-injury recovery and followed questionable team orders on the most suitable Olympic course I will probably ever race on. I am frustrated with myself for following orders rather than my usual race instinct.

Four days later I ride in the road time trial, two laps of a 23.8 kilometre circuit with a 12 kilometre uphill and a nine kilometre descent. The event is won by Swiss favourite, Fabian Cancellara; Sweden's Gustav Larsson takes silver and Spain's Alberto Contador takes bronze.

I finish fifth. I reckon that even being there vying for a medal is a pretty good effort. I tell journalists I've gone from 'a cripple to an Olympic athlete' in the four days before my selection for the Australian team was confirmed.

What is it about me and the Olympics? I often reflect on the Olympic curse that seems to follow me.

Every four years, right before the Games are due, something will happen in my life that jeopardises my chances of performing well, or performing at all. For me, it seems there's never a clear path to the biggest sporting event in the world.

CHAPTER 14

LOSING SUPPORT

2008–2009

IT'S HARD TO UNDERESTIMATE the importance of your team when you're a cyclist. And when the team lose faith in you, it becomes very, very difficult. The problem is that you get into a difficult situation where you can't do the races that suit you, so they can actually make you perform badly if they want to. It sounds ridiculous, but if they don't want to renew your contract or whatever, they can manipulate your results in a lot of ways.

In December 2008, the team announces publicly – without consulting me – that I'm going to ride in both the Giro and the Tour.

At the time, I'm out training with a close friend in Australia. I get a text message from another friend and glance at it: '*Gazzetta dello Sport* says you're riding the Giro – are you?'

'What the ...?!' I tell my riding friend Nick what the message says.

'Well are you?' he asks.

'NO!' I say emphatically. He just laughs.

I soon learn that *La Gazzetta dello Sport* has run a story stating that I am.

For the Belgian management at Lotto, articles in the newspaper have greater bearing than written contracts.

Winning the Tour is very difficult. Winning it after riding the Giro is even more difficult. Lotto know that. Everybody knows that. The last one to do it was Marco Pantani in 1998. Only seven riders have ever completed the double.

And Lotto know that I want to give my best showing at the Tour.

This creates a lot of tension between me and the team. It doesn't help that there's a complete lack of communication. They make no effort to keep me informed or ask my opinion. They seem to have lost all respect for me.

Early in the season I'm doing an interview to promote a charity race I'm about to ride in. The journalist asks me about the news that I'll be riding the Giro this year.

'As far as I know I'm not.'

'But it was in the newspaper that you are.'

'Well, no one asked *me* about it.' There's a story for him.

My comments appear on the Cycling News website and they're republished in Belgian newspapers. It puts me in a big mess. It embarrasses the team because it makes them look unprofessional in the newspapers they and their friends read.

I speak to assistant manager Hendrik Redant, one of the few sports directors who actually answer my calls, about riding the Giro on top of the Tour. I say, 'If we're going to do this, we may as well just give the bouquet of flowers for the Tour to Contador now.'

I want to do the Tour with fresh legs and then ride the Vuelta later in the season as I'm sure it is the best way to get ready for the World Championships.

But it's not just the Giro and the Tour they want me to ride. They want me to saddle up for Paris–Nice, the Tour of the Basque Country, the Ardennes Classics, Coppi e Bartali, Ruta de Sol, the Vuelta – all these races. It's inhumane.

They're now sure I can't win the Tour de France, so since I'm being paid the salary of a potential Tour winner, they think they'd better get their money's worth out of me. So they plan on sending me to all the races where it's possible for me to get points for them and contribute to the security of their sponsorships.

It sometimes happens as a rider that you go from being treated as a human to being treated as collateral. And I hate that. We are humans, with feelings, emotions, families and lives.

I'm working towards the Tour but feel completely unsupported. And that undermines my psychology as a professional on the team. You're giving your best to someone and they're slapping you in the face for it. It feels a little like betrayal.

By now I've developed a pretty thick skin. I refuse to let them break me.

IN MARCH 2009, I ride the Coppi e Bartali a good race for training that I really like. It's held in Reggio Emilia, a city renowned for its good food, even by Italians themselves.

At the end of stage three there's a descent and then it's flat to the finish. We are a group of around 20.

There's one rider in the group who's quite fast and I'm concentrating on him, hoping I can beat him in the sprint. Roberto Damiani, the race director, thinks I won't win in a sprint. He's yelling at me to jump away solo: 'Attack! Go away! You've got to go away!'

Roberto and I first met at the '02 Tour Down Under when he was a manager at Mapei; it was my first race with them. I actually brought him with me to Lotto, as they needed a manager who had experience with a Grand Tour contender. When the team lost confidence in me in '08, he chose to side with the team, for his own employment security I guess.

So Roberto is shouting at me to go away, but I'm sitting back and waiting for the sprint.

I overhear some Italians organising themselves to collaborate, so I use that to anticipate what they're going to do, and I win in the sprint, but only by a bike throw. It's a small win, just a stage win, but my first season win, and more importantly the first season win for the team. I finish second in the race overall.

But there's a bit of friction between Roberto and me, because I've done exactly what he didn't want me to do and been successful. That doesn't help my already frayed relationship with the team.

In cycling, if you do exactly as you're told and lose, that's usually OK. If do as you're told and win, that's ideal both for you and for the team. But when you're in a negative team environment, if you do other than what you're told and win, it's probably worse than losing.

IN APRIL I RIDE the Tour of the Basque Country and finish fourth overall on GC.

A week later I head down to the Mapei centre to see Aldo. I'm scheduled for a test, but mainly I need to speak with Aldo about the paralysis I'm feeling in my career. He knows the situation I'm in and the difficulties I'm having with the team.

We do some testing in the lab. I don't like doing these tests much, it's a lot of effort. You get a bit of a training effect in doing a test but it's not like pushing yourself in the races and getting some results.

Afterwards we sit down and talk.

'Aldo, they've lost all faith in me.'

'I know.'

'Anything that goes wrong is my fault.'

He says, 'It shows. If you just didn't have all the stress, you'd perform fine, but you've got all this pressure and it's affecting your performance.'

As usual, Aldo is right. The team's lack of faith is eating away at me.

After my meeting with Aldo, I race all three Ardennes Classics followed by the six-day Tour de Romandie. After a stage one evening, I walk into David Bombeke's hotel room when I receive a SMS. I glance at the message, 'Davide Rebellin "A" sample from the 2008 Olympics non negative.' Davide? No! It is a blow not only for our sport, but he is a rider I really look up to as an example of patience, tolerance and professionalism. He was always so calm, respectful and unobtrusive in the group.

In June I ride the Critérium du Dauphiné Libéré, which begins in Nancy, France. On stage five I'm isolated between two collaborating Spanish riders on Mont Ventoux and I lose the leader's jersey. Valverde wins. Again I'm second, Contador third.

Sponsor, Marc Coucke's response is: 'Why can't you win a race like this?' Tony Rominger leaps to my defence, but it makes no difference.

I'm getting tired of seconds. And I'm getting tired of Lotto seeing me as someone who can't win.

I'm trying to do my best, but when my support structure is not only unsupportive, but also seems to be adding to my challenges, it undermines everything I need to perform for a team.

THE TOUR DE FRANCE is now less than three weeks away. There's a team time trial in it this year. I know Lotto are under-resourced and undertrained and that we're going to lose a lot of time in that stage.

But there's no open line of communication between me and the management of the team, so I have to communicate my thoughts in other ways. I have to say it to the Belgian media so they go and they write it in the newspaper and then the reporters say, 'Lotto have got to work on a team time trial', and then the team is forced to do it.

A strange but effective strategy.

I know if I'd asked them they would have said, 'No, it's too hard to organise.' But then if I'm two minutes down in the time trial and two minutes down in Paris they won't be happy with me either, and I know where the blame will be placed.

We go to a track to do some team time trial training. At the track there are journalists and photographers. Once again I'm thinking, 'I thought we were here to train.'

We don't have a training program to follow so we just start riding in team time trial formation on the circuit while the TV crew takes some footage. As soon as the TV cameras leave, the other riders say, 'Now we'll go to lunch.' Some of them leave altogether. It's a complete waste of time.

As an athlete, you have to be optimistic but realistic. If I am to ride for GC at the Tour de France, all signs indicate that it is going to be all up to me. But even if I do everything just right, and the team has not done anything to prepare for the team time trial, it is likely I am going to be penalised by two to two and half minutes there alone. For somebody who has lost not one, but two Tours by less than one minute, the prospects do not look favourable. It takes focus just to keep confidence.

One of the internal problems is doping busts. A few days before the Tour begins, it's announced that new Dutch Lotto member, Thomas Dekker, has failed a drug test carried out on a urine sample taken before he joined the team. He's suspended from the team and is out of the Tour de France. The first reserve, Charlie Wegelius, is at his local municipal office lodging papers to register his wedding. His phone rings, 'Pack your bag, you are riding the Tour.'

It's come on top of an earlier failed drug test by Austrian, Bernhard Kohl. Bernhard was the best climber in the 2008 Tour de France and finished third overall. Bernhard's sudden improvement in performance came as a surprise to everyone. A sudden rise to success is usually a red flag, but the team were desperate, so the guy who had been a surprise podium finisher at the Tour was coming to Lotto to support me in the mountains. I was training in Australia when it all came out towards the end of 2008. What had sounded to good to be true evidently was to good to be true.

But the big news of the 2009 Tour is the return of Lance Armstrong, who 'retired' in 2005 after seven consecutive Tour victories. He's coming back as part of the Astana team, which includes Alberto Contador.

I'm not alone also in wondering how fast he'll be able to go after four years out, and at the age of 38. That's a lot of time to miss, a lot of your endurance base to make up for.

And obviously he has a lot to lose. Actually, he has *everything* to lose. If he had walked away in 2005 after seven consecutive victories, his place in cycling history would have been – *might* have been – secure. He could have basked in the glory of being described as the best Tour de France rider ever. The 'miracle' – as he called his successes after having survived cancer – would have retained its power and hold on the world, including the corporate world that had so generously rewarded him.

But he's decided to tempt fate and come back.

No one knows why he's returning, and I don't think he knows himself. Does he miss the adrenalin too much? Does he miss the attention? Is he still hungry for the validation and the competition and the cameras? What point is he making? Why would he risk the scrutiny he's left behind?

I don't know what Lance's game plan is – not that I've given it much thought. At the moment my own career is consuming too much of my mind and body for me to have energy left to think about the careers of others.

THERE ARE MOMENTS IN the Tour when Lance's performance – and his team Astana's – can be described as startling. Or unbelievable.

In stage six into Barcelona, Astana go to the front to stay safe and ride tempo in the pouring rain. It's a dangerous move because we are coming into a city with wet and slippery roads.

Michael Rogers, riding for Columbia–HTC, is in front of me. We go through a roundabout and he leaves a half-metre gap for safety. Astana is riding so fast no one can move in front of them. In the line behind, no one can move from their position because they're flat out just holding the wheel in front of them.

I have a bit of extra momentum exiting the roundabout, so I move past Mick, up one position, and get on the wheel and go again. But Astana is going so fast in one line that to come out of the slipstream you can't go back in, especially at 65 ks per hour. That's how fast they're riding. It's just ridiculous. I have not seen anything like it since USPS/Discovery Channel Pro Cycling Team days.

The guys in Astana pass a message down the line that everyone should stay where they are to make it safer. But it's a moot point because no one can move up anyway, so who's going to argue? We ride the descent safely, Astana get off the front and the pace returns to normal.

At the start of stage 16 there's a 25-kilometre climb up the Col du Grand-Saint-Bernard in the Alps. I wonder why everyone is riding so fast. I'm flat out on the wheel just holding my position. I look up and see seven of the nine Astana team members riding at the front again.

I think, 'That's a relief, two of their riders have been dropped.' Then I look to my right and Popovych and another Astana rider pass me in the bunch, each with six bottles in their jersey for their teammates at the front. Not one break can stay away, yet here are these guys moving up the side like we are riding on the flat, just doing what they want.

Very demoralising.

I do have a laugh during this stage, though. I've started to get to know Bradley Wiggins in this year's Tour de France. He's quite tall with a narrow body and shoulders. Probably thanks to his background on the track, he has tremendous hip rotation, allowing him to reach a very efficient aerodynamic time trial position.

He's quite reserved but has a very quirky sense of humour that not everyone understands. Going up the second climb of the stage – the Col du Petit Saint-Bernard – the speed's getting higher and selections are being made and it's all happening, and Bradley is reciting a line out of the gangster movie *Lock, Stock and Two Smoking Barrels*.

Here he is, making like a Cockney heister, spouting dialogue: 'Yer nasty bastard ... *Boof!*' Another rider looks at him, 'What the ...?' I burst out laughing.

All this while ascending Petit Bernard. I like his style. He has made a big leap in performance this year, sitting in the first five on GC.

AFTER MY LOSS OF the 2008 Tour, the support and confidence from my team has been in a continual decline. July feels like we've hit rock bottom.

While the team staff; the masseurs, mechanics and my good friend and very trusted Sports Director, Hendrik Redant, are always there for me off the bike, it's on the road where the results are made. Teammate, Jurgen Van den Broeck is having a great Tour, battling with Franco Pellizotti for the King of the Mountains jersey and a place in the first five on GC. I'm guessing that he is delighted that I am not doing well.

Some of the other riders are becoming more and more disgruntled by the day, not that I see much of them during the stages. It's sad to suggest, but I imagine a big part of their disappointment about this Tour is that they will not be going home with as much prize money as they were hoping for. After consistently bringing in a reasonable amount of prize money, especially in the last two years, I don't get any pity from that department.

Even worse, though, is the tension between me and Herman Frison, who is the second team director at the Tour. It's been so bad that I actually wrote a letter, months before, to team management about his ill motives, lack of skills, and poor communication skills.

In stage 20, he's a big part of creating problems that lead me to be dropped on Mont Ventoux. On the climb to Ventoux he comes alongside me in the car yelling something. I can't understand a thing he is saying, nor can he of me. The discussion gets heated so I resort to blunter means of communication, I hurl a water bottle at him. It hits him right between the eyes. Unbeknownst to me, sitting next to him is an 'important politician' who had just captured this on his brand new iPhone. Somewhere in Belgium is some interesting footage of me finally cracking with this guy.

After the stage, Herman threatens to send me home. 'Can I go home? I'd love to get away from you' I replied. The threats cease there.

I finish the Tour an abysmal 28th overall. Like all of the riders in the team, I cannot wait to get away from the toxic environment and get on with my life.

TEAM PROBLEMS HAVE NOT hampered the performance of the winner, Alberto Contador. With everything going on in Astana, for him to still win the Tour de France makes me think of him as one of the strongest of the Grand Tour riders. If you saw him not dressed as a professional you'd never guess he was a pro bike rider. His muscles look soft and don't have much definition.

Lotto are annoyed at me for my poor performance. Traditionally, I distribute my prize money among the other riders but this year I didn't get any. So the riders on the team are annoyed too.

Lotto announce that I won't be the sole leader of the team in the future. I don't know what the future holds for me exactly. All I know is that I'm deeply unhappy and still have a year to run on my contract.

My mind is on the World Championships in Mendrisio, right near my home. I know the course well, I know it will suit me. Nearly every other year the Worlds are not a peak priority for me, but this year they are. Up there with the Vuelta. Seven years into my road career, this is the first time I've geared my whole season around a one-day race.

Lotto tell me they want me to come to Belgium for a meeting. I say, 'I can't. I'm at a training camp at altitude. You come to me.' I'm in a remote location in the Italian mountains trying to build up to a good Vuelta and World Championships.

Two of the Lotto management make the journey down to visit me in Pontresina, Switzerland, not far from where I am training. Tony joins to understand what this unusual meeting is about. The Lotto management list some 'unprofessional' acts, not wearing the correct casual shoes, wearing an undershirt other than the one supplied from the team, amongst other trivial matters as opposed to the real problems. They also attempt to reduce my salary for the following year.

OK, this is obviously ridiculous now. Mentally I make a switch, 'Forget about the results, just train and enjoy racing. If the team don't want results, so be it.'

IN SEPTEMBER, I RIDE the Vuelta and take the leader's jersey in stage eight. I'm riding well now because I have given up going for GC at the Tour de France which has left me with a bit more in reserve than I am used to having at this stage of the season.

Then, because of hopeless team organisation, I lose the leader's jersey in stage nine. A good break of nine riders goes away and all we have to do to keep the overall lead is keep the break at a safe distance and ride into the finish for tenth place. We couldn't hope for a better situation.

Then the team starts riding faster, Gilbert asks them to slow down but they ride faster. I ask them to slow down but they ride faster. I try yelling at them, only to be ignored. The rules state that you cannot raise your hands off the handlebars towards another rider, so I can't do anything more than yell...

The gap to break is reduced. Alejandro Valverde attacks on the small climb near the finish and joins the break with Dutch rider, Robert Gesink and me following. We come into the finish for the bonus seconds and I try to pass Gesink on the shorter inside line.

Gesink gets out of the saddle and starts sprinting for the line. He's is very uncoordinated when he gets out of the saddle to accelerate. He's waving his 'farm gate' (very large bicycle frame) around like it's a rodeo and we nearly hook handlebars as I try to go by him. I have to slow down. Valverde gets the bonus seconds and the jersey.

After we cross the line I have some words with Gesink and then the team, but I see I'm wasting my energy, so I try to save it to get the jersey back later in the race. Never argue with an idiot, they will bring you down to their level and beat you with their experience.

THE FAMOUS BOTCHED WHEEL change debacle on the climbing stage to Sierra Nevada is a truly testing moment. It's not the team's fault but embodies the frustration I am experiencing.

Just before the Monachil summit on stage 13 – the penultimate climb – I get a puncture and need a wheel change, so I call for help. But the team can't get to me because the car is stuck in traffic. Why? Because Spanish TV – on a motorbike – stops in the middle of the very narrow road and no cars can get past. A TV motorbike should stop on the *side* of the road – no one is allowed to block the road.

As I've already learnt from racing in Spain, the TV coverage is terrible. And here they are blocking my way for a chance to win a Grand Tour.

The cars are blocked and my team car is 10 or 15 cars down the hill. I'm losing crucial time.

In the race you have the race director behind and then a neutral spare car. If someone goes in a breakaway, the spare car is the first car to be there. The neutral spare car is there for everyone, for a spare wheel or even a spare bike. It won't be your own but it's a bike and you can finish the race.

Neutral mechanics arrive to fix my problem but are not able to change my wheel quickly enough. It's very unprofessional, not even competent.

Some other riders have already had trouble with the neutral spares. The situation is complicated by the different brands of wheels held by the neutrals for incidents like this. We're using Campagnolo components. Campagnolo has switched from 10 to 11 speed. The neutral mechanics have to know which teams are using 10 and which are using 11. They don't, and that's apparently why the wheel change takes so long.

The guy gets the wheel and he can't put it in. I'm thinking, 'Man, get out of my way and let *me* put it in and I'll go.'

As I stand there waiting, the only strategy at my disposal is to remain calm. 'Stay calm, 'kids' is my most repeated line on race radio over the years. And now it's *my* turn to hold my anger in. Getting angry sets off the body's flight, or fight response – I'm going to need that later.

Our mechanic, Nick Mondelears, back in the team car, is pretty sure that something's gone wrong. Thinking cleverly, he gets my bike off the roof and rides it up the road to me.

By now I've been standing there for one minute and 23 seconds, and I'm eight seconds down on GC. Nick's actions save me from losing another minute or more.

Meanwhile my rivals are charging down the other side of the Monachil. Valverde and the other GC riders have capitalised on my problem and collaborated to increase the gap.

There is no water bottle on the new bike so I take a water bottle from the car while I'm on the climb. You're not allowed to do that, so to add insult to injury, I'm later given a 10-second penalty.

I am starting to make time on them again, but if there's someone in the lead group who's behind me on GC they're going to ride with Valverde to help him move ahead of me on GC. Sammy Sánchez is with Valverde, but fortunately for me he gets dropped.

I cross the finish line in eighth place. I'm now over a minute and a half behind Valverde on GC. I only have the time trial to make time back.

The bitter irony for me in all this is that Valverde is meant to be serving a sanction for being involved in the Fuentes scandal.

I'm just gutted. At the end of the stage I say, 'I don't deserve this shit.'

It's painful just to think about it. This was Australia's best chance so far of winning a Grand Tour, and the opportunity was blown through circumstances beyond my control.

When the stage is over, I get into the bus, and for the first time ever after a race, I cry.

NEXT DAY I ROLL out. The start is in Granada. There are a couple of stages to go. But there's something wrong with my bike. I'm trying to go back to the team car to get it checked out when a Spanish fan grabs me to get something from me. I untangle myself from his grasp and ride off to the sound of his curses and insults.

I'm thinking, 'With everything that Spanish cycling dished out to me yesterday, today I get sworn at by a Spanish fan. Oh, please.'

I get back to the car and fix what I have to fix. And get back to the start. At the start line, I run into one of my PE teachers from high school, Mrs Trager, who, by chance, is in Granada on holiday. She's thought, 'Oh, the Vuelta's on, I'll go and see if Cadel's there.'

Mrs Trager and I say hi, exchange a few words. It's so refreshing to have my mind pulled out of the sphere of cycling for a moment.

We're riding in neutral at the start of the stage and Stuart O'Grady and Dave Millar come up to me.

Dave says, 'You must be the angriest person in the world of cycling right now.'

Stuey offers me commiserations. 'It's only a grandy,' I say with sarcasm.

'What the fuck? That's so wrong,' he says.

Yeah, we're only talking about the win in a Grand Tour here. Dave and Stuey understand.

I try to get the time back in the time trial, but Valverde rides a good time trial. I finish third, 1 minute 32 down after losing 1 minute 23 seconds for the botched wheel change and a 10 second penalty for taking a bottle, 1 minute 33 seconds in all. At least I'm on the podium.

I like Valverde on a personal level. He's certainly had his dealings with the dark side of the sport, but I judge him by his genuine friendliness, mental toughness and desire to race. He has big calves and thick ankles (unusual for a cyclist) and usually sports a good suntan. He moves his upper body quite a lot and that is accentuated when he gets fatigued, something to note when you are going against him, as I so often have.

I rode against Valverde when he was at Kelme in 2003 and 2004 and I was at T-Mobile. Here was this young rider who was winning in bunch sprints and hilltop finishes and we were all saying, 'He's incredible. If he could time-trial he could win anything, this guy.'

And then he beats Erik Zabel in a bunch finish one day at the Vuelta a Valencia. Then the next day on the hilltop finish he's there racing for the win against the pure climbers. The following year he comes back and he wins a time trial and everyone is thinking, 'Oh no, he's learnt to time-trial as well, this guy's going to be unbeatable.' I've had a few head-to-heads with him. He's a tough competitor.

Now, fans are cheering him on the roadside and Spain is at the head of the national rankings, but the fact that he was even permitted to race during this period feels unjust. The fact that no Spanish athletes or staff implicated in Operation Puerto have been sanctioned is a knife in the back, not just to me, but everyone who wants a cleaner sport.

I GO HOME TO Stabio and next day I go for a ride.

I roll out of the gravel driveway, turn left and head towards the Villa D'este, an opulent hotel on the shores of Lake Como where my travel manager and friend, Troy de Haas is staying. The security guard is reluctant to let me in but eventually relents. After catching up with Troy over a coffee and taking a photo with the guard, who has now changed his tack, I take the back roads home passing over some of next weekend's World Championships course. Some Dutch and Belgian spectators are already camped there.

I'm trying to put the injustice of the Vuelta behind me. I remember what Chiara's always told me. 'La ruota sempre gira.' The wheel always turns. My luck will change.

SHORTLY BEFORE THE WORLD Championships, the Australian road team hold a meeting to discuss race tactics: nine riders and a team manager.

It's going to be a particularly hard Worlds, in fact many on the team are not even expected to finish the race. Some are here to focus on the time trial, others are here to ride on the front if necessary and help the leaders with getting food and bottles, staying with them if they have a problem and generally looking after them. If the leaders are successful in winning or placing in the medals, everyone in the team will be financially rewarded, which is fair.

First the team votes on who will be the team leader, or leaders.

'OK, who wants Cadel?' the manager asks.

Only I put my hand up.

'Who wants Simon?'

Seven vote for Simon Gerrans, one rider abstains.

After the vote, one of the riders comes over to me, 'If you win, you still have to pay you know?' I remain silent. Later I try to explain to the sports director that I have based my whole year on this race but he is dismissive. 'You saw the vote'.

I have become exceptionally good at dealing with lack of faith this year. In the end it's about the love of riding, which, even in my darkest moments, never leaves me.

Even if the Australian team don't believe in me or want to support me, I'm still going to go and race hard for the Worlds because on my bike is where I'm happiest.

The wheel always turns – my luck will change.

And maybe it will happen soon.

JUST A FEW KILOMETRES from home, right where the finish line was for the 1971 World Championships in Mendrisio, is Ciclosprint, a bike shop run by Ermanno Bossi, an exceptional bike mechanic.

When I first moved here to Stabio in 2005, Aldo recommended I go and see Ermanno; Aldo knew him because Mapei was a sponsor of the Mendrisio Under 23 club. And it turned out that Ermanno lived across the road from my apartment in Stabio.

Ermanno is a laid-back, warm-hearted guy who runs a much-loved local hangout. On the wall is a photo of Ermanno in his pro-racing prime riding his bike. I'll often wander into the shop and see local riders buying a new bike tube or parents buying their child a bike for Christmas. It has what all good bike shops have: the ever-present rubber smell of brand-new bike tyres.

He has always been available to me and this year particularly so. I have spent a lot of time working through problems with the bikes supplied by the team – long conversations and hours in the shop. I train around the roads of Mendrisio then ride straight to Ermanno to describe the problems I am having. He often shakes his head in disbelief but always finds solutions to my problems.

AFTER 10 YEARS WORKING with me, Tony Rominger knows how unhappy I am, and that I need to find a better environment.

Some months previously, Tony pitched an idea to BMC, an American-registered Professional Continental team that is looking to build a Tour de France team and needs a strong GC rider. He knows BMC owners, Andy Rihs and Jim Ochowicz. He's suggested that if I were recruited, the team would have a fairly good chance of gaining a wildcard entry into the 2010 Tour de France.

American, George Hincapie has been BMC's biggest signing, announced at the start of September. George was a key *domestique* for Lance Armstrong on all seven of Armstrong's Tour de France victories. He also rode for Alberto Contador in 2007 when Contador won the Tour de France. George's reputation in the cycling world has suddenly brought a lot of credibility to BMC, even though they're not yet part of the ProTour. Soon after George signs, the recruitment announcements keep coming. They include Dutch rider, Karsten Kroon, Swiss rider, Steve Morabito and Italian, Alessandro Ballan.

Signing riders of this calibre is a statement to the world of cycling that BMC is a team with serious intent. But they still need an established team leader to win a Grand Tour.

I'M AT THE AUSTRALIAN team hotel in Varese for the World Championships in two days time. The phone rings. Jim Ochowicz.

'Hey Cadel, I'm in Europe for the Worlds. Do you have time to meet?'

I've never met Jim. A former cyclist who raced for the United States in the 1972 Summer Olympics, Jim has probably had the most influence of anyone in breaking America into European cycling. He was instrumental in bringing the first American team – 7-Eleven (later Motorola) – to the Classics and Grand Tours, including the 1986 Tour de France, where they took the yellow jersey in the first week.

The highlight of 7-Eleven's seven years as a team was the win by Andy Hampsten in the 1988 Giro d'Italia, the first by an American. The team later rode under the sponsorship name Motorola, with Australian, Phil Anderson on board. Jim helped George Hincapie get his first break in 1996.

Jim was confident it was the start of big things for American cycling, and he was right. American, Greg LeMond won three Tours de France, Lance Armstrong seven, and Floyd Landis one before it was stripped from him. Jim knew the Americans were coming. He's a visionary with a global view.

He also seems to be a person I can trust. Charlie Livermore, who managed the Volvo–Cannondale mountain bike team where I finished my mountain-bike career, worked with Jim and only told me really good things about him.

'Can we catch up?' Jim asks me.

'Jim, the only day I can meet is Saturday. The race is the next day.'

He says, 'Won't that distract you? I don't want to upset your concentration.'

'The timing's fine, Jim. Let's meet.'

I'm keen to meet him and find out about the future of the BMC team. All I know is that I'm in a dark tunnel. I just want to know if there is light at the end. I'm thinking maybe Jim Ochowicz *is* that light.

We meet in a little bar in Varese, a town 20 minutes' drive from my home. We have a chat, he asks me some questions. He's seen me frustrated at the races, dealing with all this rubbish.

Then he says, 'You're known as a difficult rider. You have all these demands. Why did you have a bodyguard at the Tour?'

I think, 'That bloody bodyguard idea!' I can see how that looked bad.

'No, Jim,' I tell him, 'I didn't want a bodyguard at the Tour. That was Lotto's idea. All I want to do is race my bike and get the best results I can and be as professional as possible.'

Jim looks at me. 'You just need a team that has confidence in you.'

Did I just hear that? Light-in-tunnel moment.

'Yeah, Jim, that's all I want.'

Nine months of frustration and anger have created a lot of tension in my body. I've been riding all year with a massive handbrake on. But Jim has just released it.

PART TWO

TAKING *the* LEAD

CHAPTER 15

THE WORLD CHAMPIONSHIPS

2009

THE FINISH LINE FOR the World Road Championships of 2009 is three kilometres from my front door. Mendrisio is the nearest major town to where I live, and I'm often here to shop or go to a particular restaurant I like.

But crucially, I know the course well; I've ridden it countless times in training. It's the biggest one-day race in the world and it's virtually in my backyard.

When it's cold in the winter, I do most of my training along the shores of Lake Como. It's 15 kilometres from Stabio along tiny back roads. Go through Genestrerio, past my good friend Luigi Zanini's impressive cantina, and the computer shop where I get my laptops looked after. Turn right at the roundabout near the Peugeot dealership and up towards Novazzano, then descend La Torraccia di Novazzano towards Chiasso and over the border into Italy, to Cernobbio. Soon you're at the foot of Monte Bisbino, a 15-kilometre climb up to 1325 metres altitude or, for flatter training, continue 15 kilometres north along the lake towards Argegno and the climb up to Val d'Intelvi, most of which is exposed to the morning sun.

To return, on the same route, go up La Torraccia and descend towards Genestrerio, where you can either turn left to get straight back to Stabio, or take the slightly less busy route that will take you up to Ligornetto then home.

How many times have I ridden up La Torraccia? Countless times, in the rain, in the snow, in the heat – fresh and stomping (riding well), or exhausted, empty and creeping (riding badly). On 27 September, this five-kilometre section of road – the last stretch of many quiet, usually comfortingly lonely training rides – becomes the last five kilometres of the pro-men's World Championships course.

The course itself is difficult and the climbs are reasonably hard but not incredible. It's a one-day 262-kilometre course suited more to the pure climbers than the Classics guys. It is one of the better Worlds courses for me since Stuttgart in 2006.

It had been such a challenging and frustrating year. I'm 32, and if you believe what Lotto – and others in the cycling world – are saying, I'm done.

I've woken up this morning feeling much lighter after yesterday's meeting with Jim. Everything just flows. I am riding well. I have a World Championships almost on my doorstep to race, but most of all, I am conscious of a light at the end of the dark tunnel that my season has become.

For the first time in ages I feel a sense of hope.

A BIG GROUP GOES early and for a time it looks to have a chance to stay away for the finish. Mick Rogers is in the move so despite some panicking from my teammates, I think we should just stay calm and see what happens. Simon Clarke stays with me during the race, getting me feed bags and bottles so I can avoid the mess that the feed zone is at any World Championships.

As the race goes on, the field is shrinking though attrition. I'm drinking a Coke on the main climb, Acqua Fresca ('Fresh Water'), as I close gaps between the riders being dropped. 'Shit' I think to myself, 'I'm on quite a day here'.

The attacks mark the start of the real contenders' race. I see a chance to jump across alone to what looks to be the selection for the final. I go across, on the Acqua Fresca climb again, passing riders as they are being dropped off the back of the dozen or so riders left in front. As I get onto the back of this group it gives me a moment to see all of the riders and make a quick overview of the situation. I think, 'There are three Spanish riders here, and the first of them to get away will stay away'.

Fabian Cancellara, the Swiss time trial specialist from Bern, is there too. I first met Fabian in 2002, and we trained together on a few occasions, as he lived only 45 kilometres from Lugnorre, my home at the time. He was a first-year professional on Mapei's GS3 team, the development squad. Fabian was the biggest of the pool of talent Mapei were conditioning for the future.

Michael Rogers once said of him, 'That guy has no idea how strong he is.' Fabian went on to make great use of his abilities. He's one of the few big talents in the world of cycling who can get everything out on the road and onto the results sheet. He has an amazing ability to concentrate, probably the greatest asset in his treasure chest of talents. As a manager who worked closely with him once said, 'Five minutes before a time trial you could tell him his house was burning down, with his family inside, and he would not budge.' His focus was so strong.

Cancellara has ridden exceptionally well to get to the front group, this not being his preferred type of course. On the downhill it's windy and technical, so even though you are descending, you have to pay a lot of attention. One turn, in the village of Gorla, is quite sharp and narrow, a right-hand turn of more than 90 degrees, so you have to concentrate just to stay in front.

We're in the final lap and there are nine kilometres to go. There's a long, fast sweeping left turn. This is where the first of the Spanish riders, Rodríguez, goes away between the lane dividers which instigates the move of Russian, Alexandr Kolobnev and me.

I follow Rodríguez through one of the gaps. You're going very fast, and unless you've anticipated such a move, you can't follow because the gaps are small. At race speed, Kolobnev punches across and there are three of us again at the front.

Seven and a half kilometres to go. It's pretty clear now that we've got a very good chance of all being in the medals. The Worlds are a different kind of race: everyone is there for the win. The winner of the World Champs gets the privilege of wearing a rainbow jersey for one whole year, and of keeping those rainbow stripes on their jersey for the rest of their career. The most honourable stripes in cycling. For this, riders change their mentality for the Worlds, the added pressure and expectations they put on themselves to win, not to place, or do well but to win, changes the dynamics of the race. Everyone is racing to win.

At the foot of the Novazzano climb the other two are looking at each other. I'm thinking, 'You idiots, I wouldn't be doing that if I were you.'

They leave a small gap so I go solo from the front.

That's all it takes. One look away, one tiny gap.

I increase the gap then I hit the bottom of the climb, La Torraccia, and extend my lead. I know every metre of this climb. This road is the one I take home from training. These are *my* roads.

I know the climb so well. I'm thinking, 'Is it possible to ride the first section using the big chainring?'

I decide to try to do the first half in the big chainring and then I'll see for the second half.

I go up in the big chainring, which you'd normally never think of doing because it's just ridiculously hard. But I find I can stay in the big ring because today is one of those days.

At the top of the next climb I have a 28-second gap.

Of all the kilometres I've ridden around in the world so far in my career, those six kilometres have been the best I have ever done. Fortunately they are the final six kilometres of the World Championships and it can all be seen on TV.

We've already raced 250 kilometres but I have a Tour and a Vuelta in my legs. I need a Grand Tour in my legs to be competitive over 250 kilometres, mostly because I race a long season. And riding all year with the handbrake on means I haven't been able to dig into my reserves and truly empty myself.

In this moment, I put absolutely everything that I have down on the pedals. I have to increase the gap between me and the two behind, and behind them there are another eight or nine riders who are possibly going to close on them.

The last lap, the last climb of the World Championships is the moment on a bike when it's like being at a rock concert – you cannot hear yourself think. The crowd is going mad, all cheering for their various countrymen.

At four kilometres from the finish a lot of Spanish fans have gathered. As I go past the crowd is completely silent. I go a bit further up and there are a lot of Italian fans and absolutely everyone is in complete silence too.

My father-in-law asked me a year ago, 'Where should we watch the Worlds from in Mendrisio? Acqua Fresca?'

'No, no … La Torraccia is what will matter.'

And so it is. I get to the top where I can hear Chiara and my in-laws. They seem to be the only ones happy to see an Aussie come over the hill solo, in front.

I don't think I've won it yet. Way too early to relax. In 1999 I had been this close to winning a world cross country title and lost it, so I know too well that it's not over yet. I've lost so often by so little in my career that I've learnt never to take anything for granted. It ain't over till it's over, till a medal is being put around your neck. And even then I'd want to check.

Two kilometres to go. I'm alone.

Am I living this moment or am I dreaming it?

There's a motorbike with a TV camera operator following me; it's just me and the motorbike. I keep going as hard as I can, even though I'm pretty sure I can't be caught. As long as the motorbike is with me I've probably got a 30-second gap. I don't look back. I just go.

Riding those last few kilometres I experience a surreal flood of emotions. It's been a year of being talked about as 'the nearly guy', who lost close races, who couldn't win the big ones. Cadel Evans? Great rider, races gritty and clean, gutsy and honest, but keeps getting beaten by tiny margins because of circumstances very often out of his control – whether it's lack of team support or bad luck.

It's been 15 years since I placed second in my first World Championships. There have been many placings since, but tough competitors, circumstances, and sometimes people outside of the race have proved beyond my capabilities to overcome. The elusive 'World Title' has remained elusive for fifteen years.

These setbacks have, unknowingly to me at the time, served as lessons: every loss has something to teach; every period without a victory, every close-but-not-quite result motivates you to work harder and smarter. To an athlete whose very existence is judged by their sporting results, these lows seems like the worst thing in life at the time, but they are the very reason the highs are so high.

FOUR HUNDRED METRES TO go. 'Just keep at it', my key words of advice in moments of difficulty throughout my career.

I keep going and cross the finish line.

I give a kiss toward Stabio, and a kiss to Mendrisio – to thank the people from there who've had faith in me.

The first person I see after crossing the line is the press officer from Cycling Australia, who is standing there crying.

I ride up to her, still in a surreal state, and ask, 'Cadel Evans, World Champion?'

She can't speak at first, then says, 'Yes, yes, yes, yes, yes!'

I'm being pulled and shoved in every direction. Everyone's trying to talk to me, take my photo, hug me, kiss me, get an autograph, get an interview. It's a very intense, unbelievable, moment.

I'm swept along, guided from reporter to drug test to official to the official press conference. I seem locked in a moment I know I'll remember all my life.

This is what redemption feels like. And vindication. Some had relegated me to a pawn, but I have just taken the crown. It's a mix of joy, relief and a certain nasty satisfaction at seeing the disappointment in some of my teammates' faces, who I suspect will feel no joy at all for my win.

CHIARA HAS HITCHED A ride on the photographer's motorbike to get to the finish line from her spot on top of La Torraccia, three kilometres away. We have the photo presentation and the people who've had faith in me are all there. Ruiz, the physiotherapist in Mendrisio, David Bombeke, Ermanno Bossi from the local bike shop, a beaming Aldo Sassi, Dr Squinzi, the owner of the Mapei company, which is sponsoring the World Championships. And, of course, Chiara, who has dedicated herself to motor-pacing me in preparation for this event, and whose support of my cycling career has been invaluable.

La ruota sempre gira. And today my luck has finally changed. To become World Champion is a high point in any road cyclist's career. I tell reporters afterwards, 'The world's been telling me for years I can't win big one-day races because my job is to win stage races, and then today I come out and win the World Championships. I don't quite believe it.'

I've won seven World Championship medals up to this point – junior, Under 23, elite, mountain bike cross-country, road time trial – but I've never been able to win a gold one.

The win changes people's perceptions of me. I'm 32, and once you get over 30 in cycling, if you don't perform then people seem to get the idea that you're too old.

I get back to the team hotel, my roommate, Simon Clarke gives me a hearty handshake. I go and have a shower and then have a quiet but very satisfying beer with David Bombeke. We don't say much, we have no need to.

Later Shayne Bannan makes a speech. He lists all the events Australia has won up until this point. There are quite a few – Stuart O'Grady's Paris–Roubaix, Michael Rogers's World Championships time trial wins, a couple of Hamburg classics with Robbie McEwen, stages in the Tour and the Giro. He congratulates me on a great effort.

The newspapers are reporting I'm the first ever Australian world road champion, but it was Jack Hoobin from Melbourne who won in the amateur division in 1950, when there was a title for both amateur and professional cyclists.

Well done, Jack. Proud to be second.

IT'S LATE IN THE afternoon now. I'm getting a lift home, still in my gear, from my friend Shayne Bannan, who is driving the car of the national team.

The phone rings. Jim Ochowicz.

I know Shayne is going to become the manager of a new ProTour team – which at this point is confidential – so, as always in cycling, it is probably wise not to reveal too many of my plans. So I answer the phone in an anonymous manner and don't mention any names.

Jim says, 'Hey, Cadel, I'm really happy for you. You really deserve this. I wish you all the best with wherever your future takes you.'

'Thanks for the thought,' I say.

It's a gracious phone call and I'm touched, but I sense disappointment in Jim's voice. Without revealing anything to those in the car, I say, 'And that little project that we were talking about? You know, for me this doesn't change anything. For me everything's the same.'

Then I sense a hurriedness. I'm guessing that Jim wants to hang up the phone and call Andy Rihs to say, 'We're still in the game.'

After the race, Chiara hangs the rainbow jersey on the bedroom wall and says, 'If this is still here in the morning, it's all true.' Next morning we wake up and it's still there.

The doorbell rings. It's Italian TV.

'Where's your jersey? What do you mean you're not wearing it?'

'I'm not wearing it because it's up there on the wall.'

I answer some questions at the front gate, then Chiara and I head off to the local café, Molly and a TV crew in tow.

Chiara takes the jersey with her. The whole town is delighted with their adopted Australian. We walk out and everyone in our street is waving and beeping their horns and shouting their congratulations. We go down to the café and get our breakfast.

AND LIFE GOES ON. A week after the Worlds I have to go to Peccioli in Tuscany for the Coppa Sabatini (Sabatini Cup). It's where I did my first race as a *stagiaire* with the Saeco team in 1999. And they give me the same number. It's 10 years almost to the day that I raced here, finishing 12th, I think.

My teammate, Phil Gilbert is racing and I help him out by positioning him for the last short but hard climb up to the finish. And the guys at Lotto are saying, 'Here's the World Champion, pulling the Belgian guy.'

Gilbert wins. All are happy.

A couple of days later I come fourth in the Giro dell'Emilia (in Italy's Emilia–Romagna region), then I race the Giro di Lombardia around Lake Como.

The descents in Lombardy can be dodgy. Some feature one of my pet fears: massive walls on both sides of the road, leaving no margin for error if you come off the bike. And on some of the sharper turns you can't see around the next corner, which always makes me nervous. It's not so much the sharp turns that worry me, it's being blindsided, which can be very dangerous.

That's one of the aspects of cycling that's always intimidated me. The slippery roads in Lombardia aren't great either.

Italian rider, Mauro Santambrogio is away on the last climb – San Fermo della Battaglia is its full name. I know that Mauro is going to BMC next year, but I can't say anything at this point. And here I am, chasing Mauro back, which is kind of a strange way to get to know him.

San Fermo della Battaglia is close to my home in Stabio. I know it quite well because I've trained here a fair bit for the race. I can see Phil Gilbert winning this race if I bring back the breaks.

I go up to Gilbert and ask him, 'How are you?'

'Yeah, I'm good, I'm good.'

I say, 'OK, let's go', so I get on the front and close the gap to Santambrogio and Swede Gustav Larsson. Here I am in my first big race in the rainbow jersey; I don't have the legs to win on my own today, but together Phil and I can win. I pull the break back and I am done for the day.

It's another victory for Silence–Lotto, and I suppose I've won some fans back in Belgium, pulling back the breaks so that Belgian rider Gilbert could win the Tour of Lombardia. I'm happy to work for Phil in the race and finish 10th.

Gilbert is having a streak of wins, including a stage at the Giro, and the overall win at the Ster Elektrotoer in the Netherlands in June. When he's fit and lean he has very well-defined calves, a real natural on the bike. He moves his upper body a lot, looks around a lot. Off the bike he's a real practical joker. When he's racing he's more serious.

I suppose we've had a mixed sort of friendship. The first time we had anything to do with each other, I was in a breakaway at the Tour de France in 2005, and no one wanted to ride with me.

I said to Gilbert, 'No, no, no, I'm not going to attack you on the climb, I'm not going to attack you on the climb.'

And my team director told me, 'You're going to get caught, you're going to have to go away.'

So I convinced Gilbert and the others in the breakaway that I wasn't going to attack them on the climb. But when the situation changed I had to attack the break.

So, of course, I attacked, and he was furious with me for years thereafter.

This finish at the Tour of Lombardy is probably one of our best moments together in a sporting sense, where I was committed to him and he was able to deliver the result that he wanted – that we all wanted.

VELO CLUB MENDRISIO IS the organising club of the World Championship that 'Nostro Australiano di Stabio' ('Our Australian of Stabio') won. This is fitting for a small club renowned for its successful development of junior and under 23 riders.

I am the recipient of the Mendrisio d'Oro (Gold Mendrisio), a prize awarded to the rider judged by Velo Club Mendrisio to be the best of the year. I'm in good company here: others winners have included Greg LeMond, Sean Kelly, Eddy Merckx and Bernard Hinault.

Sean was one of the best Classics riders of all time. From 1977 to 1994 he won nine Monuments and 193 professional races, including Paris–Nice seven years in a row. Now he does the commentary for Eurosport. I like his commentary style; he's very quiet and softly spoken. There are times in the race to be excited and times to stay calm.

They called Bernard Hinault 'The Badger', and some say he was the most talented rider ever. He was a very successful, aggressive rider with a huge personality. Among his 10 Grand Tour victories are five Tour de France titles – 1978, 1979, 1981, 1982 and 1985. In 1978 he scored the Giro d'Italia–Tour de France double before he was 24. His tally of Tour victories is second only to Eddy Merckx's tally of 11, and he is the only rider to have finished in the top two in every Tour de France in which he competed. As the last French winner of the Tour, he remains a legend in his home country.

After my win, I want to thank Ermanno Bossi at the local bike shop, so I ring him to say I'm bringing some things down. I take my ProTour jersey, the World Championship jersey with my race number on it and the bike I won the race on, as well as a yellow jersey from the Tour de France. It's an acknowledgment of his role in my success. The jerseys and the bike are still there.

The priest from the Ghisallo church also writes to me asking whether I'll consider donating a World Championship rainbow jersey to put on the wall. Of course, I'm honoured to. To win a jersey worthy of entering such a sacred place in the world of cycling is maybe one of the least famous but most honourable accomplishments of my career.

In the world of cycling, wearing the rainbow jersey changes your life. After the win, I am asked an annoying number of times: 'Has it changed you?' No – I live in the same house, I do the same training with the same coach on the same roads. The only thing that's changed is that now, everyone perceives me in a different light.

ATHLETE
OF THE MONTH

28
C.EVANS

Cadel Evans

My first time in the media spotlight, *Bicycling Australia Magazine* 1993. This was my first year racing the national mountain bike series. I am riding my first competition-level bike – an aluminium frame with a Shimano Deore XT groupset. By today's standards, the bike was relatively heavy and the forks flexed absurdly, but it was a huge improvement on the equipment I had previously ridden. (Phil Latz/*Bicycling Australia Magazine*)

I look back at a simple but happy childhood. My true passions in life, cars, bikes and food were discovered early.

With my mother Helen in Atlanta after the first ever Olympics mountain bike cross country race in 1996. I was the second youngest rider in the race, riding to ninth. It was not an optimal performance as I was bit overwhelmed by the whole Olympics show.

Wellington, New Zealand, 1997, a breakthrough moment in my career. When people were not expecting it, I came though to win my first ever mountain bike World Cup race at the age of 20 years and 1 month, still the youngest ever male rider to do so. A fact I am proud of.

(Barry Durrant/Getty Images)

At the Sydney Olympics, September 2000. A big day, but a big disappointment –
seventh place. Inexperience cost me and the attention I received at the race was
overwhelming for me. All lessons learned for later. This Cannondale CAAD 5 was
a relatively simple, light and reliable bike. When you got it going on a fast technical
single track it really flew. (Adam Pretty /Allsport)

The Giro d'Italia 2002, in the days before helmets were obligatory. Although I always
preferred to wear a helmet, our Lazer helmets were not the lightest, and in the third
week of my first Grand Tour they gave me neck problems, so on some of the later
mountain stages I raced without. (Reuters/ Stefano Rellandini)

ABOVE: Aldo Sassi in his office – the place where everything was planned, calculated and assessed. The empty chair is the very chair I nearly fell off two days after the 2006 Tour, when Aldo calmly looked up from his calculator and told me that Floyd Landis had been cheating.

(Richard Baybutt)

LEFT: Wearing the *maglia rosa* at my first Giro d'Italia, 2002. This was another breakthrough moment in my career when I proved to the cycling world I could be a serious contender in three-week stage races.

(Franck Fife/AFP/Getty Images)

On the front of my first team time trial at the 2005 Tour de France with the Davitamon Lotto team. It was the first time the guys had to ride a TTT for GC. We finished eleventh, a better result than I expected. (Robert Laberge/Getty Images)

Stage 9 of the 2008 Tour de France, just after the crash that maybe cost me the race. I'm getting patched up by the race doctor. Robbie McEwan was alongside me helping me though the process. (Joel Saget/AFP/Getty Images)

Riding behind Lance Armstrong and Alberto Contador during the 2009 Tour de France. When Armstrong came back to racing, his body looked different, his arms and legs looked much more defined and cut. This year he was missing a team that could ride in the wind for him from the beginning to end, resulting in a lot of crashes for him. (Reuters/Eric Gaillard)

My four-legged therapist, Molly. Chiara brought Molly along to the Tour on a couple of occasions, knowing how therapeutic it was for me. From a year before my first Tour, until a year after my last race, little Molly was the one constant through all of the highs and lows. She succumbed to a tumour a year after I stopped racing. (Patrick Hertzog/AFP/Getty Images)

German photographer, Timm Kölln took this shot for his 'The Peleton' project, seeking to capture the fatigue of Tour riders immediately after they had crossed the finishing line of a stage. Timm asked me to 'Look like you are tired' — I didn't need to pose.

At the 2008 Beijing Olympics with my trademark post-race towel around my neck. It may help deter illness when you are in a run-down state. I did see Bond in one of his earlier movies doing the same thing, so at one point in history it was cool. (Jamie Squire/Getty Images)

ABOVE: Climbing La Torracia during the 2009 World Championships in Mendrisio – one of the best rides of my career. In this moment, I was solely focused on getting absolutely everything onto the road to get me to the finish line as quickly as I could. A dream moment for any cyclist. (Gabriele Putzu/AFP/Getty Images)

LEFT: Finally, 15 years after my first World Championships podium, I got to stand on the top step and receive the jersey. It was well worth the long and arduous journey. (Bryn Lennon/Getty Images)

Crossing the finishing line at Montalcino, stage 7 of the 2010 Giro. This was one of the better rides in my career, a day when all of my cycling experience got put on the road for all to see. (Luk Beines/AFP/Getty Images)

The 2010 Tour was the first opportunity I had to race on cobbles. I would have liked to have tried a Tour of Flanders or a Paris–Roubaix, but having always been on very strong Classics teams, and having so many other goals in the season, I never had the chance until then. (Bryn Lennon/Getty Images)

David Bombeke – 'Da Bomb' – keeping me out of pains way at the 2010 Tour de France. At the Tour, everyone seems to have this desire to touch and grab the riders, making it difficult and quite painful when you are injured, in this case with a fractured elbow. (Tim de Waele/Corbis via Getty Images)

Jim Ochowicz and Andy Rhis, team manager and team owner of BMC Racing Team respectively. Thanks to the faith and vision of these two gentlemen, I had the opportunity to get everything on the road and onto the results sheet with a professional and supportive team. (Tim de Waele/Corbis via Getty Images)

Climbing the Col Du Galibier, stage 18 of the 2011 Tour de France. This was probably my best day at the Tour ever. I drew on every bit of experience from the previous 20 years of racing – a test of strength and calm under pressure. (Tim de Waele/ Corbis via Getty Images)

Racing the individual time trial of the 2011 Tour de France – a day when everything just flowed. Countless hours were spent developing the bike and fine-tuning this racing position. Although it was an extremely low position, the bike still handled very well on the downhills. (Radu Razvan / Alamy)

Immediately after crossing the finish line on the Champs Elyseés in 2011 – the moment I finally let myself accept victory of the Tour de France. The video of the moment still brings a tear to my eye. (AP Photo/Laurent Cipriani)

From this moment onwards, my life changed. (AP Photo/Laurent Cipriani)

At the start of stage 10 of the 2013 Giro d'Italia: one of the more glamorous moments of a pro cyclist career. (Bryn Lennon/Velo/Getty Images)

Final podium of the 2013 Giro d'Italia: To be able to share such a moment with your son is a beautiful thing for a father. (AP Photo/Fabio Ferrari)

Stage 16 of the 2014 Giro d'Italia, a stage that probably should have been cancelled. It is on days like this that an office job sounds very appealing... (Tim de Waele/Corbis via Getty Images)

With good friend Simon Clarke on the start line of my last race, the inaugural Cadel Evans Great Ocean Road Race. Simon was second that day, I finished fifth. (Mark Gunter/AFP/Getty Images)

My last race, my last moment with a race number on. It could not have been a nicer way to finish my competition career. (AAP Image/Jaimi Chisholm)

Celebrating with race winner Gianni Meersman. Racing in Australia was always a pleasure – I feel very welcome, appreciated and respected in my home country. (Con Chronis)

CHAPTER 16

BMC

2009–2010

CYCLING IS AN INTERESTING mix of teamwork and individualism. When you win a race, your team has won as well. You draw on your individual talent and efforts, but they alone can't win you a race. You need to rely on your teammates to play the roles they've been assigned. Everyone is depending on each other.

I once asked the Australian sports psychologist, Noel Blundell, about how we can best reconcile the mentality of the individual athlete with that of a team player. He said I had 'asked the single most difficult question in my profession'.

I've had probably 100 teammates. There are only 500 or so professionals in the ProTour rankings, and only 200 of them score points. So after a while you get to know everyone pretty well.

I've changed teams five times – once with great sadness (when the Mapei team shut down in 2002), and this time with great relief (now that I'm leaving Silence–Lotto for BMC). One was forced, one was fraught. No two experiences of arriving at or leaving a team are the same.

Generally you join a team and your situation as a rider changes. Maybe you increase your capacities, maybe you decrease them.

A lot of team success comes down to money. If they are able to attract quality riders and staff then it's a good base. If you consider the top 20 ProTour teams, there's a strong correlation between the quality of the team and the budget.

But it's not always the money that attracts a rider. You look at what's going to provide you with a good environment to race in. What opportunities will the team offer? Big race starts and good teammates to help you or to work for? A secure long-term future? Is the team organised in the races? Are they organised in looking after health, training, and material needs of the riders? What is the nationality of the team? Maybe a team has a rider, sports director or coach you know and can trust?

In the end you choose the team that's your best option. But first you have to have options; a good rider will have several, while some riders will have only one, and it could be a far from ideal option.

Nearly every team is registered in a particular country, and has a certain degree of bias towards riders of that nationality. Euskaltel, for example, want to have all Basque riders in their team. Astana has a lot of Kazakh riders on their team. The team I'm about to join, BMC, is an American-registered team.

I've always been a foreigner in foreign teams. It's only now that Shayne Bannan is looking to put together an Australian ProTour team that being in an Australian team is a possibility.

As a foreigner in foreign teams, you always have to bring in a few more results than the national riders to receive equal treatment and recognition. It keeps us Aussies hungry, but it is frustrating to see individuals get lazy and complacent due to the easier road that has been paved for them solely because of their nationality.

BMC has a Swiss sponsor, but the main goal of the team is to increase BMC's brand awareness in the American market and it has many American managers, staff members and riders. So while it's an international team, it has a distinctly American mentality – a mentality that has brought some refreshing changes to the world of cycling in the past few years.

Being sponsored by a bike manufacturer brings a number of benefits. We riders have close working relationships with BMC engineers, so modifications, improvements and individual requests for particular equipment are dealt with efficiently. The company is all about cycling, and cycling performance products, which creates an environment much more in line with our personalities as riders than that of a corporation from another sector.

There are 20 teams in the ProTour, and up to 30 riders on each team. All the ProTour teams will race in all the ProTour races, and they'll each field between six and nine riders at each of those races.

I've been on teams with 28 riders where the only place I see teammates is at the meeting at the start of the year and the meeting at the end of the year, because we rode race programs that were completely different. With me being a climber and them being a *rouleur*, we were never sent to the same race.

At Lotto I only ever rode three or a maximum of six races a year with Robbie McEwen: the Tour Down Under, maybe the National Championships or World Championships, and the Tour de France. They were the only races we were both suited to. While I got to know him as a teammate from our time spent together away from the races, I didn't actually race with him very much at all.

THE DAY AFTER THE Giro di Lombardia in October 2009, Matt Lloyd and I race the Coppa Lella Mentasti (Lella Mentasti Cup), a two-man team time trial race in Stresa on the shore of Italy's Lake Maggiore. We come 12th. As soon as it's over, I head to my first BMC team meeting.

It's the first time I've met Andy Rihs, though I know him as the man who went through hell as the owner of the Phonak team, having watched Phonak rider, Floyd Landis's disqualification after having 'won' the Tour de France in 2006.

A successful Swiss businessman, Andy's a big, jovial guy and a passionate cycling fan. His connection to pro cycling goes back to 1998, when he became a shareholder in Grenchen-based bicycle company BMC. Looking to find new ways to provide exposure and increase market share internationally for his company Phonak Hearing Systems (now Sonova), which makes cochlear implants, Andy believed a successful cycling team could achieve that. In 2000, he bought BMC outright and launched the Phonak cycling team (using the slogan 'We race for better hearing').

His plan for exposure worked. Consumer awareness of the Phonak brand grew from 20 to 70 per cent in the six years the team was alive.

When the team dissolved after Floyd's disqualification, it broke Andy's heart. He has said that the moment it was revealed that Floyd had failed a drug test was the worst moment of his life.

However, after just a few months out of the sport, Andy and BMC needed to get back into racing – easily the best way to test and give credibility to high-performance equipment. Andy announced he intended to create a new team that would take the name of his bicycle manufacturing company BMC. Jim Ochowicz came on board as manager and co-owner two years later. And it was in this new team that Andy placed all his hopes and dreams of winning a Grand Tour. And maybe of healing a few wounds along the way.

Andy's determination to build a successful team – US-registered, Swiss-owned and Belgian-managed – was obvious from the start. His enthusiasm for the project was evident the moment you met him.

He could not have been more welcoming to me. We've arranged that this evening I'll be introduced to the other guys in the team as a likely recruit. At this stage, only Jim and Andy know that I might be coming to the team; the others have no idea.

Everyone's sitting there. Andy says, 'We've got one more guy who's coming to the team next year ... Here he is.'

I walk into the room. Here I am, a few weeks in as World Champion. George Hincapie's eyes light up.

I think it's a really nice surprise for him in particular. When we've ridden together on opposing teams I'll see him from a distance. We're friendly but don't know each other well. Now we'll have a chance to ride together.

If George is pleased that I'm joining BMC, I'm happy he's already there. George is a Tour veteran. He knows much more about winning the Tour de France than I do. Having that on my side, after coming from a team that didn't even have a GC rider before I joined, is fantastic.

After the meeting, George and I sit down and chat. We talk until the early hours of the morning.

George asks, 'You'd like to go well in the Tour?'

I look him in the eye. 'George, I have come to this team to *win* the Tour de France.' I say it pretty firmly.

He smiles. 'Yeah, okay.'

George gets a pretty close-up view of my ambition on this night. Maybe my words sound arrogant to him. Confidence can often be misinterpreted as arrogance. I think George has a preconceived idea of who I am and he wasn't expecting this side of me. Competitors can underestimate you, which is more advantageous than most people realise.

I don't know what George did when he rode with Lance Armstrong and I don't want to know. I've never asked him. In 2006 George said that he'd stopped doping and was doing whatever he could to work against that culture. I take his word on that.

A WEEK LATER LOTTO announce that I have exercised the buy-out clause of my contract and will not be with the team next year. It is a hefty purchase, the single most expensive purchase I've made in my life, but I see it as an investment in my future. While speculation goes on about which team I will go to I get the BMC contract thoroughly checked by a lawyer before taking the next step.

I'm waiting at Melbourne airport early Monday morning, ready to fly to a function where I will be surrounded by media, all wanting to know about my future. I'm still waiting for the okay from the lawyer, I am calling Switzerland every five minutes. 'Is the lawyer back from golf yet?' Just as I am boarding the plane, I get through and receive a very welcome 'okay'.

Philippe Gilbert is the first person to ring and congratulate me. He knows what I've been dealing with at Lotto. He says to me, in a sneaky kind of tone, 'Oh, who knows, maybe we'll be teammates again one day.'

I hear a few murmurs in the cycling community: 'Oh, the last years of his career, World Champion, taking the money, going to a pro continental team...' the normal speculation and innuendo newspapers are filled with.

Although I am stepping down from a WorldTour team to the second tier pro continental level, I have done my research, this team has a great future.

After two extremely near misses in two consecutive years, I still see the Tour as unfinished business. I want to give myself every chance I can to go one step better.

Going to a developing team without a licence to ride the Tour de France is certainly a risk. But I look at BMC from a business perspective: from where I stand, all the signs suggest they will succeed. Team BMC are on a strong growth curve, and at the helm is Andy, a proven hard-headed businessman with an appetite and passion for racing success. It's a team that is doing everything correctly and is underpinned by stable economic backing. Its plan is to race in the Tour de France. What's going against it? If the Tour de France organisers assess the merits of giving BMC a start, the case seems pretty strong.

BMC have recruited well. Dutchman, Karsten Kroon, 'KK', is a solid *domestique*. He's a good friend of Stuey O'Grady, who's told me, 'He's an awesome bloke – you'll see.' Stuey's right: Karsten's a funny guy, great company, and a very loyal team member.

Italian, Alessandro Ballan is best known for winning the World Championships in 2008. Like many of the top riders he does not look strong. He has soft-looking legs that aren't particularly defined. Like me, he's quite knock-kneed, and hangs his head very low, his most notable characteristic on the bike.

I've always liked Ale. He's always been friendly, always smiling, and I've always said hello to him at races. And now we're teammates. On the team, I soon grow to like his attitude. He's quite laid-back about his training and racing but he really knows how to race. And getting in position with him in the bunch is great.

When he leads you into the peloton, Ale will take you on a wild ride. I'll often follow him up the side, jumping up on the kerb, ducking under tree branches, dodging mirrors on vehicles and scraping in between riders. Ale does it because he's a good rider and he can. When you're following him he always looks like he's just about to crash, but that's just the way he rides. It's highly effective.

American, Brent Bookwalter, 'BB', is a similar age to me, with fair, sensitive skin, always doused in sunscreen. This unassuming, quiet, polite, thoughtful, well-educated biologist has little experience racing in Europe. Like George Hincapie and others, he's brought an entire audience – that of North America – to the ProTour race circuit. He is a fearless rider. It amazes me how he can use his aero handlebars in time trials, round wet roundabouts and the most technical corners, when most would not think of even having their fingers off the brake levers.

Italian, Manuel Quinziato has a distinctive style on the bike. He has a very long torso and quite short legs for a bike rider. He's very dark and tanned. He loves rock music, and is often seen sitting in the team bus wearing enormous headphones.

Like all good *domestiques*, he's always looking behind to make sure his teammates are where he wants them to be.

He'll say, 'I have to take you here, go here.'

'Manuel, let's just save a bit of energy,' I'll reply.

'No, no, I've got to get you here.'

'No, no, I've got to save energy for the final, hold back a bit, please.'

When we're both riding well, we work really well together.

And joining BMC is the start of a friendship with Swiss rider, Steve Morabito. I first saw Steve when I was feeling completely exhausted in the line at Geneva Airport on our way to the Worlds in '02. He's someone else I've always said hello to. Sometimes I've wondered if we'd be on a team together one day. And now we are, and he becomes one of my strongest friends in cycling.

And then there's a new recruit who's twice come second at the Tour de France and has just become World Champion – me. I'm the first rider since Bernard Hinault who could make a serious play for the yellow jersey while wearing the rainbow jersey.

All of the necessities are in place. Now it's up to us to put it altogether and turn it into results.

THE TEAM HAVE SOME pre-conceived ideas about me. In the world of cycling, rumours and gossip spread quickly. Very quickly. Upon joining a new team, it is your reputation – based on those rumours that precede you.

It's funny to hear rumours about yourself. I assure BMC that I just want to race my bike to the best of my ability.

The only person I do bring over with me is David Bombeke, with whom I've now worked with for some years. David and I make a great team. Though he's an osteopath, David works closely with me in preparation, training and at the races, so he effectively plays the role of a *soigneur*. *Soigner* is French for 'to care for, to look after'. And David cares for me, and everyone on the team for that matter.

As for the rest of the behind-the-scenes team, BMC are being as particular about the staff they recruit as about their riders.

I've worked with a lot of bike mechanics. At BMC I work with chief mechanic Ian Sherburne, and later with Antonio Biron – 'Biro', we call him. Biro goes to all the races with me. He lives reasonably close to me, and is very helpful in keeping the measurements of all of the bikes in order. He is, in my mind, the best mechanic in the world. Every mechanic has a certain amount of ability, but it's how much they want to work that separates a good mechanic from a great one.

Biro knows exactly how I like to have my bike set up and keeps detailed notes to the millimetre: left brake lever, right brake lever – because I have my brake levers at different heights, which is a really unusual thing. I also use two rolls of handlebar tape and gel inserts hidden underneath, just to make things more comfortable. People get onto my bike and ask, 'How do you hang on to it?' because the bars are so big, but they're also very comfortable. And when you're trying to go as fast as you can down truly rough descents, that really matters.

Former cyclist Fabio Baldato, whom I've known distantly for years, comes on board BMC as a race director. Georges Lüchinger is appointed media officer. Both are high-calibre professionals and exceptional people. Both will become dear friends.

Fabio, who rode professionally until he was in his early 40s, is a real gentleman. With his efficiency and his long experience in professional cycling, he is critical to the team. I first met him in 1999 when I was a *stagiaire*, preparing for the Under 23 World Championships. He was one of the few professional riders (other than the Australians) who would say hello to me. It's the sort of thing you never forget, which is a good thing as I may have been the one who decided if he came to the team or not.

Making the transition from rider to sports director is a bit like moving to another planet. As a rider, it's all about the details. If it's raining outside it's *you* who gets wet and cold. If the team need you to use a certain type of saddle that doesn't work for you, it's *you* who literally has to live with the 'pain in the arse'. At the other end of the spectrum, as a sports director you have to think long-term; the budget needs to be allocated carefully to balance young potential and old experience, expensive proven performers and more affordable 'one-hit wonders' who might pull out a big ride once a season. You have to deal with the big picture of up to 30 riders, maybe 60 staff servicing these riders, 150-plus bicycles, 10 to 15 vehicles, plus a couple of trucks and buses.

Riders who have had to rely on tactics rather than exceptional natural talent, and who have a methodical and organised approach to training and racing, often make the best sports directors. Fabio was such a rider, and from what I can see, he is making the transition well.

Georges Lüchinger lives in Liechtenstein, the principality between Austria and Germany. He has worked as a soccer and hockey commentator, and he was the Liechtenstein national team soccer coach for a while, so he has a good perspective on sport at a high level.

Georges is a key reason why I'm able to perform well at BMC. Calmness has always been what I've most needed as a rider and Georges is able to create that environment for me. I feel protected by someone who doesn't need to use aggression to keep things together. In a high-tension world of ruthless timeframes, and demanding riders, directors and media, the man is unflappable. He never panics, he never catastrophises, never sweats the small stuff. He always sees the broader picture.

Georges becomes my liaison with the world. The way we work together is pretty simple. I say to Georges, 'These are my goals; this is my list of priorities.' And he works it out for me.

He understands the psyche of an athlete. He understands how to manage me, and at stressful moments that's invaluable.

The more high-profile I become, the more I need a buffer between me and the many demands of the media. For me, Georges is gold. He is that buffer.

At Lotto I felt like I was being used – told to go and do this interview, do that interview, go here, go there – deceived and manipulated. And I'd try to say, 'Hang on, I'm racing a Tour de France, all my competitors are in the hotel resting quietly and I've got to be here, there and everywhere.'

Georges doesn't operate like that.

He and I both understand that the best way to generate good publicity for the team is to win races, so we don't do much that will compromise that. It's soon evident that Lotto were wrong: I've never needed a bodyguard. What I've always needed is a Georges.

And it helps that he's respected and liked by people in the cycling world, including the cycling journalists. I think that being told 'Not today' by Georges is the most palatable way to have an interview request turned down.

He and I have a pretty efficient way of managing journalists' requests. We try to be available and fair to everyone. Everyone who is not on our 'black list' at least.

THERE IS A GREAT spirit in all parts of the team, and I feel support from the top down. BMC is expecting big things, and so am I.

My first race with the team is the Tour Down Under in Adelaide in January 2010. BMC have been given a wildcard to compete.

The Tour Down Under became a ProTour event a couple of years ago, and is the first ProTour race of the year. It's turned into a very popular event. I find it's kind of like being in the Tour de France, in the sense that you're racing in hot weather, often through vineyards. But there aren't nearly as many traffic jams as there are at the Tour de France.

At the Tour Down Under is where I first come to experience George Hincapie's calmness in tricky moments.

In stage three, I go away over the race's last climb into Stirling, wearing the rainbow jersey. I'm following all the sprinters, including Robbie McEwen and Graeme Brown. 'Brownie', the stocky sprinter from Sydney, can be fiery and unpredictable on the bike, but he's jovial and relaxed when he's off it. He's a big talent from a very successful track background who can't seem to get his full potential onto the results sheet in Europe. Maybe it's down to difficulties of cultural integration, or possibly a love of Belgian pastries.

The finish is really hard. In the last kilometre all the sprinters get dropped. Valverde's watching me and I know what game he's playing: he's waiting for me to launch a sprint so he can use me as his lead out. But I'm thinking, 'No, I'm going to play it your way.'

Suddenly, Manuel Cardoso, the Portuguese national champion, hits out over the top of us to win the stage – his first pro win – and I'm third behind Valverde.

After the race George is chilled out. 'How was your day, Cadel?'

It's like we're chatting about an ordinary day over coffee.

'Valverde pipped me in the sprint, I came in third.'

'*What?!* If I knew you were such a good sprinter I would have helped you more, why didn't you say?'

'Ah, no worries. Next time'

I'M ROOMING WITH MAURO Santambrogio at the Tour Down Under. And the first thing that strikes me is that he sleeps in an AC/DC T-shirt. What the hell?

Ben Stiller's just had a movie out, and looking at Mauro's haircut, his mannerisms and the way he walks, I'm thinking, 'That's Ben Stiller! I'm rooming with Ben Stiller!'

Then by chance we're sitting in the bus, about to start the Tour de France and someone says, 'Um, Cadel, do you mind if Ben Stiller comes into the bus and says hello?'

'No problem,' I say. So Ben Stiller comes in and says hi.

Afterwards I'm thinking, 'Oh, shit, Mauro Santambrogio and Ben Stiller were just in the team bus at the same time and I didn't take a photo!'

IF I HAD TO pick a word to describe the feeling at BMC at this point, it would be 'momentum'. Every day it feels as if we're moving forward. We riders are all getting along well, and the team management make sure things run smoothly. We're becoming stronger, faster, more efficient, more effective.

But you can't expand this quickly without some growing pains.

In the other teams I've ridden with – Mapei, T-Mobile, Lotto – I've seen the things that bring success but I've also seen the things that undo success.

I read an excerpt from Andre Agassi's autobiography, *Open*. He writes about losing a grand slam because he was worried his wig was going to move. It's amazing how at the top level of any sport, the smallest details can undo all the hard work.

In cycling, a moment's inattention can make the difference between winning and losing, being competitive or just being a number in the race, finishing the race on your bike or in an ambulance. It could be a bolt that comes loose, getting too wet and cold, riding on an uneven road and getting a puncture.

And at BMC, small things like inexperienced riders and mechanics working with new equipment present more than the usual range of teething problems. All the hard stuff has been done but they're shaky on some of the little details – the little details that can put you out of a race.

In February, a rider in the breakaway in the Tour du Haut Var in southern France gets dropped when his seat slides down. Another can't sprint because his handlebars move after hitting a large pothole. Simple things, but correct torque settings and appropriate carbon-fibre binding products take a little time to master in the adverse early-season European conditions.

Not that these things hold us back for long. Noises are made and the problems are soon fixed.

IN MARCH WE'RE IN a few season-opening races. The first is Strade Bianche (White Roads) – a beautiful race to ride as a lead-up to Tirreno–Adriatico, and perfect for testing equipment and bike setup for the Giro d'Italia. It's in the Tuscan hills around Siena and you're riding on beautiful roads; the gravel on the roads is quartz so they really are white.

This one-day professional race only started in 2007. I've heard about it, read about it, and thought, 'That's a race I'd like to ride one day, even if only for the curiosity factor.'

What I find so interesting about Strade Bianche is that it evokes the old days of cycling, how the sport was 50 or 80 years ago, before they rode on asphalt. And of course gravel roads have less traffic so they allow more possibilities for cycling through beautiful countryside. It has inspired a whole new type of bike designed to go on gravel roads. I don't know what came first – the amateurs riding on the gravel roads or the fans watching the pros ride on the gravel roads and then going and doing it themselves.

Strade Bianche is also a very competitive race. A lot of the top Classics riders are there racing to win, not because it's a big race, with points, or because of pressure from teams and media to perform, but because they love to ride nice races. It's so refreshing to see. You go there and Alessandro Ballan, Fabian Cancellara, Slovak, Peter Sagan, Greg Van Avermaet and Philippe Gilbert, big Classics riders, are all racing flat out for the win.

'FABIO, *TI DISPIACE SE guido io*?' I ask Fabio Baldato if it's OK if I drive. '*Per meglio capire il percorso.*' To understand the course better.

It's a rainy morning outside the little medieval hilltop town of Montalcino in Tuscany. I love this town and its justifiably famous Brunello red wine, but today it's all business.

I've just raced the Strade Bianche and it's a couple of days before the start of the Tirreno–Adriatico. The BMC team have gathered for some course reconnaissance for the Giro, three months away. It's the first of many course recons Fabio and I do together and the beginning of a very close friendship.

Fabio looks over at me. 'You want to drive? Sure, you can drive.'

It's probably the first time he's been asked this by a rider. I've arrived on the team with a reputation for meticulous preparation, so Fabio's not all that surprised. We swap seats.

'Can you take some video of the corners?'

I tell Fabio I want video of the start of each section of dirt so I can watch the videos back on the morning of the race as a small reminder of what is ahead.

'OK, sure,' he says. I sense a note of doubt in his voice.

As we drive along I am getting a feel for where to and how much to brake for the corners, shifting the car manually to get a better sense of the gradient of the climb, marking parts of the course mentally, like I did for years as a mountain biker.

The next day I ride the same course on my bike, checking out the stage. I ride the last kilometre five times. I lock this information away, along with what I learnt yesterday.

Fabio and a couple of other guys from the team are having espressos at a little café beyond the finish line. I finish my recon and ride to the café.

The guys are getting ready to leave. Fabio's got a cheeky grin on his face. He looks up from his coffee. 'So have you learnt the corners yet?'

I smile. 'Yep. Learnt the corners. All good now.'

The guys at BMC are going to have to get used to me and my leave-nothing-to-chance style: the way I'm going to try to help BMC win a Grand Tour.

It's innate in me, and it's been reinforced by Aldo: preparation is everything. The more of it you do, the more you can control the variables. And there are a lot of variables in cycling. What did Benjamin Franklin say? 'If you fail to prepare you are preparing to fail.' It's what I've based my career on, ever since I started giving myself points in the performance diary when I was a teenager.

All the BMC guys know is that the new guy in the team has brought a new way of thinking, a new approach, one that I'm convinced is going to help shape the team for the next five years.

THE TIRRENO–ADRIATICO IS A good race to do because it usually features a team time trial that is useful preparation for the Tour de France.

A pro stage race in Italy, the 'Race Of The Two Seas' (running from the Tyrrhenian to the Adriatic), is among the first stage races of the season. It's a favoured preparation for the classics riders in anticipation of Milan–San Remo.

I'm looking forward to finally being able to race in the Tirreno. I've wanted to ride it for my entire career. I haven't been deeply involved in racing the Classics, but I like the idea of having a go at the Tirreno's steep, short climbs, and being away from the bad weather of the Paris–Nice cannot be a bad thing.

Finally I come to BMC and I get to choose the races I want. And so in 2010 I get to go to the Tirreno–Adriatico, and in the rainbow jersey.

'Oh yeah,' they say, 'we're going to do a stage race', and they go in with no expectations. It's the team's first WorldTour stage race and thanks to George Hincapie's sharp eyes, I sneak in for third overall.

One day after a stage Ivan Basso comes up to me. He says, 'You have good equipment.'

And it's not just the bikes he's referring to. It's also our MAN bus (as in the German brand name). MAN is known to make the best buses, and the most expensive. You don't go and buy a MAN bus if you're putting together an inferior team. These are the kinds of small details that show Andy is in this for the long term.

On the road we are now performing well together. People see we're at the front and riding well. In George Hincapie, I'm seeing first-hand what a great *domestique* and road captain is, and as Brent Bookwalter and Micky Schär gain experience, I can have complete trust in them too. I feel I can leave my GC in their hands, which has a transformative effect on my riding.

George's attitude towards me changes when we start racing together; he soon ditches his preconceived ideas. We begin to develop a strong mutual respect and a great bond for what I think will be a very long-lasting friendship.

George has a nice style on the bike, and moves through the peloton easily, thanks to his skills but also because he's highly respected by his peers. The main angle I see of George in the peloton is looking behind to make sure I'm OK on his wheel. He becomes my closest and possibly most effective support rider, an extra tactical mind, and most importantly of all, an extra set of experienced and focused eyes on the road.

He's such an integral part of this stage of my career. He's the man who's established the good mentality that BMC has, and the true gentleman of the peloton. I have nothing but compliments for him – the way he prepares and conducts himself as a professional is exemplary. When he rides with us he is the first guy to go to bed and the first guy to breakfast in the morning; the first guy to say no to having a glass of wine with dinner and the one who always refuses dessert. He's a great influence on the mentality of the team as a whole.

I admire him on two levels: as a person he's warm, friendly and polite, and as a rider he has so much ability that he sacrifices for his team.

He'll come up to me in a race and say, 'Hey, we should go in front, these guys are doing something.' Or, 'I feel a bit uneasy about being behind these guys so let's move up.'

And George will take me up; we'll move up out of the wind and we'll sit in position. George is very well respected in the peloton and we move up in a group of three or four. Other teams will let us in because they know we mean business, and we're not just in front to be on TV, we're in front to do something in the race.

I've become a point of reference in the peloton for where to position and when to ride in front. I know this because in some races, riders are focused just on me. They follow me. I don't miss too many splits or important moves. Thanks to experience, I have a reasonable sense of safety and energy conservation. On a few occasions I have even had riders angry at me when for some reason, I haven't made, or choose not to make, an important move.

In my role as a GC guy, I've always had to concentrate for every second of the race: I've had to watch every breakaway, I've had to watch for the chance of a crosswind, a narrow crossing, a dangerous section. It's very fatiguing but it's how I've learnt to position so efficiently. I've often needed to risk being badly positioned in the peloton, because I won't have the energy to be there at the end if I don't roll the dice with some audacious moves.

Now all of a sudden at BMC, I can allow my concentration levels to drop because the other guys have my back. And because I don't have to concentrate nearly as much, in the moments when I do, I'm so much fresher mentally. I can focus so much better and perform so much better. Riding with a team that's willing and able to complement me makes so many new things possible.

AFTER A STAGE OF the Tirreno I call Aldo.

'How are you, Aldo?'

He says, 'I don't feel well, I've got a bad headache.'

I call him the next day at the office. They tell me, 'Aldo didn't come in today, he's got a headache. Call back tomorrow.'

I'm a bit concerned. I think, 'Hope he's OK.' From my own experiences with headaches, if you have to go home, it's pretty bad.

The next day I call the office again.

Terrible news. They tell me the doctors found a tumour, and that Aldo's in the hospital having brain surgery.

What?!

It's all happened so quickly. Turns out they found four tumours.

I can't get my head around it. I can't believe this has happened to such a life-force of a man, a man whose whole professional life has been devoted to helping others improve themselves, become stronger, be able to do superhuman things on a bicycle, be the best athlete they can be.

Aldo, for all he taught me about training and fine tuning my body for road racing, above all has been the man who has always been there for me when others haven't. The low points of one's career are when you really need support.

They remove the tumours but they are not sure if Aldo is clear of the cancer.

A few weeks later I call him.

He says, 'Cadel, no matter what, we're going to win this Tour de France, even if it's the last thing I do in my life.'

THE TEAM IS GROWING, hoping to go into the ProTour. They've requested a wildcard entry to the Tour de France this year; Andy and Jim have been in discussions about it for over a year.

In April, a week before the Amstel Gold Race in the Netherlands, I'm at a camp in Sierra Nevada, Spain, training for the Giro d'Italia. I'm riding up the climb, right past the place where I was gapped by Valverde during the botched wheel change in the Vuelta six months earlier. David Bombeke is following me in the car.

I have a tiny robust waterproof mobile in my pocket. I hear it vibrate. It's a text message. Almost no one's got this phone number, so if a message comes it's probably important, and I often check it even if I'm riding at threshold up a climb.

I'm thinking, 'That's right, they're announcing who the Tour de France team wildcard entries are today. Better have a look.'

The text says BMC has been granted a wildcard entry.

Great. One less doubt in our minds. I breathe a sigh of relief and continue on for the remaining 15 kilometres up to the hotel.

I LIKE GOING TO the one-day Amstel Gold in Holland mostly to get my legs going for Flèche Wallonne and Liège–Bastogne–Liège. I've raced the Amstel Gold twice before and know the course quite well.

This year I ride with Dutchman, Karsten Kroon, who is a great fun guy to have on the team. KK used to ride with the Dutch Rabobank team, that I know like to criticise inconsequential details, so when he gets taken right past the entire Rabobank team by one foreign teammate who happens to have a rainbow jersey on, and delivered to the exact spot where he needs to be, KK is pretty happy. Afterwards KK tells me it's the best positioning he's ever had in the Amstel Gold Race. He goes on to get ninth. He is as proud as punch to be on TV for his family and friends. I am more than happy to be there for someone else, without the expectation of team results on me.

Holland has fantastic infrastructure for commuter cyclists. But this means it's very dangerous for pro cycle races, because they have so much of what we call 'road furniture' – so many things to crash into. There are lane dividers everywhere, and every town you enter has a narrow descent with a speed hump to slow down traffic. You just have to ride in the middle of the lane, and if someone doesn't crash in front of you or beside you, you're going to be OK.

But as Karsten says to me, 'At least in the Netherlands you know when the obstacles are coming, as opposed to Belgium, where they're just random.'

A FEW DAYS AFTER the Amstel Gold I go to the Ardennes Classics without much racing but with a lot of training in my legs, and it all comes together. I race the Belgian Classic La Flèche Wallonne and win, having jumped ahead of Contador within the final 100 metres of the climb up the Mur de Huy. Contador is second, Joaquim Rodríguez third. I'm at my best in anticipation of the upcoming Giro, and I've taken the time to check out the course in training with sports director John Lelangue. When I did the finish at training speed, I saw that I could start my sprint much later. So I do, and it's BMC's first win for the season.

While the race has gone well for me, unfortunately, Karsten has had a horrible crash. I don't know what happened but he has the biggest bruise on his face afterwards.

I only find out how badly injured Karsten is later. In the race I've gone back to the car and I've asked John Lelangue, 'Is Karsten OK? I heard he had a crash.'

'Yeah, yeah, he's OK,' he says.

Then straight after crossing the finish line, I'm asked by a journalist about Karsten. 'Oh, he's OK, he's fine,' I say, because I've been told he is. I've been given the information that Karsten is

'OK' – 'OK' in this sense being 'Well, he had to go in an ambulance, he went to hospital, but he's going to live.'

So the quote from me in the newspaper the next day? 'Oh, Karsten? Yeah, he's fine.' And there's a picture of him with half his face swollen up like a football, bright purple.

But that's bike racing. In the culture of racing there's a language that's used. If you have a crash and then get up and ride you're 'OK'. If you don't, you're 'not OK'. Basically that's how it goes. 'Not OK' could be broken arm, broken shoulder, broken face, broken leg, unconscious ... or worse. Getting up and riding, maybe with bruises, maybe with lost teeth, maybe a broken bone, you're 'OK'. Race 'communication', the yelling that goes on between rider and director at 40 to 50 kilometres an hour, is nothing like other forms of communication we're used to in this 'communication age'.

It is a good result for the team, but with Karsten's crash and injuries it was a mixed day. Later at the hotel I get in the lift to go down to dinner quite satisfied with our win when Jim gets in, 'We have had a positive.' It took me a while to register. What?! Who?! Thomas Frei has tested positive for EPO and is out of the team. Of course my mind goes to the possible consequences. Could this affect the future of the team? After the investment I had made to get here, it's a real concern.

Despite this setback, winning a Classic in the rainbow jersey is special, something that hasn't been done for quite a while. I become the fifth rider to win the Flèche in the rainbow jersey, joining Ferdinand Kübler (1952), Rik Van Steenbergen (1958), Eddy Merckx (1972) and Claude Criquielion (1985). Most of all I'm happy to get some results that will put an end to the 'curse of the rainbow jersey' talk that bores me to tears.

WE BACK THIS UP with a good showing at the Liège–Bastogne–Liège, where I come fifth.

It's a relief to have broken through in the Spring Classics, and again, it puts a lot of work into my legs for the Giro d'Italia, now just a couple of weeks away. A Grand Tour requires five or six months of training and four to six weeks of specific work at altitude and recon work on the stages themselves.

It'll be my first Grand Tour with my new team. But the closer we get to the race the more exposed I feel. Earlier in the month the team are forced to suspend Alessandro Ballan and Mauro Santambrogio, after they were linked to an investigation into doping at their former team, Lampre. Then just before the race starts, Steve Morabito comes down with the flu, and pulls out. Our number of experienced riders is being reduced by the day.

Our preparation becomes a bit messy towards the end. As we're squeezed for time, Brent Bookwalter and I go directly from the Ardennes Classics to a mini training session on Passo del Tonale, the finish for stage 20. We pick up Mauro on the way. Because I understand Italian and English, I spend four hours in the car on the phone to his lawyer and the BMC team lawyer, who are trying to rectify the situation. I'm already exhausted from the week of racing in the Ardennes; now I'm getting very frustrated. It amazes me how some fully-grown adults cannot look after themselves, but if I don't take care of Mauro's affairs, nobody will.

Things pick up after this. We stay in a nice hotel on top of the Passo del Tonale and train well. In the end Mauro's suspension is lifted and he's allowed to race. Ale Ballan won't be racing, but he comes up and stays with us too, to train and say hello.

As we're descending the Passo di Gavia and passing through the town of Ponte di Legno, there's a small wedding taking place. The bride and groom see my rainbow jersey and wave and cheer. It's the rainbow effect ... and hopefully a good omen for the coming Giro ...

CHAPTER 17

THE CURSE OF THE RAINBOW JERSEY?

2010

AT THE GIRO IT'S just like any other season: I'm here to do my best and get the most out of myself for me and my team. The only difference is I have a different-coloured jersey this year.

The team get off to a pretty good start. Brent Bookwalter, at his first Grand Tour, is second in the opening prologue in the Netherlands, which is won by Brad Wiggins. I'm third. It's a great learning experience for Brent.

The next day Brad Wiggins gets held up, Brent gets held up and I go into the pink jersey.

But we don't have a team who can support a pink jersey.

We're already three riders down, and the other experienced riders, like George Hincapie, have been entered into the Tour of California. That race is very important for BMC as an American-registered team.

In stage three, with 10 kilometres to go, I'm looking good, then I come round a corner and the whole Sky team has crashed. I lose around 40 seconds, along with the *maglia rosa*; it's taken by Alexander Vinokourov.

Stage seven is 220 kilometres from Carrara to Montalcino, racing for 50 kilometres along the Tyrrhenian coast then inland towards Pisa and the first climb at the town of Volterra. In the pouring rain.

The hilly finale of the stage takes in the famous *strade bianche*, usually dusty but today slippery in the rain. I've prepared for this well. I know exactly what tyres I'm going to use and I've organised to have a bike specially set up for the gravel roads, and another for the fast new asphalt leading to the gravel. The team have prepared two other bikes, which sit on top of the car ready for me to use later.

The right equipment is going to be critical today. Tyre selection is a tricky call and depends on the race. Cycling is all about efficiency. In a one-day race, you can take a risk because you're there for all or nothing. But when you're in a three-week tour racing for classification it's also about consistency and reliability. One puncture at a bad time means your three weeks are going to be compromised.

As a GC rider you have to be more conservative and go with a surer bet, which means heavier tyres, despite their higher energy cost. You need to put reliability before performance. The priority is not losing time overall, as opposed to going for lighter tyres and risking everything just for the stage win.

I choose a light, fast setup so I'm fresher for the important part of the race. A lot of the others are riding their 'Paris–Roubaix' tyres – special tyres that resist punctures in a 'cobbled classic' – with heavy wheels, which have a higher rolling resistance and therefore use more energy. They're designed for the slippery, rough cobbles in the famous French stage race.

I think they've chosen the wrong tyres. Many agree. Before the stage start my competitors are looking at the equipment I've chosen. They see I've got aero wheels and fast, light tyres. I think they're thinking, 'OK, Cadel's riding the fast stuff, so we'll do that too.' I notice some go and start madly changing their wheels or tyres at the last minute.

Inside I smile. There's something gratifying about seeing your own race procedures mimicked so faithfully.

IT'S RAINING HARD AS we ride off. Visibility is poor, sometimes nonexistent, and the course is misleadingly marked.

But the preparation is paying off. And saving that little bit of energy on lighter, faster tyres is making a big difference in the final.

Because of my mountain-bike background on the dirt, I know that bikes behave very differently in the wet. Brakes and gears do not work as well, visibility is terrible. You have to let the bike go where it wants to, and you basically steer with the rear wheel. It's kind of like a Motocross rally. It's a classic mountain bike day.

The BMC brakes are so good and you can go very fast on the descents. We are using Easton wheels and SwissStop brake pads made in Mendrisio. The brake surface is smooth and consistent and the brake pads are so adhesive you can brake really hard with them. It's useful in the wet. Andy Rihs always says, 'I don't want a rider to say they were disadvantaged by equipment.'

Coming into the last three kilometres of the stage, I'm at the front. Alexander Vinokourov and Damiano Cunego are with me and Cunego knows what he wants: to get to my wheel in the final sprint. Vinokourov is also trying to stay behind me for the sprint. They both want to stay behind me, but *I'm* trying to get behind *them*.

Cunego is there for the stage. I'm there for GC, so I have to keep us moving to maintain the gap behind, but he knows this so he's trying to work me over to win the stage.

Heading into Montalcino, we get to one of the corners where I've done the recon with Fabio. I can't see much in the pouring rain. I'm so glad I did the recon because it means I'm able to feel my way forward.

I'm trying to stay with Cunego. But he's misled by the confusing signage and bad conditions and goes the wrong way. I don't follow him, relying on my memory of the final kilometres rather than what I can actually see. In the rain and the fog I'm thinking, 'I'm sure I've got to turn right here somewhere.'

I go on the front way too early. It's *pavé*, and I know there's a chance I could crash, because these stones are slippery and dangerous. In this situation, leading out early is safer.

Cunego's back on my wheel and he's probably thinking, 'Oh, this is great. Here I am being led out by the GC rider.'

I come into the last kilometre. I know the last corner because of my recon. The last left turn up to the finish looks intimidating, but with a good line and a bit of risk it is possible to take it flat out and carry the speed through to the line.

I'm thinking, 'Damiano, if you can follow me around this last corner you deserve to win.'

He can't, and he doesn't. I make the last corner, and my speed and momentum allow me to stay in the big chainring and maintain my gap to the line.

I've won the stage. I'm dirty, wet and cold, but I'm happy because by winning the stage I've jumped from 16th to second on GC. Perfect, on a day that will be remembered by aficionados for years to come.

The photos from that stage of me soaked through and covered in mud have become quite famous. It has come to be known as 'the mud stage'. People have commented on the grit and determination I must have had to summon up to win in such conditions. I'll let that myth continue to be perpetrated, because I wouldn't want to rewrite history. But for now I'm just pleased that our careful preparation came together so well. Andy and Aldo will be proud of this.

THE PLEASURE OF HAVING ridden a clever strategic stage is short-lived. Two days later, straight after stage nine to Cava de' Tirreni – won by Australian Matthew Goss – I start to feel feverish. 'Why am I so tired?' I ask the team.

I get back to the hotel and crash onto the bed in my wet clothes, unable to move. It's only the second time ever that I've been unable to take off my bike clothes to go to bed. (The first was after Floyd Landis's incredible performance in stage 17 of the 2006 Tour.)

Then I keep having to go to the bathroom. It's a long and horrible night. By 2am I'm leaking everywhere, throwing my pyjamas in the bin while my roommate Mauro Santambrogio snores in the bed beside me. I'm trying to be as quiet as possible, knowing the strict code of never waking a sleeping athlete. It's one of the times when I wish I had my own room.

Next day I wake up hot and sweaty. I make my way gingerly to the breakfast room. I eat a bowl of white rice – good carbs, and with its neutralising effect it won't upset my stomach further. I probably shouldn't, but I can't *not* have a coffee.

While I'm eating my white rice I bump into Italian rider Gilberto Simoni, who's doing his last Giro d'Italia. Gilberto notices the rice. He has the good radar of an experienced rider.

'You're sick, aren't you?'

'Nah, I'm fine.'

'You're sick.'

Of course I'm trying to hide it. Vulnerability is what your competitors can use. I'm sweaty and weak, and that's before I've pushed a pedal.

I go and see the doctor. He tells me I have a temperature of 39 degrees and that I shouldn't start. 'You should probably go home,' he says. But he leaves it up to me to decide.

It's a lot to throw away. I tell the doctor I'll just start and I'll see what happens.

I put three pairs of extra shorts in my rain bag. I'm a bit scared that I'm going to have a bit of an attack while wearing the rainbow jersey, and if I stop on the side of the road the TV's going to follow me. I'm not thrilled at the idea of footage of me running across the fields to the bushes to answer a *serious* call of nature.

Somehow I get through the stage – finishing 32nd – and hang on to my second placing on GC.

But it doesn't help that stage 11 the next day is the Giro's longest: a one-kilometre ride to sign on and a 256-kilometre stage. And to really cap it off, the weather is appalling. What the hell?

The sign-on to the stage is three kilometres away from the team parking, so we decide we'd better leave early.

I'm not feeling great. I'm heavy and sweaty. Even riding to the sign-on I'm scared I'm going to get dropped because I'm so weak with fever. Naturally I want to avert that embarrassment.

Then we're told, 'Neutral's at 10 ks.' Ten kilometres to the official start of the race.

Then after 10 ks, 'Neutral's been extended, it's going to be at 14 ks.'

So we're riding along ... 14 kilometres ... 15 ... 16 ... 'OK, we're coming up to kilometre zero.'

No – neutral's actually around 20 kilometres away. So we've ridden 23 kilometres before we even start the race.

Then the stage begins.

Vinokourov still has the *maglia rosa*, but his team's not controlling the race. Then the attacks start happening.

We get about 20 kilometres into the race and a breakaway goes off with 56 riders in it. I see Richie Porte go in there. I think, 'This is a dangerous breakaway.'

I can barely see in front of me and I'm feeling like hell. Australian, Richie is sixth on GC, in the front group. It's his first Grand Tour.

The riders gradually fall away till there are around 40 left in the breakaway. I believe Vinokourov is waiting for me to react with my team to close the gap, but I'm not going to put my team on the front because if they start riding I might get dropped.

He's probably waiting for *me* to do something and *I'm* waiting for *him*.

Even with the fever I manage to stay in the GC group. David Bombeke is driving behind in a Volkswagen Caravelle van doing 30 kilometres an hour, knowing I'm sick and thinking that I'm going to pull out any moment.

So we ride to the first major climb. It starts hailing, there's a bit of snow around and it's a pretty miserable day. Mauro Santambrogio, riding behind me, pulls out of the race. It's too much for two others in our team, who also pull out. Wow, if only they knew what *I'm* going through and *I* haven't stopped yet.

Here I am, high temperature and not sure I can even make it to the finish, and there are still 40 guys in front. There's no one to ride behind because half the peloton has been dropped.

Eighty kilometres to go. All the GC riders are thinking, 'We're going to have to ride here, everyone's going to ride.'

Stefano Garzelli, who's eighth on GC, says, 'We've got to do something.'

I say, 'No, I'm not riding, I'm sick.'

He says, 'No, no, we've got to ride.'

So the first 12 on GC start riding together. Competitors are riding for each other to save the race. If we don't, we're all out of GC.

I can do turns at the front but I can't pull. I'm just too weak.

At 10 kilometres to go, the computer says I've ridden around 280 kilometres. On paper it was a 256-kilometre stage. It was three kilometres to ride to the sign-on, the neutral was more than 20 kilometres so it's about 290 kilometres on the bike today – mainly in the snow and rain. And according to the doctor I should have gone home yesterday.

The break's down to eight minutes from 20, so by this time the breakaway has already finished. Richie Porte's got an eight-minute lead and takes the pink jersey.

I first met Richie in September 2009, when he was reserve for the Road Worlds team. He comes across as shy and very reserved. Suddenly finding himself in the *maglia rosa* at his first Grand Tour, Richie has come to the fore quickly.

I cross the finish line in 52nd position. There's still pouring rain and it's cold.

David Bombeke rushes up to me and asks, 'Are you OK?'

Poor David has spent 10 hours in the car today, as miserable as I was probably. Expecting I would pull out any minute, he was on hand ready to take me to the hotel or hospital.

OVER THE NEXT FEW days I start to do better. I place second in stages 15 and 16, and work my way back to fourth on GC.

But in stage 19, from Brescia to Aprica over the formidable Passo del Mortirolo, my luck turns again.

Once more, I'm doing what I think is the right thing in choosing my gearing, not looking at what the others are using. But this time it works against me. The Liquigas–Doimo team – which includes top GC riders Ivan Basso and Vincenzo Nibali – all have smaller, compact gearing. And because of this they can ride in a more varied rhythm.

The weather at the Giro can be bizarre at times. Here we are, riding down a valley, and it's 25 degrees and humid. Then we ride up to the top of Mortirolo and it's raining and eight degrees. With all the sickness I've had, I'm already at my limit, and riding with the wrong gearing puts me over that limit. So just near the top of Mortirolo I get dropped.

I come to the first corner and I haven't used my brakes for the whole climb because I've been riding uphill in the warm. All of a sudden it's cold. At BMC we use fantastic brake pads, but there's an incredible difference between how they behave when they're cold and when they're warm. When they're warm you don't have to brake till the last possible second.

I'm trying to bridge back to the group so I'm going as fast as I can. Suddenly I've got no brakes. I start going right off the road and nearly crash into a camper that's parked there.

We do a lap around the valley and finish in the town of Aprica. I'm three minutes off the lead and finish the stage in sixth place. The three Italians in the break hold the gap. How they managed to stay away, I'd like to know, but there was no television coverage and no way of finding out.

The next day, racing from Bormio, there's a headwind up the valley leading to the final climb up the Passo del Tonale. On the climb, I've ridden three kilometres solo from the GC group, trying to bridge across to the breakaway. Johann Tschopp is in the lead, and I've come into the last 500 metres and seen him just ahead. He finishes six seconds in front of me.

I finish the Giro fifth on GC and win the points competition. I can't deny I'm disappointed. If I'd stayed healthy I could have been so much more consistent throughout. It's one of those times where I wonder what could have been.

Ivan Basso wins, David Arroyo takes second, Vincenzo Nibali is third. Nibali was called up at the last minute to ride the Giro, then *Boof!* he comes third, and everyone's saying, 'How could you do that?' But he's been performing at a much higher level than I have. I've been on a pretty downward spiral, my body exhausted and unable to recover from illness. As my performances in the Grand Tours have been diminishing, his have been on the rise.

Personally I'm disappointed, but I'm really proud and happy for the team after our good showing. It reinforces Jim Ochowicz's message when I joined: 'If you do everything right, the results will come.' At Lotto it was 'You didn't win. You have to win, you have to win.' That's not a healthy attitude for athletes to have. It puts unnecessary pressure on them, especially the ambitious self-motivated athlete.

What BMC are smart enough to realise is that the sport is evolving. In this period, races are becoming closer, small details make the difference between podium or no podium, winning or losing. We've demonstrated at the Giro that thoughtful and strategic use of equipment and course preparation can make that difference.

It's how I want to think of myself as a rider – coping well with varying conditions and terrible weather. Before my win in stage seven I was smart and experienced in the preparation of my equipment, and during the stage I was patient and waited for the right moment. I won not just with brawn but with brains as well.

BMC's aim is to test their equipment in the toughest conditions at the highest level to develop the best possible bikes. So doing this meticulous equipment preparation and bringing it all together to win in those conditions, probably the filthiest conditions of any race of the year, are the things we're really about as a team and a company.

I go home and start getting myself ready for the Tour de France. I have five weeks to get myself right, two of which will probably be spent getting the Italian grit out of my skin.

AFTER MONTHS OF BUILD-UP to three weeks of waking up each morning and asking myself: 'What's on today? Is it an important day? Is it a *very* important day?' With the answer arriving in a flood of adrenalin that gets me through the day.

For four or five days following a Grand Tour, I wake in my bed and think, 'What day is it?' I feel Molly asleep on my feet and realise that it's over. I roll over and try to go back to sleep.

Physically, my body is tired. Mentally, my mind is exhausted. It is a struggle just to put cycling clothes on to go for a ride. But once I am out on the bike, I can ride the big chainring up any climb I choose to do. My mind demands rest, but my legs cannot stand to go without a workout for very long. My body can work, if my mind can push it.

After my first Tour in 2005 I said to Robbie McEwen, 'I can't wait to get home. Just, you know, to go for a walk with the dog, relax and not have a schedule.'

Robbie looked at me. 'When I get home, I'm sitting on my couch and I'm not getting up for a long time!'

Not many people in the world are able to do what professional cyclists do. It's a truly gruelling sport, which is part of its great appeal both to us riders and to cycle fans. Part of the satisfaction of watching professional cycling is being amazed by this level of aerobic and mental endurance. The question is always hovering, 'How are they doing this?' Followed by the thought, 'I am glad it's not me.'

It's not really natural doing what we riders do. You ask so much of your body and mind and it almost always responds dutifully. And then you take a breath for a moment and reconnect with the world, and eat a brioche with your coffee in a tiny act of rebellion, before having to start preparing to do it all again.

Because it's time to refocus: the Tour de France is just around the corner.

BY JUNE, ALDO'S HEALTH is in a frightening decline, but still he pushes on, preparing me for the Tour. 'I'm going to work at this like it's my last Grand Tour, because it probably is,' he scares me by saying.

He suggests I go to an altitude training camp; we choose Valais, Switzerland, where Steve Morabito lives. Aldo sends me out to do some tests. The specs sound savage.

'Aldo, I don't know if I can do that,' I tell him.

He looks at me with a shrug. 'Well, if you can't do this, forget about the podium at the Tour de France.'

OK, now he has my full attention.

I go out on my bike and warm up on the flat. I give all of my spare clothing to Fabio who is following me in the car as if I am in a race, then I head to the climb, hit the 'SET' button on my SRM and start the test.

For the first ten minutes I can maintain the required power, but once I go above 1200m altitude, I am absolutely flat out staying near the target outputs.

I do good roll out and return to the hotel. I call Aldo. He tells me, 'Take a two day rest and try again.'

'Two days rest? Isn't it better to train?'

'Try again in two days. Call me then.'

I go back two days later, do the same warm up, go the same climb, hit the 'SET' button and go...

It's 20 minutes of high-powered output. And when I say 'high-powered', there are probably 10 people in the world who could do it on a good day.

In the first part of the test I'm right on target to hit Aldo's benchmarks. But right at the top of the mountain a car pulls out in front of me and scrambles my time.

Later I download the power files and email them to him. I explain about the car. I'm nervous as I wait for his reply. Whether I can admit it to myself or not, if Aldo says I can't make it to the podium of the Tour, then I know I won't be.

Aldo writes back to me, saying, 'That's good enough.'

THERE'S A LOT OF talk in the press about why no one in this generation has won two Grand Tours in a year. Well, maybe there's not enough time to recover from a monster race in May before racing in a similarly gruelling event in July. Maybe there's not enough time to balance recovery, work and tapering your loads towards such a draining race. These days it takes six weeks to do it properly, and the races are just five weeks apart.

Despite many attempts, no one has been able to repeat Pantani's double of 1998. (Not that anyone wants to imitate his mysterious death from a cocaine overdose on my birthday in 2004, after years of persistent doping allegations.)

Aldo's reason for being, professionally speaking, is to coach an athlete and see him win the Tour on training alone. I want to be that athlete.

AFTER RECOVERING WELL FROM the Giro, Steve Morabito and I had a brief, quiet but effective training camp up in the Swiss Alps. The Tour came around quickly but working in solitude and tranquillity, we were recharged and ready.

The tour starts with a prologue in Rotterdam. Lance Armstrong gets fourth on the day, 22 seconds behind Swiss prologue specialist, Fabian Cancellara who completed the 8.9 kilometres in an impressive 10 minutes. German, Tony Martin takes second, David Millar takes third. I lose a disappointing 39 seconds to Cancellara,

Andy Schleck loses a disastrous 1 minute and 9, greater than a 10 per cent deficit over a very short distance.

The race then heads through Belgium and towards France where BMC's Classics strength shows on a much-anticipated stage three, over six sectors of cobbles finishing just short of the infamous Arenberg Forest. It's not a place of major significance if you were to visit on a quiet day, but in the world of cycling, when the Paris–Roubaix passes through, it is almost always a scene of action and drama.

The Tour is revisiting the cobbles, not the pretty and precisely cut *pavé* that is used in towns and villages across Europe for aesthetic reasons. Cobbles are very different – large hand-cut stones used on farm roads to allow cars and tractors an easier passage in the wet. This is something that needs to be ridden to truly comprehend.

George Hincapie, with all his years of riding the cobbles says to me before the start, 'Today is not the day to be friendly to anyone'.

Things start to get heated in the lead up to the first section of cobbles. It is an interesting affair with all of the Tour riders in a classics rider's situation.

Marcus Burghardt is taking me on the right, Steve Morabito is behind me for added security. We are on a very smooth, fast, narrow road approaching a ninety-degree right turn. There is a small canal running parallel to the road. This is one of my landmarks for 'Have to move to the front now'.

Someone elbows my right quad. 'Whatever' I think to myself. Then they elbow my hip, 'Who the fuck?' I look, its George, 'Oh shit, lets go!' *Whoosh* … we are in the first fifteen.

We can see the first sector of cobbles in the distance now. George moves up on the left as only he can. We enter the cobbles among the first five or so. I am yet to see a breath of wind. George is in front of me, riding on the dirt a few centimetres to the left of the cobbles. He goes a little off-balance, his front tyre skimming the sharp edge of the cobbles, puncturing the sidewall. As I pass on his right he says, 'Shit I've flattened man'.

I think 'George, all that skill, all those Roubaix's ... you dumb-arse!'

I hear a pile-up behind. Only three GC contenders, Andy Schleck, Ryder Hesjedal and myself, get through to the small group that goes all the way to the line.

I do not test my luck any further and mark Thor Hushovd's attacks conservatively. I come in third behind Thor and Geraint Thomas. Just passing the first big pile up and taking one to two minutes on most of my competitors is like a stage win for my GC points. I go away from the finishing line kicking myself for not risking a little more in the final kilometres.

After the chaos of the cobbles, nerves start to settle in the group and we make our way south towards the 'middle mountains' of the Jura.

SEVEN KILOMETRES INTO STAGE eight – 189 kilometres from Station des Rousses in the Jura Mountains to Morzine-Avoriaz in the Alps – five riders fall down in front of me and I topple over with them. It seems like a soft landing and I think nothing of it.

I get back on the bike, but as I ride along my left elbow feels a bit sore. John Lelangue, in the team car, asks, 'What do you want to do?'

I say, 'Let's stick to the plan.'

I finish the stage. I manage to come fifth and take the yellow jersey.

I feel a sense of pride on the podium, to have to cover the rainbow jersey with the yellow jersey. This hasn't happened in the sport for a long time. The Tour de France organisers are happy too. We may be a Pro Continental team, but we have justified our place in the Tour.

That evening my arm starts to hurt badly, but I don't want to face the possibility the injury may be serious. It's a rest day tomorrow. If I can ride into yellow with a sore arm, it can't be too serious. I try to sleep.

The next day, team doctor Max Testa takes me to get an X-ray. He tells me, 'You've got a broken arm.' Great. Now I have to ride 2000 kilometres in the Tour de France with a broken arm.

I'm told it's the best possible break you can have: a hairline fracture in my left elbow. As Max Testa says, a stable fracture – small, but very painful. I don't need a cast. But I do need rest. The main thing is to avoid movement, which will open up the injury. I'm going to see how I go, riding one-handed if I need to.

Each hour it gets worse. I go for a ride and every hump and bump in the road causes pain.

But I'm in the yellow jersey so I don't want to abandon the Tour. It's my first Tour de France with BMC and I feel a strong obligation to keep going, for Andy, for the team. I think, 'If I can take the yellow jersey with a broken arm, I can ride the rest of the race with a broken arm, can't I?'

It's my second Grand Tour with the team, and as GC rider I feel a strong responsibility not to pull out. We are building this BMC project and the goal of the team is to be part of the ProTour and go to the Tour de France in 2011. BMC are still a second-division Pro Continental team, and according to some we don't even deserve to be at the Tour. We have a point to prove.

If I can hold on to the handlebars and ride, I'll find a way.

Only four people know about my arm: Dr Max Testa, Jim Ochowicz, David Bombeke and Fabio Baldato. I don't say anything to my teammates because I don't want to ruin their confidence. 'Yeah, we're riding for the yellow, but the leader's got a broken arm.' Not the message to inspire them.

Lucky it's a rest day. By the evening the pain in my arm is really kicking in. My arm is throbbing and I can't sleep. I can't find a way to lie in bed comfortably.

UNFORTUNATELY, THE NEXT DAY'S stage, the ninth, is over 200 kilometres including an ascent of the Col de la Madeleine. David has wrapped my arm in tape and the mechanics have raised my handlebars so they're more comfortable.

My arm is really hurting. Riding is opening up the injury and stopping the healing process. Oh my God, what's going on here? I can't even follow the group.

Someone from our team starts to ride on the front and I get dropped. I come back, but I'm trying to hide the injury from my team and also from the world.

It's no good. I can't ride. I'm dropped on the final climb of the race. I lose 8.09 minutes. I go from first to 18th on GC at seven minutes 47 behind Andy Schleck, who's now the Tour leader.

I cross the line in 42nd place. Mauro Santambrogio has ridden with me and is rooming with me. It's loud at the finish, so I yell in his ear, 'I'm sorry, I have a broken arm.' He can't believe I was able to keep going.

Jim Ochowicz decides that it's best to speak about my injury publicly. I tell the press: 'I suffer on my bike every day but I do it with pleasure. The guys and the team have supported me and believed in me in this whole project. I'm so sorry to have let them all down.'

My Tour de France is pretty much over. After the stage I think, 'Well, OK, I can't win the Tour so I'll just ride to stay in the first ten.'

After a while, 'OK, the first twenty-five.'

I'm in survival mode for the rest of the Tour. I just want to finish.

Considering what I've been through, 24th on GC by the time we reach Paris is probably pretty good.

BY EARLY SEPTEMBER I'VE recovered enough to ride the one-day Paris–Brussels race.

It is my first participation in Paris–Brussels, a race normally for sprinters, although this year it's slightly hillier. It's a good test of equipment because you ride along on really smooth, fast roads and then you hit sections of *pavé* and potholes. I've never hit so many potholes at high speed. Because you're riding in the peloton you can't see the holes, and because you're in a race you're going very fast so you hit them extremely hard.

I'm getting ready for the World Championships in Geelong as defending World Champion later in the month, and I don't want to take any risks. So I stop to change my bike after hitting an enormous hole. The group splits behind me and by the time the car gets to me I'm out of the running for the race, which is a pity because I would have been in with a bit of a chance.

IN LATE SEPTEMBER, I'M motor-pacing with Dave Sanders, one of the coaches of the national team, along Beach Road, one of the main inner city cycling thoroughfares of Melbourne. It's the day before the Geelong World Championships, and perhaps the last day I'll wear my rainbow jersey. I'm feeling good, training well, and we're going fast and passing other groups.

As I ride along in the rainbow jersey – hard won a year ago in Mendrisio – I hear a rider say: 'Look at that wanker, he thinks he's World Champion.' It's the only time I've ever been insulted for wearing the rainbow jersey.

Among all the responsible cyclists who ride there early each Saturday morning there's undoubtedly a few who stand out for their irresponsible riding, or their unfriendliness and unsociable manner. They sit on the wheel, not sharing a turn, they disregard the personal space of others, not considering they may want to ride alone, or they aggressively sprint past for a hilltop or an imagined finish line. That behaviour is for racing, when everyone has a number on his or her back. Where there are rules to abide by and commissaires to enforce those rules.

But for the most part I like meeting people out cycling. It can be a hard sport, but on a bad day a complete stranger will help you out, riding in the wind for you when you are tired, offering you food or water when you are hungry and dehydrated or a tube when you don't have any more spares.

An older more experienced rider should offer encouragement and advice to younger less experienced ones. Act as an example to follow. A beginner should be welcomed to the sport, not made to feel intimidated because they are yet to learn the mysterious unwritten rules that cyclists follow.

Cycling allows people from different backgrounds to come together, enjoy life, improve their health and fitness, maybe race and push each other, test each other, help each other to enjoy the experience through the common bond that is a bicycle. That is the true spirit of cycling.

THE 2010 GEELONG WORLD Championships are the first elite road world championships Australia has ever hosted. I'm proud that the Worlds are being held in my home town – or at least the nearest big town to my home in Barwon Heads. It's a special feeling to be racing in Australia as World Champion with a number one on my back. But to stay calm and focused I try to put the sense of occasion of riding at home to one side, and to treat this like any other race.

The Geelong course is less well suited to me than the previous year's course in Mendrisio. There are fewer climbs and long flats between them. In preparing for the race, I've worked very hard and done everything right, but because of the broken arm in the Tour I haven't had the lead-up that I wanted. I never seem to race a great World Championships unless I've done the Vuelta leading into it, which hasn't been possible this year. So I'm a little bit underdone, but reasonably fit.

In the final it looks like we are in with a good chance. Philippe Gilbert is the overriding race favourite. He and I spend everything we have getting away on the hot climb, so when we're caught by the sprinters we have nothing left. In the end, the race comes down to a larger group sprint, won by Thor Hushovd – not a pure bunch sprinter but a pretty solid sprinter. It does not go our way today, but 'that's racing'.

I would have preferred a better result but Geelong couldn't have hoped for a better day of racing. For years afterwards, the World Championships help Geelong's profile and boost its credibility as a host of international sporting events. The Geelong people are so grateful and appreciative to have a World Championships in their city.

IN OCTOBER, I RETURN to Europe to race the Giro di Lombardia, the last race of the year, right near my home in Stabio. I love this Classic, but like so many other years, I get to the end of the season exhausted.

We're riding up the famously severe Muro di Sormano. I've always found the descent on the other side a little unnerving with many blind late-apex corners hemmed-in by walls. I know well that in October it can get some really slippery patches because of the sap from the leaves that drips onto the road, which explains the regular crashes there.

I've been dropped on the Ghisallo so I'm not with the front group. Seeing that I'm not going to make it back high in the placings, I take it easy on the descent in the rain. You don't need to pedal much down this one. In fact, it's steep enough that you don't need to pedal at all.

Alongside Lake Como, I go round an easy curve and slide out. I hit the ground and bang my head. Luckily it's a stretch without walls.

The director of the Sky team comes over.

'Are you OK?'

I sit there on the ground for a minute. 'Um, I don't know ... maybe not.'

I slowly climb back onto the bike and ride around the edge of the lake, then back to the bus in Como, sorry to end my 2010 season so quietly.

THEY TALK ABOUT 'THE Curse of the Rainbow Jersey', where the wearer is jinxed for the year he spends as World Champion. It's cycling's version of the Bermuda Triangle. I *have* had a bit of bad luck in 2010, but I don't go in for curses.

A more rational perspective would be that as the wearer of the rainbow jersey, any race you start, any finish you near, or any break away you try to enter, you stand out from the crowd. Every rider has bad luck during the season, but few riders are scrutinised and studied like the World Champion is. If the World Champion has bad luck, the world of cycling is there to observe, analyse and discuss.

Also, when you wear the rainbow jersey, every day you race you are seen as a favourite by all of your competitors. This makes winning more difficult than normal, perhaps resulting in a lower victory count for the season. It still is however, the most prestigious, most sought after, most envied and beautiful jersey in cycling.

ALDO'S HEALTH IS IN fast decline. The capabilities of the most incredible mind I have had the fortune to learn from are diminishing at a horrifying rate.

I regularly go to his office to catch up. Now he can't fill in a spreadsheet for the annual calendar. I ask him questions about threshold power and speed on a climb, things that I can't calculate, and he still rolls the numbers off out of his head. But he can't fill in a simple spreadsheet.

One day we have a long talk. He tells me, 'I'm sure you can win a Grand Tour. I hope for you it is the Tour de France, because that's the biggest and most prestigious. And if you do that, you will become the most complete rider of your generation.'

In November, I fly back to Australia. On 12 December, I get a phone call. Aldo has died. He was surrounded by his family, and was peaceful. He was 51.

I can't make it back in time for his funeral, but the Aldo I know would have preferred for me to stay in the warmer weather and not miss any training; he was a very objective person.

On my website, I can't resist sharing some of the Aldo I knew:

I can only hope now that his family can recover from their suffering, and Aldo can rest in peace. Even in rest, I would not be surprised if he is still watching over us, calculating climber's outputs and VO2 max results.

I am very grateful to have been able to work with Aldo, but even more, for his contributions, along with the Mapei company, to the clean side of cycling, and support of all those who believe in it. There are very few people who realise just how much he did in his quest to win the big races drug-free.

MONTHS LATER, I'M IN the final 10-kilometre time trial at Tirreno–Adriatico and I'm going flat out but it looks like I'm going to lose the lead in the last stage.

Then I think, 'Aldo will be so disappointed if I lose.'

So I drill holes into myself in this time trial and maintain the lead.

For once, there is something external pushing me. It isn't a team director encouraging me – for me that never works because I have always been my own source of encouragement. But this is different, this is Aldo, and right now I am riding so Aldo won't be disappointed.

I've heard of this before: people striving to impress those they've lost, not wanting to let them down. And I don't want to let Aldo down.

From this point on, my 2011 season is a string of consistent performances, leading up to, and including, the 2011 Tour de France, the race Aldo always wanted to win above all others. The race he never got to see.

He's gone, but I still work according to his philosophies, principles and beliefs, with dedication, conviction and pride.

Aldo is never really far away.

CHAPTER 18

'WHAT'S GOING ON WITH CADEL?'

2010–2011

I CAN'T SEE MUCH. Just a few metres ahead. That can happen when you're riding in heavy snow.

It's one o'clock in the afternoon and I'm descending Monte Bisbino, west of Lake Como, a few kilometres from home in Stabio. I carefully choose the time when I go riding to maximise the amount of sunlight on the climb and to coincide with the warmest part of the day. One degree above zero is better than one degree below. But it's still cold for a guy who was born in the Australian desert, so I've rugged up in five different layers: a thermal undershirt, two jerseys, a Windtex vest and a Gore-Tex jacket over the top. I've got some hot tea in my thermos, and some Cailler chocolate bars in my pocket just to be sure I stay warm. Being this insulated against the cold, simply not feeling it, has its own attraction.

I start on a steep climb. In no time, my glasses are steamed up, my gloves are wet, my breath looks like a small cloud, I'm covered in muddy grey water.

It's Christmas Eve and I can see smoke struggling up from the snow-covered roofs. As I ride past the houses I can smell the delicious aroma of Christmas lunches being prepared: polenta, minestrone, maybe with some gorgonzola melting in the polenta. As I ride I try to guess the smells.

There is no one out today. No cyclists, not many cars. Why would there be? Most people are keeping warm inside their houses, maybe wrapping Christmas gifts in front of the fire. The last place most people would want to be today is riding their bike along an icy, snow-encrusted country road.

But we're not most people, we are cyclists. And I'm probably even more extreme than most. Why else would I be loving this experience, this chance to push myself, to test myself against nature, to see how I go in the worst of conditions? All in complete tranquillity, with the elements as my insulation from the outside world.

When it hurts, when it's hard, and when not many other people could do it, that's when I come into my own. I like that there is no one around to tell me to stop or slow down. The fact that half of my competitors are at home having a day off makes it even more satisfying.

CHIARA AND I HAVE had seven Christmases in a row in Australia, which has been wonderful – spending time with my mother and her family, catching up with friends and being in Barwon Heads, which has that magical laid-back gelato-licking insouciance that you see at an Australian beachside town: kids playing beach cricket, people sitting in street cafés with their lattes and newspapers, lots of people riding bikes.

I have friends who own and run a provedore in town that's one of my favourite places in the world to get a coffee. It's got a very European feel about it, with a communal table in the middle where people sit and eat paninis and read the day's papers, then take a casserole or some prosciutto and cheese home for dinner. It's become a reassuring touchstone for me on my visits back home.

This year, Chiara understandably wants to have Christmas with her family in Gallarate, which I am more than happy to do. So here I am, experiencing my first European winter since I was a junior, but a real winter this time, with snow and sub-zero temperatures. Most consider me crazy for opting for this over summer on the beach, but the peace and quiet, the long nights and short days, the winter food and fashion are all a novelty, and it's very enjoyable.

Apart from the magical scenes in the mountains, there are other advantages for a cyclist to staying in Europe for winter. I'm not just building a useful training base, I'm also acclimatising myself to conditions that may easily occur in the new cycling season. And there's less traffic, less noise and very few riders out.

AT BMC'S FIRST RACE for the season, a few of us are squashed inside the small team camper, putting on our shoe covers and getting warm-up oil massaged into our legs.

Ale Ballan walks in. He looks at my legs and sees an abundance of prominent veins: a sign my training is going well.

Ale's impressed. 'Whoa, shit – what have you been doing in the off season? When Ivan Basso looks at your legs he's going to be psyched out.'

'*Speriamo*,' I reply. Let's hope so.

The event we're at is the Giro del Friuli, a little one-day stage race held early in March in Friuli Venezia Giulia, on Italy's northeast border. It's a second-tier event that teams ride to get ready for the Classics. I first rode it as an Under 23.

The smaller one-day races aren't easy by any means, but the level's not like at the big one-day races, and there aren't the same expectations. So you can go there and enjoy yourself more, and often perform better than usual because you're under less pressure.

On this occasion, it's pouring rain and there's a mighty crosswind, and BMC all get caught behind and look a bit silly.

As a lover of Italy, I enjoy all the races I do here, from the Giro to the small events like this one. You go and stay in a small, family-run hotel where you meet really nice people. The owners seem proud to have riders staying with them. Often we arrive at a new hotel and are welcomed like we are regular visitors.

I have many memories of sitting in small hotel dining rooms eating beautiful traditional meals, trying some of the local specialties and chatting to the waiter or owner over a glass of wine. Yes, a glass of wine. It seems like the right thing to do in this setting, and it has a discernible relaxing effect, which is precisely what I need to recover from the day's riding and get in the mood for another day on the bike.

2010 WAS A YEAR packed with training and racing. I did two Grand Tours, two sets of course recons and two sets of training camps, then travelled to Australia for the World Championships. I didn't race as much as some other years – maybe 60 or 65 days throughout the year – but I did 110 days of training camps. It was a lot of time away from home, but it meant I built up an excellent training base.

Mapei coach, Andrea Morelli takes over the role that Aldo Sassi has had with me for so long. I've known Andrea for quite a while but now that we're working together closely we develop a strong relationship. We sit down and discuss where BMC is at as a team. I tell him what I think the team can do better and the possibilities for the year ahead.

In my training we've cut down the early season high-intensity work a little, so I have more energy to work on more specific aspects. Having the freedom to choose exactly the race program I want allows me to move into the season slowly, which I haven't often had a chance to do.

As a team, BMC are constantly developing. In my second season with them everything is functioning better. And this year we've been given UCI ProTour (now WorldTour) status. We're feeling good for Spring Classics time, and while no one is openly talking about it, we think we've got a pretty good Tour de France in us.

My main goals for the first half of 2011 are the WorldTour stage races while trying to be present at the Ardennes. The Tirreno is going to be my first little peak for the year, so I'm nicely working myself up to it.

A week after the Giro del Friuli we race the Strade Bianche. I'm still in need of some racing to get going, and unable to follow the best guys in what has now become a classics specialist race.

Just after the team car passes me, my seat breaks. Strade Bianche: harsh conditions that are perfect for testing equipment.

Ale Ballan comes in second to Philippe Gilbert. I ride in with the main group for 30th place.

Four days later it's time for the Tirreno. By now BMC are getting into the swing of things.

There's one moment in a long stage from Chieti to Castelraimondo that encapsulates where we're going as a team. We're riding and George Hincapie sees the group is going to split. I'm not paying attention. George calls out, 'Hey Cadel, quick, quick, go in front, go in front!'

George knows he has to refocus me. He takes me up to the front, puts me in position then slips behind. The group splits, I go in front and I take the leader's jersey.

He's caught me at a time when I was nearly out of contention on GC. It's the act of an experienced campaigner. I ride strongly from that point on. George's sharp eye has ensured that I stay on track. It was both a tactically smart move and, coming from a close teammate, a gesture of faith and encouragement.

The next day in stage six we're on a pretty tough, steep finish around Macerata. Ale and George get on the front and make a selection for the last steep finishing climb.

Soon all of us – the BMC team – are riding on the front absolutely flat out. Being in this knot of BMC riders is such a confidence boost to everyone on the team.

As a tactic to encourage the others I've taken a breath and taken a moment to calm down, and I've said to them loud and clear over the radio: 'Really good work, guys, *ottimo lavoro*, really good work.' Hearing me over the radio they think I'm sitting behind going easy, so they're extra motivated to ride hard.

I'm ahead on GC and looking like I might win the stage as well. Italian, Michele Scarponi and others start attacking but I cover them.

I know this finish from racing last year; a very steep pitch to a hard right turn into a flat road before quickly taking a sharp left and the steep narrow medieval cobbled road to the old town centre. I sprint to the bottom of the cobbled grade where no one can pass me.

The win says a lot about how quickly BMC has grown into a great team. George, Ale, Brent Bookwalter, Micky Schär and Steve Morabito are all riding well and are a great support to me as I ride for GC.

The team didn't have any expectation of winning so they don't even have a podium bag. But I take it as a compliment, we are performing above expectations, though obviously still have some room to improve.

I see a change in the guys' psychology at this point. We really start motivating each other for the rest of the 2011 season. Going to the Tirreno and winning when we had no expectations has been an important turning point for us. It feels like suddenly we understand each other. And from this point on, we get stronger and stronger. It's the first stepping stone on the journey to the Tour de France.

DAYS LATER WE RACE the Volta a Catalunya (Tour of Catalonia) in Spain. With the Tour of the Basque Country, it ranks equal second in Spanish road races behind the Vuelta a España.

During the race, spectators on the roadside are holding banners, protesting that the UCI is being unfair in their treatment of Alberto Contador. Contador's 2010 Tour de France victory has been questioned because he's tested positive for the banned drug clenbuterol. Contador has come out with a story about eating contaminated meat. It's all a bit hard to believe. He has been cleared by the Spanish Cycling Federation, triggering the UCI and WADA (World Anti-Doping Agency) to lodge appeals.

After all the doping scandals in cycling, when there's a story like this, people don't believe it and take the side of logic rather than of the athlete. And so for the most part the cycling world thinks Contador should be sanctioned. The feeling I have is that Contador shouldn't be racing. As riders, we're a little appalled that the Spanish are protesting against the UCI, rather than against the rider who's been accused of doping.

I have a problem with the way Spain handles these issues. This is a sport that's done a lot to clean itself up and made a lot of progress in the fight against doping. But in Spain it seems as though they're 10 or 15 years behind the rest of the world in terms of their mentality to people who don't abide by the rules.

I'm a bit tired at the Volta after the Tirreno–Adriatico and finish sixth overall. Contador wins, despite all the controversy surrounding him. Another example of his amazing mental strength.

A COUPLE OF WEEKS later I'm out training on my Cyclo-cross bike on some unfamiliar tracks on the Monte Generoso, near Stabio. At the bottom of a steep descent I lose it and try to bail off the bike, hitting my knee on the top tube in the process. Turns out I've bruised my femur. The doctor is clear: you're out for a while. I have to pull out of the rest of the Classics – the Amstel Gold, the Flèche Wallonne (which I won last year) and the Liège–Bastogne–Liège.

While I'm disappointed, it's a chance to give my body a break. The other upside is that it enables me to concentrate on other aspects of my preparation.

So I pay attention to my diet and I look at all the other aspects. I do a review of my training and my race program, and it helps me refocus. It consolidates the great base of training I have from two Grand Tours and the Worlds last season. What I need in terms of a training load is already in my body. I've given up some training time, but the fact that I'm able to rest means I don't lose much of this load, and I'm a lot fresher, more motivated and better able to concentrate than I would have been.

I want to be ready to ride the Tour de Romandie in late April.

I see my physio Luca Ruiz, whose clinic is near my home in Stabio, for treatment two or three times a day, and undergo all sorts of ultrasounds and other treatments to shorten the recovery time. I am super-motivated to recover quickly, and I'm helped in this by the great people I have around me. We're able to shrink a recovery time of four weeks to just 10 days.

I get back on the bike and start slowly. The first day I ride for 30 seconds in the morning to see how it feels. In the afternoon I do a minute and a half. The next day five minutes. Three days later I can do 40 minutes. The day after I do an hour and start applying a bit of pressure.

Still, I can only ride for very short periods, so I make every moment count. Instead of bashing through a six-hour ride thinking, 'I've got to do this many kilometres, I've got to eat this and do this', I say to myself, 'I'm going to do 450 pedal strokes, and I'll make every one of those strokes as effective as I can'.

After a week I feel I'm not far away.

IN LATE APRIL, I'M fine to race in the Tour de Romandie. As I hoped, the rest has done wonders for me physically and mentally. This time last year, I was already exhausted.

It's sometimes funny what fate has in store for you. What looked like the end of my Tour campaign at one stage is a boost to it three weeks later.

I take the lead in the time trial on the second-last day of the tour. I ride a good tactical time trial and I'm able to bring back a heap of time on the very last hill and beat Vinokourov to take the leader's jersey. BMC go on to win the tour.

My teammates are intrigued, and I think impressed, that I've been able to return to the road after my injury so quickly and so well. They're saying, 'He's been out for two weeks, he comes back and he wins. What's going on with Cadel?

I have a great group of people around me who trust my judgement and experience, and so far, it's all coming together. Let's 'keep at it'!

AFTER THE TOUR DE Romandie David Bombeke, Ivan Santaromita (who is also coached by Andrea Morelli) and I go to a training camp in the Sierra Nevada mountains in Spain. We do four days of intense work on the road, sleeping and training at altitude. These big blocks of training will replicate the toughest stages of the Tour de France.

I work super-hard, riding multiple days of 4000 to 5000 metres of climbing.

Ivan is an excellent trainer, but we choose different approaches. He will sleep in while I get up and do core training with David Bombeke before breakfast and then do the big rides. I'll be doing extra training and getting less sleep for recovery, so Ivan will drop me on the last climbs of the day. He'll outdo me in training, but our race results speak for themselves.

It shows the difference between someone who trains to train and someone who trains to race.

IN MAY, I DECIDE to take on a new Australian manager: Jason Bakker, a former Victorian cricketer who has launched his own management company. I don't know Jason well, but I enjoy his company and I find his knockabout manner reassuring.

Jason grew up in coastal Geelong, Victoria's second city after Melbourne, and he's a bit like Geelong itself: no bullshit about him. I have a feeling we're going to work together well. It means I'll have much less to worry about off the bike so my time will be used much more efficiently.

ON 5 TO 12, June we race the Critérium du Dauphiné, the last lead-in race before the Tour de France. It's regarded by riders as a dress rehearsal for the Tour.

I can't understand why some of the other Tour contenders don't ride the Dauphiné leading into the Tour, because we do the same time trial as the one that's in the Tour de France. So I go there to ride that time trial like I'm riding the time trial at the Tour. Perfect practice. We do all the training, try all the different equipment, and have everything decided and ready to go so that when we ride this same course at the Tour we are hopefully in a good position. The downhill is quite technical and the Dauphiné gives me a chance to ride it in training and in race conditions, which I know will be really helpful in the Tour.

It's my worst stage race for the year in terms of how I feel on the bike. I'm really suffering from allergies and I'm just hanging in there after an enormous block of training. One day the group gets split in the crosswind and we get caught behind.

Everyone's getting overexcited with the build-up to the Tour. One day, Chiara is trying to call me before she goes to bed and there are people in my room and I can't take the call.

It makes me realise, 'This is ridiculous that my own wife can't even speak to me. Everyone just calm down.'

Then my roommate Ivan Santaromita gets sick, so I'm in a room by myself, and all of a sudden I start riding better.

I improve so much that I end up finishing second, to Bradley Wiggins. The race is his arrival as a force in professional cycling. Bradley finished fourth in the Tour in 2009 but had slipped back to 24th in 2010. He's been incredible in the Dauphiné. I'm a bit surprised, because I thought he'd crack in the mountains. But no cracking. It's an enormous leap forward for a guy who has never even tried riding GC in mountain stage races in previous years.

I can't work him out. I see him and I think, 'If you could do that good a season for one year, the other 10 years, couldn't you have done something more?'

WITH THE TOUR NOW just a few weeks away the media begin reporting the odds for the winner.

I'm far from favourite. That burden falls largely on Alberto Contador, who won the Giro three weeks ago. The case against him for doping at last year's Tour has yet to be heard by the Court of Arbitration for Sport, and meanwhile he's free to race.

Also in the favouritism mix are the Schleck brothers, Andy and Fränk, Alexander Vinokourov, Levi Leipheimer, Ivan Basso and Bradley Wiggins.

Levi Leipheimer is an American rider I've never got to know very well, even though I've raced against him for years and years. Back in the '90s when I was a mountain biker racing in America, I would race against him at races like the Redlands Bicycle Classic, a stage race we used to do for training before the mountain-bike season. He's quite a calculating rider, and probably the most aerodynamic time trialist of all of the professionals.

Ivan Basso is from the same area as Chiara. He and Chiara were born in the same hospital, almost a year to the day apart. Chiara's parents went for years and years to his parents' butcher shop.

He started in road racing around the time I did. I raced against him when I was Under 23, and he was a good rider, not exceptional. And then it all started happening. He became the Under 23 World Champion, then he won the young rider's jersey at the Tour de France in 2002. Early in his career, he was probably too lean, then he went to Team CSC in 2004 and put on weight and developed into a Grand Tour winning machine. He was incredible for a few years, then a few things changed, but he still came back and won the Giro in 2010.

He used to be renowned for smiling on the climbs, people would compliment him for it which was very annoying if you were already being dropped while pushing 6.5 watts per kilo.

After winning the Tirreno, my odds of winning the Tour are reported as around 27 to 1. I am a little surprised, but guessing how the odds are drawn up, a little smug too, given the form I'm in. I don't think I'm deluding myself; barring mishaps I can't see how I won't end up on the podium. A female friend of mine puts some good money on me to win.

It's not just me who's riding well at BMC. The whole team are humming along really nicely, and flying right under the radar. We are a team that is in its WorldTour debut, preparing for our second Tour de France. I understand why the cycling world is underestimating us and we have no problem at all with that.

TO GET TO THE Tour de France we planned to fly from Malpensa in Milan, but an airline strike means we have to change plans. Half the team are training in Livigno, about a four hour drive from my home in Stabio, so we all met at Lugano Airport, where Andy Rihs has organised for his private plane to pick us up and fly us to France.

It's a calming experience compared with the disrupted travel arrangements of some of the other riders. Most of them are stuck at airports, and probably frustrated by that. There we are, already at our hotel in Britanny – even though it's an awful little place – and getting ready for the Tour to begin.

When Andy and his brother fly in, they give them a poky little room overlooking a tyre shop. He's naturally used to better accommodation, but he doesn't mind at all. He's too excited about another Tour and I get the feeling he has a lot of confidence about how we might go. There's such a great mood in the team that it doesn't matter that our hotel isn't five-star. For me, as long as the sheets are clean and it's not too noisy, it's fine.

We are isolated from the Tour 'excitement' in our modest surrounds and so go about our work with the minimum of distractions. Three teammates have birthdays this week, so that allows us some levity, but we all know why we are here. So while the attention of the world is turning to the Tour, and to the Schlecks and Contador in particular, we have time to do what we need to do: focus on the job.

It's an ideal build-up to the 2011 Tour de France.

CHAPTER 19

CHASING THE YELLOW JERSEY

2011

NOTHING FEELS WRONG.

By now I'm programmed not to trust. I've learnt not to trust teammates to be there for me, not to trust race directors, not to trust fate.

Too many times I've been isolated on a mountain climb with not a teammate in sight, watching a Contador or a Schleck ahead of me surrounded by a bevy of teammates. My chases have often been solo and my efforts have had to be greater than those of my competitors who are lucky enough to be blessed with team support.

But this year is different. In the BMC team there are no internal power struggles. There is no jealousy or gripe about me as team leader. Sports director, John Lelangue works *with* me on strategy, not against me. My private space and recovery time are respected and protected by Georges Lüchinger. Andy Rihs is always present and enthusiastic. Sports director, Fabio Baldato is, as usual, super-organised and supportive. And I have George Hincapie, the greatest super-*domestique* you could wish for, right by my side. As a Classics rider George will do his own thing and get great results, but then he'll commit himself completely to the team at an event like the Tour de France. As a GC rider, to have that kind of loyalty on your side is extraordinary. Alongside George, I have a team of young and talented riders who share the same dream: to win a Tour de France.

John Lelangue knows how I operate. He knows I need communication and open-mindedness, and he provides that. Racing is in his blood. John's father was a sports director who worked with Eddy Merckx among others. John remembers riding in the team car when he was eight, listening to his father help Eddy win. John raced a bit when he was young but he didn't aspire to be a rider; he always wanted to be a sports director.

Although he's French, John has a very American approach. He speaks with an American accent and is very optimistic in that American kind of way. As an Australian, I might find that constant optimism a little hollow, but I soon learn it's better to be optimistic than pessimistic in a sports team.

Working with John is simple. We'll discuss things like what races I'm going to ride and it's always easy. I'll give him my strategies for a race, he'll suggest his and we'll put them together. It always seems to work.

All I want is a clear shot at a Tour. I keep getting told I'm too old to win one. I don't think that's true and I want to prove it. But I just need three weeks without bad luck.

Everyone on the team is focused. We have new, even better time-trial bikes, which will give us a real advantage in the team time trial. Everyone is fit, healthy, happy and confident. This is our chance to show Andy Rihs who we are as a team and how much we've developed.

I've experienced a lot of wrong in teams over the years. And now, on the eve of the Tour de France, nothing feels wrong at all.

CALM.

It's as important in road racing as any piece of equipment, any smart race strategy, any block of training. And in the high-pressure moments of a Grand Tour it's not easy to achieve.

Some people have an idea of sport where it's all about a fire inside you, a rage of burning energy. It's not like that. I would call that over-arousal. A cycling event like a Grand Tour is so long and gruelling that you can't be over-aroused for three entire weeks.

My main plan for achieving calm is to have everything prepared so well that I don't have any niggling doubts. Then I'll take a moment to reflect on all the preparation I've done, conduct a little review of myself. Have I analysed the course details well enough? Have I got the most appropriate clothing for the weather? Have I got an ideal nutrition plan? Have I got a good, practical plan that I've been through with the team? How am I psychologically? Am I nervous? Indecisive? Anxious?

Achieving calm is not easy when you're one of the favourites for the Tour de France.

If you're doing well on GC you rarely get a second alone. You leave the team bus and instantly everyone's around you. It seems wherever you go, everyone wants your attention. You want to be directing your attention towards the race, but in the end, you have to direct all your attention just to staying calm.

For us riders, we just want to get the race started. Day one is your first chance to see how you measure up against your competitors. People around you are nervous because they hope all the preparation has been done – whether it's the mechanics who've prepared the bikes, the directors who've prepared the planning, the coaches who've prepared the riders, or the riders who've prepared themselves. So these people make those around them nervous.

Day two is much easier. Things settle down and you start to see a nice rhythm develop – depending on how your stage one went, of course.

I look at the results sheet after stage two, and first I look for how many GC contenders finished ahead of me, then for how many finished behind me – and whether it was by a little, or a long way.

After the first week, I've already lost track of what stage we're up to. It's a psychological strategy: I just don't count them. If you think, 'Oh, well, it's stage seven, that means 14 stages to go', and you're already tired, that weighs on you mentally.

For most observers, stages are remembered and recalled by the start and finish towns and the stage number. For me, stages are imprinted in my mind by the points at which a climb, descent or narrow road starts, who was in the breakaway – who won the stage.

I try to have a long-term view, and not get lost in these details. Sure I analyse, but I concentrate on mundane things, like: 'What's the weather going to do? What's the wind going to do?' On TV they're talking about the stage distance and the towns it passes through, but to win the Tour, the town names are irrelevant.

I try to restrict my thoughts to: 'I'm healthy', 'I'm recovering', 'I've lost this much time on GC', or 'I'm this far back from the other contenders' or 'I'm this far in front of the contenders'. I'm just focused on everything that relates to performance, which is good for performing, but probably often takes away from my enjoyment of the race. But this is where I think I'm a real elite sportsperson – I'm here with a job to do.

The Tour de France is won over three weeks by not losing time, not crashing, staying healthy, being good in a few stages and looking for opportunities everywhere else.

I was told that Lance Armstrong once said you win the Tour de France with two good time trials and two good attacks in the mountains.

He's probably missing a few elements, though. I think the Tour de France is won two weeks before Christmas the year before, when you're working your way up a snowy, wet road and you're building a body and a psyche that you can activate six months later.

IN THE OPENING STAGE, Philippe Gilbert continues his great season. When he attacks in the last kilometre I find myself blocked in and can't get out to follow him. When I do get out, it's too late: Gilbert has made a gap. I try to close on him but can't. Gilbert takes the first yellow jersey and I'm second. I get to wear the green jersey as compensation.

In the following day's team time trial, we lose two riders in the first five kilometres. Far from ideal but everyone left rides very well and we finish second to Garmin by a mere two seconds. Thor Hushovd takes the yellow jersey. I am the 'carrier' of the polka dot jersey.

In the first week of the Tour, the team are focused on making sure I stay safe. That means positioning well without expending too much energy, staying near the front when there is a greater chance of a crash, and drifting back in the wheels to relax when it's safe to do so.

A promising sign for the race comes in stage four to Mûr-de-Bretagne, and it happens in a surprising way.

Someone runs into my derailleur, bending it, rendering my gears almost unusable. I have to change bikes. There are just 10 kilometres to go, along narrow roads.

George Hincapie sees it. I'm not as calm and collected as I appear to be.

'George, I think I need to change bikes. Shall I do it now or wait?'

'Change it now.'

Thanks, cool-headed George.

There are 180 riders to pass to get back to the front. Steve Morabito and Brent Bookwalter take me back to the peloton, and Marcus Burghardt then takes me to the front, past the whole peloton, down the edge of the narrow road, sometimes in the dirt; I don't even know how he found the space. He drops me off near the front and George takes me to the last steep climb and then I'm able to start following the moves. There's a little sprint at the end and I beat Contador on the line to win the stage.

The team have snapped into action, and we've quickly overcome the time lost on the bike change. It's teamwork like I've never experienced before, the most amazing collaborative effort I've ever seen. It reinforces that everything the team are doing is right.

I'm not the only one who thinks BMC have a strong chance. One day George takes me aside just before the stage start. He's very serious, almost aggressive. 'Listen, I was just talking to Ivan Basso. He was following you yesterday and he says he's never seen anyone ride so strongly. Dammit, you can win the Tour de France!'

I say, 'George, stay calm.'

But George is being uncharacteristically firm. 'Cadel, I mean it, you can *win* it.'

'Stay calm, George, stay calm.'

SUPERSTITION, REASSURING ROUTINE, OR just plain procrastination? Interesting question.

I know riders who use one seat for their entire career. I've had teammates who will only ever use one type of chamois in their shorts.

A lot of bike riders have little habits, and I do too. My small quirk is that I'll hang on to anything that's working well for me. So even if I have 20 new jerseys in my cupboard, if I've raced really well in a particular jersey, I'll keep wearing that same jersey for a week or two weeks, or maybe a whole Tour de France. I'll keep it until I have a bad race and *then* I'll change it. If I raced well with certain numbers yesterday, I'll keep the very same numbers today. I'll take the pins off carefully one by one, clean the numbers, and pin them onto my jersey, maybe the same jersey, the next day. The same applies to gloves, undershirts, sunglasses and so on. We all have our quirks. 'If it ain't broke, don't try and fix it.' A philosophy I have tried to apply my whole career.

I was doing a little review one time and I realised that I bought a little race bag in 2003 and years later I was still using it. In the bag were scissors and Band-Aids and safety pins. I'd taken them to every race I'd been to for years. I was given a tiny Leatherman pocketknife for my 21st birthday, that I carry with me, it's been travelling around the world with me for 18 years now.

AFTER STAGE EIGHT'S TOUGH little finish to the Super Besse, the race organisers can't make up their minds whether it's me or World Champion, Thor Hushovd who should take the yellow.

For once, I don't want to be in yellow, I want to save the team for later. And I definitely do not want to wait around in the rain while they work through the timing to see who is leader.

Thor and I are of a similar age. We first raced together as Under 23s – at the 1998 World Championships in the Netherlands, where Thor won the time trial, and at the 1999 Transalsace International in France, where he won a few of the sprint stages.

He's incredible when he's good. Despite all his success as a rider, he's so solidly built he looks like a Viking on a bike. He can be amazing uphill for his build, and one of the better descenders of our generation. Turns out Thor's team Garmin–Cervélo were faster than BMC in the time trial by a minuscule 47 hundredths of a second. Thor takes race leadership, which he retains for seven days. This suits us just fine.

The mountains are coming up and it's perfect for us to be sitting behind the leader.

Not being in front means the team will miss out on the publicity. But fortunately my days at Lotto where they craved the publicity associated with being in yellow are over. At BMC we're just focusing on what step of the podium we can stand on in Paris. Our marketing ideas are those that motor sport are built on, 'Win on Sunday, sell on Monday...'

IT'S BECOMING A TOUR of crashes. Bradley Wiggins and Chris Horner crash out after a touch of wheels in the 218-kilometre stage seven from Le Mans and quit the Tour.

In the 208-kilometre stage nine, from Issoire to Saint-Flour, there's a horrific pile-up at the 100-kilometre mark that ends the hopes of Alexander Vinokourov and Jurgen Van den Broeck.

Later in the same stage, the driver of a French TV car swerves into a group, striking Dutch rider Johnny Hoogerland and sending him flying into a barbed-wire fence, which causes some terrible cuts on his legs. It is captured on TV, horrible to watch but an important lesson for us all. Johnny still has the large scars on his legs today.

Later in the stage, BMC are in the lead group and we take a right turn onto a short but steep climb. Because of the hard, fast and very aggressive start to this climb, the group is falling to pieces behind George Hincapie and me. I look at my SRM PowerMeter and see that I'm riding on George's wheel at a very high 440 to 460 watts – not a level even an elite rider can hold for an extended period of time, and, of course, we still have more than four hours of racing to go for the day.

I look to the front and see two riders – Luis León Sánchez and Sandy Casar – drift away up the road into the rain and haze. I think to myself, 'Anyone who can attack now deserves to win.' Just at that moment, Frenchman, Thomas Voeckler punches away from our select group of less than 20 riders and bridges across to the two riders in the breakaway. 'Wow, that's really strong,' I think. Voeckler goes on to take the yellow jersey.

Thomas is a French breakaway specialist with a very distinctive style on the bike. As a non-cycling person once said to me, 'He looks like one of those clowns at Luna Park, where you put a ball in their mouth to win a prize.' As he rides his head swivels from left to right, acknowledging everyone who calls out his name encouragingly.

Thomas isn't known for his popularity in the peloton or, as it happens, in some crowds. Maybe it's just his proud French manner but he gives the impression he is superior to the rest of us. His only friend in the peloton is teammate, Pierre Rolland. But they both seem to be quite happy that they only have one friend each.

Pierre is quiet and reserved, and very similar in physique to Andy Schleck: tall and slight. He also races like Andy, riding quietly at the back of the smaller races, and showing himself and his limits at the big ones.

Although a particular character, Voeckler's a talented rider who can pick and read the breakaways really well. He's physically very strong, but it is his placidity when everyone else is panicking and missing opportunities that permits him to put in a fast and strong acceleration when the time comes to bridge across to a break.

VOECKLER KEEPS THE OVERALL lead in stages 12 to 14 through the Pyrenees, and I'm right behind him on GC. I've been hovering between second and third place since the start of the Tour.

By stage 18 we're into the Alps. The 200-kilometre stage from Pinerolo in Italy features the highest climb of the Tour – up the Col Agnel then over the Col d'Izoard with a finish on top of the Col du Galibier – the highest finish in Tour history. I'm trailing Voeckler by more than a minute.

Voeckler seems to have ridden beyond himself in the mountains thus far, so I'm expecting him to crack at anytime. I don't think he has the climbing ability to hold on to yellow, so he's probably gone. It's the Schlecks, Alberto Contador and Sammy Sánchez who are my biggest threats.

Until the gap between me and the yellow jersey blows out to two minutes or more, the Tour is BMC's to lose. To win you have to risk losing. You have to play the game.

Andy Schleck is over two minutes back from the lead on GC. He knows it's his last chance to take more time from me before the time trial in stage 20 if he wants to win the Tour.

On the second big climb of the day, the Col d'Izoard, Andy takes that chance and attacks.

He needs a really big time gap, and to achieve that he has to go from a really long way out and make a risky move. I could follow, but his brother Fränk is there. If I followed then Fränk would go too. I think, 'Why don't I let him expend energy now, let him be fatigued and then I'll bring it back later?'

It surprises me how fast Andy's group are racing from the Col d'Izoard to the Col du Lautaret. They're in a headwind in the upper part of the valley. Andy doesn't have any teammates to ride behind now. If you're riding to a climb with a climber, you don't ride very hard, because you've got to save energy to follow the climber on the climb. So how Andy manages to motivate them to ride so hard I don't know.

I go back to the car to speak with John Lelangue. 'John, we're losing the Tour de France, we've got to do something. And we've got to do it now. There's no one to ride and no one's going to collaborate with us.'

He suggests I try the only thing left: collaborate with Voeckler.

I give it a go. 'Thomas, let's ride together?'

But his response is: 'You're the king of the Tour here, it's not my job.'

This is an example of Thomas Voeckler's mindset: he would rather compromise his own chances of being on the podium than help me win the Tour de France. So he's not going to ride. Neither he or Pierre Rolland are not going to help me. I'm not at all surprised.

These are the kinds of things you need to be attuned to when you're riding. It's all part of the game.

We're riding on the flat and the riders in my group are blowing up one after the other. Voeckler is there with me, hanging on to the yellow jersey much longer than most thought he could. He has teammate Pierre Rolland in support.

Amaël Moinard and Steve Morabito give everything to come back on the descent of the Izoard but are only capable of doing one big turn each. Euskatel is the only team left with some riders, but they too are only capable of one turn each. Everyone is exhausted. This is exactly the situation Andy Schleck wants. He also has the advantage of having his brother there keeping tabs on things.

We start the climb up the Col du Lautaret and I know I have to chase. I know I can claw time back from Andy in the time trial, but I have to limit the damage so the job is not impossible.

But no one seems to want to take up the chase with me. I'm isolated. All my teammates have been dropped. It's all up to me. I know that if I want to win the Tour I'll have to do it by myself. And right now.

It isn't just grinding up the climb, it's now a matter of fine judgment. With my support now gone, I have to work out how hard to ride and when. I know I'm going to have to ride hard all the way to the end, and I also know Andy will probably attack with three kilometres to go. I know the harder I ride, the more tired I'll be, but the harder I ride, the more riders I can drop. It's a balance I have to find.

Andy was trailing me by one minute and 18 seconds at the start of the day. At 14 kilometres remaining, he holds a four-and-a-half-minute lead.

At this point Alberto Contador rides up and asks, 'Do you want me to ride? Because we've got to ride.'

He's right – we've got to ride. I start riding with him.

It's a key moment in the Tour. Contador has less to lose than I do, but he's taken the initiative and triggered my move. He knows he can't win the Tour, but he doesn't mind if I do, whereas others like Voeckler *do* mind.

Sometimes I've been in that position, where I'd rather salvage second or third, and help someone else win. Sometimes, you get accused as a rider of not racing for the win, but if you haven't got a chance to win and you can guarantee second, sometimes you have to race for that.

Maybe Contador is hoping to keep fifth place on GC. I don't know what his psychology is at this moment. But whatever it is, I'm really grateful to him.

With nine ks left, I'm still trailing Andy by four minutes. It seems like a winning margin. Now we're losing the Tour. It's pretty much down to what happens on Galibier.

John's on the radio giving me time checks and encouraging me. To conserve energy, I'm not talking back.

At eight ks to go, the gap is three minutes 45 seconds.

John comes onto the radio. 'Cadel, you're doing great, this is fantastic. Don't worry, it doesn't matter what happens in this Tour de France, you've already proved you're a champion.'

But as I ride I'm thinking, 'Fucking hell, if we don't win this Tour now, I'm going to be so fucking mad!'

So I ride and ride.

Then I hear: 'Contador's struggling behind! Contador's struggling!'

I keep going. This information puts energy into my legs. I decide to up the pace a bit to test him, to see whether he really is struggling.

Then I hear John say, 'Contador's dropped. You've dropped Contador.' As any cyclist would understand, when you are riding Contador, the best Grand Tour rider of this generation, off the wheel on a climb at the Tour de France, it is a solid morale boost.

Ivan Basso comes through to do a turn.

I say, 'Ivan, get out of my way, you're slowing me down.'

There's nothing polished about this. I'm hammering away on the pedals, not pulling back for a second, putting it all on the mountain.

I have to ride within myself because I still have Fränk Schleck in my group and he's going to try to attack me if I get too close to Andy.

I don't have a choice but to stay calm. I have a three minute gap to Andy Schleck to close and I have all of the GC contenders on my wheel trying to take advantage of this situation.

'Just keep going.' I say to myself.

Three ks to go. In our group are Voeckler, Rolland, Fränk Schleck, Ivan Basso, Damiano Cunego and Contador, who's made it back to the front. I'm waiting for an attack from Fränk or one of the others, maybe Rolland or Voeckler. I have a feeling Pierre wants to ride. But he doesn't.

Two ks to go. The gap is three minutes and five seconds.

With one k to go I'm still at the front. Still no one is attacking me.

I think, 'This is good.'

Three hundred metres to go. Andy gets across the line, followed by Fränk, then me. Voeckler hangs on to his GC lead by 15 seconds. More than half the field receive a 20-point penalty for finishing outside the elimination cutoff.

I've dropped to fourth, but I'm only one minute and 12 seconds behind.

It's a great and gutsy performance by Andy. People are saying that it's been an epic stage in Tour history, a battle between Andy, in front and exhausted, and me, dragging the remnants of the peloton up the mountain.

In those 9.5 kilometres on the Col de Lautaret and the Galibier, 17 years of racing experience at the top level have been put to use. It's like a 30-minute window that reflects my entire career.

It reinforces the fact that patience, persistence, good tactics and a refusal to give up are potent weapons.

It's certainly among my best ever performances, and one that was captured by the cameras for the world to see in all its drama.

THEY SAY IF THE Tour had ended then it would have gone down as one of the epics.

But it wouldn't be right if there wasn't an annoying incident to take the gloss off the moment.

A cameraman is trying to film inside the van where I'm trying to get changed. He's knocked over my bike and is now standing on my precious beloved machine like it's a pile of rubbish that has been blown under his feet by the wind.

'Excuse me,' I say.

No movement.

I'm annoyed now. 'Please have some respect, get out of the way.'

I try to close the door and I don't care if he gets caught because he's been warned. I am human and I want some space. I'm bloody exhausted and this guy is aggravating me with his lack of respect.

The close access the media have to riders is a great opportunity for them to portray the sport and its difficulties, tell the story, communicate their observations. But it also gives some unscrupulous individuals a wonderful excuse to mistreat, torment, manipulate and provoke participants into acting out of character. In the Information Age it seems it only requires 10 seconds of video footage on YouTube or a 'fact' written in black and white on Wikipedia to summarise who you are as a human being.

It's an unpleasant – and, I feel, undeserved – end to what has otherwise been one of my best ever days on the bike.

Putting the experience behind me, David Bombeke and I head down the mountain in a team van. I am utterly exhausted but quietly satisfied with the day's efforts, and I can tell David is satisfied too.

I get back to our hotel near Briançon, and find my very comfortable room has an enormous bathtub. I should not keep my teammates waiting but I can't resist the opportunity to unwind and release some of my pent-up stress after the biggest and possibly most important day of my Tour de France career. So I run the water and peel off my Lycra. I need to be alone and reflect on the day. Just be, quietly.

I sit in the bath and enjoy the soothing, warm water.

Out of curiosity, I download the data from my SRM PowerMeter. 'Shit.' It's the third week of the Tour and I've just ridden the equivalent of a World Championship.

How many calories burned today? I better have a big dinner!

We have another 'very important' stage tomorrow. That's stage 19 from Modane, 109 kilometres, all mountains, no flat. There are three famous climbs: the 16.7-kilometre ascent on the Col du Télégraphe, the northern passage of the 18.1-kilometre Col du Galibier (we climbed the southern side today) and the notorious 13.8-kilometre Alpe d'Huez.

I sink into the warm embrace of the bath, trying to distract myself from the thought of it. I start to feel human again, and see the funny side of this cycling life.

The bath is a saviour but time is ticking by, I really need a good meal and I do have quite a few stories to tell my teammates.

As I head into the hotel restaurant, I make a conscious effort to stand up straight and not look exhausted in front of the 'BMC Boys.' I sit down to an enormous plate of pasta or two. We know we've done something pretty incredible today.

THE NEXT DAY IS a short but very intense stage. Shorter for a Tour rider is not better, shorter means harder. It starts with a 14 kilometre downhill before a very high-speed approach to a tricky narrow entrance to the Col du Télégraphe – the first climb of the day.

Gorge Hincapie takes me up the right side of the group just before the left turn under the narrow underpass, I am way back in the field but carry my speed to weave through the group to make it to the front. Just as I reach the front, Contador attacks, I continue my epic passing manoeuvre and latch onto the back of the breakaway with Andy Schleck, Sanchez and Voeckler.

Then something doesn't feel right with my bike. We are using super-light quick releases – the part that holds the rear wheel in – and they're not binding tightly enough. It feels as though the rear wheel has moved within the frame and it's touching the brake pads.

And this is my torment: if I didn't have such a sensitivity to every tiny detail of my bike it wouldn't bother me. I wouldn't think about it.

I change bikes which puts me back in the main group, behind the break containing all of the GC contenders. Again, we are on the ropes.

What George, Steve, Brent and the others thought was going to be a relatively relaxing ride in the mountains turns out to be an 'everything is on the line to lose' situation again. John Lelangue has alerted the guys to be ready via the race radio. Marcus Burghardt has dropped back from a group in front of the GC guys to ride with me until the others catch up. George organises the guys on the road in reverse order of climbing ability, one turn each, everything they have. One by one, they do their turn then peel off and get dropped to grind away to the finish on their own.

Between the Télégraphe and the Galibier, there is a small descent; it seems to pass by in about 45 seconds, not quite enough for the legs to rest between one climb and the other. This makes the two climbs feel like one 34 kilometre ascent up to 2600 metres.

Steve Morabito is the last guy left as we near the top of the Galibier. He has done altitude training with me leading into the Tour and is performing well.

In the distance, we can see Sanchez. Steve does his last turn to try and launch me across to Sanchez on the steepest pitches of the day. I cannot quite get across to 'Samu' on the climb and have to close the rest of the gap on the descents. It is not a day to take note of the unprotected drops off the edges of the road, the same road we had raced up the previous day. I make it back to Sanchez, and he makes it back to the group containing Andy and Contador on the descent to Le Bourg d'Oisans and the start of Alpe d'Huez.

After the dramatic start, Alpe d'Huez is a relatively relaxed affair. I just need to stay with the Schleck brothers now. I am thinking about the next day's time trial.

I finish the stage in fourth place but my GC status is strong. Voeckler has slipped to fourth on GC and I've kept my deficit on Andy to 57 seconds and Fränk to just four. Now all that's left is a 42.5 kilometre time trial in Grenoble on the penultimate day.

That night we stay in a hotel on top of Alpe d'Huez. In the restaurant there's a party atmosphere and a big buffet, but all the riders know the job isn't done. And we know we still have a day to make sure nothing gets in the way before Paris.

A lot of the publicity caravan staff are staying in the hotel. For them it is one of the last chances for a party. For us, it's business as usual.

I go to bed and unfortunately the party is still going on.

I don't really mind. It's 11pm, and I know I need sleep, but I can't help enjoying the music. They're playing the Eurythmics, a band I like. I lie in bed quite enjoying the music from the party.

Then they play 'Sweet Dreams (Are Made of This)'.

Oh, come on. I smile in the dark at the song choice and soon drop into a deep sleep, just trying to go with the flow, trying not to analyse the timing, trying not to analyse the hugeness of the day ahead, trying not to analyse anything. Just being content and satisfied with the job we've done so far.

CHAPTER 20
INTO PARIS

2011

I WANT TO GET to the start a bit earlier than usual because traffic can be a problem at the Tour. So we leave at 7.30 even though my start is scheduled for 4.12pm. Annie Lennox has kept me up a bit the night before. But that's okay. Years of not going to bed early have conditioned me for today.

Getting there early turns out to be a smart move. The traffic is shocking. We have to wait for hours to go through a tunnel and only just have enough time.

Steve Morabito and I go out on a recon to check the course, with John and David behind us in the car. It's almost identical to the course we raced on in the Dauphine just a few weeks ago.

It is important for me to get out on my time trial bike, test the legs, allow them a little time to adapt to the different position. I get a feel for the tyres sticking to the asphalt and the aero time trial brakes and their capabilities.

I am normally very focused during these reconnaissance rides, but today I see a special cycling fan, an elderly Belgian gentleman, Lucien Blyau, who has become a friend of mine over the years. I see him at every big race in France, always on the second to last climb handing out small bottles of Coca-Cola to the riders. I rarely get a chance to take one in a race because at that moment it's usually starting to get serious for GC guys, but I am grateful for his years of generosity and admire his passion for the sport.

For months, David Bombeke has been carrying a small gift in recognition of our gratitude. Now the moment has arrived – David reaches out from the car and hands Lucien a rainbow jersey.

After the recon with Steve I go back to the bus and sit in my usual seat up the back, listening to some Paul Kelly. Apart from the brilliance of the songwriting, there's something about Kelly's voice I love.

My teammate Manuel Quinziato comes up and shakes my hand. He says, 'Capo, I just came up to say good luck.'

'Hey, Quinzy – win, lose or draw, tomorrow night we're going to party like it's 1999.' He smiles and heads out for his time trial.

ONLY FOUR TIMES IN the Tour's history has a rider come from behind to take the lead in the final time trial. But I'm not thinking about history, I just want to be able to get everything on the road today.

I've been in this situation before, on just two occasions. Your mind wants to win, and once you start riding, deep inside you know whether your body is capable or not. It's best not to analyse it, just be sure to minimise the chances of mistakes. And let it happen ...

I roll down the start ramp.

Everything feels right.

I'm getting good feedback from John in the car. And I'm going faster and faster and faster. I get to the downhill and our race preparation starts to show.

I record the second-fastest split of 20:33 at the first intermediate mark at 15 kilometres. Andy Schleck goes through the same mark in 21.09, 36 seconds slower than me.

Now I'm descending. And the further I go, the faster I go. I surpass the 57-second mark after just 34 minutes of racing.

I'm flying now. By the second intermediate mark after 27.5 kilometres, I'm ahead of Andy by 1:42.

Up ahead there's a guy standing all alone beside the road. It upsets my concentration for a moment. I think to myself, 'Idiot, get back to work.'

John stops giving me updates on German time-trial specialist Tony Martin, who's riding well.

By now I'm virtually in yellow. Not that it is in my mind. I am focused on getting to the line as quickly as possible. John's worried I'll crash, but I'm having the time of my life.

I get to a section where you can cut the corner really straight, but there are potholes around on the crest of a small rise. In training I've jumped over them, to avoid puncturing or damaging a wheel. In the race you're going 20 ks faster. I go to jump over them and the bike launches off the ground and goes a bit higher than expected. I'm really flying. If a gust of wind comes now the time trial bike will be blown sideways. But I land OK.

From there it's onto the flat. I'm putting every molecule of myself onto the road.

It's strange. I'm barrelling along and I can't feel my legs. But they're going as fast as I need them to go.

I must be in the lead of the Tour de France now. But I haven't actually won it yet. I've still got to get to the finish line, so I take the last corner cautiously.

I cross the line in one piece. David is there waiting. He looks as though he does not know what to say or do. I give him our much used hand signal to indicate 'all okay' and ride on to get some of the lactate out of my legs. It's not over yet.

Tony Martin wins the stage. I'm seven seconds behind. I'll start the final stage from Creteil into Paris with an overall lead of one minute 34 seconds on Andy Schleck and exactly two and a half minutes on Fränk.

As I head for the team bus all I have to do is stay upright on the bike. Sounds easy, but I've often dodged dogs or people on bikes or people taking photos, so I take extreme care.

I get to the bus and raise my arms, big smile. Scream. All the guys are hugging each other.

Brent Bookwalter's face is one huge smile. He says, 'Man, I've never been so nervous about a time trial in my life.'

They've been sitting there with sweaty palms, because it's their race as well.

For them, I'm a brother on the bike, and during that time trial everyone was on the bike with me, because we're a little family and this matters a lot, for all of us.

I see John Lelangue. With a hint of sarcasm, I say, 'John, you didn't give me the time checks on the downhill, we could have won the stage.' I'm joking, of course.

He says, 'Yeah, we know why.'

They knew I had it won. I hug John.

David Bombeke, 'Da Bomb', is there of course. It is our seventh Tour de France together, through all of the highs and lows, he has always been there. However, never have we been so proud or as satisfied as this moment.

It's a day when I feel very close to this group, and grateful for their talent and their efforts, and it's an amazing feeling winning this Tour as part of a team where we all know how much we've all been through – all the training and suffering on the bike and sharing of experiences that make up the strange life of a professional cyclist.

There are a thousand stories when you're in a cycling team, a thousand triumphs and a thousand losses. When you've won a Tour de France together those stories make up an extraordinary narrative that only we guys on the team can ever call our own. I'm guessing these shared experiences will stay with us forever.

AFTER THE TIME TRIAL I am called to a press conference.

When I walk into the room all the journalists stand up and clap. Later people tell me this is the first time it's happened at the Tour in living memory.

To get a standing ovation from journalists? That is not something I had ever considered possible, but I am truly touched by the recognition of those from whom I have often had to place mental and sometimes physical barriers.

Although some in the media tell a different story, I do not have a problem with those journalists who are professional and at least a little courteous. I strive to do every aspect of my job as best as I can. Like anyone with a job that has stresses, expectations, pressures and responsibilities, I do not have time and energy to waste on people who act disrespectfully, unprofessionally or create problems for me, as any decent person would understand.

But as I walk into that tired space under an old sports stadium, there is no doubt that they're all behind me. Here there is no feeling of being interrogated by individuals looking for a controversial quote. It is not about dissecting why an athlete in the heat of the moment didn't do this or that as seemed obvious to those watching on television.

Today, on the eve of a Tour victory, they know it's going to be possible to write that hard work and commitment have won through at one of the world's toughest sporting events. After all the dark days when stories of the Tour have been dominated by drug cheats, they're acknowledging a rider who's clearly won with legs and heart alone.

And it's not just about me, it's about the health of our sport. It's a victory for all those who want to make the difference on the bike, not in the bus beforehand, or the hotel room afterwards.

Those of us who've been involved in this sport for a long time – journalists, organisers, staff, sponsors, riders – are all in it because we love it. That shared passion – despite our conflicts, disagreements and different goals – is what brings us together in an atmosphere of mutual respect. And it's this mutual respect – not the number of newspaper sales, not the number of views on YouTube, not the number of race wins or the number of zeros on a team contract – that I hope my win will be remembered for.

I hope that this victory brings more to my sport than the 'first Australian', or a 'non-cycling' nation's victory. I hope that this victory is a basis for the sport to move on from dark days to a healthier brighter more credible future.

BACK AT THE HOTEL I'm still on routine, so I go to David Bombeke's room for the post-stage massage. He's not expecting me.

I walk in. He's probably thinking, 'The Tour de France winner's just walked in, wants a massage, better give him one.'

I lie down on the table. My phone rings. It's an unknown number so I let it go to voicemail.

I check the message. It's Andy Schleck.

I ring back. 'Andy, everything OK?'

'Yeah, yeah, I just wanted to say that I probably won't see you much tomorrow, and I just wanted to tell you that you really deserve to win this race, and if I'm going to be beaten by anyone, I want to be beaten by you … And congratulations.'

'Thanks Andy. Good of you to call, really appreciate it … Hey, Andy – one day you and Fränk and I will sit down and we'll have a beer together to celebrate this. Because congratulations to you, two brothers on the podium, that's fantastic.'

Andy says, 'Oh, OK, I'll hold you to that.'

We hang up. David continues the massage.

I say, 'That was really nice.'

David says, 'Oh, shit, that was Andy? That was really nice, wasn't it?'

I'm touched by Andy's call. This is what sport's about: thrash it out on the road and be respectful later. Andy must be devastated at not having won, yet he still takes the time to call the guy who did. All class.

I GO BACK TO my room and get into the bath.

There's a knock on the door. Georges Lüchinger.

'Cadel, Julia Gillard's on the phone.'

Hey? The Australian Prime Minister has called.

'Hi, Julia, how are you? I'm just having a bath.'

Julia says, 'I hope it's a nice warm one.' Then she says, 'Congratulations, the country's very proud of you. How do you feel about a public holiday in your name?'

'Well, of course I would be honoured but, how does that fit with the nation's economy?'

'Err … not very well', she replies.

I say, 'Julia, do what's best for the country. I don't want to upset Australia's GDP for the sake of the Tour de France.'

She laughs. 'Oh, thanks. I'm very glad to hear that.'

THE LAST STAGE OF the Tour is always the ride into Paris, and along the Champs-Elysées. For me it's just a formality. The only thing that will stop me from winning the Tour de France is a stray dog on the road or an idiot on a motorbike. All I have to do is not crash.

As I ride along, someone in a team car hands me a flute of champagne. The imminent winner is supposed to ride along holding champagne. I find it a little repetitive to see the same photo of the Tour winner riding with a champagne flute every year.

I say to the guys in the car, 'Do I have to? Don't you have any beer?'

They say, 'No, no, you've got to have it here.'

So I'm riding between the kerb and the team car, with one hand on the brake lever and the other holding the champagne flute when a TV motorbike crashes in my path. I manage to pull up before it, without crashing or spilling any champagne.

I hand the flute to John in the car, saying, 'You drink this, I'm going.'

I pedal towards Paris, and finally cross the finish line.

I get off the bike and grab all my teammates and hug them.

This is it. We've finally won it. I've always wondered how it would feel.

We do a lap of the Champs-Elysées, soaking it all up. These are magical moments that the guys on the team will forever share.

We'll always be the ones who did this together.

That will never change.

THERE'S A LIGHT WIND as I stand on the podium in the shadow of the Arc de Triomphe. I'm in the heart of Paris, holding a toy lion from Tour sponsors Crédit Lyonnais and wearing a weary smile. There's an Australian flag around my shoulders, and the wind has caught it and blown it up to look like a Superman cape. That's one friend's perspective, anyway.

Standing there, I feel all sorts of emotions at once. The first and predominant one is relief. That finally, after all these tries, I've done it. This time, nothing has stopped me.

This time, I cruised across the finish line in a super-calm state. This time there were no circumstances I couldn't control. This time there was no bad luck or near misses. This time there was no need for anyone to ask, 'Can you win the Tour?'

No need for any of that. This time I've done it. I've won the race I've dreamt about since I was a little boy, ever since that day in primary school when the teacher told us about a gruelling French bicycle race.

Another emotion I feel up on the podium is pride. Pride in myself, that all the work I've done towards achieving this dream has finally paid off; pride that my four-year-old team have won cycling's biggest race in their first season on the WorldTour.

And as images of me draped in an Australian flag are being beamed around the world, I feel proud of all the Australian cyclists who've gone before me, who've worked so hard for so long to compete in and try to win this race. I'm the first Australian to do it, but so many have helped me get there.

I'm proud and grateful for the support of John Lelangue, Jim Ochowicz, Andy Rihs and Tony Rominger. These people had faith in me when many others in the world of cycling didn't. And now, their faith has been justified.

I also think of all the people who've said I couldn't do this, that another Grand Tour was beyond me, that I was too old. I'm grateful to them, too, because their negativity has provided me with priceless motivation. Being doubted and underestimated is something I've grown to enjoy.

A lot happens in those moments when I'm standing on the podium. Photographers are snapping away. I'm focused on looking straight ahead, making sure my hat and sunglasses are on straight; these photos may be used for years to come. Then I'm looking up at my face on the screen and listening to Tina Arena sing 'Advance Australia Fair'. But it's only later that I'll fully appreciate the moment.

As the Tour winner I start my victory speech in French. It wasn't planned that way. Everyone is speaking French around me, the person asking me questions is speaking French, I'm listening and thinking in French, so I start talking in French.

It then occurs to me, 'There are quite a lot of Australians here, I should probably repeat this in English, shouldn't I?'

So I repeat my spontaneous but honest little speech and I can hear the Aussies come to life in the crowd. I don't think the Australians in the crowd realised it was me talking.

Andy and Fränk Schleck, both French speakers, are standing next to me on the podium. At one stage I ask, 'Was my French correct? Did I say something wrong there?'

Andy said, 'No, no, it was very good, Cadel.'

Once I'm off the podium, it's back to 'work,' interviews for various countries in various languages, a drug test, many warm and firm handshakes and hugs, all in time to meet the guys for the lap around the Champs Elysées. It takes a while, as we try to say 'g'day' to every Australian there.

'Cadel! Well done, mate!'

'Hey, Cadel! You bloody won! How do you feel, mate? You must be bloody exhausted. I know I am, and I was only watching.'

And now I want to see Chiara. She comes up, hugs me, big smile.

'What have you done!'

What *have* I done?

Eventually I head back to the hotel with Chiara, still wearing the yellow jersey. My new life as a celebrity has apparently begun. I now have to enter hotels in a different way. I'm told, 'There's a hotel next door, so you enter that hotel and everyone will think you're staying there, then go in the back door of *this* hotel.'

When we finally reach our room there's a bottle of champagne on ice waiting for us, courtesy of the hotel owner.

A knock on the door. It's my friend Martin Whiteley, who commentated at my first mountain-bike race when I was 14. It's hard to escape the symmetry. I had dinner with Martin during the training camp before the Dauphiné a few weeks ago; it was near where he lives in Spain.

I introduce Martin to Chiara. It's just the three of us in the room.

I twist the cork.

'Would you like a glass of champagne Martin? I won a race today.'

So here I am, in the yellow jersey, in a Paris hotel, sipping champagne with my wife and an old friend. I'm a long way from that little 14-year-old on a mountain bike, bouncing around on the dirt tracks, wondering if it was possible to make a career out of riding his bike.

AT CHARLES DE GAULLE Airport in Paris we're in the little bar we always go to. There's one healthy meal you can get there, a packet salad.

I take the salad to the table and open it up, and a silverfish walks slowly over the top.

Real life isn't taking long to kick back in.

SOMEONE IS MISSING IN Paris.

Aldo Sassi isn't here to witness this. My much-admired and occasionally intimidating coach would have loved this – how BMC trained and recovered, how tactically smart and consistent we were, the way we rode together as a calm, united team.

It was everything he and I talked about. It was the vision he was trying to instil in all the riders he worked with. Aldo's work with us meant we were clever in the crosswinds, conserved energy when we needed to, made good equipment choices, made course reconnaissance integral and did everything possible to be in the best physical shape and to be the best professionals we could be.

And in the Tour de France BMC did all this to perfection, on every level. Our Tour de France was a distillation of his life's work, a summary of everything he believed in and taught. The way we raced was exactly what he would have wanted. We've put his philosophies to use on the road, and into the results sheet.

I know he would have been super-proud of me. He knew I always worked hard, doing it Aldo's way.

I decide to take some of the flowers from the podium to Aldo's grave. It's the perfect way to honour the enormous contribution he made to my career and my life.

The day after we get home to Stabio we drive five kilometres to the cemetery, and are taken to Aldo's grave by his daughter Valentina and her boyfriend. I tell Valentina how much her dad meant to me, how much he did for my career, what a great man he was.

It's very moving. We stand at his grave and put my Tour race number, 141, on his tombstone with a bouquet of flowers. I reflect once again on all the work we did together – all the analysing of data, all those crushing training loads he expected you to do. Most of the riders he coached couldn't do them. I worked until I dropped for Aldo. I didn't want to let him down, or disappoint him.

I've come here to thank him for all he did for me. But more than that, I've come because this was the culmination of both our life's work.

Everything he lived for has come together in this Tour de France. And it's so profoundly sad that he never got to see me win.

A CALL COMES THROUGH from the Premier of Victoria, Ted Baillieu, 'Can you make it back to Melbourne, we would like to honour your victory.'

The message is brought to me by my manager, Jason Bakker. Jason's life has changed overnight, just as mine has. Jason came to France to experience the Tour; he certainly picked a good year to do it.

When he started his management company a year ago he signed me and Tasmanian rider Matthew Goss. He only had two clients, two cyclists. Then Matthew Goss became the first Australian to win the Milan–San Remo one-day Classic that year and I won Tirreno–Adriatico, and suddenly he was managing the number one and number two bike riders in the world. I don't think his life has been the same since.

In Australia, the media coverage is huge. Greg Baum writes in Melbourne's *Age*:

> *Temperamentally [the Tour] suits Cadel. He is a singular combination of diesel engine and violin, able to chug away at metronomic RPMs for hours at a time, but also delicately strung, obsessive about health, hygiene and appearance, a reclusive, sensitive soul who is married to an Italian pianist and cares about his little dog and Tibet, but on the road is steely and indestructible ... Which leaves me only to declare that if Cadel Evans's victory in the 2011 Tour de France is not the single-most heroic Australian sporting accomplishment of all, it is at least the equal of any preceding it.*

I'm honoured by his words. And as far as character assessments go, his is pretty spot on.

(My interest in Tibet came from my favourite fictional character Tintin, as it happens. My love of this nation caused a mild controversy before the Beijing Olympics in 2008, when I wore an undershirt that read 'Free Tibet' under my Silence–Lotto jersey and was fined by the team for doing so. The next year I was fortunate enough to meet His Holiness the Dalai Lama in person.)

I fly home to Melbourne for the parade (I still say 'home' about Melbourne). The airline staff are very nice, and put Chiara and me right up the front of the plane.

I decide I'd better make the most of all their stocks of fine French beverages. I'm not a big champagne drinker, but as we've been put at the front of the plane, I think this is an appropriate moment to indulge.

In Melbourne, Mum picks us up from the airport, like always, 'What's news Mum?' I look up and see a three-storey high billboard saying 'Congratulations Cadel!' with a photo of me on the Tour podium.

'Nothing, everyone's just talking about the Tour', she replies.

The reception in Melbourne is beyond comprehension. All of my family are there, with about 30,000 others. The streets of the city are lined with people, all wanting to congratulate me. I have never seen sport reach so far into the heart of the public.

That night I go back to Mum's house – she still lives around Plenty – and we drive along the very same roads in and around Diamond Creek, Nutfield and Hurstbridge where the whole dream started. We get back to Mum's quiet block of land, to pause, have a rest, hang out together. In the paddock, the horses are standing wearing their rugs; July in Melbourne is a lot cooler than July in Paris. We sit down by the open fire like so many times before, open a bottle of wine and begin to talk. Mother to son, friend to friend.

We have so many things to catch up on. Winning the Tour de France is one, but there are so many other things a mother needs to ask her son who lives in another country.

Then I go to bed and sleep for hours.

WINNING THE TOUR MEANS so much more to me than I can get my head around at the time. I've put this pressure on myself for such a long time. For years people have asked me: 'Can you win the Tour? Can you win it?' It's not like they ever say, 'Oh you can win the Tour, keep at it, you can win it, keep at it.' It's as though they ask with a fair dose of doubt. As though they don't think I can.

After you're asked this nearly every day for years, unfortunately it starts to change your own way of thinking. It weighs on you. Whether consciously or subconsciously, it's there in your head. It starts gnawing away at you, and you start to believe it may be true. Maybe you *can't* win it. Maybe the doubters are right.

So the win is a vindication, especially the way we've won, riding so well as a team and overcoming setbacks. It makes all the second places easier to live with.

I've had to deal with those second places for three years. The agonising closeness has become an epic element of my story. I've been 'the nearly man'. Every press conference you go to and every interview you do, you're asked about it, and it just gets a bit tiring after a while. After all, coming second in the biggest bike race in the world is not bad.

Now that I've won, I'll never have to deal with that any more. Suddenly it's all been erased from people's minds.

There were many winners that day. The whole BMC team – all the riders, the *soigneurs*, the mechanics, the sports directors and management, Georges Lüchinger, everyone who has put in so much effort. A racing team is like a family, except the family is on the road for much of the year, living right next door to each other and sometimes in the same room. Even families don't have to do that. But when we won, it certainly felt like we were a family, everyone happy for each other.

I'm especially happy for the head of the family, Andy Rihs. Having been through the trauma of the Floyd Landis disqualification in 2006, to come back and start a new team and win the Tour in the way we did – turning a small domestic American team into a Tour de France powerhouse – was extraordinary and so well deserved. It was a fantastically memorable day for him.

Speaking to the media, Andy called my victory an 'honourable' one. 'This old story was a very sad story,' Andy told the VeloNews website's Brian Holcombe, referring to the 2006 scandal with Landis. 'I have to say I have to strip it off of my mind. I did that because I don't want to stay on that level because nobody believed it, but when you drop from the sky without a parachute, it's not fun.'

Tony Rominger was so excited for me when I won the Road World Championships in 2009. And now I've won the Tour he says to me – and this really touches me: 'Finally my dreams have come true. One of my riders has a better *palmarès* than me.' I'm really quite blown away.

If I hadn't won the Tour I would judge my career very differently. After all the close calls and bad luck, I feel as if I deserved to win the Tour, so if I'd missed out, I would have felt a little bit robbed, to be honest. I've always had the legs to win it, but through misfortune, or just lacking a tiny bit, I haven't always had the chance to get it all down on the road. I think I could even have won more than once.

SOON AFTER THE PARADE in Melbourne, I travel to America for the Tour of Utah, known as America's toughest stage race. It traverses the states of Utah and Wyoming, over 1213 kilometres at altitude. It's been an incredible month, just highs and highs. I am looking forward to getting back to training for my next race.

A bike race is a fantastic way to showcase the spectacular scenery that Utah has to offer. I'm thinking 'Wow, I'd really love to come back to this race because it looks like lovely countryside to ride in. Here are some people who have a real belief in cycling.'

Afterwards I'm training near Park City in Utah in preparation for our next team race, the Tour of Colorado. We're out riding along a quiet back road among the prairies of Utah and a car comes along.

'Cadel! Great job at the Tour de France.'

'Oh, thanks!'

Another car comes along five minutes later.

'Cadel! Great job in the Tour de France!'

Wow. Everyone watches this race.

2011 IS THE FIRST edition of the Tour of Colorado, or the USA Pro Cycling Challenge as it's officially known. When I heard that race was starting and it fitted in after the Tour de France I wanted to do it, knowing how beautiful Colorado is to ride in and knowing that in America if they're going to put on a race, they're going to put on a nice race.

Andy Schleck is here too, so they end up having the first and second placegetters in the Tour de France at their event. I come eighth overall.

Walking back from dinner one evening, I see a bar and decide to drop in and see if any familiar riders are there. Andy and Fränk walk in.

'Guys, about that beer we were going to have ...'

So we sit down and I shout them the beer I promised we'd share one day.

A true sign of respect and sportsmanship.

IN OCTOBER, I DONATE a yellow jersey from my Tour de France win to the Madonna del Ghisallo. It will join my World Championship jersey donated two years earlier. An official ceremony is held in the chapel. I'm blessed by the priest and presented with a medallion bearing the insignia of the Saint of Cyclists.

I feel very honoured to have two jersey's worthy of a place there.

MONTHS LATER, I'M DRIVING to meet a friend for dinner one evening. It's just about the first moment I've truly had to myself since the Tour. In your car no one can see who you are and so there's no one to talk to you.

So I'm driving along and suddenly I think: 'Shit, that was really good, wasn't it? I won the Tour!'

It's months afterwards. But my life has been so busy that I just haven't had time to reflect.

What I've certainly noticed is that people have started treating me differently, looking at me differently. I felt this after the first Mountain Bike World Cup race I won in 1997, and again after the World Championships in 2009, but because this is the Tour de France it's on a different level.

To be honest, I find it a little disappointing: I'm being judged only on my results.

Of course, I'm the same person now as I've always been.

The same person who fell for riding a bike at 14.

The same person who is never happier than when I'm out training.

The only difference is that the 14-year-old kid has made a career in cycling and secured its greatest victory.

CHAPTER 21

YOU'RE ONLY AS GOOD AS YOUR LAST RACE

2011–2012

AS IF 2011 HASN'T already been amazing, the final days of the year turn out to be the most incredible of all.

Back in 2009, Chiara and I decided to start a family, but in contrast to most, we started with adoption. Our lives revolved around my cycling. I was aware of how much energy and effort my career needed, and how little time I was left with afterwards for a so-called normal life. We both sacrificed a lot for my career, and I wanted to ensure that other aspects of our lives were being nurtured. One of those was our desire to have a child.

In the process of starting a family through adoption we were led to Ethiopia.

In December 2011, our plans come to fruition and we fly out to meet our new baby boy. We arrive in Addis Ababa on Christmas Day 2011.

During the adoption process, I decide to keep up my training. Chiara doesn't want me going out riding on unknown roads, so

I ride the rollers every day, morning and night. I do about 600 kilometres on the rollers over the time we're there.

Becoming a father is a greater transformation than I could ever have imagined. Robel changes me overnight, as all children do. Up till now, I've been an independent operator, able to jump on my bike and train when I need to and to travel whenever necessary. Now I'm responsible for a beautiful little boy who has become my first priority in life. Everything – training included – comes a distant second.

Athletes are often role models, especially for young people. When you become a father, immediately you're a role model for your child in everything you do. How you speak to people, how you eat your dinner, how you scratch your nose – they absorb everything you do.

On the basic level, being a father makes me even more careful always to wear a helmet when I pick Robel up from school. His friends know that Robel's father is a bike rider: 'He wears a helmet so we should too.'

Instinctively, professional athletes are programmed to be selfish. Instinctively, fathers are programmed to be self*less* – good ones, anyway.

It's a tension I'm committed to resolving. I have a feeling it won't be hard. My career and my commitment to my son are both coming from a place of love. Surely I can do this ...

But I'm about to be severely tested.

IT'S MARCH 2012. I can't get out of bed.

I'm the reigning Tour de France winner and I'm meant to be preparing my defence. But I'm not the same person as I was eight months ago. I feel reduced, a shadow of who I was. In the morning I look in the mirror and my face is puffy, with bags under my eyes. I look at my reflection and wonder why it looks back at me seeming 10 years older than it was just six months ago.

CADEL EVANS

I'm just so tired. It's a tiredness like I've never felt before. I've reduced my training and optimised my recovery but I can't enjoy it because of this exhaustion.

Like a lot of athletes, usually I don't need much sleep, which is a good thing because it gives you much more time to get things done. Normally, unless I'm sick or really tired, I can't stay asleep for more than seven or eight hours. Now I wake up after 12 hours of sleep and all I want to do is go back to bed.

What is the matter with me? When I do get out of bed I'm finding it hard to garner the energy to climb onto my bike, let alone ride it for training.

I've been a little tired for a few weeks, and felt I was starting to get sick. Then from the start of the 2012 season I had a string of health issues, which was uncharacteristic for me. Just small things, but they kept setting me back.

One morning in February I got up after 13 hours of sleep and went for a ride. The plan was to do 130 kilometres of training, including efforts.

I had four espressos and got on my bike. I rode five kilometres down the road and I saw a small patch of grass in the snow. It looked so enticing. Ten minutes into a four-hour training ride, all I wanted to do was stop and lie down on that grass and go to sleep.

Instead I stayed out in the cold, pushing one pedal stroke at a time through the four hours of planned training and efforts, and returned home, even more exhausted.

I'm still doing the same amount of training and racing, but with about 50 per cent of the recovery capacity I previously had. I can race well for one or two or even seven days, but after that I always go into decline.

After all I've learnt and refined over all my years as an athlete, suddenly I'm having to relearn everything, because suddenly everything has changed.

THE CRITÉRIUM INTERNATIONAL IS a pro stage race held in late March in different areas of France – not part of the WorldTour, but a race that's raced hard by all who participate. This year it's moved to the island of Corsica, birthplace of Napoleon and famous for its stunning scenery.

There are three stages over two consecutive days. There's a sprinters' stage and a hilly stage and a time trial, and it's sort of like two one-day races, where all the sprinters and time trialists go flat out on one day and climbers go flat out on the second. But if you're there for GC you've got to be there for both and it's actually quite a tough race. German rider, Jens Voigt and French riders, Raymond Poulidor and Emile Idée have all won it five times.

I'm feeling terrible and I don't want to go to the race because of the logistics of getting there, but I've been called up unexpectedly by the team and they really want me there. Half my luck: Andy Rihs picks me up in his plane and we get there in no time.

In the race, it all comes together very quickly. It's a pleasant surprise to come first in the time trial in stage two, and I actually end up winning overall as well. It's great to get a result for the team, and gives me some much-needed encouragement after I've put in so much effort but been repaid only in fatigue.

There's a nice bonus too. As it's a ASO race – organised by the people who run the Tour de France – I win a Crédit Lyonnais lion like those given to the yellow jersey wearer on the podium of the Tour de France.

I get home from the race that night in time for dinner. I sit down at the table and I put the little lion on the seat next to Robel. He looks at the lion and his face breaks into the biggest smile. It makes the victory extra-sweet.

AS AN ENDURANCE ATHLETE, the first thing you learn is that fatigue is inevitable. Being tired is never an excuse. It's endurance sport's equivalent to 'I can't be bothered', just the poorest, easiest excuse you can give.

I see one specialist sports doctor after another. Five in total. No one can say for sure what is wrong with me. I'm worried mainly because all the medical opinion is saying I just need some rest.

It starts causing tension with the people I work with.

AS JUNE APPROACHES I still feel terrible.

The doctors are still saying, 'Cadel, you're fine, you just need to rest.'

So, I continue on with my training as I have done for so many years, paying special attention to my recovery. Having just became a father, the sleeping routine of an 18-month old child fits in neatly.

I'm very close to my usual numbers in training. But with less capacity I only have one option to make the difference, and that is mentally. To reach these numbers I have to push myself harder, suffer and hurt myself more than I ever have before. This is not only pushing my body over its physical limits, but it's also pushing me over my psychological limits.

I am regularly falling ill, just small things, but enough to affect my training and racing, which in this line of work is another stressor to deal with. My body is letting me down, and despite all my experience, I am not experienced at doing this job with such a small engine. It is a difficult time for me.

WHEN JUNE ARRIVES I'M well enough to ride in the Critérium du Dauphiné. Whenever I ride this race I always find myself up against someone who's going really well. I win the first road stage but finish the race third overall to Sky's Bradley Wiggins and Michael Rogers – which is better than I was expecting.

Leading up to the Tour things start to come unstuck very quickly. I haven't recovered well from the Dauphiné and I can't do much training.

As defending Tour de France champion, I'm feeling the pressure of others' expectations piling up on top of my own. Indeed, I'm expected to win. I try to shelve my exhaustion, try to put it away somewhere so I can deal with it later. I decide to approach the Tour with high hopes of being on the podium again, because of what the doctors are telling me.

In late June, I'm still not in good shape. I feel absolutely exhausted all the time. Why is my body letting me down? Aside from injuries, it never has before.

THE FIRST WEEK OF the Tour goes OK. I'm second to Sky's Chris Froome – now racing under an English licence – on the first hilltop finish in stage seven, which puts me up into second on GC. It's a little frustrating, because I went with Steve Morabito to do reconnaissance of this stage but they hadn't built the bit of road where the last corner was, so the recon's value was rather diminished.

He beats me in a sprint to win the stage. He's ridden on the front for three kilometres and then he still wins. I'm thinking, 'Woah, this is impressive. If he could ride for himself it would be interesting to see what he could do.'

As I understand, Sky have a video course analysis system that may have helped Froome judge the finish better. Maybe it was technology surpassing traditional course reconnaissance. Or maybe it was just good luck for Froome and bad judgement by me. After how the year has gone thus far, I am very disappointed not to get a much needed result at the Tour.

The next day I'm second again in stage eight, from Belfort to Porrentruy in Switzerland. But then as the second week continues, I don't have the ability to recover from one day to the next, and it puts me on a cumulative downward spiral. In stage 11, a tough course through the Alps, I'm just slipping further down GC and the world is watching. When you're getting dropped in the Tour de France and you have a number one on your back the attention is not welcome.

It is the encouragement and an occasional pat on the back that gets me through. While some are happy to see me struggling, it's guys like Steve Morabito, and Fabio Baldato who know I'm doing everything I can but am stuck at half speed.

MY FRUSTRATION INCREASES IN stage 14, when I'm one of 30 riders to suffer multiple punctures after tacks are spread on the road near the summit of the Mur de Péguère, the final climb of the 191-kilometre ride to Foix.

We don't lose any time, because the peloton sportingly slows down, but I'm furious. It's only a suspicion, but I can't dismiss the thought that it's Spanish fans who've thrown the tacks, and the fact that the breakaway leader and eventual winner of the stage is Spaniard, Luis León Sánchez does nothing at all to weaken my conspiracy theory. It's unfortunate that a few instances can give all Spanish fans a questionable reputation.

In the pre-race meeting, John Lelangue twice repeated: 'Watch out for the crazy Spanish fans.' I suddenly think back to the Tour in 1992 that started in Spain, and the tacks that got thrown on the road after Indurain passed by. I can't help but see a similarity here.

BECAUSE I'M RACING SICK I've really only got the capability to do maybe the first 15 stages. I'm dropping further on GC each day, and in stage 16, my American teammate, Tejay Van Garderen moves one place ahead of me.

Tejay has arrived at BMC this year as a very promising rider, a very good time trialist and certainly a good Grand Tour rider. He's long and lanky on the bike, with a fair bit of hip rotation and narrow shoulders, which have helped him become the good time trialist that he is.

There's a moment as we're getting ready for the final time trial when I realise the team are preparing to put their GC hopes in Tejay rather than me.

Normally John Lelangue follows me in every stage I do. But this time, Fabio Baldato walks in and says, 'I'm following you in the time trial.'

'OK,' I think, 'John has decided to follow Tejay. I'm not the best guy so John doesn't want to follow me any more.'

This is quite a reality check. A year ago, we were here in a position to win the Tour de France. My results were the cornerstone of the team's existence. The managers and directors involved me in many of the important decisions. My experience, knowledge and position in the team was highly respected and highly valued. Now that I am slowly sliding down GC and out of contention for the podium, I don't register in the thinking of management or the directors. I am no longer the king on the chessboard, I'm more like a rook or a bishop – my capacity to move is being restricted.

I have some support on a friendship level, from guys like Steve, Fabio and Quinzi. However, these guys don't run teams, they don't run cycling, they can offer support but they can't rectify the situation.

How things can change in a year of professional sport. When it's going well it is great, everyone is there to support you and work with you to make sure everything synergises. When it is going badly, support is minimal. Blame flows your way. Problems accumulate quicker than they can be resolved. It is *very* tough.

But that's sport. People who come into it from the outside think it's brutal and unfair, but that's just the way it is: hyper-competitive. You're only as good as your last race.

BRADLEY WIGGINS WINS THE Tour and I come seventh. Team Sky show they are the guys to beat in the big stage races. It's a huge leap for a team that showed little promise when they formed barely two years ago – winning only in sprints and the occasional prologue.

Chris Froome really comes to the fore for the first time. Froome made his presence felt when he beat me in the first hilltop finish to La Planche des Belles Filles in stage seven. Then we saw later in the Tour that he was maybe even better than Wiggins, certainly as a climber.

He has a personality that's quite clinical, like his racing. Clinical but effective. It seems he has the same approach to his training and his preparation: it's all about numbers and doing what needs to be done, and it doesn't involve a great deal of spontaneity or intuition. But it's working for him, and maybe he's going to become one of the best Grand Tour riders of his generation.

AFTER THE TOUR, I am exhausted as always, but this time, rather than the 'so tired I can't sleep' fatigue, it's a 'I can't stay awake anytime of the day fatigue.'

A few days after the Tour I fly to London. Still disappointed by my Tour result, I'm having to shape up quickly for this event. It's the Olympics, after all, and probably my last one. I want to enjoy it, but above all, I want to perform well.

In London, we stay on the outskirts of the city to train more effectively, but I'm struggling to get out of bed each day. The Australian team director, Matt White pulls me out of the time trial, even though the Olympic protocols don't permit us to call in a reserve time-trial rider.

Monitoring the various indicators of fatigue, I find all of the signs are discouraging. I need a good rest, but I only have two days until the road race, and in those two days I need to do at least one 'pipe opener' – a hard ride to get everything going – then recover a little from that effort. I have one 'hit-out' behind a motorbike and cannot even recover from a few moderate hours of mid-level intensity. I go into the Olympic road race exhausted.

The Olympics are, of course, a unique event; only the World Championships are similar in dynamics. Because we race as national teams, we go head-to-head against the very guys who were teammates, maybe even roommates, at last week's Tour de France.

With a freshly crowned English Tour champion taking part, the road race is attracting a lot of interest. The London course takes in the various sights of London, along a twisting and turning course of varied road widths, on the way out to a very nice circuit. With great weather, there's a wonderful ambience in the English countryside.

The circuit, characteristic of English roads, is generally narrow, requiring good positioning to stay consistently in front. It's a vicious circle: the further back in the field you drift, the harder it gets, the more energy you need to move up, the more fatigued you become, and the further back you go. Typical Worlds or Olympics style. I quickly find myself struggling away at the back, and it just gets worse as the race goes on.

My performance in the race is abysmal, but in terms of enjoyment this is probably my best Games ever.

Previously, I had been so focused on my preparations for, and performance at the Olympics, I don't think I ever adequately appreciated the international flavour of the games. That is, until one evening when I'm having dinner with Stuey O'Grady.

We're sitting in the dining hall with all the other athletes. Stuey says, 'Cadel, you know this is the finest collection of physical specimens in the whole world right here?'

'Wow, that's true, isn't it?' I reply.

We both look around the room. The best athletes of every sport from everywhere in the world are here in this dining hall. All these different people, with every build you can imagine, because every sport's so different.

The weightlifters look like they could eat the marathon runners for breakfast. The swimmers with their V-shaped bodies are top-heavy compared with us bike riders, with our hard quads and minuscule upper bodies.

There's a sport appropriate for pretty much every body type in the world, and we see them all here tonight.

Amid the worry about the poor performance I feel is coming up, I try to be in the moment. I sit there thinking, 'There are the Ethiopian long-distance runners, there are the American sprinters, there are the Ukrainian weightlifters and there are all the Russian gymnasts and the wrestlers – wow, it's incredible, isn't it?'

My problem is always that I'm so hard on myself. As with previous Games, I could have enjoyed this moment more. After all, how many people get to go to the Olympics? Programming myself to assess life by race results has made me a good cyclist. But maybe there's a disconnect. But maybe there's something I'm missing. As a young rider, I remember someone telling me quite firmly. 'Don't forget to smell the roses! Don't ever forget that!'

AMONG THE RIDERS AT BMC who can relate to what I'm going through is Philippe Gilbert, who's just switched over from Lotto this year. He had his best year in 2011 and then this year he's had health problems like me. Dental problems that have started a string of setbacks. We've both rode poorly at this year's Tour de France.

Another new team member, Thor Hushovd, has had to withdraw from the Giro, the Tour and the London Olympics thanks to an unknown illness. He's hardly made a mark this season.

I've won the Tour in 2011, Thor Hushovd's become World Champion, and Gilbert's had his best year ever, with a string of victories that put him top of the UCI WorldTour rankings. And at the start of 2012 the cycling press are telling us, 'We're going to be the dream team in 2012, how's anyone going to beat us?'

Then all of us have suffered from various health issues and gone on to have one of the most disappointing seasons of our careers. We've gone from the 'dream team' to a trio of under-performers all in one year.

Gilbert, Thor and all I have this in common: none of us is used to performing so poorly, so mentally we don't have the experience to deal with it.

The expectations put on riders who have been World Champion, and done well in the Grand Tours, are much higher. And cyclists who are under-delivering get nervous and stressed. That's certainly the way I'm feeling. And I don't know what to do about it. Outwardly you become intolerant and impatient and you become a bit more difficult to work with.

So I see Gilbert a little bit in that situation too, which of course is never going to help a friendship.

Thor is somewhat different. He and I have spoken as colleagues throughout our careers, but it's not until we became teammates this year at BMC that we spent much time together. Initially, the cycling media try to create friction between us, reprinting a quote from a year previously saying I didn't want a sprinter in my Tour team … it's true I didn't want a 'pure' bunch sprinter, but Thor is so much more than a sprinter.

THINGS ARE CHANGING AT BMC. Tejay is 25 and finished the Tour fifth overall, I am 35 and managed seventh. These results seems to have overwritten all previous results and the contributions I've made to the team outside of races. Resources and efforts are quickly shifted away from me, windows of opportunity are hurriedly closed.

In the end: you are judged by your race results alone. If you perform well on GC at the major events, your year is done. Lock it away. You're safe. You've done your job.

It's happened before. I performed badly in 2009 in the Tour de France, but my year was redeemed by winning the World Championships. In the end it was an OK year.

In August I get a phone call from the team saying that they want me to do the Giro. As in, they *don't* want me to do the Tour.

They've lost faith in me as a Tour de France rider. I will lead the Giro team, Tejay will lead the Tour team. I guess that's the end of my Tour career.

I'VE BEEN SEEING DOCTORS for months now. I ask all of them, 'What is the matter with me?'

At first they all say, 'You're just tired, have a rest.'

In late August we're at the USA Pro Cycling Challenge in Colorado, where finally a diagnosis comes through.

After many tests, Dr Max Testa has found an abnormally high count of viral antibodies in my blood. I'm told I have a form of chronic fatigue syndrome. It's a relief to know what the problem is because I'm very rational about these things.

IT'S A DIFFICULT TIME for me. As a cyclist you're often alone, so when you're not on the bike you need strong people around you with big hearts.

David Bombeke is one of those.

As a rider you're often concentrating so much on your career and the endless pursuit of performance and results that you lose perspective. Whether it's your health or bad luck or injury, or issues in your personal life, your psyche gets pushed in one direction and another and you can't control it. Because you're in the middle of it, you struggle to have a good overview of the situation you're in.

This is where a great *soigneur* can be really helpful. A *soigneur* who knows you really well, knows your situation, knows what you're dealing with, and has a bit of a wider perspective.

A good *soigneur* knows when you're doing well and knows when you are not, because they can feel it when they give you a massage. The muscles in your body say a lot about you, and the *soigneur* can read a lot about you this way.

David is in some ways my *soigneur*. As a qualified osteopath and physiotherapist he probably doesn't want to be called a *soigneur*, but it's just a name. David is invaluable to me because he knows me as a person. He understands my psychology. He sees me when I'm good and he sees me when I'm bad, when I'm happy, when I'm overly stressed or angry, when I'm winning, when I'm losing. David sees all sides to me.

He'll say, 'Hey, calm down', or 'Don't let that person bother you', or sometimes 'How do people get so far while being so stupid?' But usually it will be, 'We need some Johnny Cash today.'

David is such a trusted friend and ally in a year when I really need one.

VERY FEW PEOPLE OUTSIDE my close circle know how ill I've been since January, and that is frustrating because the expectations on me are high, even for a healthy person. I feel like I have not only wasted a season because of illness, I have paid for it with my physical and mental wellbeing.

At the end of August, the Max tells me, 'Stop racing and go home and sit on your couch for two months.'

Great. If I had known that in February, maybe I could have come back and done a good Tour and Olympics.

So I stop for two months completely. No activity whatsoever, which, because I've recently become a father, is a bonus. I'm able to spend a lot of time with my little boy Robel, which is a blessing.

ON OCTOBER 10, THE United States Anti-Doping Agency releases a damning 1000 page report labelling Lance Armstrong a 'serial cheat' who was at the heart of a systematic doping conspiracy. It unleashes a media frenzy around the world. Naturally this is confronting for everyone involved, myself included. After all, I was there trying to follow Lance on the climbs of the 2005 Tour de France. The maelstrom rolls on sparing no-one. I am even asked questions about my meeting over a decade ago with Michele Ferrari. When I met with Dr Ferrari, I had no idea what he was involved in. All I knew was that he worked with a lot of riders. He gave me good advice, and based on his advice I made a good career choice. He was later associated in the media with many riders and methods of questionable reputation. If people want to associate me with them too, then so be it. I can only imagine Aldo Sassi turning in his grave in disgust.

Nine days after the report is released, closer to home, Stephen Hodge steps down from his position as vice president of Cycling Australia. When I see my friend and one-time manager some months later, he explains that it was 'Just not right' that he be involved with sanctioning riders for misconduct that he himself was guilty of during a darker period of our sport.

I hope that his brave admission is understood in the context of the period and the particular team environment he found himself in. Stephen has done so much for cycling in our country. It's never black and white.

FOR THE REST OF 2012 it's about recovery and slowly getting ready for the new year.

Most cyclists are creatures of habit, and I'm no exception. I like a solid plan. A solid plan that brings solid, reliable results. I cannot guarantee I will win, but I like to be able to guarantee I will perform well. All of a sudden, it's like I've been given a whole new engine to work with, but someone's taken out my V8 and replaced it with a little turbo four-cylinder thing, which doesn't have nearly as much torque and seems to require a complete rebuild after just one week of racing. And I'm having to learn how to do that.

I feel like I'm starting all over again.

CHAPTER 22

BEGINNING OF
THE END?

2013

IN THE OFF-SEASON, ON the flight from Europe back to Australia, I usually find some time to think, reflect and plan for the following year. This is a time when I look back at what I have done, look at where things can be improved and put them into a plan for the following year.

Going into 2013, it is very unsettling to not be able to plan. How is my body going to recover after being ill and being pushed so hard when it was ill? For the first time in an 18-year career, I plan more for recovery than training.

In addition, I am now a father as well. Cycling seasons come and go. A bad year can be rectified with a good year. But a year lost seeing your child growing up cannot be recuperated.

A road cyclist often leaves home for one, two, three or even four weeks at a time. When you go to the airport and an infant or toddler starts crying and screaming when they realise you are going away, it tears at your heart.

But if you stay at home and don't perform up to expectations at the next race the team look at you and ask, 'Why didn't you do a training camp?' or, 'Why weren't you at altitude like the guy who won today?' Worse still, you might go away from your family to be the consummate professional, and either do not get selected for the race you are training for or get a start, only to be taken out on the first day by some idiot in the peloton who is not paying attention.

Your child is only a baby once. You only get one shot at being around in these critical years, and I'm not going to miss them.

Everyone tells me, 'Appreciate it now, because it goes by quickly.' They could also be talking about my career.

I'M RIFLING THROUGH A drawer, looking for my Motorola cycling top. I need it because I'm going for a ride.

It's 1993. A young American called Lance Armstrong has just become World Champion in Oslo, Norway. Young Lance rides for the Motorola team and he's just taken on the world and won. He's 21. I'm 16, still at high school, have only been riding for a couple of years and this victory has grabbed me.

The young Lance Armstrong. What kid into cycling wouldn't think he was great? American, brash, confident, powerful on the bike. At this stage there aren't many non-Europeans who are winning in cycling. And here's this young guy, an English speaker, charismatic, taking them on and winning in a sport almost totally dominated by Europeans.

The day he wins in Oslo I go for a ride with a friend, Russell Collett, after school. I'm wearing my Motorola team jersey. Most boys my age wear Australian Rules football scarfs – and if I was more into Aussie Rules I would wear the scarf of the Geelong Cats. This isn't my thing. I think this Texan guy, Lance Armstrong is cool.

Twenty years later, in January 2013, after years of suspicion, allegation and always-fervent denial – usually in the tone 'How could you possibly suggest this?' – Lance Armstrong finally admits, to interviewer, Oprah Winfrey, that he's lied about doping, and that he doped before winning all seven of his Tour de France titles.

The interview is one of the biggest stories in sport. In any sport, ever. 'It was a mythic perfect story, and it wasn't true,' he tells Oprah. It was, Lance said, 'one big lie that I repeated a lot of times'.

It's cold, it is matter-of-fact, and it stuns the world.

There've been doping scandals before – Festina, Puerto – but Armstrong's explosive revelations are a watershed in the sport.

The day he reveals his deceit to Oprah, the sport of cycling changes. It's probably right to say that never again will a rider – or a team of riders – be able to operate the way Lance and his team did. The sophistication of doping tests is now such that cheats will be found out much earlier and 'impossible' feats will remain just that.

There follows, of course, a media frenzy. It's actually quite surreal that after Lance has spent years doing everything in his power to protect his dirty secret, now it's all come flowing out at once.

The world is transfixed. I am more disgusted. I don't want to dignify it by watching the interview on television as it's transmitted. I go about my life and read excerpts afterwards.

My opinion of Lance after everything that's come out in the press in the last few years hasn't changed much. Lance is quite a good bike rider but my main impression has always been that he's a very astute businessman.

I follow the Armstrong saga as it unfolds along with millions around the world. The difference is that I rode against him, and saw up close – up *very* close – how he raced. Before he rode away from me at least.

On a personal level, I was always quite respectful of him. I never bothered him when I raced and he never bothered me. I was never a target of his bullying or harassment. He never tried to manipulate or intimidate me. On that level, I never had a problem with him.

I never saw him outside of the races but in a race I'd say, 'Hello, how's everything going? What do you think of this rider or that rider?'

We had a similar upbringing, because like him, I came from another sport and was quite successful as a young athlete (he was originally a triathlete), and was the only child of divorced parents, as I was. That's where the comparison ends, though.

My initial feelings of amazement after the Oprah interview – not at the revelations but at his decision to dope – are soon replaced by the same emotion I've had towards dopers throughout all my years in professional cycling: a certain numbness. For most of my cycling career that is precisely what's got me through times when it felt like every second rider was doping.

I've had to stay protected inside this bubble that I've made, and that strategy has usually worked. I've had my program of training and racing and looking after myself and making sure I'm the best prepared professional I can be.

Of course, I've talked about it with friends, family, teammates, team managers, team doctors and sports directors. How could you not? It's been right up in our faces so often, and it's had an impact on how we've gone about our race strategies when riders from other teams have been banned. But I've never dwelt on it. I've never over-analysed.

My friend, George Hincapie rode a lot with Lance Armstrong in the last three of the teams they were in. George helped Armstrong win several of his seven Tour de France victories, riding as a loyal and reliable lieutenant. George has never spoken in any detail to me about what happened in those teams.

One day, though, we're having a meal together and talking about some of the results in the 2005 Tour de France. I name a certain rider. 'What about him? He was clean, wasn't he?'

George looks at me. 'Trust me, he wasn't.'

'What about that one?'

'No, no, not him either.'

Well, I'm not going to keep asking. What's the point?

After that conversation with George we never speak about it again.

I find what he's telling me demoralising. It gets to the stage where I don't want to know *what* he knows. There's a very good reason for that, and it's to do with morale. As an athlete, I don't want to know about this stuff because I don't want to get demoralised.

No, best not to know. Ignorance is so underrated. In this instance, not knowing is far better than knowing.

I GO INTO THE 2013 season hoping things are going to turn around soon. In February, I fly to the Middle East to compete in the Tour of Oman, a new pro stage race. Middle Eastern countries see the value in large events, especially cycling events that showcase landscapes and scenery so effectively. The Tour is part of the UCI's plan to expand cycling's reach around the world. Co-owned and organised by Eddy Merckx, the event was launched in 2010, with Fabian Cancellara winning the inaugural edition.

It's always interesting to see another country and the race organisers put us up in a sensational hotel with large well-appointed rooms with ocean views. When I'm in places like this I sometimes get a little too much 'holiday relaxation'.

There is no culture of cycling in Oman. But apart from the weirdness of seeing no one on the sides of the road watching the race, it's good to ride in the warmth of desert roads. It does actually rain while we're there, very briefly, but it dries up even more quickly.

I'm very happy to have the chance to ride in this race. It's a beautiful race in a dusty, rugged but gorgeous landscape, and we get a few insights into a vastly diverse culture.

Not that it's an easy ride. It's my tenth season on the road, but my first season post chronic fatigue and its associated disruptions. I still want to be at my best to be able to fight for good results in all of the races, despite the diminishing amount of confidence the team may have in me.

Fortunately things are looking pretty good by stage four, which finishes with a climb up Green Mountain; we only race up the first six kilometres of a 20-kilometre climb. It's incredibly steep, but I finish second to Chris Froome by 24 seconds.

I finish the Tour of Oman in third place after Chris Froome and Alberto Contador. Coming third is quite a relief. After the illness last year, I didn't know what level I was going to be able to return to, which was a difficulty in itself. So it's nice to have a good indicator at the start of the year that things might be starting to drift back to normal.

BUT MY OPTIMISM MAY have been a little premature.

In early March I come 28th in the Strade Bianche, then a few days later it's time for the Tirreno–Adriatico. It's a race in which I've done well in the past; all things being equal, I can do well again.

But it doesn't work out for me. I can't follow the best guys over the climbs and I finish in 22nd position.

The doctors are still saying, 'You need to rest.'

I'm resting as much as I can, but I have a life, I'm a husband and a father, and as a professional athlete I have to do a certain amount of training and racing. Pro cycling coaches, team managers and sport directors understand 'recovery', but 'not training' does not even enter into their thinking. All of this limits how much rest I can get. And so I'm stuck between a rock and a hard place.

It's become a tradition for me to get a ride back from the Tirreno–Adriatico with Stefano Cattai, a former Italian pro rider and now in charge of BMC company–team liaison. He was one of the very first people from the BMC 'family' that I met back in 2009.

Back home, I get a phone call from the team. 'We want to meet with you, Cadel.'

I'm thinking, 'OK, what's going on here?'

On 16 March, the night before Milan–San Remo – which I won't be racing – Jim Ochowicz, John Lelangue and Max Testa come up from the team hotel in Milan to meet me over dinner in Como.

We meet at the Albergo Terminus, an elegant old hotel overlooking Lake Como, just across the road from the ferry wharf.

Jim has been coming to this hotel since he ran the 7-Eleven team in the 1980s; it's a favourite haunt for both of us. The hotel maître d' here has worked in films as a George Clooney double, and if you half close your eyes, there's a remarkable similarity.

We sit in the lounge area. Jim goes to speak, but before he says anything I ask, 'Do you still want me to ride the Giro this year?'

Jim does the talking. 'We think you should ride the Giro. It will give you the base that you're missing to do a good Tour de France.'

I'm thinking, 'So now they want me to race the Giro – great. But to do a Giro – Tour double? I don't allow myself to think it's impossible, but it will almost certainly compromise my chance to perform well at the Tour.

But I don't say much. I just tell them I'll think about it.

Actually, there's not a lot to think *about*.

When you're winning the races, you get more choice. You're in a much stronger position to shape your own race schedule. After the struggles of 2012 and the subsequent results, I'm not in the best position to be calling the shots. The decision is made much easier by the fact that the Giro is a race I genuinely love.

The reasoning behind it, from the team's point of view, is that, considering my age and experience, all the indicators show that in past seasons I perform better when I have two Grand Tours in my legs rather than one. Ideally, those two Grand Tours would be the Tour de France and the Vuelta, but at this point I'm underprepared after last year, and there's only the Giro to get me into shape before the Tour de France.

I've only ridden the Giro and the Tour in the same season once before, in 2010. I was disappointed with both performances, but that was exclusively due to illness and injury. And, of course, the following year was my best year at the Tour ever.

It's true that all of my best performances have come in seasons when I've raced two Grand Tours. Riding the Giro and shaping up well for the Tour seems unlikely. But not riding the Giro and shaping up well for the Tour seems *even more* unlikely.

There's an underlying philosophy here, too. As a professional athlete, if you do what the team tells you and you perform badly, the responsibility for the bad performance is shared. If I throw my weight around, say I want this and that and go against their wishes, the responsibility of the under-performance is all on my shoulders.

Our meeting at Albergo Terminus comes to an end. Jim, John and Max drive back to the team hotel for Milan–San Remo. I don't know how poor John will stay awake driving the team car the next day in the season's longest race. I make the 20-kilometre drive home, and by the time I'm there, I've developed a skeleton plan to prepare for the Giro. The next day, I go out training with the Giro as my main objective in mind.

A WEEK LATER, I race the Critérium International once again, but I don't have enough in me to perform well.

Then in April I ride the Giro del Trentino, one of the great 'training races', held in the Trentino–South Tirol region of northern Italy. It's not part of the WorldTour, so not as important as far as points, team rankings and future contracts are concerned. But because it's such a nice race, with an optimal slot in the calendar, a lot of the top riders go there to fine-tune their fitness for the Giro by racing hard on the climbs. It always ends up being quite a competitive little week of racing, in great scenery, and without the expectations and nervousness that the bigger races are often choked up with.

It's a rushed period for me, squeezing in the necessary course reconnaissance, altitude camps and the usual specific training in both climbing and time-trialling, but also testing and training with a specific uphill time-trial bike. A new experience for me. So I go to the Trentino, still in need of progress, but considering the short time frame, it's not going too badly.

The team scramble to get together for the team time trial on the first day, after travelling all the way up to Linz in Austria. We're disappointed to lose a discouraging amount of time to the victorious Team Sky.

I struggle through three other stages, making modest improvements along the way, to finish fifth on the last mountain stage. A reasonable result behind Vincenzo Nibali and Mauro Santambrogio, now racing for Vini Fantini–Selle Italia, who catches and passes me in the closing kilometres. They also end up first and second on GC, while I place eighth. Nibali is making all sorts of statements on the road. He is looking good for the Giro in a few weeks.

BY THE TIME WE start the Giro, things are starting to come together. It has been a crammed and stressful preparation, but it seems like it has been productive.

Mark Cavendish from the Isle of Man (Omega Pharma–Quick-Step) is having a great opening week to the *Corsa Rosa* (Pink Race).

I like Cav. Above all, I like his passion to race. I see him as a rider who hates training as much as he loves racing. Therefore he shows up at the start of the year, a long way behind his competitors.

But if he does not push himself much in training, he pushes himself very, very hard racing. I once heard a rider say this about him: he only just wins the sprints in the first week of a Grand Tour, and by the third week he wins them by five lengths. Because he doesn't train much at home, he's fresher to race better and harder, but also, he gets the training effect of the race. Because he has not expended all that physical and mental energy in training, when times get tough and he is hungry to win, he is bullet-proof.

George Hincapie, who rode with Cav at Team Columbia (formerly T-Mobile), once said to me about him: 'When he gets there you think there's no way in hell he can get over this climb but if he thinks he can, you've never seen anyone who can push themselves as hard.'

My first memories of racing with Cav are his first Tour de France in 2008: you're riding along and there are 10 ks to go before a sprint finish. You move towards the front to be safe, but also you don't want to get in the sprinters' way. And you hear people behind you swearing and cursing, 'Oh, shit, here comes Cav', and sure enough, from behind you, *Boof!* you get a shoulder barge or an elbow in the backside, and you're saying, 'Ten ks to go, really, please!'

I think banging into people as he's coming through is his way of getting himself psyched up for the finish. I think that's a little bit unnecessary, especially as some of us are there for the GC of the race; as GC contenders we're not exactly a sideshow.

He has grown up and calmed down since then.

TWO WEEKS INTO THE Giro I find myself second overall, with Vincenzo Nibali leading. It is a pleasant surprise, after an abysmal 2012.

But we're riding with some newly developed components that haven't been tested properly, and certainly haven't been tested in bad conditions. And the Giro of 2013 is the epitome of *bad* conditions, the worst conditions at a Grand Tour in years. If we're not racing in torrential rain, we're riding in the snow.

The extreme conditions are accentuated by extreme stage routes that often have to be changed. The climb to Sestriere in stage 14 is omitted because it's thought to be too dangerous to descend on the icy roads. An avalanche risk shortens stage 15's climb up the Col du Galibier. And stage 19 in northern Italy is cancelled, which means the omission of the mountains Passo di Gavia and Passo dello Stelvio.

The inclement conditions are a test, both of our skills on the bike and our ability to resist the cold. It's a test of equipment as well – newly developed components that had not made it to the market yet. It turns out I am the guinea pig in these conditions.

In stage 20 in the Dolomites, there's a freak snowstorm as we head for the mountain finish at Tre Cime di Lavaredo. The weather is ridiculous and, as prepared as we are, it's not enough for these extreme conditions.

But for me, the biggest issue is being a guinea pig for the new equipment. I'm generally happy to help BMC and its partners develop and improve their products, but in this case it really backfires on me. Colombian, Rigoberto Urán sees my gears jumping, so he accelerates, and because I'm limited to larger gears with this new equipment, I can't follow. He jumps into third place in the stage and second place overall.

The equipment problems limit my capacities to put what I have on the road. I've been second on GC for most of the race and I fade on the last climb, overtaken in the last two kilometres on the final snowy mountain finish.

Equipment testing and development is part of my job, but in this moment there are some in team management rubbing their hands together every time I falter or underperform. So while my extreme conditions testing was of benefit to some, I will be judged by most as having slid backwards on GC. It's nasty timing for me.

After this freezing stage, my body feels numb. I can hardly walk up the stairs of the bus. Someone has to undress me, because I've got no dexterity whatsoever: my hands are so cold there's no blood circulation.

On the bus I stagger into a lukewarm shower. My body's so cold that even at 20 degrees the water scalds my skin. So I have a 15-degree shower and slowly turn the warm water up. I'm filthy, covered in diesel stains, which have got embedded up my nose, in my ears, in my eyes. I stand in the shower scrubbing away at my quads, shins and backside because they've got black stains on them. This evening the dirt leaks out of my eyes, a startling sight for the people I'm talking to over dinner.

I stand there under the shower and after a long while the stains are gone and the numbness has begun to fade. But of course by this time, everyone else is on the bus and they want to get into the shower too. I ask my teammate, Ivan Santaromita how the race was for him. He says, 'That was the coldest day I've ever had on my bike.'

While equipment cost me a place on GC, which I'm absolutely furious about. In my mind, I really could have got second in this Giro. But considering I wasn't even sure I'd be ready to race, third place at the Giro d'Italia certainly isn't bad.

It means I've now stood on the podium of each Grand Tour and I am quietly proud of that. Of course I'd rather have been on the top step of the podium of each Grand Tour, but anyway …

The result has been much better than what I was expecting, and I'm surprised and relieved. I've been questioning whether I'm still capable of performing at the top level. It will be nice to improve on this at the Tour.

IT'S A TIGHT TURNAROUND, six weeks between the Giro and the Tour. Just as you're calming down and recovering from the first one, you need to be putting your foot on the gas to get ready for the next one.

We have a good plan for the Tour. The problem is that the Giro has wiped me out. I start the Tour empty, and it shows. It's similar to my experience in 2010, but this time I've had even more trouble recovering in between the two races.

Stage eight, the first mountain stage of the Tour, includes an 18.6-kilometre climb up the Col de Pailhères and finishes at the Ax 3 Domaines ski resort. As we come into the last kilometre of the climb, I can see the Team Sky guys on the front and a long line of riders behind them. Just the sight of them all increases the fatigue in my legs and makes me question how competitive I can be on the last important climb of the day.

When we start the last climb towards the finish, I am struggling. But it's not the sort of struggle of two years ago when I might have dropped 170 of the world's best bike riders and been amongst the 10 in front. I'm struggling, and only 140 riders have been dropped, and there are still 40 guys in front of me … I'm looking ahead and counting them, seeing them all and knowing I'm not going to be able to follow. I am a long, long way from being competitive here, nowhere near the standards I've always set myself.

I'm absolutely destroyed by the end of this Tour de France. It's pretty clear I haven't fully recovered from last year's virus. I finish 39th: my worst Tour result ever.

IN AUGUST, A COUPLE of weeks after the Tour, Tony Rominger rings.

He tells me as diplomatically as he can: 'You should focus on the Giro or one-week stage races.'

It's not what you want to hear as a rider.

I hope Tony's wrong, years of this have conditioned me not to believe it, but not long afterwards, Jim Ochowicz calls.

'Forget about the Tour next year, Cadel. Focus on the Giro.'

I'm glad Tony rang first, because it's prepared me for this.

All I can think of afterwards is: 'Forget about the Tour?'

In one way it's nice to be able to concentrate on the Giro, because in my heart I want to race it and race well. But my head is saying: 'I'm not a Tour de France rider any more.'

For 10 years the Tour de France has been the race I have worked for, based my career on, planned my life around, what I am known and recognised for, what I get out of bed everyday to work for. And now I have to let it go?

My third in the Giro in May shows I can still ride at the highest level. And now I'm being told I'm no longer going to be given the chance to ride the race that has meant so much to me.

I try to be rational about it. But I'm sad.

This is how quickly things turn around for a professional athlete; you're only as good as your last race. It's a phrase worn thin by overuse, but every athlete in the world knows it's true. So I won a Tour de France? That was two years ago, almost ancient history.

There've been a few key moments since I've joined BMC when Jim has said things that I didn't want to hear but I needed to. He's offered his views about things outside my professional life, too, and I respect him for that. He's been a little like a father figure in that way.

After the shock has died down, I tell him how much I appreciate his courage as a truth-teller, when the truth was the very last thing I wanted to hear.

I'm no longer a Tour de France rider. Officially.

I guess I have to start learning to accept that this is the beginning of the end.

MEANWHILE, MY SEASON CONTINUES. In September, I race the Tour of Alberta in Canada. It's a new race in the cycling calendar, and I'm keen to be a part of it and continue my tradition of participating in the 'inaugural' of new races.

I have great memories of Alberta province, from the races and training I did there in my mountain bike days. One of the most amazing rides I ever did was a training ride towards Banff and Lake Louise in Alberta. Stunning country.

What distinctly stands out about the Tour of Alberta is how incredibly fast the roads are. We go for a training ride in Edmonton, Alberta. The only way to ride out of car-centric Edmonton is to ride on the freeway out of the city and get onto some country roads. We get on these roads and they are just so incredibly fast compared to any roads I have ridden on.

On the first training ride I do, I notice the numbers straightaway. 'Mm, must be training pretty well, we have a 36-k-per-hour average speed.'

Then we do some efforts and I'm riding at 55 ks an hour when normally I'd be doing 45 or 48 on a good road in Europe. Riding in Canberra during my AIS days, for the same effort I'd be doing 40, where roads are very slow and dead. And here the roads are hard, dry, straight and smooth, with no roundabouts, so we're doing ridiculous speeds.

People often ask me why I didn't go in breakaways as a rider. Well, normally in Europe, no one wants to collaborate with me in a breakaway because I can go uphill and go pretty well all day. I'm also reasonably fast at the finish.

In America, though, people get in a breakaway and they want to race and they race to the end.

At the Tour of Alberta, a break goes early in stage four, so I jump across and enter the group of seven or eight riders. To my surprise, they are happy to collaborate for the 100 or so kilometres until the sprint. Of the remaining five riders at the end, I'm able to sprint fastest and win the stage. I'm not sure they'll be riding in breaks with me any more.

Because we're getting ready for some longer days on the bike in upcoming races, Marcus Burghardt and I decide to motor-pace halfway back to the hotel to get some extra distance after the stage.

As one of the 2011 Tour team members, 'Burgie' will always have a special place in my thoughts. The big, quiet, incredibly dry-humoured German took a while to soften up and be himself around us initially, but when he did, he really came to be valued by the team.

I say to him, 'Burgie, look at your computer.'

We're going a little bit downhill, and we're doing 70 ks an hour. Then we get out on the highway and it's steeper.

'Um, Burgie, don't look at your computer now but we're going really fast.'

We're riding at 110 kilometres an hour, motor-pacing behind the car. At these speeds we ride all the way back to the hotel and still don't get enough hours.

These are very fast roads.

OUR NEXT TWO RACES, held soon afterwards in Québec province, are the Grand Prix Cycliste de Québec and the Grand Prix Cycliste de Montréal, two recent additions to the WorldTour. Both are one-day 'modern Classics' that I want to experience at least once in my career. I'm always keen to participate in new races in countries around the world with emerging cycling cultures. It's interesting to see how cycling is accepted and developing, but I also have a long-term view of hoping to help – even just a little – the globalisation of our sport.

The two Grands Prix Cyclistes are highly competitive, though coming just before the Worlds in the calendar makes them difficult to manage if the Worlds are in another time zone. The longer travel and time zone changes are another challenge to overcome in the quest for reaching your peak, already a difficult task at this late stage in the season.

This year my role is to help Greg Van Avermaet. I finish 18th in Montreal and 12th in the second Grand Prix Cycliste, held in Quebec City. Then we all head back to Europe to get ready for the Worlds in Firenze.

I go up to a quiet little mountain retreat near Steve Morabito's house to prepare. The course this year is a tough one and I want to give myself every chance at being in the hunt for another world title.

Normally the women's race is on the Saturday and the men on the Sunday. For so many World Championships, the weather is bad to terrible on the Saturday and fantastic on the Sunday. This year though, a storm is predicted for the men's race.

We go to sign on for the start and the clouds open, a downpour like you would expect in the tropics rather than in Tuscany. There are a few early crashes on the wet roads that lead us out to the main circuit but it is on the circuit that staying upright really becomes difficult. After just a few laps, the bunch has been significantly reduced by crashes.

A few laps in, Simon sees me in the group and says, 'Follow me down here on the right, they are all crashing on the left.' I hesitate a moment then follow. Two guys hit the brakes in front of us, Simon squeezes though the small gap that is left and continues. Following him is Dave Tanner and then myself. Dave goes down, I hit him and then bounce onto the barriers.

Lying on the road the pain in my right tibia is horrendous. I sit up. The Australian team director, Brad McGee comes over, 'Are you ok?'

I look at my leg and can see it actually swelling up. Brad takes one look at it and calls the ambulance.

They lift me into the ambulance, Dave Tanner is next to me, Sam Sanchez is in there lying on a stretcher. One or two other riders are here with us. I am sure I have broken my leg. The ambulance driver asks where we want to go, I'm the only Italian speaker there.

'To the hospital'

'Where is it?' he asks.

'What? Have you got a navigation system?'

'No. Have you got a phone?'

'No. Have you?'

Wet in my lycra with what feels like a broken leg, this is starting to infuriate me.

A young race volunteer gets things organised and we arrive at a nearby hospital. Sanchez is still groaning on the stretcher. Wives and girlfriends are there waiting for battered loved ones. The hospital is right out of the 1960s, clean and tidy but certainly not modern. The staff are very helpful and X-ray me quickly, to tell me the news I want to hear, the pain is severe bruising, not a fracture.

A few days later, I am riding back from the local café when Fabio calls me, 'Are you okay to race Lombardia?

'I don't know... I still can't train yet.'

'I need to know. We have to pull Burgie out the race and he is due to leave this afternoon. Can you ride or not?'

It's one kilometre to my local café and I have lost enough skin off my backside that it's impossible to sit on the seat of my town bike for that distance. Two hundred and fifty kilometres next week? 'Err, no I won't be able to ride.' Season over.

WHAT COULD GO WRONG?

We're at a friend's farm in Scone, thoroughbred horse country in the Hunter region of New South Wales. Simon Clarke and I are getting away from cycles and teams and schedules and race books and returning to our roots as country kids. There are no bicycles in sight, but there's a pretty awesome range of mechanised vehicles we have our eyes on, vehicles where your legs sit there quietly and your wrist does all the work.

I have always loved cars – anything mechanical, really. This stretches back to my childhood with Dad. We'd spent hours together pulling engines and gearboxes apart and I came to have a reasonable understanding of the workings of engines. From a young age, I was driving tractors, cars and riding motorbikes on his farm.

Simon and I have vowed to talk about anything but cycling. Of course we do, though.

It's late afternoon. I'm bouncing along on the back of a quad bike that Simon is driving. The sun is fading and the shadows are getting longer on the paddocks, stretching towards a line of elms. We are two guys hanging out on some cool machines.

I call Simon off when I have visions of him bouncing off the steep road down the side of the mountain. I start driving and he urges me to take off up an embankment.

'Will this make it?' I ask.

Simon is confident, 'Yeah, these things can go anywhere.'

And then suddenly it isn't so cool. When we try to ride the quad up the embankment it slides backwards and beaches itself.

Soon I'm up to my armpits in the mud, trying to put rocks under the wheels of the quad so that we can get some traction to get it out. Simon remembers I'm wearing a Swiss-made watch, probably quite valuable, a present from the TAG Heuer CEO on winning the Tour de France.

'Shouldn't you take that off?'

I say, 'No, they told me it can survive anything.'

We've both faced many challenges in our cycling careers. This is just another one.

But for all the rocks I've put under its wheels we can't get the quad out. Now it's dusk, and we can't see much at all.

We have to return the next day to pluck the quad out of the swamp with our friend's dune buggy. It takes us weeks to wipe the smiles of our faces...

The timing has been perfect. I have a lot of decisions to make about my career, and I want to avoid having others make them for me.

PART THREE

FINISHING
the RACE

CHAPTER 23

THE DECISION

2014

AFTER THE 2013 SEASON, there are changes going on within the BMC team at the management level, and some of them involve their approach to me.

The main plan for the year is to do well at the Giro d'Italia. Now that I won't be doing the Tour de France, it's the race I want to concentrate on.

This year, Jim has given me the opportunity to choose all the riders and staff for the Giro. It's a great indication of his faith in me. I take up his offer, thinking this will be my last chance at a Grand Tour, and I'm able to put together a fantastic team.

Part of my role this year is to get the team off to a good start, to get some points straightaway for the team rankings. In 2013, these were pretty average, 11th in the world rankings, which wasn't nearly as good as we should have been. A big part of the team's goals is to improve this for 2014.

The team's best seasons are when we get off to a good start. So the plan is to do the Tour Down Under in Adelaide in January and get some momentum going for 2014.

We have a rider on the team who, while not especially well suited to the Tour Down Under, is usually capable of performing well in the early season. That rider is ... me. I've always thought the Tour Down Under was a fantastic event, and while it'll be tough to be so far away from my little guy Robel for a month, it's the first time in 10 years that I won't be riding the Tour. So I can go into the season early without having to hold anything back for later.

I start my season with the Australian National Championships in Ballarat. It's the first time I've raced in the Nationals since 2005. I come into the finish with Simon Gerrans confident I will be able to beat him in a two-up finish to win. I get out of the saddle to sprint and can't accelerate at all. I have to settle for second.

Simon, riding for Orica–GreenEDGE, turns out to be the one to beat at the Tour Down Under too. He is leading on GC at the start of the race, but after a slower first couple of stages I win stage three and we get the jersey. Simon snatches back the lead at stage five, however, and ends up beating me on time bonuses by just one second.

Being an Australian team, the Tour Down Under is very important to Orica–GreenEDGE, and they work for it accordingly. They've sent a very strong team here, all very focused, experienced and suited to the race. I've fallen just short of winning the Tour Down Under, but I've got BMC off to a solid start, worn the leader's jersey, won a stage, and created some good momentum for us to take into the year, which was what we needed.

But the second placing means there's even more pressure on me. Every rider knows there's nothing better than race wins on your side when you're talking about new contracts. I know my results this season are going to dictate the future of my career.

I'VE BEEN HAPPY TO start the year going for wins in the early races. But by March I just can't concentrate on riding. I'm struggling with some of the team's requirements for this year. I want to deliver as a professional, as I always have, but I feel constrained.

I get the feeling there are new additions to BMC's management who believe I need some pressure put on me to perform. Don't they know how much pressure I put myself under already? I'm my own harshest critic. They must know that for someone as methodical as me, someone who has always worked with systems and routine and self-imposed high standards, applying even more pressure won't help, it will hinder, but maybe that's what they want.

I have enough pressures in my life off the track right now, more than I can deal with. I find out I may not be seeing as much of my own son in the future, which has more of an effect on me than I want to relate. The team, and Jim are very understanding and supportive of this, which means more to me than they will ever know.

The focus on performance and results you find in cycling and sports more generally is so obsessive that the very people who are cheering for the men and women who achieve these high standards forget that these men and women are human. Inevitably, we all have to face difficulties in life and these affect our wellbeing and sometimes even our ability to function.

When you are in a profession where a 2 per cent drop in performance is obvious, everyone is asking why, but personal lives are personal lives, they cannot always be talked about publically. If people don't hear a reason, or are given an explanation that they don't want to hear, they invent their own reasons. In cycling, if you are over 34, that reason of course is, 'You are too old'.

I can't concentrate on riding, and it's showing. When I'm at Tirreno–Adriatico and getting dropped on a climb in a group of 50 because I've got anger and tension in my body, the team see this. Before the final stage, they send me home and tell me to come back when I'm ready.

I find this a very fair and considerate decision. I don't think there are too many teams that care much for the wellbeing of riders and staff as much as BMC do.

I TAKE SOME TIME away from racing to settle things. After a few weeks I meet with Jim and Dr Max Testa, again at the Albergo Terminus by Lake Como. Max encourages me not to ride the Giro, he says with everything going on in my life right now it will be too much stress for me emotionally and physically. I know this might be my last chance at a Grand Tour and a good chance too. I don't know if it is desire, pride or stubbornness, but I want to go ahead with the program. Jim and Max agree, and we go back to work.

The short break has done me good. By early April I'm getting back to normal and able to ride the Tour of the Basque Country.

I'm sharing a room with Sammy Sánchez, who's new to the team this year. I've ridden against Sammy for many years as an opponent, on the Euskaltel–Euskadi team. We've often found ourselves going head to head in stage races like this one, the Tour de France and the Vuelta a España. Euskaltel are renowned for having bike riders who crash a lot, but Sammy's a good bike handler and a very good descender – among the best downhill GC riders of our generation.

When you're racing against each other you never get to build a relationship, or talk to each other on a personal level. It's only this year that we've developed a friendship.

When he joined BMC, I noticed many similarities in our styles – how we train, how we prepare, our attention to detail, especially when it comes to maintaining our equipment. I think Sammy positions too conservatively in semi-crucial times of the race, but otherwise we're very similar.

Outside of the sport we also share some common likes and interests – American muscle cars, Swiss watches, Mediterranean food.

It is great to finally ride with a Spanish teammate who knows this part of the country well. But I'm not riding very well and I come seventh overall.

LATER IN APRIL, I head to the Giro del Trentino for the second year in a row.

Again, the race opens with a team time trial. This year, with better planning and a motivated and organised team, we're able to win the opening team time trial, with Italian Daniel Oss crossing the line first. He puts on the first leader's jersey in Torbole, beside Lake Garda.

I feel this is very appropriate: the hardest workers on the team should get the opportunity to lead in team time trials. The GC rider, if he's a worthy leader, will have his chance to wear the leader's jersey at the other end of the race. In this case, the stage winner is not only one of the team's most valuable 'gregarios' (*domestiques*), but also the hometown boy, who grew up in Trento. And it turns out that I *do* have a chance to wear the leader's jersey at the other end of the race, as BMC are able to keep it all week to win the event overall. A solid encouragement leading into the Giro, that helps me refocus and concentrate on the task at hand.

THE GIRO BEGINS A couple of weeks later. I know this may well be my last Grand Tour, my last three-week race. So I want to make sure I put things in perspective mentally and concentrate on the riding.

The first half of the race goes well. In line with the increasing trend at the Giro and the Tour of including countries other than Italy or France, the race begins in Belfast, Northern Ireland. We have a great team of guys who are not only very trustworthy and capable, but guys who are also an absolute pleasure to race with.

Again we open with a team time trial, and come third this time, better than we expected, since we lose two riders during the stage. Stages two and three are bunch sprints in Ireland. I'm happy to share a Guinness with the team as we farewell the Emerald Isle.

During stage four, finishing in Bari in southern Italy, there are very public discussions on the danger of the race, due to the slippery roads. At the request of my colleagues I have firm words with one of the race judges about how dangerous the finish might be. Several riders, me included, appear on TV firmly arguing that the final lap of the race should be neutralised – meaning that times for GC will be taken with one lap of the circuit (8.3 kilometres) still to go, leaving the sprinters to race for the stage victory. With 42 kilometres to go, organisers agree to our request.

We have three finishing laps in Bari, the GC riders, myself included, position well for the last intermediate sprint some distance from the finish. The sprinters and sprint hopefuls then take over for the finish. Entering into the last kilometre, no one has crashed. Shit, what have I done? I've convinced the organisers to cancel a stage for nothing. Five hundred meters further on, 86 guys hit the deck.

In stage five it also pours with rain just before the finish and I can barely see where I am going. I stay very tentative on the last descent because the roads are incredibly slippery. There is a split after the descent, which has the other BMC guys worried. But we just make it back to the front group before the last short pitch to the finish and I use what little I have left in my legs to get second in the stage behind the unlikeable Italian rider, Diego Ulissi. This moves me up into third place on GC.

I enter the waiting area for drug testing after the stage and find Ulissi sitting in the cold in his shorts and undershirt, drinking a beer. I'm a bit taken aback. I am not surprised when he later gets a nine month suspension for failing a test taken during this race.

Stage six is more of the same 'Giro drama'.

There are 11.2 kilometres to go and everyone is trying to get on the front. I'm riding at the front with Steve Morabito, Manuel Quinziato and Daniel Oss, all waiting to move. Daniel is doing 74 ks per hour on the flat to position me so I can enter the last roundabout in the first three before a sharp left and slight right turn onto the final climb.

The roads are wet, but we in the front group manage to get through the narrow roundabout safely. As the peloton hits the roundabout, someone hits one of the reflectors on the road shoulder, there's a clip of wheels and *Boom!* riders fly everywhere. It's a shocking pile-up. Russian squad Team Katusha lose three riders, Giampaolo Caruso, Angel Vicioso and team leader, Joaquim Rodríguez, who suffers bruised ribs and a fractured finger. His chances of winning his first Grand Tour are now over. Race leader, Michael Matthews (Orica–GreenEDGE) has to ride without teammate Brett Lancaster, who has broken his hand.

Michael and I are two of the eight riders who escape the mêlée, riding at the front. Michael goes on to win the stage and I'm third in the race and second on GC, having gained 53 seconds.

As I am racing up the final climb, I am so preoccupied with the crash that in the final sprint, I run half a metre wide and let Michael Mathews slip though and win the stage. I come second, and am furious at my own stupidity.

The crash triggers some discussion: should Michael Matthews and I have waited before climbing towards the abbey at the top of Montecassino?

The conventions of what to do if there's a crash are open to interpretation. Some say that if you aren't involved you shouldn't ride. Others say once the race is on, it's on, go for it.

There is no doubt that at the time of the crash the race was definitely on. If you stop, or even hesitate to think about waiting, you lose your position and your chance at winning. We put together a team, in particular Quinzi and Daniel, knowing well that these situations would arise and that we have to prepare for them. The first step of winning a Grand Tour is not losing it.

You have good luck and you have bad luck. No one in the peloton knows that more than me.

IN STAGE EIGHT TO Montecopiolo I finish fifth, and it's enough for me to take the *maglia rosa* for the third time in my career. And suddenly, there's a fundamental change in me. The attitude I've always had as a professional athlete – look ahead, work now for long-term goals, do everything within my capabilities to maximise my potential – has been put on hold …

I know that 2014 may be my last year racing. And I know that this is probably my last chance to perform well at a Grand Tour. So I realise it's time to savour it. After 20 years in professional cycling,

I know I have an opportunity I may never have again: to be in the moment and appreciate where my racing career has taken me.

I've always been rational about the Grand Tours. I'm there to win and not get distracted. And riding through beautiful towns and villages in Italy provides a *lot* of distraction. All the colour – the little cafés, the medieval roads curving through ancient villages, the excitement on the faces of spectators on the sides of the road, waving their signs and shouting their support, the little kids thrilled to see professional riders in *their* part of the world, *their* village, *their* town.

For 20 years I've always had a job to do, so I've often been blind to this beauty. This scenery that people come from around the world to see is my workplace. I've focused so much on the job I've had to do that I've rarely stepped back and simply taken the time to smell the roses.

But on my fourth day in pink, I'm riding along in the front with the team and have a moment of real revelation. The stage goes from Collecchio to Savona, and we're heading towards Italy's west coast, and riding through a string of little towns.

It's a great group of guys I'm with: Daniel Oss, Manuel Quinziato and Brent Bookwalter. The breakaway has gone and the sun is shining and as we ride through these villages people are standing along the sides of the road watching.

And I'm thinking, 'Isn't this great! Aren't we lucky to be here today!'

We pass through one town and all the people are out on the streets – in the town centre, outside the schools and the shops, out the front of their houses. And they're holding signs and cheering for their favourite riders in the Giro, and I hear some calling my name.

As I ride along I'm looking at all these people – grandmothers and grandfathers, mums, dads, teenagers, kids, people of every age – and I realise that these people are always going to remember the day the Giro d'Italia passed through their town, passed by their place of work, passed by their school.

And you know what? If they only remember one rider from today, they're probably going to remember the rider who was in the pink jersey. And that's me.

Maybe that little kid standing in the schoolyard there on the right, when he is 20 or 30 or 50, is going to tell his children that the Giro d'Italia passed through here once and the Australian rider Cadel Evans was wearing the *maglia rosa*.

And he may remember that for the rest of his life.

And I think, 'That's beautiful!'

At this moment I realise that I've become part of the history of Italy, this wonderful country I love so much, whose people I've spent so much time with. I'm now a small part of this country's history and culture, forever.

For me it's a revelation. Late – but better late than never.

I'M GLAD I ENJOYED and appreciated that moment because downhill is where I go in the third week of the Giro. That stage to Savona is the last stage when I wear the pink jersey. I barely scrape into the top ten in the following days and start slipping down the GC table.

I cannot shake a feeling of deep sadness during this last week of the Giro. Sadness because I've lost the chance to do well in a race I've spent a lot of time and emotional energy preparing for.

And then there's the weather. It's still the worst weather at the Giro in years. For the riders it isn't just gruelling, but also, in some stages, dangerous.

The chance of good weather in the Italian mountains in May is so slim that these stages really shouldn't be used in the Giro. Almost every year it's a problem. Stages either get cancelled or should be. I think the Giro should keep its character and persist with stages in bad weather, but not when there's over 50 per cent risk of snow.

Stage 16, a punishing mountain stage from Ponte di Legno to Val Martello, really should have been cancelled. It's a day after American BMC rider, Taylor Phinney had a pretty horrific crash into a guardrail at the US National Championships and broke his leg badly. We are all shocked by Taylor's accident, another reminder of how dangerous this sport can be, especially in these conditions.

At the top of the Passo di Gavia it's achingly cold and I'm feeling numb on my bike. It's snowing, but it's not soft snow. It's what the Americans call 'frozen rain'. They're not snowflakes, but somewhere between small hail and snow.

I'm wearing four pairs of gloves, but my hands are still paralysed and I can't use the brakes very well.

My glasses are frosting up from the snow so I take them off. But it's so painful with all the snow in my eyes. So I quickly lick my glasses to try to defrost them, literally, and I can't even do that. I put them back on and dive on the brakes to make it around the next switchback.

I'm riding down the descent of the Gavia and it's very windy and it's hard to brake. I have lost sight of the GC group ahead. I have nearly lost sight of the road itself.

After the Gavia torment is over we face the next challenge: the imposing Passo dello Stelvio. There are 36 switchbacks on the ascent and 48 on the descent in the snow, with almost zero visibility.

It's one of the few times in my career when I've thought, 'I don't care about GC, I'm just going to survive this.' Robel hasn't come and visited me at the Giro and I'm missing him.

I think, 'I just want to see my son again – but not from a hospital bed.'

The organisers finally neutralise the group when Movistar is at the front. They sit up and spread across the narrow road. Except for Nairo Quintana, he slips off the front and bridges to the breakaway. We are all furious.

Usually, I enjoy testing myself in extreme weather. My high level of preparation has even given me an advantage when the weather is horrible. But racing in these conditions is ridiculous.

I know that organisers and TV producers like the drama of riders battling the elements – if the viewers can actually *see* any riders. But there has to be a point at which continuing a race should be regarded as irresponsible. This is one of those times.

You do wonder when race organisers believe that point occurs. Is it when a rider dies?

AS HAS BEEN THE case since 2012, in the third week my body cannot recover between one day and the next, causing an almost exponential downward trend. I have all the classic over-reaching symptoms: fluid retention, loss of appetite and sleeping difficulties. In this state, it becomes a race of limiting losses.

It's been a good start but a very disappointing finish. I came third in stage one (with the team), second in stage five, third in stage six and third in stage twelve. In the penultimate stage, the infamous Monte Zoncolan climb – the hardest climb I have ever raced – it's looking like I could finish the tour seventh on GC, but I can't hold my position and slide back from seventh to eighth at 12:00 behind the leader.

Nairo Quintana is the first Colombian ever to win the race, a great effort by him. He was in a class of his own in the third week, and although the Stelvio incident was to his advantage, it seemed very unlikely he would have been challenged.

He is a unique rider. He is known in the world of cycling for not showing any signs of fatigue. It is almost scary how little his expression and riding style changes over the course of a stage. He shows little, and speaks even less. In the peloton he bounces round like a ball in a pinball machine. It's very disconcerting.

After the last stage on a tough little circuit in Trieste, RCS Sport, the organisers of the Giro, arrange to have Dire Straits play a concert for us. Any of the anger about the Stelvio stuff-up quickly subsides. After spending three weeks together in our professional roles, it is nice to be able to put the race behind us and socialise with the organisers, the sponsors and everyone involved.

AND THAT WAS MY Giro d'Italia. A good start on classification, but a finish far below our goals and expectations, not even a stage win. The team, and I gave this Giro everything we had. This was important for me, to know that I had not cut myself short and to truly accept that I can no longer be a successful lead rider in three-week stage races.

I *do* want to ride the Vuelta a España in August to be there for Spanish teammate, Samuel Sánchez and help him finish as high as possible. I also want to try to do a good World Road Championships in Spain in late September. Subconsciously, I know the Vuelta is my very last chance to ride in a Grand Tour, whether I acknowledge it consciously or not.

Of course, now I'm feeling pressure from the team. The media are noting in their stories that my contract is due to end at the close of 2014. It's being written that BMC have made their plans – that instead of me, they want Tejay van Garderen to be the new team leader. Sometimes, we as riders find out about our futures by reading about them in the newspapers ...

What's happened to my performance? Has it deteriorated because of the illness I had in 2012, or because of my age, or because of issues off the bike that I'm dealing with? Is it a combination of all of these? I just don't know.

The problem is that athletes find these realities hard to absorb. You don't accept these things. You train yourself not to accept them because otherwise they bring you down. You have to learn to shut them out because sometimes everything's against you.

I've fought my whole career, and that fight is still in me. The fight is so ingrained in me that my automatic first response is to battle against the forces I'm facing.

Here's how you think: even if everything's against you and you don't accept what's happening and you keep fighting, well, maybe you'll find that one-in-a-hundred chance that you can get through this difficulty.

And often you do. Often I have.

It's a coping mechanism, I suppose. The most important person who has to believe in you is you. Doubts and negativity are corrosive for an athlete. You need to have an enormous belief in yourself and your abilities, especially when no one else does.

AFTER THE GIRO, I opt to do the Tour de Suisse. An ambitious plan, but without the Tour de France my summer feels very empty. Why not profit from some post Giro condition and hang in for a modest GC or maybe try on one to two stages?

I've only been to this pro stage race – a preparation race for the Tour de France – once before, in 2005, when I was injured and couldn't get ready for the Dauphiné.

It's one race I would have liked to have been able to concentrate on a bit more and do better in, because I live in Switzerland and it's a beautiful race. But it clashes with the Dauphiné, which is the race I always opted to do because it works better for my Tour ambitions.

The Tour de Suisse is a fantastic race to ride, with beautiful roads, beautiful mountains, beautiful scenery. Usually there's at least one time trial and several mountain top finishes. The only downside is that it has the slowest motorbike riders of any race. Swiss people are such good, law-abiding citizens that they don't know how to ride beyond the speed limit. But in a bike race you have to go far beyond the speed limit.

After inspecting a house to rent in the morning, I ride from Stabio to the Hotel Delfino in Lugano, just 25 kilometres away and close to the start of the Tour.

I settle in to the hotel room with trusted friend and teammate, Steve Morabito. After all our time together in the lead up to, and during, the Giro, it's almost as though I have missed having him around. He seemed a little subdued when I arrived, but as I was distracted with my life outside of racing, I did not think much of it at the time.

I get a call from Jim Ochowicz, who says he wants to meet with me.

We meet outside the hotel restaurant on the evening before the prologue. We sit down on two old chairs, at a small round table with a lamp in the kitsch style you often see in Switzerland.

It's just before dinner. I have no idea what this is about.

Jim says he has to leave soon and seems keen to get to the point. 'I just want to have a quick talk with you.'

'Jim, can we speak tomorrow?'

'No, no, I've got to fly out this evening.'

I think, 'This is strange. It seems urgent.'

Four years ago, Jim said to me: 'I'll know when it's time for you to stop and I'll tell you.'

Back then I thought, 'Oh, OK, well, one day that will come, but I'll know myself ...'

And now here we are.

Jim pauses. 'Cadel, there's not a place for you in the team next year. I think you should stop racing.'

Couples are walking past us, going out to dinner. Someone laughs loudly in the hotel restaurant.

I look at Jim.

'OK, Jim.'

As a professional rider, I've had a lot of time to practise hiding my emotions. This is one of those moments when on the outside I may be showing very little. Inside is a different story.

After this short and sharp discussion with Jim, I immediately telephone Tony, and he's shocked. He told me just a week ago, after speaking to Jim: 'For you there is always a place in the team.' Two weeks ago I also received pretty firm indications from the team that if I wanted to go ahead, I could. Reading between the lines, I'm guessing there's someone else in BMC management who's influencing the direction of the team.

In politics they might compare this to the Night of the Long Knives. Somewhere else in the Hotel Delfino this evening, two other BMC riders – Steve Morabito and Martin Kohler – have also been told they won't have a place in the team next year. Dinner this evening is a grim affair.

With a race the next day it hasn't been ideal timing, but Jim wanted to tell us face to face and I respect that. A lot of communication with riders is by email. And I've worked with team managers who won't return text messages just to avoid confrontation. At least Jim has shown more guts than this. And when you hear that it's time to stop from someone like Jim Ochowicz, who understands these things very well, you listen.

NATURALLY, I GO INTO the prologue distracted. I'm still exhausted from the tough last week of the Giro, and it doesn't take me long to realise that doing the Tour de Suisse wasn't such a great idea. But once again, my athlete's denial gene kicks in – that capacity to block all the negative indicators out of your mind and get on with the job. It's a gene that has served me well for a long time.

I suppose you have these moments in life where there are things you have to deal with. They just take time to process.

I have to get away and do some thinking. What do I do next? Change of career? What do I do if I'm not a cyclist? Still work in cycling somehow? Something else? Is this the end of living in Europe? Do I return to Australia?

I speak to some friends about it, people who know me – sports director Fabio Baldato, my manager in Australia, Jason Bakker.

Before the time trial at stage seven I also speak to Andy Rihs. Andy is a good man with a good heart. We've always got on very well, and I admire what he's achieved in business, his ethical standards and his passion for cycling.

I ask, 'Andy, what do you think about this whole thing?'

'You know what?' he replies. 'You're much better to retire when you're up near the top than when you're down near the bottom.'

He's right.

I take Andy's words to heart because I respect his observations. He's never raced as a professional cyclist but he understands the world and the business of sport.

'Retirement' has been a word I have always tried to avoid using, to me it means 'giving up'. Andy's words are a big help in changing my perspective.

THE END OF MY contractual period is 31 December 2014. This is crucial now, of course, since they're not renewing my contract. But it was two years ago that Jim Ochowicz first asked me about the future of my career.

I replied, 'Well, can I ride the races in Australia? Can you ask the UCI if that's possible? I can ride the races in Australia for a while for BMC, and then I'll stop.'

This was long before I knew I was going to have the issue forced on me.

Then, as time went on, I wanted to race longer. I want to do another year or maybe another two years on the WorldTour.

But now it's not going to work out that way.

I'm motivated to do another two years and I'm told I should retire. I'm struggling to accept it. I'm an athlete. Tell me I'm retiring? I'm not going to believe you. For better or worse, this is the psychology of an athlete. It's the classic athlete's response.

But when I think about it later, I'm glad Jim stood up to me. I know I'm getting old. I'm 17 years older than some of my competitors. And I know they have a huge advantage over me; naturally their bodies recover much better than mine.

At 27 your body can handle illness and you can come back again and again. At 27 you've still got a lot of potential. At 37, people don't have much faith and confidence in you any more. So even if you work hard and stay committed, you might be able to get over health issues, but a lack of faith in you means your opportunities are fewer.

My body did the right thing by me for so long. Part of that was good management by me and people close to me like David Bombeke. Part of it was luck. I always used to have the answers. Now it's becoming clear my team don't believe I have the answers any more.

At 37 you might think you have a year, but for a team to invest in you, you've got to do one or two years, and that's when doubts creep in. The media are saying I'm too old and that perception takes hold. People start thinking this and it doesn't matter what you do, unless you go out and win something extraordinary.

And if your team is losing faith in you, you're not even going to be leader in the big races. So all of a sudden your chances even to perform are limited. Even though physically you can do it, the opportunities dry up. The doors close on you pretty quickly.

This is the moment when you need good people around you to give good advice, because to do your job as an athlete while also having some wider perspective is probably not possible.

I've had good people around me, right at the time I needed them.

I'VE THOUGHT ABOUT ALL this too much. I need to get away.

My friend, Martin Whiteley invites me down to Granada in southern Spain to spend some time kicking back and trying to sort out my head.

Martin lives in a beautiful house near the Sierra Nevada mountain range, and I always catch up with him when I do training camps there.

I really trust Martin. We've known each other for about 22 years. He knows what I'm like, both professionally and off the bike. I don't think there are too many people I can say that about.

It's wonderful to be away from cycling for a few days. I need to clear my head. I need to talk. I just need to be somewhere different and work things out.

At Martin's I wake up and have coffee and breakfast and chat for a bit, then he goes away and does some work. I get my bike and I ride to the top of Sierra Nevada and back again.

It takes four or five hours, probably a 40-kilometre climb if you go through Granada to get up there. I ride the Monachil stage, where the infamous wheel-change debacle happened in the Vuelta in 2009.

It's a sunny day up in the mountains. There's no one around. I ride to the stretch of road were the wheel drama occurred. Back then the whole cycling world was watching; today, it's just me.

I get off my bike and stand at the exact spot. I even take a photo of it. The memory of it is strong, even though the pain of it was ameliorated a little by winning the World Championships a week later in Mendrisio.

It's strange being here. The life of a cyclist is not normally one of reflection; there's always too much happening. Today, though, I'm reminded of the piece of bad luck or incompetence, or both, that I've so often been a victim of.

I keep going on the bike. It's not so much the training load I'm focusing on today. It's more the chance to breathe this superb mountain air, to be by myself, and to have a think about where my life is going.

I ride up to the ski resort of Sierra Nevada, then continue as far as the asphalt goes, and just because it's in my cycling DNA, I ride on the gravel road for a while to get up to 2800 metres altitude. This mountain, Mulhacén, is the highest in Spain, 3479 metres above sea level. I ride as high up the mountain as my skinny tyres permit; after that point you can keep going but you have to hike or ride a mountain bike.

I stand here and look out over the Mediterranean. The sky – a cobalt blue today – is smudged here and there with streaky white clouds. There's not a sound. From where I stand I can see Africa.

Apart from marvelling at this beauty, the main feeling I have at this moment is relief – relief that the pressure is finally off.

I suppose I've come to realise that there's no longer going to be a lot of expectation on me to perform at the highest level. Right now there are certain factors – my age, my health, my personal worries – that are holding me back from performing at that level, and I can't do much about them. As an athlete you can try to control all the factors to optimise your performance. But the factors you can't control have a hold on me.

At this point, I think, 'You know what? After everything I've done in my career, after all these years, all the achievements, it's as if the world of cycling needs me to prove myself yet again. And you know what? I don't feel I need to do that.'

I RIDE BACK TO Martin's, shower and come down for a gin and tonic. It's a beautiful evening, so we sit outside by the swimming pool and talk for hours in the warm Spanish evening. I pour out all the things that are happening in my life. A lot of it has been bottled up inside me. It feels good to vent, to release it all.

I tell Martin that I'm not sure I'm ready to stop, but part of me feels it's the right decision to make. I tell him what Andy had said – that it's better to leave when you're on top. I tell him about my sense of denial, my feeling that even at 37 I still have a lot to give.

I know that this is a key moment for me – a rare one, too, when I focus on the reality of stepping away from something I've been doing for 20 years, more than half my life, and face the reality that I don't have much time left to ride professionally – with the camaraderie of a team around me, with the expectation of being a team leader on my shoulders, with a role as mentor to younger riders and advisor to the team management.

Any sportsperson will tell you: it's hard to let go.

By the time the evening is over and I've wandered off to bed, I've arrived at a decision.

I've accepted that it's time to end my racing career.

CHAPTER 24

THE FINAL SEASON

2014–2015

BEING DRUG-TESTED HAS BEEN a daily issue in my life for my whole career. As a participant in the most drug-tested sport on the planet, it's just something you get used to.

In 2011, I estimate I was tested 40 times or more. When you're a favourite for the Tour they come and test you every week, normally in the morning or after a race, but sometimes in the evening.

In 2004, WADA (the World Anti-Doping Agency) introduced 'Whereabouts', which requires athletes to be available for one hour every day between 5am and 11pm for testing at home during out-of-competition periods, or at their hotel during races.

Ever since then, four times a year I've had to get my laptop and type in my expected whereabouts for the three months ahead to ensure the UCI knows where I am so they can drop in and test me wherever I am, any day of the year. You have to nominate where you'll be sleeping each night and give them a one-hour window each day. I'll have to continue to do this for six months after I retire too.

I always say early in the morning because normally I'll be at home then. I might be asleep, but if they ring the doorbell, the dog will bark and wake me up and I'll answer the door. (A faulty doorbell is a dire matter for an elite cyclist.) My local cycling group in Barwon Heads meets at 8am, so if I'm riding with them I'll have my drug-testing window from six till seven.

During races it might be different. At the Vuelta, for example, the stage starts are very late, so you usually nominate a later drug testing window, in the last hour of the sleeping period.

Drug-testing is always a (necessary) invasion in athletes' lives. Obviously – when you have someone staring at you while you're peeing in a cup. But like most, I want our sport to be clean. And part of that is making the job of drug testers easier, which means making ourselves available to them.

The problem is that bike riders travel a lot. I calculate that over my years in professional cycling I've done an average of 45 flights per year. And you're sleeping in a lot of different hotels. During the Tour de France, over 21 days, you stay in about 17 different hotels.

It isn't easy to do, all that drug testing. The protocols in every country and culture are very different. In Australia, for instance, they're fastidious about the rules, which makes it difficult, because if you have a busy life, the rules are almost impossible to follow. You can't afford to make any administrative errors, because in the public eye they won't be seen as administrative errors, you'll be painted as a drug cheat, even if you're not.

This is where drug testing becomes a little bit difficult: if someone who's organising your travel for you changes your hotel address and they don't tell you until the last minute, the responsibility is yours.

It's the same with taking medicines you may need. Medication for illness or injury is always a minefield. If you get sick out of hours and you have to go to a pharmacy and get medicine, it can be difficult contacting your team doctor to ask, 'Is this one OK?' There are many cold and flu medicines that contain the banned drug pseudoephedrine.

'Tainted supplements' are another big thing you've got to watch. It's been proven that if a manufacturing plant produces medicine for one company one day and the next day makes maybe amino acid supplements for another company, there can be cross-contamination. If the first medicine contains something that's on the banned substance list, the drug tests are so sensitive that there could be a trace of that drug in the amino acid supplements.

Protein powders are among the most widely used products that come with this risk. If someone is trying to do the right thing by protecting their health and they get a tainted product, it's probably going to ruin their career, which is pretty unfair. BMC hands out a list of suggested supplements in each country around the world – buy this product here, buy that product there. And fortunately the supplement industry has introduced its own certification system for non-tainted products, which makes life easier for everyone.

There's a lot of information available for cyclists on what over-the-counter drugs you can and can't take, but you have to concentrate hard to stick to the rules.

Most riders go out of their way to try to do the right thing. But it's not always easy. We have wives, we have friends, we have family, we like to go on holidays, we get caught in traffic jams, planes get missed, life is life for us too. And if you need to change a medicine or change your whereabouts, sometimes you just can't get online because there's no internet access. We all know that in the end, if we make a mistake, it's all on us.

Mistakes in cycling get a lot of attention, but I'd like to reinforce that cycling is doing more than any other professional sport to combat this. Cycling is not the richest sport in the world, but the percentage of its earnings that are spent on fighting cheats is a true indication of how serious the sport is about the fight.

IN JULY, FOLLOWING THE Tour de Suisse and the break in Granada, I fly to the US to ride the Tour of Utah which starts on 4 August. I want to race it mainly to use the high-altitude training to get ready for the Vuelta and the World Championships.

We have a two-week training camp before the tour. There's a holiday feel to the trip. It's a relief to be in America, away from everything and everyone and just train and live the life of a bike rider. It's a relief to feel a distance from what is going on back in Europe.

I stay with Andy Blank, an American ex race driver that I met when I came to the Tour of Utah as a spectator in 2011. We've since become good friends. It's great to hang out with Andy and his wife, to be in a real home and not a hotel. I watch the Tour de France stage finish each morning, then Andy and I go riding together and I do my training.

As well as some group training, I take some time to train alone, and I'm loving it, climbing up these big arid mountains, knowing I haven't got long to go in my career.

I realise how much fun I'm having, doing this ride with no one watching, taking in the beautiful scenery, letting myself be in the moment, absorb what's going on around me, rather than grinding up mountains and flying down them with one purpose. Reminds me of that day at the Giro.

Finally, *finally*, the journey has become just as crucial as the destination. I make a mental note: I've got to come back here after I retire.

THE TOUR OF UTAH is a well-run race which I hope will grow to become a big part of cycling. I've made such a group of friends here – Andy included – that I feel quite at home. To ride in Utah is very different from riding in the Tour de France or the Giro. It's not a highly classified race but the altitude and highly motivated American riders make it a hard one to win.

The start and finish of the race are in Park City, a town I know quite well. At the training camp before the race I try to motivate the guys in the team. I tell them, 'After this race, we're going to my favourite place, the High West Distillery. It's one street back from the finish line on the final day.'

On stage four, we're riding towards a hard finishing climb, up Powder Mountain. I'm struggling a bit, and I see my Belgian teammate Ben Hermans, who's riding well.

I say, 'Ben, if you're in front today, you go and ride your own race, OK?'

So he rides away and gets second. I'm ninth.

The team car comes up to me and I'm asked what happened and why Ben Hermans was in front and I say, 'Yeah yeah, I told him to do that.'

Near the end of the race, after a slow start, I am coming good again and starting to really enjoy it. It must be because the pressure is off. At the Giro and the Tour de France it was all about my result. In Utah I am able to enjoy the race for what it is – to look around a bit, to enjoy the company of my teammates, none of whom know I've decided to stop racing.

I win from a breakaway at stage six, the snow summit stage I was helicoptered to in 2011. It's been a good day, but the ride back to the hotel isn't.

I'm riding back down the hill and all the cars leaving the race finish have created a traffic jam, several kilometres long. I'm riding down the left-hand side of the road, into opposing traffic, but the road is closed on that side so there are no cars coming.

Then I see a police car behind me in the distance and assume it's here to open the road.

Then I hear a siren.

I think, 'That's strange, the policeman's driving down the wrong side of the road. I'd better stop and get out of the way because it might be an emergency.'

But the car pulls up right behind me. The policeman gets out, yelling at me.

'What the hell are you doing? You could die doing that!'

'Doing what?'

'Don't you realise what you're doing?'

I'm thinking, 'Compared with what I've just done in the race, riding down the wrong side of a closed road with no traffic is as safe as houses.'

But he doesn't see it this way.

This seems to be a normal strategy from an American policeman, trying to intimidate and scare you. I'm a bit used to it because it's not the first time it's happened to me.

I try to tell him I'm a professional rider and know exactly what I'm doing, but this is just infuriating him further.

He carries on yelling. Then he starts to write me a fine and he asks my name.

'Cadel Evans.'

'Spell that for me.'

'C-A-D-E-L E-V-A-N-S.'

He asks my address.

'Via Capriccio.'

'Spell it.'

'Capriccio. C-A-P–'

'Where's that?'

'Switzerland.'

The cop gets halfway through the word 'Switzerland', scoffs and sticks his notebook back in his pocket.

'Get on your way, don't do it again.'

In the meantime, all the people who've watched the race are driving past me slowly in the bad traffic. They're all taking photos and putting them on social media.

Not the best end to an otherwise great day, but it takes nothing away from my affection for this race, the people who run it and that gorgeous Utah scenery.

THE LAST STAGE THE next day is a mountain stage with a big climb over Guardsman Pass, then a descent to the finish in Park City.

I'm going over the top of the last climb with a young rider. What happens with some of the young American riders is they think they're racing with other young American riders, and they can work them over and take advantage of their generosity or lack of racing nous. Er ... I'm not a young rider, and I know all of those tricks, very well. I've had them played on me before and I've also played them on many others.

This young rider catches me as we near the crest of the climb. There's a little headwind, just enough to make sitting on the wheel advantageous.

'Come on, take a turn.' I say. 'I can't.' he replies.

'Don't make me angry, you idiot,' I'm thinking. 'I know if you catch up to me on the climb you must be riding better than I am, and the difference between cooperating and not cooperating with you could be the difference between fifth and sixth on GC.'

In frustration, I accelerate to gap him, then as he closes back to me we're approaching the first technical corners of the downhill. I accelerate again to demoralise him and get some speed for the first switchbacks on the descent. I keep up the speed and increase the gap behind me and close towards the riders in the front group.

I'm approaching a right-hand switchback; I remember the corner well from training. The slightly off-camber right turn looks deceptively difficult, but the surface is very good, and there is a nice rounded kerb on the exit of the curve that you can use in case you're carrying excessive speed through the apex.

There are a couple of people standing on the footpath at the exit of the corner; they dive into the grass as I approach. I am up on the footpath, then back on the road, then I accelerate over a little rise and have to brake to avoid the cars following the front group. I slow down, tack onto the back of the group and wait until the last two left-hand turns, which I've ridden twice before the stage start.

We've come in to the last corner and there are three or four riders in front of me. I go into the corner, not taking any risks, but I pass everyone and get a gap, and carry it to the line to again win the stage.

The prize for the stage win is a bottle of whisky from the High West Distillery, where we already have a booking for the whole team tonight as a bit of a celebration. After telling the team about High West, I've been thinking about the dinner every morning during my pre-breakfast ride on the rollers. A little carrot on the end of a stick in front of me.

I need to celebrate tonight. This could be the last stage victory of my career.

It's been nice to race the Tour of Utah with the young guys and get sixth place on GC. Tom Danielson, a rider from Colorado, wins the tour. Chris Horner, now at Lampre–Merida, is second. Ben Hermans has done really well, riding into fourth overall on GC.

I do the podium for the stage win, the drug control, the media. I decide to ride home because I need some more kilometres in my legs for the Vuelta in a couple of weeks.

I FLY BACK TO Europe for the Vuelta and perform very poorly, which is disappointing. But I'm here to support Sammy Sánchez, and he ends up fifth on GC, which is a great result for the team.

The legendary Miguel Indurain is at one of the stage starts, which is not far from where he lives in Pamplona. This is the man who first inspired me to ride the Tour de France when I started cycling seriously in 1991.

I've already met Miguel a couple of times over the years. In 2003 at the Grand Prix Miguel Indurain, a race in Spain, Miguel was at the start line and I shook his hand and was absolutely awestruck. He came across as quiet, and so calm and composed – just as he used to be on TV. And it struck me that a real champion is a champion on the bike but also in life. I've always felt he was exactly that.

'Big Mig' seems to make that impression on everyone. I was invited to a dinner in Adelaide on the eve of the Tour Down Under in 2008, a year when I wasn't competing. My mother heard that Miguel Indurain was going to be there so she rings me up, 'Can I come to Adelaide with you?'

Miguel arrived with his wife Marisa and I had to go up to him more quickly than anyone else did, like a fan. 'I'm sorry to bother you,' I said,' but I just want to introduce you to my mum because she'd be delighted to meet you.' She shook his hand and was quite awestruck. He was very understanding and accommodating. Then my mother told me 'That's why I wanted to come'. Wow! ... And I thought she came to give me moral support!

This third meeting with Miguel is quite different. By this stage I'm performing pretty badly and I know I'll be ending my career soon.

We speak about retirement and Miguel is friendly about it. I say, 'Miguel, I'm going to be in your shoes shortly. In fact I'll be there in a few weeks.' I say with a smile.

THREE DAYS BEFORE THE World Championships we have a small press conference.

'Cycling built me as a person, it's been more than half of my life; it's amazing what this sport gave me,' I say. 'It's given me all I could dream of.'

'I've had some regrets and bitterness, but I go away happy and know I gave the most I could. I know I inspired people to take up sport. I tried to always be the best professional, whether it was in the results sheet or outside of that.

'For me this is not the end, but the beginning of a new chapter of my life in cycling.'

I'm asked whether my Tour win in 2011 was a bright light after years of doping darkness. 'I hope so. I can only speak about my own credibility.'

And that's it. I answer a few other questions and we wrap up the media conference.

IT DOESN'T HAPPEN FOR me at the Worlds this year. I'm not able to put all the work I'd done on the road and I don't finish the race. It kind of confirms I've made the right decision.

The Tour of Lombardy in October is going to be the final race of my career in Europe, and I find that perfectly appropriate given that it's held just down the road from where I live. It's my home race, a beautiful event that I've always wanted to win.

It's my ninth start at this race and each edition is slightly different. This year it begins in Como, just 22 kilometres from Stabio. The course winds through the villages that sit high above Lake Como, past the Madonna del Ghisallo – the shrine to cycling that has become a special link to me with Italian cycling – then across through Bergamo, looping up through the hills north, Colle Gallo and Passo di Ganda, before returning back to Bergamo.

It's a beautiful clear autumn day by Lake Como. There's a wonderful atmosphere at the race. It feels great to be around people who are being so supportive and gracious towards me. Riders from the other teams – as well as *soigneurs*, mechanics and other cycling people I've known for years – congratulate me and wish me all the best.

People in the crowd approach me respectfully and with some nice messages: 'You've had a fantastic career, I hope you can finish well today.' So many people tell me they're grateful for what I've given to cycling. I really appreciate that.

Robel comes to the sign-on in the Piazzo Como with me. He sees all the people cheering and taking photos and he loves being in the middle of it. I'm so glad he's here for such an important event in my life.

It's great seeing people I know who've turned up for this race. At the start line I see my friend Marina Romoli, a cyclist who had a very unfortunate accident years ago and is now in a wheelchair. Next day there's a photo of Robel, Marina, her dog Marilyn, and me in *La Gazzetta dello Sport*, which is really quite touching for me.

I've come here quite relaxed and wanting to enjoy the race. Today it's not about me. Phil Gilbert is the team leader, and my role is to ride in support of Phil and Sammy Sánchez. But I do feel sad that my racing career in Europe is coming to a close, and I want to finish off strongly.

I'm not riding very well today but Sammy Sánchez and Phil Gilbert are. There's some immature jealousy between a couple of the BMC riders in the final kilometres, which is very disappointing as it really compromises the team's chances.

I've gone back to talk to Fabio Baldato in the car.

Fabio asks, 'What's going on?'

I say, 'Oh, there's a little bit of immaturity going on in the race tactics here.'

Fabio looks at me. '*Si Lo vedo*', yes I see, he says.

'I'm so not going to miss this crap.'

I take Phil to the final climb and position him well. That's my job for the team done for the day. And it's taken everything I had left.

I cross the finish line and take a few breaths. It feels strange. I don't know whether to feel relieved, sad or fulfilled. Maybe I feel a bit of all three.

All I know is that something huge in my life is over.

I have no need to rush anywhere, no need to start the recovery process for the next race. It's been nineteen years since my first race in Europe. Nineteen years I have been coming to race with a number on, inside the barriers, rolling out from the start, crossing the finish, in the middle of the show. From now on, I will be on the other side of the barriers.

I agree to a TV interview. The last time I was on this particular television program I had a towel wrapped around my neck and a big beanie on to minimise my chances of getting sick.

This time I sit in just my jersey, nice and relaxed. No race tomorrow. Or the next day. Being totally relaxed is not a natural state for me, and at this moment I'm enjoying it.

And that's the end of BMC's 2014 season. The guys say goodbye and head off for their Christmas holidays. I wonder when I'm going to see them all again. I hug Fabio and farewell our *soigneurs* and shake the hands of a few media people who have been covering cycling for as long as I've been in it, and I head home.

Robel asks, 'Why were there so many people there today, Papi?'

'It was the Giro de Lombardia. And it was my last race here in Europe.'

'OK. How many more races to go?

'Three.'

I END THE 2014 season knowing I have only three races left in my career: the Tour Down Under, the National Championships, and the inaugural Cadel Evans Great Ocean Road Race.

My manager, Jason Bakker and I have been working on my race for two years, and now it's finally locked in for 1 February 2015. It wasn't conceived as my swansong, but fittingly, it's turned out that way. It will be an ideal way to see out one chapter of my life and welcome a new one.

In December, I fly home to Australia and spend some time at Barwon Heads training with friends along the Great Ocean Road. Then I head up to stay with my mother. It's been a while since I've seen her and we have a lot to catch up on. Leading into the last lot of races, my plan is to get away from the holiday traffic and train on the roads around her house, the roads I cycled on as a teenager.

For the first time in a long time I'm training enthusiastically, energetically. Like a junior, but wiser and more experienced.

As ever, Mum is a good listener and a wise counsellor. We settle in for a few of our long talks in the living room, overlooking the horse paddocks and the undulating country beyond.

Mum still loves her horses. On the mantelpiece is a photo of the horse that kicked me in the head when I was eight years old. Thirty years later I still reflect on how much that incident taught me about overcoming setbacks.

I remember being inspired as a young rider by reading an article about Greg LeMond, titled 'What Does Not Kill Him Only Makes Him Stronger'. I've heard that same phrase so many times since. But it sums up my career as much as it does Greg LeMond's. My greatest victories have been won in adverse conditions, when the odds have been stacked against me. While it was good training and a reasonable amount of natural talent that enabled me to race for those victories, it was my experiences gained though losing, during the bad times, that taught me the lessons I needed to turn the good results into big wins.

As I prepare to wind my career down, I find myself reflecting on where that career started, on these same country roads – riding the same climbs, timing the same loops.

Now, 20 years later, I'm back breathing this country air and feeling the sort of peace I haven't felt for a while.

It's wonderful to be home.

JANUARY 2015. IT'S THE last month of my racing career. I'm trying to look at it with a professional mind: performing as well as I can in the races and fulfilling as many requests as possible off the bike for the team.

I'm looking forward to my last three races.

First up on 11 January are the National Championships in Buninyong, a suburb in the Victorian city of Ballarat. I come in eighth, one place behind my good friend, Simon Clarke. Then I get ready to race the Tour Down Under, starting on 20 January.

My Australian teammate, Rohan Dennis is probably the favourite. I notice Rohan seems excessively nervous in the days leading up to the race. Racing in his hometown, it is to be expected.

Some of my teammates are glancing at me with a hint of doubt in their faces. Am I here to race hard or just to wave to the crowd?

Something happens at the Tour Down Under that's been happening to me a lot lately: I find I'm enjoying myself. Usually racing is gruelling, and can only be enjoyed later, on reflection. This time, the burden of dealing with things I normally find stressful is lifted from me. I know I'm not going to have to deal with any of them for too much longer. It means I have a level of patience and tolerance that I've never had before.

For once, I like being the centre of press attention, being pulled left and right to fulfil the constant requests.

An interview? Hey, no problem.

A photo with a fan? Sure.

Today, as I ride in the final stage through the Adelaide Hills, burnt by recent bushfires, I see it all. Here we are, cycling along roads where just a few days ago fires raged. I see the scorched trees and the still-smouldering earth. As I ride along I can still smell the charred countryside. It's a grim reminder of the loss and trauma that fires so often cause in Australia.

As we head towards the city of Adelaide for the finish, I see my competitors around me – some of whom will step up and do great things in the sport, maybe even win a Tour de France. I see such hope and ambition on these riders' faces, like the hope and ambition on my face nearly 20 years ago when I rode in the inaugural Tour Down Under as part of the national Under 23 team – my first time racing with European professionals. My journey on a bike is about to end, but theirs can be anything they make it, and I wish all these guys around me every success.

Today I see all this. And I see something else too. I see myself the way the fans watching the race probably see me: as a guy who's just about to finish an amazing 20-year journey. A guy who is feeling happy, a guy who finally knows how to live in the moment.

I'm still enjoying the race as I sprint for the finish. My sacrifice for Rohan Dennis has paid off: he's first on GC and I'm third, with Richie Porte (Team Sky) between us.

It's very late in the day to be appreciating what I've had for 20 years, but today I am hyper-aware that when I stop racing my life will change in untold ways. I start to imagine my world without competitive cycling, and I'm not sure what that will look like.

As a professional cyclist you learn to deal with a lot of different situations. But you only retire once in your career. It's a big psychological leap. I'm about to leave something I've done more than half my life.

And in the middle of all this, I have a race to organise.

WHEN THE IDEA FOR a one-day race in Melbourne and surrounds was first suggested it may have seemed a little far-fetched. Years ago, it seemed a long way from Europe. How could it fit into the season? Why would riders want to travel so far for just one day?

But as globalisation changes the world, cycling becomes more international. Teams are made up of riders from a wider range of nationalities. The companies and organisations funding the teams have larger markets. Cycling has spread to more countries, where there are large communities of avid followers.

The international cycling body, the UCI, has an agenda to grow and globalise the sport, to add new events to the world calendar. We want to complement their ambitions.

The Tour Down Under is an excellent example of a race that riders really enjoy being at. A race that is held early in the season because of the southern summer. Surely it could be enhanced by another race in close proximity, to kick-off the start of the world cycling season? We can add a race to the world cycling calendar without additional travel logistics and expenses for teams and their riders while offering an opportunity to train and race in good weather.

It started out as a far-fetched idea, but with the support of state and local governments, a great team of people and the endorsement of the UCI, it is becoming a reality.

My Australian manager, Jason Bakker has spent huge hours making sure everything is in place for the inaugural Cadel Evans Great Ocean Road Race. I've put in a huge amount of work too – giving advice and recommendations about the Elite Men's Race, including thoughts about the course, the teams, the riders, the media; and organising the Women's Race and the People's Ride.

As an organiser in an eponymous race there's the added pressure of hoping the event goes well, that the riders find it a good course and that the crowd enjoys it.

It's a rare experience to ride in a race with your name on it and I feel very privileged to have had the chance. The event is a fantastic opportunity for me to continue to give back to the sport, and hopefully it will still be going in 50 or even 80 years' time.

It's been an interesting challenge going over to the side of race organisation. You want to create a race that riders want to ride. Take the Strade Bianche, for example – it's not part of the WorldTour but everyone wants to ride it, and that creates a fantastic event because you're bringing out the passion and enthusiasm of the best riders in the world.

The race needs to work for the teams: the timing, distance, difficulty, and training benefits have to be just right. The race also has to be interesting, ultimately unpredictable, like a good movie when we don't know what the outcome will be until the very last moment.

I want to promote the sport of cycling and encourage people to get involved. And that's why we've included events in the program for non-professional riders. I don't want to close down somebody's street and tell them they can't have anything to do with the race other than to stand at the side of the road and watch. I know it can be a bit discouraging for females coming into the sport and I'd like that to change, which is part of why we have the Women's Race.

I'm bringing an event to an area that has a special place in my heart. My home in Barwon Heads is 20 minutes' drive away from the starting point in Geelong. I'm excited about leaving a legacy in my town, and about riding through it. In 2009, I proved to the cycling world that I was the best rider in the world, and I did that three kilometres from my home in Switzerland. Now in 2015 I'm going to ride in a race just a few kilometres from my home in Australia, the race in which I'll say goodbye to cycling.

There's a symmetry in that I like.

CHAPTER 25

THE LAST RACE

2015

THE RAIN COMES DOWN early.

I hear it when I wake up in my hotel room in Geelong. 'Not ideal,' I think. For the riders – including me – the roads will be slippery. And for the cycling fans – well, I hope they show. So much work has gone into this event, much of it by Jason. Starting up a new race is not easy, but everything has worked so well I'm only left wishing for the rain to stop.

My race preparation has been a long way from ideal. As an organiser of the race I've been busy with last-minute details. Three nights ago I went to the airport to pick-up Robel who had just flown in from Switzerland with his mother. I've finally got to see him after three months. It's been wonderful to spend time with him, even if staying up until one o'clock in the morning was not within the 'disciplined athlete' guidelines. I want to have him present at such an important day for me. And at age four, he might be able to remember something of it in years to come.

I get up early Saturday morning to see the People's Ride off. The prime minister has donned lycra and rolls off in front of 4000 others.

Despite the rain there's a great atmosphere in Geelong today. ABC Melbourne has set up an outside broadcast. There are TV crews and photojournalists at the start. The former State premier, Ted Baillieu is here. (Ted was instrumental in getting me to fly back to Melbourne in the middle of the season to attend a civic reception in Melbourne after my win in the Tour de France.) Mayor Darryn Lyons is here too, as well as about 40,000 cycling fans.

The 174-kilometre course begins on the Geelong waterfront, sets out for Thirteenth Beach at Barwon Heads and then winds down to the Great Ocean Road past the world-famous surfing spot Bells Beach, before heading inland and returning to Geelong to complete three laps of the 2010 World Championship course.

I do interviews before the race. I have never felt a greater responsibility to be an ambassador and a spokesperson.

I tell a presenter:

I'm kind of looking forward to the next phase of my life. I really don't know what to expect. I've raced nearly every race on the cycling calendar over 20 years, I've never raced my last race and I've never raced a race through my home town so it's all new for me today. I'm just grateful we can have this event, grateful to the people of Geelong who made it possible ... I want to first of all enjoy it, stay safe and of course I am a racer and I'm not going to give up until I get to the finish line.

The Cadel Evans Great Ocean Road Race has attracted 120 riders from 14 nations. Of the 20 squads, eight WorldTour teams have been invited, so some excellent riders will be here. It's great to have such a high quality field, and I'm proud of the spirit surrounding the event.

AND SO TO THE race.

The enthusiasm of the riders is evident from how hard they race right from the start.

A breakaway goes in the first kilometres. The rain eases, the roads dry. The group calms down as we pass through my hometown of Barwon Heads. The streets are full, and from the bike, everyone looks like they are having a great time. I am grateful, but slightly distracted.

I can't concentrate fully because I'm looking at it through my race organiser's eyes, checking whether everything is where it should be, that cars aren't parked where they shouldn't be, that the riders are safe on the wet roads. But I'm also there riding for the win.

We head towards Bells Beach. I hear some sprinters complaining about the steep pitches on Bells Boulevard. One sees me, 'Cadel, what did you put this in for?'

We come out to the view over Bells Beach, one of my favourite views along the coast, it always provokes a sigh of contentment every time I ride there. Bells Beach is famous for its surfing history, but today it's the starting point of our short King of the Mountain climb. Names are painted on the roads, the spectators here are the hard-core cycling fans, not abundant, but noisy and keen to see some suffering. From a race organiser's perspective, this is looking very promising.

The speed picks up as we head inland past Paraparap and Moriac towards the circuits in Geelong. Riders are bustling for position for the right turn onto Barrabool Road. There is a tailwind and speeds are high.

Team cars are trying to get past, I do the polite thing and get out of their way losing position in the process. We take a right turn onto the very road I have done more hill repeats than I can possibly count. I look up and see the group splintering. My heart sinks, here I was being polite, and now I am behind several splits in the crosswind.

I can count the number of times I have been dropped in the crosswind in my entire career on two hands. And here I am, dropped in my own race. Shit, I have to get to the front.

This is great, the guys are racing like it's a Belgian Classic. I find teammate, Micky Schär and we make it back to the front as the field regroups. We hit the laps in Geelong, only 60km to go now. The main climb on Challambra Crescent reminds me of the World Championships here five years ago. The field is reduced again, the sun is out and it has warmed up considerably.

Micky comes up to me with 10 ks to go. 'Take a bottle, take a bottle.'

'No, no, I'm fine, thanks.'

'Are you sure?'

'Yeah.'

Micky throws the bottle away in disbelief.

Five ks to go. This is new territory for a cyclist. Here I am riding a race and thinking, 'There are too many parked cars here, we need to put the no parking signs out earlier next year.'

I'm a race organiser and ... that's right, I'm also a cyclist! Mental note: deal with the parked cars later. Right now I've got a race to win, if I can.

Four ks to go.

Back to the race.

PHIL LIGGETT: Cadel Evans, riding like the champion he has always been throughout a career that spans almost 20 years, first of all the maglia rosa in the Giro d'Italia, finally got to finish third in that race, then won the Tour de France, became the professional road race champion, won Flèche Wallonne, now retiring on his own roads, just down the road from where he lives, and he's in the leading group.

MATT KEENAN: And he's retiring on his own terms, racing against the best in the world.

LIGGETT: And at the moment, beating them as well ...

It's looking like this group is the deciding group and Cadel Evans is in it with 3.6 kilometres to go.

OK, keep going. Race for the win. Last chance.

I've got to get onto the wheel of Belgian, Gianni Meersman (Omega Pharma–Quick-Step). We're going downhill and Meersman's pretty quick in the finish. But there's a headwind, which will slow him down a bit.

I *have* to get on Gianni's wheel.

I know this, but I'm thinking, 'Hang on a second ... We should mark this out next year as a tow-away zone. Maybe from Saturday onwards ... No, hang on, we've got the Women's Race on Saturday. Maybe we should do it from Friday just to be sure. Or Thursday – but I don't want to inconvenience the locals –'

What just happened?

Simon Clarke has pushed me off Gianni's wheel.

'Stop thinking about tow-away zones!'

I could fight back, but Simon is my best friend in cycling; I'm not going to push him off the wheel. We've got a lifetime of friendship after this race ends.

But as a competitor I've got to try to take Meersman's wheel and anticipate the sprint.

'Stay focused,' I hear myself say.

KEENAN: Inside the final two kilometres in the career of Cadel Evans.
LIGGETT: This is going to be the nail-biting finish we always wanted as we say goodbye to Australia's greatest cyclist. Seven hundred metres to go in his last cycle race and he's still in with a chance of winning. Cadel Evans is going out on a very high note indeed here, in the front group of nine as they race for the finish. Three-quarters of a kilometre to go ...

I go to start my sprint.

Then, as a cramp and dehydration hit, I think about that bottle that Micky tried to get me to take. I really should have.

I grind on anyway, legs hurting.

Nearly there now. The crowds are lining the finish in Geelong. I can hear the muffled voices of Matt and Phil on the PA. The crowd's noisy because they sense it'll be a close sprint finish.

I'm gratified by how hard the group is riding. And that works perfectly, because it splits the group up, and what could have been a bunch finish ends up as 10 riders sprinting it out for victory.

Gianni Meersman wins. Simon Clarke is second. I finish fifth.

I've had so many things going on in my mind that I've let my concentration lapse. I'm a little disappointed about that. But at the same time, I got pretty much everything out on the road, right to the end.

I climb off my bike for the last time and head towards where I see Robel waiting for me.

I've been speaking to my son for months about retiring, and counting down the races.

'How many races has Papi got to go?' he'll say.

'Four.'

Every time he asks, 'Why?'

'How many races has Papi got to go?'

'Three.'

'Why?'

'How many races has Papi got to go?'

'Two.'

'Why?'

Then one day I say, 'Papi's got one race to go.'

I've missed Robel hugely. Right now, my sadness that my racing career has just ended is mixed with happiness at seeing my little boy. And in the swirl of emotions I also feel a real gratitude towards the people who have come to my race, to see me one last time.

I like the fact that a young promising rider has come through and won the race. And Simon came second. I'm very happy about that.

Twenty thousand people have gathered in front of the presentation podium. Everyone cheers. 'Do You See What I See?' by Hunters & Collectors pumps out of the speakers.

I walk out onto the podium and see a sea of people, holding up signs and cameras and cheering.

I'm thinking, 'This is probably the last time I'm going to stand on a podium and I'm just going to appreciate it.'

The sun is out now in Geelong.

I tell the crowd:

I have to say from a rider's point of view I was very happy to make the front group today. It wasn't a very hilly race but it was windy conditions ... it was a really solid, hard, aggressive race and I have to thank my competitors and also the crowd for spurring all the competitors and creating an ambience which really made for ... nearly a Classic ...

I give my last proud and very emotional wave, and step down from the podium and into the next chapter of my life.

USUALLY AFTER A RACE I'll try to roll the legs out with a short ride, get warm and dry with the trademark towel around my neck in a hope to ward off illness.

This time there's none of that. I have no race tomorrow, or next week, or next month. That's it.

I'm back to being a polite race organiser. It's my name on the race and I want to make sure everyone's had a memorable day.

I feel privileged that so many people have come to see me in my last race. People are being very kind. They say, 'Thank you, and congratulations on a fantastic career.'

I'm very grateful for that.

I sign the empty bottle of podium champagne for mayor, Darryn Lyons. I do a television interview on the foreshore. I pose for some photos.

This evening there'll be a drinks party with all the riders, and later a party at a nightclub in Geelong. It's going to be a long night.

Robel is excited by the crowds. He isn't counting down the races any more. He knows it's the end.

I say, 'Guess what? That was Papi's last race.'

'Why?'

This time I have an answer.

'So I can be with you.'

CHAPTER 26

A NEW LIFE

2015–2016

THE CYCLE OF THE professional cyclist – from beginning to retirement – became clear to me after I'd been riding for a few years. It goes pretty much like this:

After four years, if you're a talented young rider who works hard you will have built up a good base of training, got a bit of an idea about how your body works and gained some racing nous. If you started as a teenager, you'll still be a junior, or maybe in the Under 23 class. If you're particularly talented, maybe you'll be good enough to become a professional.

You learn to race and be a good professional; that will take two to four years, so you're 23 or 24 now. Then you learn to train well and race well and learn about team dynamics. So now you're 25 or 26 and you're going well, you get more opportunities, maybe more results. If cycling is chess on wheels, maybe you're a knight now, maybe you are even showing the capabilities of a king.

And you perform well for two or three years. You know the moves you can make. You know the strategies of your own team and that of most of your competitors.

Then your body starts to change. And you have to make adjustments. You now have the mentality to let your body deal with training and racing, but you need more recovery time. Now you're almost 30, but with experience, and hopefully more opportunities, you do two to four great years.

Over your career you've learnt to push yourself and load and load, training your body to deal with training and racing. This mentality to do more, more, more stays with you. But as you get older you can do less because you've got this massive base and you don't need to build on it. You just need to maintain and stimulate that base.

You finally learn all these things but then time constraints become an issue. Maybe it's because of your results, or becoming a parent, and you have to adjust your training and lifestyle accordingly.

Your body's capacity to recover changes and you have to learn how to reach the same level with less training and at this point injuries and illnesses take a much greater toll. Any performances below expectations, and the world of cycling begins to mutter, 'You're too old'. Opportunities decrease accordingly. It might be time to learn how to play chess for real.

Maybe if I'd known all this earlier I could have used these philosophies better, but I was always driven. Sometime I worried I was not doing enough. A touch of laziness in a driven athlete – in balance – can be a good thing; many a driven athlete has exhausted himself or herself in training before the competition has even started.

I was three months away from retirement and frustrated one day because I couldn't go training because of some logistical issues. I was getting ready for the last race of my career and I was still trying to do everything as well as I could.

I was riding with Simon Poidevin, former captain of the Wallabies rugby union team. He told me, 'As an older athlete, one day too many of recovery is always better than one day too little.'

Wise words.

SOON AFTER I MOVED to Barwon Heads in 2003, Matt Farrell, my friend who took me to my first mountain-bike race some 13 years previously, was staying a few days with me. He'd just started riding again after university. So we decided to go and meet up with the local cycling group, outside Hendry Cycles in nearby Ocean Grove, at 8am.

It was a very mixed group of people and personalities – doctors, dentists, students, the local policeman, the local councillors, a panel beater, a retired engineer who raced professionally for a short period, a physiotherapist, a landscape gardener, and one Tour de France hopeful (me). Everyone was very polite and respectful. They shared turns at the front, rotating through the group 'Belgian style'.

I went back the next morning, and the next and the next, and in the off season the following year, and the next year, for 10 years. It gets me out of bed punctually and allows me to pass the first hour or two of my training in company. And, as for any group of weekend cyclists, it's the allure of a coffee and a chat after the ride that can be the inspiration to get on our bikes together. I join them if my training allows, otherwise I go 'to work' and continue my training ride.

We meet at various locations, depending on how fast we want to ride and how social we feel. This is my connection to another part of the cycling world, my community and friends away from professional cycling.

In February 2015, after the Cadel Evans Great Ocean Road Race, we meet up again. The landscape gardener and the policeman no longer ride, the physiotherapist has moved away, the retired engineer is not an elite-level Masters cyclist any more, but everyone is still very polite and respectful, sharing turns at the front. The Tour de France hopeful has retired as well, but he has some stripes on his sleeves now, and a lot of stories to tell if anyone wants to talk about cycling, but no one usually does.

The guys don't ride as far or as fast now. But we still look after each other, we still make a mutual decision on which loop to do to suit each other's desires. We race each other when we're good, but when there's a strong headwind or crosswind we ride tempo together. We make it hard for each other and we make it easy for each other, depending on who's there and what shape and mood we're all in.

The not-so-young only follow me a little way down the Great Ocean Road. I meet others or continue on my own, not to train, just to be out on my bike, enjoying the sun on my skin, the salty air, the beautiful views, and a good coffee and a muffin.

The Great Ocean Road, which stretches from Lorne to Portland on Victoria's south coast, is one of the truly spectacular roads in the world. With its hairpins, gullies, occasional clifftop drops, and allover incredible scenery, it is a cyclist's mecca.

You ride along a winding road often just metres from the beach and the Southern Ocean. As you ride you smell the salt and hear the ocean's roar. There is no protection from the wind, so the riding can be tough, but the scenery is so beautiful that you don't mind.

Sharing this with others is the essence of cycling, its great gift.

IT'S A FEW WEEKS later and I'm back in Stabio, my home away from home. It is time for Robel to get back to kindergarten and for me to get back to my normal life in Switzerland. What is a 'normal life'? My life has been dictated by racing and training programs for the last 20 years. Now life is no longer ruled by my world ranking, or the number of races I have won, or my threshold power, nor my skinfolds. I am no longer trying to perform with, and beat the best riders in the world. I am not on TV being analysed by followers of the sport for every race I win or lose.

I still love riding, maybe even more so now that the only expectations on me are my own. Now it is about the pleasure of climbing to the top of a mountain to enjoy the view and barrel down the other side. To feel fit and to be healthy, to feel the physical and emotional liberty that riding brings.

I've arrived home to a new routine. Some mornings, I walk with Molly down to the local café and sit with an espresso and read the paper. The people in the bar are my friends. They've always treated me like a local, never a celebrity.

In the afternoon, I'm home looking at the lawn I should be mowing. I'll get around to it soon. I pick Robel up from school, chatting to the other parents as we wait for our children. Sometimes I ride there, sometimes I walk, then we amble back home together, Robel and I, and plan dinner. Maybe I'll do a barbecue. It's wonderful spending time with him.

A few months after retiring, I'm riding from Stabio to Como on a brisk spring morning and something strange happens.

Someone passes me on a bike.

I'm thinking, 'Shit, someone passed me! That hasn't happened for a while.'

I have to laugh: even while riding a fixed-wheel bike, carrying a backpack containing my street clothes and doing 55 ks an hour, I still have this competitive streak in me.

AFTER HAVING PUT SO much energy into racing, I know I have a lot of energy to put into other areas of my life. Some time ago, Andy Rihs and I were talking about my career after racing. He said, 'You need to be challenged.'

And so what I'm finding is a really nice challenge is working with BMC as a Global Ambassador. I feel a real loyalty to BMC. It was their belief in me that gave me the opportunity to win the Tour de France among many other races.

Part of my role involves helping the company make better products. I'm finding that even more satisfying than I expected. Like anything at an international level, making the best bikes in the world is challenging. When we get a new product line going and it's popular and successful, I get a real buzz out of it.

I needed to find a buzz from something, because I was getting such a buzz out of racing. For years I felt as though I was adrenalin-dependent. And when I took the adrenalin out of my life I wondered, 'What's that going to feel like?'

Working with BMC is a great excuse to stay on my bike and keep fit. And it gives me a structure. It means I can stay in Switzerland which gives Robel continuity at his school and other networks, during the times when he's living with me. Of course, I have other things going on in Australia, principally my race in Geelong.

In my new role at BMC, I'm often asked about equipment by everyday cyclists. It's not hard to spend $10,000 on a bike. People like equipment. It's sometimes difficult to answer these questions, because for so long my equipment has been provided for me by my team and if it's good, I never question it. As a rider, the first thing you have to do is finish the race. So I've always leant on the side of reliability rather than lightweight performance. And because you're riding the Tour de France, more than 3000 kilometres in three weeks, your bike's also got to be quite comfortable too.

When they're setting up a bike, teams use the range of equipment with which they are supplied. At BMC, we obviously use BMC products. Then we'll use a certain brand of handlebars, a certain brand of components. A non-professional in the market has a choice of equipment – maybe 50 different handlebar choices. As a professional, you might have a choice of three.

But now that I'm working with BMC in equipment testing, I'm learning about other stuff on the manufacturing and development side. It's important that I know the quality and characteristics of the competitors' equipment. I find that's actually really interesting.

I test all the different bikes at each price point we offer, always with the same handlebars, seats and components. So it gives me the capacity to feel just the frame, which is what we're working on. I can feel the subtle differences between each frame much better.

I test bikes for BMC at a circuit at Valle di Muggio where I used to train, not far from Stabio. There are two test laps – one of seven kilometres and one of twelve, which is the steepest and most demanding section of road in the area.

In testing equipment, I ride on a difficult course in bad conditions and I try to push the bike to the limit of its descending, climbing, braking and traction capacities. I'll push the bike hard but not to the point where I might break it.

Some people tend to bash and bump their equipment and they seem more prone to breakages, punctures and so on. But since my earliest days as a mountain biker, I've always looked after my equipment as well as I possibly could. Mum never had much money, so I had to make do with really average and basic gear. And it taught me to be extra good with my equipment, to be very smooth and to have a real sensibility for every piece that I owned. I'd like to think I kept that mentality throughout my career on the road.

At the Valle di Muggio circuit, there's also an out-the-back time-trial course of around 11 kilometres. It takes me 22 minutes to ride. It doesn't have much flat in it, but it's got *pavé*, steep climbs, long fast climbs, good road, bad road, sharp corners and slow corners.

You do a time trial on each bike. You're doing exactly the same corner and exactly the same line each time. You get a good idea of the way each bike turns into a corner and how precisely it can hold a line.

Later I take notes for the engineer who's following in the car. We give a score to each characteristic of the bike, and I always try to guess the weight, just to see how accurate I am.

Bike technology has changed enormously since I started riding professionally in the late 1990s. Thanks to these advances, bicycle manufacturers are a more important part of professional racing than ever before. There are three WorldTour teams that are financed by bicycle companies – Cannondale, BMC and Trek–Segafredo.

But it's not just pro bike riders who have benefitted. The change in materials has been one big development – with frames now made of carbon fibre – but the other change has been the capacity to produce these materials in high volume for a broader market. What used to be reserved only for the very top echelon of professional cyclists is now much more widely available, much more affordable. And I'm talking carbon fibre, titanium and even electronic gears and suspension in mountain bikes. The partnerships between manufacturers, riders and consumers are now even closer, and I'm very happy to be part of the evolution that's taking place.

A rule introduced by the UCI requires professional riders to only use equipment that's available for retail sale. The equipment used by the winner of the Tour de France needs to be available for purchase by anyone.

Often non-professionals have better equipment than we do, because we have a weight limit that we can't go under, which is 6.8 kilograms per bike. This weight is based on a bike that Marco Pantani rode to Tour de France victory on Alpe d'Huez in 1998. The idea was to have a weight limit so it's not like Formula One where someone with superior equipment can perform better. It means a level playing field.

But the thing is that technology has evolved so much that 6.8 kilos is now quite heavy. Because of carbon-fibre manufacture, bikes are now lighter but still very strong and reliable. Technology has developed to the point where I believe they should review the weight limit and maybe lower it a bit, because that would give manufacturers an incentive to make better equipment across the board.

Now professional riders race on bikes that weigh less than 6.8 kilos, and add equipment to make up the weight. I added a more comfortable seat and fitted my SRM PowerMeter for training information and then my bike came up to the weight limit.

I look back at the equipment that I raced on from 10 or 20 years ago, and to ride it … you notice the friction on the cable, how hard you have to pull the brake levers, how adhesive the pads and brakes are *not*. And of course how heavy the bikes are. I look at these bikes and wonder: 'How did we ride them?' And I look back at bikes from even earlier eras and ask the same question.

Bikes are obviously a lot better now than they were 20 years ago. But in terms of sheer riding pleasure, the bikes of 20 years ago were actually really nice, because they were much simpler and much more reliable.

Thanks to developments in communication – internet, social media and better TV coverage – people can now have a better understanding of what elite racing is like compared to when I started racing. And they're sometimes appalled by the conditions we race in. Twenty years ago, when we rode in the snow, the clothing wasn't nearly as good as what it is today, and I look back and think, 'How on earth did we do it?'

As well as carbon-fibre frames, we now use wider back tyres, with lower rolling resistance and ceramic wheel bearings, and the jerseys and helmets we wear now have a much lower drag coefficient. The roads are better now as well; the asphalt is smoother, and there are more paved roads.

But what's also true is experience is what matters. The other day I was fixing the bike we bought Robel for his third birthday. It's got a lumpy, heavy chain on it and it weighs as much as my modern carbon-fibre bike but he still has a big smile on his face every time he rides it. It's that pure pleasure from just riding a bike that counts, whether you're riding a bike developed by NASA or just something that can get you from A to B.

Pure riding pleasure can come from any bike.

FOR SIX MONTHS AFTER I retire, I have to keep doing the Whereabouts program. After doing it as a rider since 2004, I was so used to it that it actually didn't bother me at all. But now, when I'm on business trips for BMC, doing Whereabouts is tricky because I'm moving around so much. In the first part of 2015 I travel to Taiwan, Taipei, Thailand, Australia and America, twice. The travel is quite intense and there are long periods when you're in a plane where you don't have access to a laptop.

I've had to say to colleagues and people I visit, 'Look, I'm still in the athletes' Whereabouts program. I've respected all of the rules to this point in my career, I don't want to have a problem now.'

It's highly unlikely they're going to test me. The drug testers understand I've stopped racing for real. I'm not just saying I'm retiring so I can go away and do something against the rules then come back. My retirement was very public. No coming back.

I retired on 2 February 2015, so the last time I have to do Whereabouts is 2 August. But for months afterwards, when I book a hotel I almost instinctively reach for my laptop to type the details into Whereabouts.

IT'S A QUESTION I am often asked. How do I feel about having ridden in an era when a lot of other riders were doping – or, to put it another way, cheating?

Ironically, it was racing against competitors that were later taken out of the sport that taught me to be a better rider, that pushed me to new personal limits, that forced me to race more intelligently and efficiently, that motivated me to train smarter, and prepare better. What I learned through these experiences, was what prepared me for the moments that allowed me get the biggest and most important results that defined my career. Those wins overcame any frustration, or grudge that I may have held towards the cheats that beat me.

Those who have made short cuts to success in our sport made short-term gains for themselves, but long-term damage to our sport. Potential sponsors do not engage with cycling, team budgets are reduced, and the effect trickles down to everyone involved.

Most unfortunately it also affects the next generation. In the 2008 Tour de France, Michael Rasmussen rides us off the wheel on the Col d'Aubisque. On television his effort looks minimal compared to the difficulty I was in behind. His own team, Rabobank, eject him from the Tour while he is in yellow. A sponsor that has not only been a huge long-term supporter of pro cycling, but also women's cycling, development programs for the U/23's and juniors, steps away from our sport.

I do look back and wonder. How did I stay there? How did I hang on the wheel for so long? How did I tolerate those that applauded the 'winner' then turned to me and criticised my race tactics, my inabilities that led me to 'lose'? How did I keep going when I am being one-two'd on a mountain by two climbers – who both later served doping bans? To lose (well, come second in) another big race then be told off by the team owner, 'At least you could have won *this* race'?

I only had my own small personal team around me, my wife, my coach, a *soigneur* friend, a training buddy to help me deal with these cutting remarks.

Of course there are some frustrations when a competitor of mine is caught. How did that affect the races I was in? What will be the consequences of their actions be to my beloved sport?

But at the same time, I see an athlete and even a colleague caught cheating, and I am happy – that is one more battle won in the war of the fight against drugs in sport.

The Armstrong case was maybe the biggest lie in the history of sport. But because the lie was proven through means other than drug testing, it is will also be the biggest deterrent to athletes who consider crossing the line from right to wrong, for years to come.

As followers of cycling become more informed about past occurrences, opinions change. Where once I was criticised for looking like a house of pain and suffering on my bike while I hung on for as long as I could on the climbs in the big races. Now, I am complimented for my endurance in the face of self-inflicted suffering.

THERE ARE SO MANY photos of me riding my bike and grimacing. It often looks as though I'm suffering when I'm on the bike. And that's because I often am.

I'm proud of those photos.

Others have sometimes looked as though they weren't in so much pain. And maybe that's because they weren't.

After the whole Lance Armstrong thing comes out, someone sends me a text: 'Cadel, how does it feel to have won more Tour de Frances than Lance Armstrong?'

I smile, and send a message back: 'That actually sounds kind of good.'

I TRY TO ENCOURAGE young people to get involved in sport. Not to be the best in the world, or to win the Tour de France, but to try cycling, see if they like it, and if they do, I encourage them to integrate it into their lives for health, social opportunities and as a means of transport. Sport can teach you so much about life. It certainly did that for me.

At times in my life, I was too obsessed with cycling, and it affected my personality and how I treated people. You become so committed to your training and preparation that you lose sight of the world around you.

I see this in a rider I know. He is so committed to his training and his diet that he pretty much doesn't have any friends. He doesn't often train with his own team because he's so committed to his personal training. I don't know what he does for meals. It's a bit of a struggle to spend time with him because he follows such a strict regime. He's too committed. As an athlete, you have to test yourself and learn what works for you as an individual and in the your environment.

I see the flip side too. I see riders who aren't committed to their training at all and the waste enormous opportunities.

You need to have an overall balance of being committed to these things but also keeping a bit in reserve, because some days you've just got to have the fight of a wild animal just to stay in contention.

These parameters are always shifting, so you have to learn what you need, what's good for you, what works for you, but then it has to be adapted to every situation. And sometimes you do everything right but you're in a team that creates a bad environment or is badly managed. They put up roadblocks for which no amount of good training can prepare you.

ONE OF MY MAIN goals after I stopped racing was to stay busy, productive and healthy, and for me to stay in cycling is the best

429

way to do that. I want to go to the Grand Tours as a fan now. I sometimes go as a BMC ambassador but sometimes I go just as a fan and say g'day to friends and some of the guys on the team.

I won't miss the stress of the last few years when I was sick, and expectations were still high but my capabilities were reduced. Maybe getting sick was a way to make me slow down, because otherwise I would have just kept pushing myself and at some point it might have just been too much. So while I was very frustrated at the time, I am philosophical about the way everything came to an end quite quickly.

I'm happy with what I did in my career. I had my time, I gave it everything and got everything out of my body. I always like to say that I was, more often than not, able to get everything out on the road. I don't have any regrets. I look back on my results and efforts with pride and satisfaction, whereas I used to look back on it and think, 'I could have done better here or there.' It was a way of motivating myself to work harder and do better.

I'm still learning things about the sport; that will probably never stop. But I don't miss racing. When I see the bad weather and the crashes and the pressure the guys are under, I don't miss it. I don't miss the egos that create unnecessary friction among the team sometimes. Or the occasional disillusionment of a *domestique* who thinks they should be riding for GC or getting more publicity.

No, I don't miss racing. I am more than happy to slow down and enjoy life. I *was* worried that I would miss the adrenalin rush of racing. But I don't.

I have some injuries that I will need to manage for the rest of my life. I have a shortened left collarbone from the series of accidents I had in 2003. It will probably never totally heal. I do yoga to maintain flexibility in my shoulder and lower back.

I have satisfaction from other challenges in my life now. The difference is that now I have time to pursue my passions. The three things I could not live without are good bread, good wine and good coffee.

Now when I go past my friend the wine-maker at four in the afternoon, he'll sometimes say, 'Hey, Cadel, come down and taste some wine.'

'Yeah, I will, actually.' Two hours later I'm thinking, 'I should probably get home for dinner.'

Oh, and I can now go on holidays. I went to Provence with a friend and stayed in a lovely hotel. Went for two rides, though, 100 kilometres each.

I didn't do holidays very well during my career. I went on a beach holiday in 2007 and again in 2011. And in 2012 we went to Crete for four days and I didn't ride. I slept very well on these rare holidays, I went into another level of decompression.

Soon after I stopped racing I noticed I suddenly had a lot more energy to do things that I otherwise didn't have to do. I feel healthier in a lot of ways. The other day I rode 100 kilometres and then I mowed the lawn. I could never do this as a rider.

As I pushed the mower around in my garden in Stabio, I thought about how new this was, that I was going to have an aperitif before dinner, that I was going to watch a movie, that I was not going to prepare my gear for an early start on the road.

I thought, 'Being retired is *very* underrated.'

FOR THE LOVE OF CYCLING

1993, 2016

IT'S DARK HERE, AMONG the massive tree ferns in the Kinglake National Park. I'm 16, flying along on my mountain bike on an awesome little single track. The ferns have grown overhead and created a tunnel, which gives the track a shadowy, dank, foresty feel. It is haunting and magnificent.

I'm flowing through a tunnel of nature, along through the quiet still air, the big tyres coping well with the slippery moss and undergrowth. Suddenly above me two crimson rosellas take off, startled by my presence. The only way for them to escape is to fly down the path. I'm following them in the gloom. They sweep and swoop, up and down, two amazing flashes of colour, flying within a metre of my handlebars as I follow them along this tunnel of treeferns.

It lasts just a few seconds. A fond and happy memory that is still with me today.

This is what cycling's about. Some of the best times of my life have been while I'm riding a bike. It's the freedom to go anywhere, the range of possibilities that such mobility allows. And it's being in the middle of nature. Up on the mountain roads I've dodged goats, sheep, deer, cows, horses and snakes as I've ridden along. I've been tearing along and a wombat has wandered onto the track in front of me. Or I've crept quietly up on an echidna as it's crossing the track, at its own pace.

One day in 1993 in the Dandenongs, in Victoria, I had an extraordinary experience. I was doing course practice with a friend and competitor, Rodney Commerford. We were riding along a narrow four-wheel drive road when a kangaroo jumped out in front of us. Then two more joined him, these huge, beautiful eastern greys. For a few hundred metres we followed the kangaroos down the track as they bounded in front of our handlebars, I could almost have reached out and touched them. Riding with roos ... from a bike you can cover distance while seeing, hearing and smelling almost everything around. It's still vivid in my mind more than 20 years later.

I like riding in the urban environments too. You see very different sights there. When you're riding in busy traffic and people are sitting in their cars, sometimes you can read the text messages of the person in the passenger seat as you squeeze by them, or you can smell the perfume of a lady in a car.

Cycling is a feeling of absolute liberty. And it's just *you*. You and this brilliant piece of simple, efficient machinery that virtually is an extension of you, of your arms, your legs, your vision and balance.

On a bicycle you can cover distances on walking trails, roads, cobbled streets, sand or snow. And if it's really steep or dangerous, you can always jump off, put the bike on your shoulder and hike or climb up or down a steep incline over rocks, water, stairs or ice then get back on the bike and continue riding.

The satisfaction of cycling has often stemmed from being alone, insulated from technology, reinvigorating the mind and body's abilities to think, navigate and register. But of course the joy of cycling is also the camaraderie, the enjoyment of sharing experiences with friends, the companionship created even among strangers when you're confronted with difficulty – harsh weather; equipment failure or accident that leaves you stranded. I always make an effort to keep a basic cycling toolkit in my car in the hope of repaying the many friendly favours strangers have paid me over the years.

After a ride I've sat with friends over a coffee or a cold drink in France, Italy and Spain and the experience of sitting and talking in an energised but relaxed state has amplified the fun of the ride. Sometimes I have had the most intense, extraordinary conversations with people as we sat in our Lycra sharing an espresso or a panini. Of course there have been lots of conversations about our sport, but we've talked about life, relationships, families, kids and life's problems too.

It was a bike that got me outside and down the road to adventures and experiences to tempt me – entice me – to go further. The journey and the destination are sometimes equally significant.

Once you've digested the natural majesty of where your bike has taken you, it's also a chance to discover yourself, which for me has been an extraordinary journey. I have learnt so much about myself through riding a bicycle in so many places around the world. I have learnt about my strengths and weaknesses. I have learnt about the limits of my body and mind, and how I've been able to push those limits.

There have been times in my professional cycling career when I've pushed myself far beyond where I thought those limits lay, when a combination of physical endurance and an inner determination to go harder produced some amazing results.

But the most satisfying thing is that the magic of cycling never died. Through all the frustrations and the injuries and the teams that lost faith in me and the injustice of being beaten by drug cheats, there was one overriding motivator.

I never stopped loving getting on my bike. Descending freely and effortlessly, climbing a hill fluidly, or even efficiently making my way through parked cars and traffic jams. I like riding downhill. That's the exciting part. I like climbing when I'm climbing well. That's the challenging part. But even if I'm climbing badly, there's usually a descent to reward my efforts.

The magic I find in cycling – the freedom of it – is the fundamental reason I've done this all my life, and will continue to do so.

CYCLING WAS THE STARTING point of a journey, a journey that started when as a young 14 year old I found peace and pleasure in being alone with a simple machine.

It started as a means of transport and independence for short trips down the road or to school. As I learned more, this simple machine took me further; to mountaintops, to far corners of national parks, and then to races. The harder I worked, the further the machine took me; interstate, nationally, internationally.

I worked harder, smarter, pushed further. I partnered with many good people, and some not so good. I was complimented, encouraged, supported and generously rewarded by some; insulted, hurt, cheated and robbed by others.

Fortune was hoped for, misfortune dreaded. One fuelled me with passion. One drained me of belief. Good fortune led to accolades and applause, big rewards, new opportunities, new adventures. Misfortune led to deep reflection, quiet time with confidants, hard lessons learned that reinforced character.

I've suffered through pain, concussion, broken bones, bruises, abrasions, scabs and scars. I've battled fatigue, illness, chronic fatigue and bad luck.

But this sport has given me the most extraordinary opportunities. It has allowed me to spend these wonderful years in Europe, living the life I dreamed about when I was a kid. It's meant that I have learned languages, learned the idiosyncrasies and manners of various cultures, and it's meant that I have been paid to keep my body as fit and healthy as anyone in the world.

Cycling has also brought me to some of the most beautiful places on Earth. I've sat in the shadows of magnificent châteaux, on the edges of famous rivers, overlooking the wild seas of Brittany and New Zealand. I've mountain-biked to amazing ravines in the Dolomites in Italy, stopped off to admire fantastic views of the Rocky Mountains in North America.

Cycling has taken me along the single tracks in the Dandenongs and it's taken me through medieval villages all over Europe, through the snow in the Italian mountains, along Roman roads in Tuscany, past wineries in California, along deserted highways in Oman and cobblestoned avenues in Poland. I've ridden past the Great Wall of China, the Duomo in Milan and ancient temples in Japan. And, a few times, along the Champs-Elysées towards the Arc de Triomphe in Paris.

From that little 14 year old with a dream, those two wheels took me so much further than I ever dreamed.

And for that, cycling, I am to you, forever grateful.

AUTHOR'S NOTE

WHEN I FINISHED RACING, my intention was to walk a five or seven day segment of the Camino del Santiago. Not for religious reasons, not for a box to tick, but to slow my life down, to have time to reflect and consider, to follow a path to greater perspective. Racing had consumed my entire adult life; it tested me, it strengthened, it hurt, and most importantly, it taught me. But how were these 20 years of intense experience going to fit into the rest of my life?

As seems to be the natural pattern of my life, time has not yet permitted me to walk the Camino. But I still needed some help to make the transition from professional athlete to an active, productive but un-stressed ex-athlete.

Writing a book? Writing is like walking. It is slow. While slow for a racer is almost always terrifying, it does allow time for reflective thinking, which in this case was much-needed therapy in transitioning to the next chapter of my life. Also, I have a lot of stories to tell, a lot of experience to share, some of which I needed to keep to myself to continue performing, right until the very last race.

As I write these last words I realise that the process of writing, reading, reviewing, editing, reflecting and re-editing – like any worthwhile experience – has been a learning experience. It has undoubtedly helped me to step back and see how the sport of cycling, and the position I occupied in the sport, are connected to the rest of my life.

The process brought many realisations, among them good and bad. I have tried to focus more on the constructive experiences of what has been an extraordinary journey.

Cycling led me to a number of crossroads in my career and ultimately my life. I owe a debt to the people who helped me make the best decisions at those crossroads. Sometimes it was a close friend with more life-experience than me, but for the most part it was one of two exceptional individuals, two cycling coaches. To Damian Grundy, and the late Aldo Sassi, thank you very much for being teachers in my sport – the sport that was my teacher in life.

While bringing these pages together helped me step away from the all-consuming life of professional cycling, it was not any easy task. But just as I had coaches in cycling, I also had 'coaches' to guide me in turning my experiences and observations into words in a book. Peter Wilmoth was instrumental in helping me get my story out and down on paper in the months following my retirement from racing. To the team at ABC Books and HarperCollins, above all the wonderful Helen Littleton, Emma Dowden and Lachlan McLaine, for their unwavering support, dedication, understanding and most of all, their patience, I say thank you. I hope you agree that I was *appropriately* slow! I also give thanks to my incredible mother – not only for giving me a strong pair of legs, but for teaching me how to use my head and heart to make the most of my talents in racing and in life.

And to my readers, thank you very much. I hope you can make use of what I have learned and recounted, and that you continue to enjoy riding, or anything in life for that matter.

– Cadel Evans